STUDIES IN BAPTIST HISTORY AND THOUGHT
VOLUME 27

Towards Baptist Catholicity

Essays on Tradition and the Baptist Vision

COMMENDATIONS

'Any book which concludes with a chapter entitled "What Keeps You from Becoming a Catholic?" promises to be nothing if not intriguing. Such promise is not disappointed in this fine collection of essays which render both the question and its committed response both meaningful and pressing. Baptists ought, both by their ecclesiology and their commitment to liberty, to be good at listening. Sadly (and illegitimately) a commitment to the integrity of the local church has sometimes muffled Baptist hearing of the broader Christian tradition as it has been confessed through the centuries. Prof. Harmon here demonstrates that this was not always the case and ought not now to be the case. Moreover, his skill as a patristics scholar gives clear shape to the manner in which a truly "catholic" Baptist theology can be rooted and can develop. Here is one of an increasing number of voices, from both sides of the Atlantic, drawing Baptists again back to their roots in the connectedness and continuity of the Christian tradition. One can but hope and pray that these voices are heard and heeded.'

John E. Colwell
Professor of Christian Theology and Ethics, Spurgeon's College, London

'*Towards Baptist Catholicity* is a book for all Christians. This volume is evidence of the catholicising tendency in Christian theology that is informed and formed by the ecumenical movement and by the findings of interchurch dialogue. Ingredient to the "thick ecumenism" of which Professor Steven Harmon speaks in the first chapter is the holistic interdisciplinary approach to the stand which a particular ecclesial community takes within the *oikoumene*. In so doing the author draws on tradition and scripture (in that order) to situate Baptist Christianity within the church of the Lord Jesus Christ. Appeal is made to church fathers and mothers—past and present, formidably ecumenical—to support this stance. Attention is given to doctrine, worship, catechesis and discipleship. *Towards Baptist Catholicity* is not about one Christian denomination. It is about the church ecumenical, and the historical, theological and pastoral concerns which ensure the integrity to envision such a church and its faith, life and witness with and beyond confessional lines. To the question "What Keeps You from Becoming a Catholic?" raised in the last chapter, this book is its own answer. One converts to the Lord, not to a denomination. The 'ecclesial and ecumenical responsibility' not only of Baptists but of all Christians is to be and become who we are in the Lord's church.'

Sr. Lorelei F. Fuchs, SA
Graymoor Ecumenical and Interreligious Institute, New York

'This is the best book I have read connecting ecclesiology, ecumenism, and the Baptist tradition with the Gospel imperative for Christian unity. Steven Harmon's proposal for a Baptist version of the Oxford Movement has revolutionary possibilities, in the Copernican sense of the word, and deserves to be taken seriously. Well researched and well argued—a work of scholarly acumen and theological verve.'

Timothy George
Dean, Beeson Divinity School, Samford University, Birmingham, Alabama

'Steven Harmon has offered in this erudite study the perspective many thoughtful Baptists have been seeking. One overarching question shapes these essays: "Can Baptists be catholic?" which Harmon answers with a resounding yes. Attentive to biblical authority, early Christian tradition, creeds, as well as the charism of Baptist life, this text pursues a reclamation project that honors the pre-Reformation commonality of western Christianity. Most significant is the author's dexterity in placing Trinitarian theology at the center of theological renewal for Baptists, weaving a nuanced understanding of biblical narrative with doctrinal construction. Rightly Harmon grounds an encompassing view of community within the communal life of God as Holy Trinity, an antidote to the endemic separatism of some forms of Baptist identity. Scholars and students will find rich construction and reflection in this collection, shaping the possibility of a new epoch of "catholic Baptists". I commend it highly.'

Molly T. Marshall
President and Professor of Theology and Spiritual Formation,
Central Baptist Theological Seminary, Kansas City, Kansas

'This is an extremely learned and important book by an author well-grounded in the history of theology. As a non-Baptist, I can only surmise its value and impact within the Baptist community. I should think its potential for re-thinking Baptist identity could be considerable. Speaking as an ecumenist, I would venture the opinion that Dr. Harmon's book could have a major role to play among all interested in the unity of the church. Its suggestion of a postmodern Baptist hermeneutic of tradition will interest many concerned about ecumenical advance.'

William G. Rusch
Executive Director, Foundation for a Conference on Faith and Order in North America

'Harmon's essays provide a welcome antidote to the poison of antitraditionalism imbibed by Christians influenced by the individualistic, anti-religious currents characteristic of modernity. Harmon not only shows how unacknowledged traditions covertly shape a Baptist tradition of anti-traditionalism, but also how critical and conttructive retrievals of ancient catholic theological, liturgical and exegetical traditions can illumine important elements of the Baptist vision now rather obscured. A must read in serious ecumenical theology for Christians concerned with living in and living out their faith traditions—whether Baptist, Catholic, or evangelical—in our era.'

Terrence W. Tilley
Professor and Chair, Theology Department, Fordham University, New York

A full listing of titles in this series
appears at the end of this book

STUDIES IN BAPTIST HISTORY AND THOUGHT
VOLUME 27

Towards Baptist Catholicity

Essays on Tradition and the Baptist Vision

Steven R. Harmon

Foreword by Paul Avis

Wipf & Stock
PUBLISHERS
Eugene, Oregon

Wipf and Stock Publishers
199 W 8th Ave, Suite 3
Eugene, OR 97401

Towards Baptist Catholicity
Essays on Tradition and the Baptist Vision
By Harmon, Steven R.
Copyright©2006 Paternoster
ISBN: 1-59752-832-3
Publication date 7/20/2006
Previously published by Paternoster, 2006

This Edition Published by Wipf and Stock Publishers
by arrangement with Paternoster

Paternoster
9 Holdom Avenue
Bletchley
Milton Keyes, MK1 1QR
PATERNOSTER Great Britain

Series Preface

Baptists form one of the largest Christian communities in the world, and while they hold the historic faith in common with other mainstream Christian traditions, they nevertheless have important insights which they can offer to the worldwide church. *Studies in Baptist History and Thought* will be one means towards this end. It is an international series of academic studies which includes original monographs, revised dissertations, collections of essays and conference papers, and aims to cover any aspect of Baptist history and thought. While not all the authors are themselves Baptists, they nevertheless share an interest in relating Baptist history and thought to the other branches of the Christian church and to the wider life of the world.

The series includes studies in various aspects of Baptist history from the seventeenth century down to the present day, including biographical works, and Baptist thought is understood as covering the subject-matter of theology (including interdisciplinary studies embracing biblical studies, philosophy, sociology, practical theology, liturgy and women's studies). The diverse streams of Baptist life throughout the world are all within the scope of these volumes.

The series editors and consultants believe that the academic disciplines of history and theology are of vital importance to the spiritual vitality of the churches of the Baptist faith and order. The series sets out to discuss, examine and explore the many dimensions of their tradition and so to contribute to their on-going intellectual vigour.

A brief word of explanation is due for the series identifier on the front cover. The fountains, taken from heraldry, represent the Baptist distinctive of believer's baptism and, at the same time, the source of the water of life. There are three of them because they symbolize the Trinitarian basis of Baptist life and faith. Those who are redeemed by the Lamb, the book of Revelation reminds us, will be led to 'fountains of living waters' (Rev. 7.17).

Series Editors

Anthony R. Cross, Fellow of the Centre for Baptist History and Heritage, Regent's Park College, Oxford, UK

Curtis W. Freeman, Research Professor of Theology and Director of the Baptist House of Studies, Duke University, North Carolina, USA

Stephen R. Holmes, Lecturer in Theology, University of St Andrews, Scotland, UK

Elizabeth Newman, Professor of Theology and Ethics, Baptist Theological Seminary at Richmond, Virginia, USA

Philip E. Thompson, Assistant Professor of Systematic Theology and Christian Heritage, North American Baptist Seminary, Sioux Falls, South Dakota, USA

Series Consultant Editors

David Bebbington, Professor of History, University of Stirling, Scotland, UK

Paul S. Fiddes, Professor of Systematic Theology, University of Oxford, and Principal of Regent's Park College, Oxford, UK

† Stanley J. Grenz, Pioneer McDonald Professor of Theology, Carey Theological College, Vancouver, British Columbia, Canada

Ken R. Manley, Distinguished Professor of Church History, Whitley College, The University of Melbourne, Australia

Stanley E. Porter, President and Professor of New Testament, McMaster Divinity College, Hamilton, Ontario, Canada

For Kheresa

'Christe Deus, pariles duc ad tua frena columbas
et moderare leui subdita colla iugo.
namque tuum leue, Christe, iugum est, quod prompta uoluntas
suscipit et facili fert amor obsequio.'

St. Paulinus of Nola, *Carmen* 25.3-6 (CSEL 30, p. 238)

Contents

Chapter 3
The Authority of the Community (of All the Saints):

Chapter 4

Chapter 5
From Triadic Narrative to Narrating the Triune God:

FOREWORD

To some, the phrase 'Baptist Catholicity' poses an intriguing paradox; others see it as a contradiction in terms. Can you really be Baptist and Catholic at the same time? Surely, if you are a Baptist, you have renounced all claims to catholicity? If you regard yourself as a Catholic Christian, you would not dream of becoming a Baptist. Through my involvement in national and international dialogue between Baptists and Anglicans over the years, I count as friends and colleagues distinguished Baptists who are as Catholic in their understanding of the Christian faith and life as I could wish and from whom I know I have much to learn about what it means to be a Catholic Christian. The author of this remarkable book is one of these.

I can identify with the pilgrimage in theology and spirituality that Steven Harmon has made over a number of years towards a sense of a church that extends through history and throughout the world; towards a appreciation of the riches of the Christian tradition; and towards a more objective understanding of the sacraments or ordinances of the Gospel than would be true of many Baptists, for whom the sacraments (particularly baptism itself) seem to be regarded mainly as a human response, made in faith and devotion, to the grace of God, rather than primarily a gift of God in which grace and strength to live as faithful disciples of Christ is bestowed.

Because Dr. Harmon is a patristics scholar (though his learning reaches far wider than that) he knows that for many of the early fathers and martyrs to be a disciple of Jesus Christ was to be a Catholic Christian—one embedded in the community of the Church with its liturgy, its rule of faith and its bishop. For the first centuries of the church's existence it was uncertain which were the Christian Scriptures. Christians indwelt the living tradition and it was this that sustained them. Once the canon of Scripture was finally discerned, the need for tradition did not fall away, for there were other pillars of the early church that depended on tradition and were related to Scripture through tradition: the councils and the creeds, the Christological and Trinitarian teaching that they articulated, patterns of worship in liturgy and sacraments, and the threefold ordained ministry of bishop, presbyter and deacon with the episcopal office playing a vital role in holding the church in unity of faith and sacramental life.

The threefold ministry is a topic related to tradition that is not addressed in this book. I am aware that some earlier Baptist pastors were titled 'bishop' and that local self-governing congregation can be seen as a diocese in miniature. But I do not think that those factors entirely answer to the concern for the unity of particular churches one with another, for teaching authority, for the pastoring of pastors and for the thickly textured fabric of visible unity—in all of which the bishop has *traditionally* had a pivotal role. However, I am running ahead of this book and I do not know what its author would have to say about that particular aspect of tradition, historicity, unity and visibility.

Newman, who is cited several times, used to say, 'If you have come this far, you can't stop here; the argument will carry you further.' Newman's own logic—or perhaps his heart rather than his head—carried him out of Anglicanism, which he had adorned by his learning and eloquence, into the Roman Catholic Church precisely during the period of Ultramontane agitation to magnify the authority of the pope and to give the status of dogma to papal infallibility and universal jurisdiction. It was authority that drew Newman and many other converts of the time to Rome. Dr. Harmon's final chapter, 'What Keeps You from Becoming a [Roman] Catholic?', only hints at these testing issues of authority. I wonder whether authority is an underdeveloped and therefore unresolved issue in this admirable volume.

We cannot live without tradition and, as this book shows, no-one—not even the most individualistic Baptist—actually does. The ideal of the solitary, self-sufficient individual engaging solely with the Scriptures is an illusion and always has been. Even the Enlightenment, with its apparent hostility to tradition, represents a turning away from one tradition, that of the authoritarian church, to another, that of classical antiquity. But if tradition is inescapable, it is also diverse and contradictory. It must be tested by Scripture within the community of theological reflection. To continue that critical sifting of tradition in all its bewildering variety remains a challenge for us all.

Paul Avis, *General Secretary, Council for Christian Unity,*
Church of England
Church House, London
Lent 2006

Preface

Towards Baptist Catholicity contends that the reconstruction of the Baptist vision in the wake of modernity's dissolution requires a retrieval of the ancient ecumenical tradition that forms Christian identity through liturgical rehearsal, catechetical instruction, and ecclesial practice. The movement of Baptists towards catholicity proposed herein is neither a betrayal of cherished Baptist principles nor the introduction of alien elements into the Baptist tradition. Rather, the envisioned retrieval of catholicity in the worship, doctrine, teaching, and life of Baptist churches is rooted in a recovery of the surprisingly catholic ecclesial outlook of the earliest Baptists, an outlook that has become obscured by more recent modern reinterpretations of the Baptist vision and that provides Baptist precedents for a more intentional movement towards Baptist catholicity today. While nine of the ten chapters that constitute this book had earlier incarnations as journal articles, book chapters, and addresses that were originally conceived for different groups of readers and hearers, these earlier versions gave voice to a common quest for a place for the catholic tradition in the contemporary Baptist vision. In their present form these once discrete publications have been revised for clarity, continuity, and cohesiveness of argument. The repetition of some material in several of the previous publications has been eliminated in the present book, and portions of some of the chapters have been expanded.

Chapter 1 is based on '"Catholic Baptists" and the New Horizon of Tradition in Baptist Theology', in *New Horizons in Theology*, ed. Terrence W. Tilley (Maryknoll, N.Y.: Orbis Books, 2005), pp. 117-34; an earlier version was presented to the annual meeting of the Region At-Large of the National Association of Baptist Professors of Religion held in conjunction with the annual meeting of the College Theology Society at The Catholic University of America, Washington, D.C., USA, 3-6 June 2005. Chapter 2 is based on 'Baptist Understandings of Theological Authority: A North American Perspective', *International Journal for the Study of the Christian Church* 4.1 (2004), pp. 50-63; an earlier version was presented as part of the Anglican-Baptist International Conversations—North American Phase at Acadia University, Wolfville, Nova Scotia, Canada, 10-13 September

2003. Chapter 3 is based on 'The Authority of the Community (of All the Saints): Toward a Postmodern Baptist Hermeneutic of Tradition', *Review and Expositor* 100.2 (Fall, 2003), pp. 587-621.

Chapter 4 is based on 'Baptist Confessions of Faith and the Patristic Tradition', *Perspectives in Religious Studies* 29.4 (Winter, 2002), pp. 349-58; an earlier version was presented to the annual meeting of the Region At-Large of the National Association of Baptist Professors of Religion at the Mercer University McAfee School of Theology, Atlanta, Georgia, 26-27 June 2001. Chapter 5 is based on 'From Triadic Narrative to Narrating the Triune God: The Development of Patristic Trinitarian Theology', *Perspectives in Religious Studies* 33.3 (Fall, 2006); some of the material on Ignatius of Antioch therein has much earlier roots in a paper written for a seminar in patristic theology taught by Robin Darling Young at The Catholic University of America in 1994. Chapter 6 is based on 'Hebrews in Patristic Perspective', *Review and Expositor* 102.2 (Spring, 2005), pp. 215-33.

Chapter 7 is based on 'Karl Barth's Conversation with the Fathers: A Paradigm for *Ressourcement* in Baptist and Evangelical Theology', *Perspectives in Religious Studies* 33.1 (Spring, 2006), pp. 7-23; an earlier version of much of this material was presented to the Philosophy of Religion and Theology section of the Southeast Regional Meeting of the American Academy of Religion, Atlanta, Georgia, 5-7 March 2004. Chapter 8 is based on 'Praying and Believing: Retrieving the Patristic Interdependence of Worship and Theology', *Review and Expositor* 101.4 (Fall, 2004), pp. 667-95. Chapter 9 is based on 'Communal Conflict in the Postmodern Christian University', in *Christianity and the Soul of the University: Faith as a Foundation for Intellectual Community*, ed. Douglas V. Henry and Michael W. Beaty (Grand Rapids, Mich.: Baker Academic, 2006), pp. 133-44; an earlier version of that essay was presented to a conference on 'Christianity and the Soul of the University: Faith as a Foundation for Intellectual Community' sponsored by the Institute for Faith and Learning at Baylor University, Waco, Texas, 25-27 March 2004. Thanks are due to the original hearers of the conference papers mentioned above whose responses and questions enhanced their transformation into articles and essays and to the editors and anonymous referees of these publications for their very helpful suggestions.

I am grateful to the editorial boards of *International Journal for the Study of the Christian Church, Review and Expositor*, and *Perspectives in Religious Studies* and to the editorial staffs of Orbis Books and Baker Academic for granting permission to publish revised versions of these articles and book chapters. John Pierce, executive editor of *Baptists Today*, granted permission to incorporate in the text of chapter 8 three slightly revised paragraphs from my article 'Do Real Baptists Recite Creeds?', *Baptists Today* 22.9 (September, 2004), p. 27. Mikael Broadway, Curtis

Freeman, Barry Harvey, Beth Newman, and Philip Thompson gave permission to reprint 'Re-Envisioning Baptist Identity: A Manifesto for Baptist Communities in North America' as appendix 1, and my co-authors Curtis Freeman, Beth Newman, and Philip Thompson agreed to allow me to publish our statement 'Confessing the Faith', originally circulated with an open letter and published online on multiple Baptist news media Internet sites, as appendix 2. All biblical quotations in this book are from the New Revised Standard Version of the Bible (Copyright 1989, Division of Christian Education of the National Council of the Churches of Christ in the United States of America. Used by permission; all rights reserved).

An invitation to deliver the Vivian B. Harrison Memorial Lectures at Mount Olive College (Mount Olive, North Carolina, USA) on 15 March 2005 provided an opportunity for a public airing of material from this book in the form of two lectures and a chapel sermon addressing the theme 'Tradition and the Baptist Vision'. I wish to thank David Hines, Chairman of the Department of Religion at Mount Olive College, along with the administration, faculty, and students of the college, for their gracious hospitality and stimulating discussion of my lectures. These members of the community of Mount Olive College, an institution sponsored by the Convention of Original Free Will Baptists, refreshed me with their deep consciousness of their connections with the early General Baptists of the Netherlands and England.

My students at Campbell University Divinity School from 1998 to the present have made innumerable contributions to this book, for these perspectives have been hammered out in dialogue with this community of people preparing for—and in many cases already practicing—various forms of congregational ministry, mainly in Baptist settings but also in other denominational contexts. One group of these students merits special thanks: Charles Bey, Aaron Findley, Patricia Freeman, William Haughton, Jason Leonard, Christopher Moore, Donald Morris, and Drew Phillips were students in the Spring 2004 offering of my course on The Theology of Karl Barth who heard the initial presentation of much of the material in chapter 7 and responded with much useful feedback. It was helpful for this Baptist to have two Presbyterian students as dialogue partners as we contemplated the work of this great Reformed theologian and its relationship to the larger Christian tradition.

Professional colleagues at Campbell University and other institutions read portions of the manuscript at various stages in its evolution and suggested numerous corrections, emendations, and revisions that have been incorporated into the text of this book. In that role Paul Avis, Bill Brackney, Lorin Cranford, Adam English, Curtis Freeman, Derek Hogan, Lydia Hoyle, Fisher Humphreys, Reinhard Hütter, Glenn Jonas, Barry Jones, John Jones, Kathy Lopez, Mark Medley, Jeff Pool, Dan Stiver, Terry Tilley, Andy Wakefield, and Ralph Wood together have exemplified the collegial dimension of what I declare to my theology students every semester: 'Christian theology must always be done in, with, and for Christian community.' My graduate assistant Tyler Ashworth assisted in the proofreading of the entire manuscript and deserves far greater compensation for this service than his meager stipend and a mere mention in a book preface.

This book owes its timely completion especially to the administration and trustees of Campbell University, who approved my request for a sabbatical leave in the Fall 2005 semester during which I wrote most of the manuscript. In particular, President Jerry Wallace, Provost Dwaine Greene, Divinity School Dean Michael Cogdill, and former Associate Dean Bruce Powers deserve thanks not only for their roles in granting me a research leave but also for their general support for research and publication as integral to the teaching mission of a Christian university. My current Associate Dean, Barry Jones, kindly kept me shielded from all manner of things that could easily have intruded upon a leave spent locally. I must also thank Willie Jennings, Senior Associate Dean for Academic Programs at Duke Divinity School, for granting me visiting scholar privileges at Duke during my leave. Regular access to the Duke Divinity School Library was a great boon to my writing, as were conversations about my project with Reinhard Hütter and Curtis Freeman of the Duke Divinity faculty.

I deeply appreciate the editors of Studies in Baptist History and Thought for being interested in this project and thinking it worthy of inclusion in this series. Series editor Anthony R. Cross and Paternoster editor Jeremy Mudditt have been immensely helpful at every stage of preparing this book for publication.

I gratefully dedicate this book to my wife Kheresa, who has been my 'paired dove' in the journey reflected in its pages since the day the words from a wedding homily by Paulinus of Nola that appear on the dedication page served, in English translation, as the preface to the order of service for our wedding ceremony: 'Christ God, draw these paired doves toward your reins, and govern their necks beneath your light yoke; for your yoke, O Christ, is light indeed when taken up eagerly and borne willingly for love' (trans. by Mark Searle in *Documents of the Marriage Liturgy* [Collegeville, Minn.: Liturgical Press, 1992], p. 31). Kheresa's theologically astute observation in our kitchen before a recent Sunday lunch serves as a fitting conclusion to this preface and segue to the book proper, for in a sentence of twenty-one words she said something that I have much less efficiently tried to communicate by writing a whole book: 'Catholics are not as bound as we think they are, and Baptists are not as free as we think we are.'

Steven R. Harmon
Campbell University Divinity School, Buies Creek, North Carolina, USA
Epiphany 2006

Abbreviations

AAS	*Acta Apostolicae Sedis*
ACCS.NT	Ancient Christian Commentary on Scripture—New Testament
ACW	Ancient Christian Writers
AILEHS	The Archbishop Iakovos Library of Ecclesiastical and Historical Sources
ANF	*Ante-Nicene Fathers of the Christian Church*, 10 vols., eds. A. Roberts and J. Donaldson (Edinburgh: T & T Clark/Grand Rapids, Mich.: William B. Eerdmans, 1993-97 [1885-96])
ASNU	Acta Seminarii Neotestamentici Upsaliensis
ATANT	Abhandlungen zur Theologie des Alten und Neuen Testaments
BapTod	*Baptists Today*
BETL	Bibliotheca Ephemeridum Theologicarum Lovaniensium
BGBE	Beiträge zur Geschichte der biblischen Exegese
BHH	*Baptist History and Heritage*
Bib	*Biblica*
BIS	Biblical Interpretation Series
CBQ	*Catholic Biblical Quarterly*
CCT	Challenges in Contemporary Theology
CD	Karl Barth, *Church Dogmatics*, vols. I-IV, ET eds. G.W. Bromiley and T.F. Torrance (Edinburgh: T & T Clark, 1956-75)
ChrCent	*The Christian Century*
ChrTod	*Christianity Today*
ChronHighEd	*Chronicle of Higher Education*
CMMC	Christian Mission and Modern Culture

CSEL	Corpus Scriptorum Ecclesiasticorum Latinorum
CSR	*Christian Scholar's Review*
CWS	Classics of Western Spirituality
DS	H. Denzinger and A. Schönmetzer, eds., *Enchiridion Symbolorum: definitionum et declarationum de rebus fidei et morum*, 36th edn. (Freiburg: Herder, 1976)
ERASCF	Evangelical *Ressourcement*: Ancient Sources for the Church's Future
FC	Fathers of the Church
FMCS	Franklin and Marshall College Studies
FT	*First Things*
GCS	Die griechischen christlichen Schriftsteller der ersten drei Jahrhunderte
GNO	Gregorii Nysseni Opera
Greg	*Gregorianum*
HHM	Harvard Historical Monographs
ICTT	Interpreting Christian Texts and Traditions
IJST	*International Journal of Systematic Theology*
InstrPat	Instrumenta Patristica
Int	*Interpretation: A Journal of Bible and Theology*
JBL	*Journal of Biblical Literature*
JEBapSt	*Journal of European Baptist Studies*
JECS	*Journal of Early Christian Studies*
JETS	*Journal of the Evangelical Theological Society*
JSNTSupp	Journal for the Study of the New Testament: Supplement Series
JTS	*Journal of Theological Studies*
LCC	Library of Christian Classics
LCL	Loeb Classical Library
LTPM	Louvain Theological and Pastoral Monographs
NGS	New Gospel Studies
NHS	Nag Hammadi Studies
NovT	*Novum Testamentum*
NPNF[1]	*Nicene and Post-Nicene Fathers of the Christian Church*, First Series, 14 vols., ed. P. Schaff *et al.* (Edinburgh: T & T Clark/Grand Rapids, Mich.: William B. Eerdmans, 1991-98 [1887-94])

NPNF²   *Nicene and Post-Nicene Fathers of the Christian Church*, Second Series, 14 vols., ed. P. Schaff *et al.* (Edinburgh: T & T Clark/Grand Rapids, Mich.: William B. Eerdmans, 1994-98 [1887-94])

NTAbh   Neutestamentliche Abhandlungen

NTS   *New Testament Studies*

OCP   *Orientalia Christiana Periodica*

OECS   Oxford Early Christian Studies

OTM   Oxford Theological Monographs

PG   *Patrologiae Cursus Completus: Series Graecae*, ed. J.-P. Migne (Paris: Garnier, 1857-66)

PL   *Patrologiae Cursus Completus: Series Latina*, ed. J.-P. Migne (Paris: Garnier, 1844-64)

PhilTod   *Philosophy Today*

PRSt   *Perspectives in Religious Studies*

ProEccl   *Pro Ecclesia*

PSSLRE   The Penn State Series in Lived Religious Experience

PTMS   Pittsburgh Theological Monograph Series

RÉAug   *Revue des Études Augustiniennes*

RevExp   *Review and Expositor*

RSR   *Recherches de science religieuse*

SABH   Studies in American Biblical Hermeneutics

SBHT   Studies in Baptist History and Thought

SBLDS   Society of Biblical Literature Dissertation Series

SBLMS   Society of Biblical Literature Monograph Series

SC   Sources Chrétiennes

SEChrTh   Sources of Early Christian Thought

SIHC   Studies in the Intercultural History of Christianity

StudChSt   Studies in Church and State

StudPat   *Studia Patristica*

StudPhil   *Studies in Philology*

SVC   Supplements to Vigiliae Christianae

TF   Texte zur Forschung

TheolEd   *The Theological Educator*

TheolTod   *Theology Today*

TLS   Theology and Liberation Series

TPMA   Textes philosophiques du Moyen Age

TS	*Theological Studies*
TU	Texte und Untersuchungen zur Geschichte der altchristlichen Literatur
WUNT[2]	Wissenschaftliche Untersuchungen zum Neuen Testament, 2nd series

CHAPTER 1

'Catholic Baptists' and the New Horizon of Tradition in Baptist Theology

'...[T]he catholic church in every place is one body, even if in different places there might be dwellings of congregations, just as members of the whole body....' *Synodal Letter of the Council of Antioch, A.D. 325*[1]

'[W]e believe the visible church of Christ on earth, is made up of several distinct congregations, which make up that one catholick church, or mystical body of Christ.' *The Orthodox Creed (1678)*[2]

'Let us, in all our supplications, remember all the members of other Churches, and ask that the choicest blessings may rest upon them. We believe, and our fathers have believed, in the Holy Catholic Church. The Church of Rome is right in affirming that the Church of Christ is catholic. The catholicity of the Church of Christ is not, however, a doctrine of Rome: it is an essential consequence resulting from the principles on which Christ's Church is founded. It is clearly written: "There is one body, and one Spirit, even as ye are called in one hope of your calling; one Lord, one faith, one baptism, one God and Father of all, who is above all, and through all, and in you all".' *Judge Willis, President, Baptist Union of Great Britain and Ireland, 'Address of Welcome' to the first Baptist World Congress in London, 1905*[3]

In 1996 a small group of Baptist theologians in the United States, the 'Region-at-Large' of the National Association of Baptist Professors of Religion, began gathering as a program unit of the annual meeting of the

---

1   *Synodal Letter of the Council of Antioch* 2 (ET of the surviving Syriac version of the letter in W.C. Rusch, trans. and ed., *The Trinitarian Controversy* [SEChrTh; Philadelphia: Fortress Press, 1980], p. 45).

2   'The "Orthodox Creed"', article 30, in W.L. Lumpkin, *Baptist Confessions of Faith*, rev. edn. (Valley Forge, Pa.: Judson Press, 1969), pp. 318-19.

3   Judge Willis, 'Address of Welcome', in Baptist World Alliance, *The Baptist World Congress: London, July 11-19, 1905. Authorised Record of Proceedings*, ed. J.H. Shakespeare (London: Baptist Union Publication Dept., 1905), pp. 2-3 (citing Eph. 4.4-6).

College Theology Society, an organization of predominantly Roman Catholic college and university professors of theological and religious studies. This meeting has served as a forum for earnest discussions of the nature of Baptist identity, set in relief against the backdrop of parallel debates about Roman Catholic identity, as well as an occasion for mutual exploration of the catholicity to which both traditions are heirs. The theme of the 50th Annual Convention of the College Theology Society in 2004, 'New Horizons in Theology', provided the Baptist theologians in attendance with an opportunity to reflect on an emerging trend in contemporary Baptist theology with important ecumenical implications: the recognition of tradition as a horizon within which the doing of theology takes place. Much of the material in this first chapter of *Towards Baptist Catholicity* received its initial hearing in that context.

Tradition is a new horizon for Baptist theology in the sense that much Baptist thought has proceeded on the basis of a radicalized *Sola Scriptura* hermeneutic that dichotomizes Scripture and tradition, with the result that many Baptists reflexively regard any post-biblical theological development as superfluous, theologically suspect, and possessing no authority for Christian faith and practice. The emergence of Baptist theologians who give more positive attention to tradition may be a counterintuitive phenomenon for some observers of recent developments in Baptist life in the United States: within an ecclesial tradition that has a tradition of dispensing with tradition[4] and in the wake of Baptist denominational controversies in which selected traditional interpretations of Scripture have become theological litmus tests,[5] several non-fundamentalist Baptist theologians are increasingly invoking tradition as a source of religious authority, reflecting on tradition as a theological category, offering constructive proposals for a Baptist or Free Church retrieval of tradition, and utilizing tradition as a resource for constructive theology. After placing this new horizon for

---

4   My language here echoes the observation of P.E. Thompson that 'Baptists have come to make a tradition of rejecting tradition, Baptist or otherwise'. Thompson, 'Re-envisioning Baptist Identity: Historical, Theological, and Liturgical Analysis', *PRSt* 27.3 (Fall, 2000), p. 302.

5   For historical and sociological studies of the recent controversy in the Southern Baptist Convention, the largest denominational expression of Baptist church life and largest Protestant denomination in North America, see B. Leonard, *God's Last and Only Hope: The Fragmentation of the Southern Baptist Convention* (Grand Rapids, Mich.: William B. Eerdmans, 1990); N.T. Ammerman, *Baptist Battles: Social Change and Religious Conflict in the Southern Baptist Convention* (New Brunswick, N.J.: Rutgers University Press, 1990); D.T. Morgan, *The New Crusades, the New Holy Land: Conflict in the Southern Baptist Convention, 1969-1991* (Tuscaloosa, Ala.: University of Alabama Press, 1996); B. Hankins, *Uneasy in Babylon: Southern Baptist Conservatives and American Culture* (Tuscaloosa, Ala.: University of Alabama Press, 2002).

Baptist theology in the larger context of the historical development of Baptist thought vis-à-vis the Enlightenment, this initial chapter will offer an overview of notable contributions to this new horizon by emerging and established Baptist theologians. This survey of the work of these 'catholic Baptist' thinkers contextualizes the remainder of this book, which is an attempt to chart a course towards Baptist 'catholicity'—i.e., towards a reclaimed consciousness that Baptists belong to what the Nicaeno-Constantinopolitan Creed confesses is the 'one, holy, catholic (Greek *katholikē*, "general" or "universal"), and apostolic church' and that they must strive after the realization of these marks of the church along with all other denominations. The horizon of the 'Great Tradition', the catholic Christian tradition that belongs to Baptists and to all other Christians, serves as a primary navigational reference point for this voyage.

Baptist Theology and the Horizon of Tradition

There is a sense in which tradition is not an entirely new horizon for the doing of Baptist theology. Seventeenth-century Baptists inherited from their forebears in the denominational traditions out of which they came or which influenced them theologically a traditional horizon that stubbornly persisted despite conscious adherence to the *Sola Scriptura* hermeneutic of the Reformation. The framers of early Reformed and Anabaptist confessions of faith could not help but read the Bible through the lenses of the ancient *regula fidei* and its Nicaeno-Constantipolitan and Chalcedonian clarifications, even while privileging Scripture as the source of this traditional horizon of interpretation. The earliest Baptist confessions demonstrate that seventeenth-century Baptists picked up the same reading glasses when they turned to the Bible as their authority for faith and practice. Baptist confessions issued during the seventeenth century are surprisingly rich with echoes of the patristic doctrinal tradition. Language and concepts of patristic origin appear primarily in Trinitarian and Christological statements of these confessions, but continuity with patristic theological formulae is not restricted to these rubrics: note, for example, the *Orthodox Creed*, a 1678 English Baptist confession that in addition to echoing patristic Trinitarian and Christological language references three of the four 'marks of the church' from the Nicaeno-Constantinopolitan Creed in article 29 and reproduces and commends the Apostles', 'Nicene', and Athanasian creeds in article 38.[6] Nevertheless, in the instance of the *Orthodox Creed* and other points of contact between the early Baptist confessions and the patristic tradition, these tend to be borrowed

---

6   'The "Orthodox Creed"', in Lumpkin, *Baptist Confessions of Faith*, pp. 297-334.

continuities, with some of this language lifted wholesale from the Anglican *Thirty-Nine Articles* or the Reformed *Westminster Confession of Faith*. These borrowed continuities served the apologetic agenda of establishing Baptists' continuity with the larger Christian tradition as well as their distinctive place within it, but they also demonstrate that the pre-Enlightenment genesis of Baptist theology took place within a traditionally circumscribed horizon.[7] As Philip Thompson (North American Baptist Seminary, Sioux Falls, South Dakota, USA) has argued, there is indeed a 'catholic spirit' to be discerned in the faith and practice of the earliest Baptists.[8]

Modern Baptists, however, drank deeply from the well of the Enlightenment's antagonism to tradition. The anti-traditional hermeneutic represented by the slogan 'no creed but the Bible'[9] served well the theological agenda of both liberal and fundamentalist expressions of Baptist theology in the nineteenth and twentieth centuries, with both types of responses to modernity claiming access to truth unmediated by any sort of interpretive horizon. In Hans-Georg Gadamer's hermeneutical metaphor of 'horizons of interpretation', a tradition functions as an interpretive

---

7   These features of early Baptist confessional literature are explored more fully in ch. 4, 'Baptist Confessions of Faith and the Patristic Tradition.'

8   P.E. Thompson, 'A New Question in Baptist History: Seeking a Catholic Spirit among Early Baptists', *ProEccl* 8.1 (Winter, 1999), pp. 51-72.

9   The slogan 'no creed but the Bible' is actually not indigenous to the Baptist movement proper but rather seems to have originated in the Restorationist movement led by Barton W. Stone, Walter Scott, and Thomas and Alexander Campbell; a variant slogan, 'no creed but Christ', emerged later in the movement (M.E. Boring, *Disciples and the Bible: A History of Disciples Biblical Interpretation in North America* [St. Louis: Chalice Press, 1997], p. 18; W. Tabbernee, 'Unfencing the Table: Creeds, Councils, Communion, and the Campbells', *Mid-Stream* 35.6 [1966], pp. 417-32; and W. Tabbernee, 'Alexander Campbell and the Apostolic Tradition', in *The Free Church and the Early Church: Bridging the Historical and Theological Divide*, ed. D.H. Williams [Grand Rapids, Mich.: William B. Eerdmans, 2002], pp. 163-80. In the latter essay, Tabbernee points to evidence that Alexander Campbell's aversion was not to patristic creeds properly utilized but rather to the inappropriate use of post-Reformation confessions to exclude people from the fellowship of the church, and Campbell in fact frequently referenced the ancient creeds in order to defend orthodox Trinitarian and Christological positions). By the time of the formation of the Southern Baptist Convention in 1845, however, it had become such a common axiom in Baptist circles that W.B. Johnson could declare, 'We have constructed for our basis no new creed; acting in this manner upon a Baptist aversion to all creeds but the Bible' ('The Southern Baptist Convention, To the Brethren in the United States; To the Congregations Connected with the Respective Churches; and to All Candid Men', in *Proceedings of the Southern Baptist Convention in Augusta, Georgia, 8-12 May 1845* [Richmond: H.K. Ellyson, 1845], pp. 17-20).

horizon.[10] In consciously dispensing with the horizon of tradition, modern liberal and fundamentalist Baptists traded the deeply textured and richly variegated horizon of the historic Christian tradition for the comparatively flat and monochrome modern horizon of supposedly traditionless reason, itself a tradition of sorts, albeit a very thin one.

The contemporary recovery of tradition as a horizon for Baptist theology may then be characterized as a constructive response to the postmodern milieu that on the one hand welcomes the postmodern critique of modern pretentions of traditionless rationality and on the other hand embraces the traditioned rationality of the Christian mind. It is not merely coincidental that serious engagement of tradition in written expressions of Baptist systematic theology has been undertaken largely by Baptist theologians who are consciously doing theology in response to the postmodern situation and in sympathy with many of its criticisms of modernity. In an essay reviewing Terrence Tilley's *Inventing Catholic Tradition* from a Baptist perspective, Mark Medley (Campbellsville University, Campbellsville, Kentucky, USA) surveys the place of tradition as a theological category in ten major Baptist systematic theologians from John L. Dagg (1794-1884) to Stanley J. Grenz (1950-2005, formerly of Carey Theological College, Vancouver, British Columbia, Canada), finding that among these only Grenz and James Wm. McClendon, Jr. (1924-2000, formerly of Fuller Theological Seminary, Pasadena, California, USA) have entered into extensive and constructive consideration of tradition.[11] Millard J. Erickson (Western Seminary, Portland, Oregon, USA), on the other hand, who has strongly criticized constructive engagement of postmodernity by evangelical theologians,[12] gives minimal attention to tradition in his major systematic theology text.[13] Openness to tradition in Baptist theology thus

---

10   The concept of 'horizons of interpretation' is developed in H.-G. Gadamer, *Wahrheit und Methode: Grundzüge einer philosophischen Hermeneutik*, 2nd edn. (Tübingen: J.C.B. Mohr, 1965); ET, *Truth and Method*, 2nd rev. edn., trans. J. Weinsheimer and D.G. Marshall (New York: Crossroad, 1989).

11   M. Medley, 'Catholics, Baptists, and the Normativity of Tradition,' *PRSt* 28.2 (Summer, 2001), pp. 119-20, n. 2. Grenz's most extensive treatment of tradition appears in S.J. Grenz and J.R. Franke, *Beyond Foundationalism: Shaping Theology in a Postmodern Context* (Louisville, Ky.: Westminster John Knox, 2001), pp. 93-129. McClendon's perspectives on tradition are summarized in J.W. McClendon, Jr., *Systematic Theology*, vol. 2, *Doctrine* (Nashville: Abingdon, 1994), pp. 468-72.

12   M.J. Erickson, *Postmodernizing the Faith: Evangelical Responses to the Challenge of Postmodernism* (Grand Rapids, Mich.: Baker Books, 1998); see especially ch. 5, 'To Boldly Go Where No Evangelical Has Gone Before: Stanley Grenz' (pp. 83-102).

13   M.J. Erickson, *Christian Theology* (Grand Rapids, Mich.: Baker Book House, 1983-85), p. 258. This brief three-paragraph treatment of the relationship of tradition to

seems to flourish where there is also critical openness to some postmodern perspectives.[14]

The New Horizon of Tradition and the Emergence of 'Catholic Baptist' Theologians

In the last few years such a noteworthy number of Baptist theologians have joined Grenz and McClendon in urging their fellow Baptists to acknowledge the authority of tradition and to explore the implications of the catholic tradition for Baptist faith and practice that they constitute an identifiable movement in Baptist theology. A 1994 essay by Curtis Freeman (Baptist House of Studies, Duke Divinity School, Durham, North Carolina, USA) calling Baptists to locate themselves within the tradition of the whole church suggests an appropriate category for such theologians: they are 'catholic Baptists'.[15] While their thought is not homogeneous, it may be distinguished from other expressions of Baptist theology by the presence of the following seven identifying marks of a catholic Baptist theology.

---

authority notes that all Christians are influenced by tradition and ascribes 'positive value' to tradition as an aid in biblical interpretation, but then cautions that 'we should consult them [the Fathers] as we do other commentaries.'

14   The critical openness to postmodern perspectives suggested here and elsewhere in this book is not a self-conscious 'postmodernism' but rather a less programmatic *sic et non* recognition that many postmodern critiques of the modern philosophical tradition are valid and that cautious concurrence with them may even liberate Christian theology from its modern captivity by Enlightenment epistemologies. Cf. the explanation by D.B. Hart, *The Beauty of the Infinite: The Aesthetics of Christian Truth* (Grand Rapids, Mich.: William B. Eerdmans, 2003), pp. 5-8, of the sense in which he employs the terms 'postmodern' and 'postmodernity' in his book.

15   C.W. Freeman, 'A Confession for Catholic Baptists', in *Ties That Bind: Life Together in the Baptist Vision*, ed. G. Furr and C.W. Freeman (Macon, Ga.: Smyth & Helwys, 1994), p. 85: 'I suggest that Baptists may more easily explore the vast resources of Christian spirituality and that other Christians may more readily receive the unique contributions of Baptist spirituality if we attempt to think of ourselves (at least experimentally) as (little c) catholic (little b) baptists.' Freeman's spelling of 'baptist' with a lower-case 'b' in this context is derived from the usage of J.W. McClendon, Jr., *Systematic Theology*, vol. 1, *Ethics* (Nashville, Tenn.: Abingdon Press, 1986), pp. 17-35, in which McClendon makes his case for rooting his theological vision in a broad yet distinctive ecclesial tradition that includes not only Baptists proper but also other denominations with roots in the Radical Reformation as well as various Pentecostal and evangelical bodies with comparable Free Church ecclesiologies. In my own usage herein I retain the lower-case 'catholic' from Freeman's suggested self-understanding but nevertheless capitalize 'Baptist', as the theologians to whom I apply this categorization belong to the Baptist tradition proper.

Tradition as Source of Authority

First, catholic Baptist theologians explicitly recognize tradition as a source of theological authority. In a journal article published in 2000 Thompson urged Baptists 'to discuss seriously the normativity of tradition', along with 'the Baptist identity's relation to the Baptist, and the Christian, past'.[16] That discussion is already well underway. Grenz included tradition in a threefold pattern of authoritative sources for theology in which Scripture is 'theology's norming norm', tradition is 'theology's hermeneutical trajectory', and culture is 'theology's embedding context'.[17] The trajectory of tradition is 'comprised of the historical attempts of the Christian community to explicate and translate faithfully the first-order language, symbols, and practices of the Christian faith, arising from the interaction among community, text, and culture, into the various social and cultural contexts in which that community has been situated.'[18] For Grenz, 'to understand the tradition of the church as providing a hermeneutical trajectory is to acknowledge the importance of tradition without elevating it to a position of final authority' in light of 'the ongoing life of the church as it moves toward its eschatological consummation.'[19] Medley echoes Thompson's concerns and reflects some of Grenz's proposals in Medley's own recommendations for a Baptist engagement of tradition: first, Baptists should explore possibilities for entering into ecumenical conversation with those who have a tradition of employing tradition as a theological category; second, Baptists might more easily embrace tradition if they move beyond an understanding of tradition as a continuity of static doctrinal propositions to a more dynamic 'retrospective' understanding of tradition as a critical, open-ended 'looking back' to the Christian past in configuring continuity for present contexts; and third, Baptist discussions of the authority of tradition might be more fruitful if they locate these discussions not in the formal theological discourse of doctrinal statements but rather in Baptist communities at worship.[20] Baptist patristics specialist D.H. Williams (Baylor University, Waco, Texas, USA) has argued a compelling case for the need of Baptists and other Free Church Christians to retrieve the

---

16   Thompson, 'Re-envisioning Baptist Identity', p. 302. Thompson contends that such a recovery of a place for tradition in Baptist faith and practice would not be an importation of something alien to the Baptist vision, citing Thomas Grantham (1634-92) and the *Orthodox Creed* (1678) as evidence that the earliest Baptists were not as disconnected from the catholic tradition as their modern descendants have tended to be.

17   Grenz and Franke, *Beyond Foundationalism*, pp. 57-166.

18   Grenz and Franke, *Beyond Foundationalism*, p. 118.

19   Grenz and Franke, *Beyond Foundationalism*, p. 126.

20   Medley, 'Catholics, Baptists, and the Normativity of Tradition', pp. 121, 126-28.

patristic theological tradition as formative of their own tradition, but he cautions that they will need to move beyond the historiographical myth of the 'Constantinian Fall' of the church if they are to do so.[21] Stephen Holmes (University of St. Andrews, Scotland) likewise has written a book that offers a critique of the tendency of Free Church Protestants to invoke their *Sola Scriptura* hermeneutic as a rationale for ignoring tradition and points to specific examples of how traditional resources can provide fresh perspectives on contemporary concerns.[22]

Place for Creeds in Liturgy and Catechesis

Second, catholic Baptist theologians seek a place in Baptist ecclesial life for the ancient ecumenical creeds as key expressions of the larger Christian tradition. It may seem counterintuitive that in the context of an enforced doctrinal rigidity in the Southern Baptist Convention, some among those who might be identified as 'disenfranchised moderates' have proposed ways in which Baptists might reclaim the proper function of the creeds. Yet Barry Harvey (Baylor University, Waco, Texas, USA), for example, rejects the mantra that 'Baptists have no creed but the Bible', contending that 'our time and effort would be better served if we attended to the question, What are the proper and improper uses of the ancient creeds and confessions, in worship and in the pedagogical responsibilities of the church?'[23] Harvey highlights the potential value of the ancient creeds as instruments of Christian education that shape the narrative mind of the church. Elizabeth

---

21   D.H. Williams, *Retrieving the Tradition and Renewing Evangelicalism: A Primer for Suspicious Protestants* (Grand Rapids, Mich.: William B. Eerdmans, 1999), pp. 101-31; see also D.H. Williams, *Evangelicals and Tradition: The Formative Influence of the Early Church* (ERASCF, 1; Grand Rapids, Mich.: Baker Academic, 2005).

22   S.R. Holmes, *Listening to the Past: The Place of Tradition in Theology* (Carlisle: Paternoster and Grand Rapids, Mich.: Baker Academic, 2002). Note the titles of ch. 1, 'Why Can't We Just Read the Bible? The Place of Tradition in Theology', and ch. 7, 'Baptism: Patristic Resources for Ecumenical Dialogue'. Holmes also treats these themes in his 2003 Whitely Lectures, *Tradition and Renewal in Baptist Life* (Oxford: Whitely Publications, 2003), and more generally in 'The Authority of the Christian Tradition: Introductory Essay', in *The Practice of Theology: A Reader*, ed. C.E. Gunton, S.R. Holmes, and M.A. Rae (London: SCM Press, 2001), pp. 55-59. A review of *Listening to the Past* published in *First Things* 141 (March, 2004), p. 55, erroneously identifies Holmes as an Anglican theologian.

23   B. Harvey, 'Doctrinally Speaking: James McClendon on the Nature of Doctrine', *PRSt* 27.1 (Spring, 2000), pp. 56-57, n. 82; cf. B. Harvey, 'Where, Then, Do We Stand? Baptists, History, and Authority', *PRSt* 29.4 (Winter, 2002), pp. 359-80, esp. 371-79.

Newman (Baptist Theological Seminary at Richmond, Virginia, USA) maintains that 'the creeds help us in knowing how to say and live the Christian story', for '[i]f we have only the individual and the Bible, then some other story or interpretive lens will easily prevail.'[24] In the period leading up to the Centenary Congress of the Baptist World Alliance in Birmingham, England, in July 2005, four of these catholic Baptist theologians in the United States issued a statement encouraging the plans of the program committee that eventuated in the Congress repeating on this occasion the liturgical act in which their predecessors participated at the inaugural meeting of the Baptist World Alliance in London in 1905: the recitation of the Apostles' Creed as a demonstration of Baptist solidarity with the larger Christian communion.[25] This statement on 'Confessing the Faith' maintained that such acts of credal confession, not only on occasions such as the Baptist World Congress but also in the weekly worship services of local congregations, would be salutary for Baptists, furnishing 'much needed hermeneutical guidance'.[26] Timothy George (Dean, Beeson Divinity School, Samford University, Birmingham, Alabama, USA) has also been active in seeking to help Baptists and evangelicals to appreciate the ancient ecumenical creeds as their own heritage.[27] Among British Baptists, Holmes

---

24   E. Newman, 'The Priesthood of All Believers and the Necessity of the Church', in *Recycling the Past or Researching History? Studies in Baptist Historiography and Myths*, ed. P.E. Thompson and A.R. Cross (SBHT, 11; Milton Keynes: Paternoster, 2005), p. 56, n. 32.

25   The transcript of Alexander Maclaren's 'President's Address' during the morning session of the Congress on 12 July 1905 reports Maclaren's call for this act and the response of the assembly: '"I should like that there be no misunderstanding on the part of the English public, or of the American public either…as to where we stand in the continuity of the historic Church. And I should like the first act of this Congress to be the audible and unanimous acknowledgement of our Faith. So I have suggested that, given your consent, it would be an impressive and a right thing, and would clear away a good many misunderstandings and stop the mouth of a good deal of slander—if we here and now, in the face of the world, not as a piece of coercion or discipline, but as a simple acknowledgement of where we stand and what we believe, would rise to our feet and, following the lead of your President, would repeat the Apostles' Creed. Will you?" The whole gathering then instantly rose and repeated, slowly and deliberately, after Dr. Maclaren the whole of the Apostles' Creed' (Baptist World Alliance, *Baptist World Congress 1905*, p. 20). In the opening session of the Centenary Congress on 27 July 2005, the assembly reprised this act, led by an actor playing the role of Maclaren.

26   C.W. Freeman, S.R. Harmon, E. Newman, and P.E. Thompson, 'Confessing the Faith', published as appendix 2 in the present volume.

27   In a newspaper interview, George explained this as a personal 'mission': 'They're [confessions of faith] important because they connect you to the whole wider Christian community. I'm a firm believer in creeds. [At Beeson] we require an essay on the Apostles' Creed as part of the admissions process. It's an antidote to radical

has argued for the recognition of the Nicene Creed as 'a central part of the tradition' that derives its authority from its 'successful repetition of central truths found already in the Bible, but because of that it has genuine authority as a privileged interpretation of Scripture, against which other claimed interpretations may be measured and tested.'[28] Paul Fiddes (Principal, Regent's Park College, Oxford, England) encourages the recitation of the creeds in Baptist worship, as 'it enables those who say the creed to be drawn anew into God's story, and so into God's own fellowship of life.'[29]

Liturgy as Context for Formation by Tradition

Third, catholic Baptist theologians give attention to liturgy as the primary context in which Christians are formed by tradition. They recognize the validity of Prosper of Aquitaine's maxim *'lex supplicandi statuat legem credendi'*—'let the rule of praying establish the rule of believing' (later abbreviated *'lex orandi, lex credendi'*—'the rule of praying is the rule of believing').[30] Although the Baptist tendency to reject forms and practices of worship deemed to be without biblical precedent has resulted in the separation of much Baptist worship from the liturgically situated tradition of the larger Christian community to which Baptists belong, several recent and current Baptist projects in liturgical theology seek to incorporate the *lex orandi, lex credendi* principle into the life of Baptist communities at worship. In keeping with the recommendation of Medley and Thompson that Baptists root discussions of the role of tradition in the first-order life of worshipping communities,[31] Anthony R. Cross (Centre for Baptist History and Heritage, Regent's Park College, Oxford, England), Christopher Ellis (Principal, Bristol Baptist College, Bristol, England), Stanley Fowler (Heritage Theological Seminary, Cambridge, Ontario, Canada), Thompson, and others have been exploring various aspects of liturgy as means through

---

individualism, and it promotes unity. Creeds are Trinitarian and very rich Christologically. We're talking about substance, not froth.' R.G. Russell, 'Q&A with Timothy George: "I'm a Firm Believer in Creeds"', *Dallas Morning News* (2 July 2005), pp. 1G, 4G.

28   Holmes, *Listening to the Past*, p. 161.

29   P.S. Fiddes, *Tracks and Traces: Baptist Identity in Church and Theology* (SBHT, 13; Carlisle: Paternoster Press, 2003), p. 217.

30   Prosper of Aquitaine *Praeteritorum Sedis Apostolicae episcoporum auctoritates, de gratia Dei et libero voluntatis arbitrio* 8; ET 'Official Pronouncements of the Apostolic See on Divine Grace and Free Will', in *Defense of St. Augustine*, trans. P. de Letter (ACW, 32; Westminster, Md.: Newman Press, 1963), p. 183.

31   Medley, 'Catholics, Baptists, and the Normativity of Tradition', p. 127, approvingly citing Thompson, 'Re-envisioning Baptist Identity', p. 290.

which Christians are formed by the Christian tradition.[32] Ellis has made an especially significant contribution to this endeavor with his book *Gathering: A Theology and Spirituality of Worship in the Free Church Tradition*, a full-fledged liturgical theology written from a Baptist perspective.[33] These recent catholic Baptist projects in liturgical theology were preceded by the contributions of Neville Clark and Stephen Winward to the mid-twentieth-century liturgical renewal movement among British Baptists. Clark's book *Call to Worship* and Winward's book *The Reformation of Our Worship* remain important resources for the Baptist reclamation of liturgy as the main arena for the theological formation of believers by the tradition of the church.[34]

Community as Locus of Authority

Fourth, catholic Baptist theologians locate the authority of tradition in the community and its formative practices. As Medley has noted, one of the most significant expressions of Baptist interest in a dynamic conception of tradition is the joint statement 'Re-Envisioning Baptist Identity: A Manifesto for Baptist Communities in North America', co-authored by Mikael Broadway (Shaw University Divinity School, Raleigh, North Carolina, USA), Freeman, Harvey, McClendon, Newman, and Thompson.[35]

---

32   See, e.g., Thompson, 'Re-envisioning Baptist Identity'; A.R. Cross and P.E. Thompson, eds., *Baptist Sacramentalism* (SBHT, 5; Carlisle: Paternoster Press, 2003); S.K. Fowler, *More Than a Symbol: The British Baptist Recovery of Baptismal Sacramentalism* (SBHT, 2; Carlisle: Paternoster Press, 2002); B. Harvey, 'The Eucharistic Idiom of the Gospel', *ProEccl* 9.3 (Summer, 2000), pp. 297-318; and the articles in *RevExp* 100.3 (Summer, 2003), a thematic issue on 'Baptists and Liturgy' edited by P.E. Thompson. Three recent dissertations and theses by Baptist scholars on these themes are worthy of note: C.J. Ellis, 'Baptist Worship: Liturgical Theology from a Free Church Perspective' (PhD thesis, University of Leeds, 2002); S.B. O'Connor, '*Lex Orandi, Lex Credendi*: An Investigation into the Liturgy and Theology of New Zealand Baptists' (ThM thesis, University of Auckland, 2001); N.C. Nettleton, 'The Liturgical Expression of Baptist Identity' (ThM thesis, Melbourne College of Divinity, 2000).

33   C.J. Ellis, *Gathering: A Theology and Spirituality of Worship in the Free Church Tradition* (London: SCM Press, 2004).

34   N. Clark, *Call to Worship* (London: SCM Press, 1960); S.F. Winward, *The Reformation of Our Worship* (Richmond, Va.: John Knox Press, 1965).

35   Medley, 'Catholics, Baptists, and the Normativity of Tradition', p. 126, citing M. Broadway, C.W. Freeman, B. Harvey, J.W. McClendon, Jr., E. Newman, and P.E. Thompson, 'Re-envisioning Baptist Identity: A Manifesto for Baptist Communities in North America', *BapTod* (26 June 1997), pp. 8-10; *PRSt* 24.3 (Fall, 1997), pp. 303-10; and reprinted as appendix 1 in the present volume.

The authors of the 'Baptist Manifesto' received their theological educations and became academic theologians themselves in the midst of the aforementioned theological controversies in the Southern Baptist Convention. They contend that both polarized parties in the conflict (variously labeled in the rhetoric of the controversy as fundamentalists and liberals, conservatives and moderates, or ultraconservatives and progressives) embraced conceptions of freedom and authority that have more to do with the modern milieu in which Baptist life flourished in the United States than with 'the freedom graciously given by God in Jesus Christ'. Drawing 'from earlier sources of the Baptist heritage . . . that have resisted modern notions of freedom and have practiced a more communal discipleship', the authors make the following affirmations: (1) 'We affirm Bible Study in reading communities rather than relying on private interpretation or supposed "scientific" objectivity'; (2) 'We affirm following Jesus as a call to shared discipleship rather than invoking a theory of soul competency';[36] (3) 'We affirm a free common life in Christ in gathered, reforming communities rather than withdrawn, self-chosen, or authoritarian ones'; (4) 'We affirm baptism, preaching, and the Lord's table as powerful signs that seal God's faithfulness in Christ and express our response of awed gratitude rather than as mechanical rituals or mere symbols'; and (5) 'We affirm freedom and renounce coercion as a distinct people under God rather than relying on political theories, powers, or authorities.'[37] Medley rightly suggests that the emphasis of the 'Baptist

---

36   'Soul competency' refers to a principle articulated by Baptist theologian E.Y. Mullins (1860-1928) in *The Axioms of Religion: A New Interpretation of the Baptist Faith* (Philadelphia: American Baptist Publication Society, 1908), in which he develops a sustained argument for the notion that 'religion is a personal matter between the [individual] soul and God' (p. 54) is 'the sufficient statement of the historical significance of the Baptists' (p. 53). The case that this is a reductionistic re-reading of the Baptist tradition through intellectual and political lenses ground in modern America is well argued by C.W. Freeman, 'E.Y. Mullins and the Siren Songs of Modernity', *RevExp* 96.1 (Winter, 1999), pp. 23-42. It is possible to conceive of 'soul competency' so as to guard against the concept's individualistic abuse: an individual may indeed be 'competent' in matters of religion inasmuch as that individual is a Spirit-empowered, church-equipped, and socially-embodied soul. Newman, 'Priesthood of All Believers', p. 55, makes a similar point: 'We cannot learn the habits and skills necessary to use, and thus to live and to be, the "priesthood of all believers" faithfully apart from the church.'

37   The document develops each of these affirmations more fully and joins them with rejections of various Baptist perversions of these ecclesial principles. For critical responses to the 'Baptist Manifesto' from Baptist historians and theologians, see W.B. Shurden, 'The Baptist Identity and the Baptist Manifesto', *PRSt* 25.4 (Winter, 1998), pp. 321-40; R.P. Jones, 'Re-Visioning Baptist Identity from a Theocentric Perspective', *PRSt* 26.1 (Spring, 1999), pp. 35-57. For additional reflections and counter-responses

Manifesto' on Baptist communities' practices of Bible reading, witnessing, gathering, and worship may be restated as an ecclesiology of the church in its local and catholic expressions as an actively traditioning community (in the sense of the Latin *traditio*, 'the act of handing down') rather than a community that merely possesses tradition (in the sense of *traditia*, 'the things that are handed down').[38]

Sacramental Theology

Fifth, catholic Baptist theologians advocate a sacramental theology. 'Sacramental' here means not only a more robust appreciation of the Lord's presence in baptism and the Eucharist than is the case with the symbolic reductionism typical of Baptist theologies of the ordinances influenced by the Zwinglian tradition,[39] but more broadly a theology that understands the sacraments of baptism and the Eucharist as paradigmatic of the relation of God to the material order that is disclosed in the Incarnation. A noteworthy exemplar of this feature of a catholic Baptist theology is a recent book by John Colwell (Spurgeon's College, London, England), *Promise and Presence: An Exploration of Sacramental Theology*, which from a Baptist perspective develops a sacramental theology in the fullest sense of that category and seeks a Protestant retrieval of the seven sacraments as enumerated in the Roman Catholic tradition.[40] Many of the contributors to a volume of essays on *Baptist Sacramentalism* edited by Cross and

---

from co-authors of the 'Baptist Manifesto', see C.W. Freeman, 'Can Baptist Theology Be Revisioned?' *PRSt* 24.3 (Fall, 1997), pp. 273-310; C.W. Freeman, 'A New Perspective on Baptist Identity', *PRSt* 26.1 (Spring, 1999), pp. 59-65; Thompson, 'Re-envisioning Baptist Identity.'

38   Medley, 'Catholics, Baptists, and the Normativity of Tradition', pp. 126-27.

39   Many Baptist interpretations of baptism and the Eucharist as 'merely symbolic' are radically reductionistic versions of the more robust theology of the sacraments as symbols advocated by Zwingli, for whom there was a real and inseparable connection between the sign and the thing signified. A recovery of this fuller Zwinglian symbolism would be a significant improvement for much Baptist sacramental theology, but as M.T. Marshall suggested in a recent published interview, Baptists need also to look beyond Zwingli: 'I've been on a mission to re-sacramentalize Baptist theology— our practices of baptism and the Eucharist. Because I think we followed the wrong Reformer in [Ulrich] Zwingli' ('A Conversation with Molly Marshall', *BapTod* 23.1 [November, 2005], p. 17).

40   J.E. Colwell, *Promise and Presence: An Exploration of Sacramental Theology* (Milton Keynes: Paternoster, 2006).

Thompson also seek to cultivate a sacramental theology among Baptists.[41] Their proposals, though far from monolithic, share in common an interest in retrieving from the larger Christian tradition this sacramental narration of the world that forms the Christian self. Especially noteworthy are Thompson's study of the political factors underlying the modern loss of an earlier Baptist sacramentality, Harvey's exploration of the political implications of a hoped-for recovery of a sacramental understanding of Baptist faith and practice, Freeman's essay reflecting on the Eucharist as divine nourishment, Newman's Baptist proposal for a theory of real presence, and Colwell's consideration of the sacramentality of ordination.[42] Beyond this collection of essays, a deeply sacramental theology rooted in a participatory understanding of the work of the Triune God figures prominently in recent books by Fiddes.[43] Fowler has engaged the recovery of baptismal sacramentalism by twentieth-century British Baptist theologians as a superior alternative to the symbolic reductionism of much Baptist baptismal theology,[44] Cross has actively advocated for a sacramental understanding of baptism by Baptists,[45] and Medley has given attention to the self-forming efficacy of Eucharistic celebration.[46]

---

41   Cross and Thompson, eds., *Baptist Sacramentalism*. A second volume of essays on this theme, also edited by Cross and Thompson, is forthcoming under the title *Baptist Sacramentalism 2* (SBHT, 25; Milton Keynes: Paternoster, 2006).

42   P.E. Thompson, 'Sacraments and Religious Liberty: From Critical Practice to Rejected Infringement', in *Baptist Sacramentalism*, ed. Cross and Thompson, pp. 36-54; B. Harvey, 'Re-Membering the Body: Baptism, Eucharist and the Politics of Disestablishment' (pp. 96-116); C.W. Freeman, '"To Feed Upon by Faith": Nourishment from the Lord's Table' (pp. 194-210); E. Newman, 'The Lord's Supper: Might Baptists Accept a Theory of Real Presence?' (pp. 211-227); J.E. Colwell, 'The Sacramental Nature of Ordination: An Attempt to Re-Engage a Catholic Understanding and Practice' (pp. 228-46).

43   P.S. Fiddes, 'The Incarnate God and the Sacramental Life', ch. in *Participating in God: A Pastoral Doctrine of the Trinity* (Louisville, Ky.: Westminster John Knox, 2000), pp. 278-304; P.S. Fiddes, *Tracks and Traces*, pp. 107-92.

44   Fowler, *More Than a Symbol*; see esp. pp. 196-253.

45   A.R. Cross, '"One Baptism" (Ephesians 4.5): A Challenge to the Church', in *Baptism, the New Testament, and the Church: Historical and Contemporary Studies in Honour of R.E.O. White* (JSTNSup, 171; Sheffield: Sheffield Academic Press, 1999), pp. 173-209; 'Spirit- and Water-Baptism in 1 Corinthians 12.13', in *Dimensions of Baptism: Biblical and Theological Studies*, ed. S.E. Porter and A.R. Cross (JSNTSup, 234; Sheffield: Sheffield Academic Press, 2002), pp. 120-48; 'Baptism, Christology and the Creeds in the Early Church: Implications for Ecumenical Dialogue', in *Ecumenism and History: Studies in Honour of John H.Y. Briggs*, ed. A.R. Cross (Carlisle: Paternoster, 2002), pp. 23-49; 'The Pneumatological Key to H. Wheeler Robinson's Baptismal Sacramentalism', in Cross and Thompson, eds., *Baptist Sacramentalism*, pp.

Constructive Retrieval of Tradition

Sixth, catholic Baptist theologians engage tradition as a resource for contemporary theological construction in a manner comparable to the *ressourcement* agenda of the *'nouvelle théologie'* movement in mid-twentieth-century Roman Catholic theology that influenced many of the developments of the Second Vatican Council.[47] For example, Baptist theologians are increasingly becoming participants in the contemporary renaissance of Trinitarian theology under the banner of social Trinitarian thought. In retrieving a perichoretic understanding of the Trinity in the Cappadocian/Damascene tradition, Baptist theologians Fiddes, Medley, and Molly Marshall (President, Central Baptist Theological Seminary, Kansas City, Kansas, USA) have discovered in the tradition resources of relevance to the contemporary context that would never have been discovered in an a-traditional encounter of the individual theologian with the biblical text.[48] As in the *nouvelle théologie*, the task of *ressourcement*, 'retrieval', is prerequisite for *aggiornamento*, 'updating'. Harvey's recovery for contemporary ecclesiology of the patristic concept of the church as *altera civitas* and the limited but significant Baptist engagements of patristic and Byzantine concepts of divinization by Fiddes, Grenz, and Clark Pinnock (Emeritus, McMaster Divinity College, Hamilton, Ontario, Canada) explored by Medley also exemplify this sort of constructive retrieval of the tradition.[49]

151-76; 'Being Open to God's Sacramental Word: A Study in Baptism', in *Semper Reformandum: Studies in Honour of Clark H. Pinnock*, ed. S.E. Porter and A.R. Cross (Carlisle: Paternoster, 2003), pp. 355-77; 'Faith-Baptism: The Key to an Evangelical Baptismal Sacramentalism', *JEBapSt* 4.3 (May, 2004), pp. 5-21.

46   M.S. Medley, '"Do This": The Eucharist and Ecclesial Selfhood', *RevExp* 100.3 (Summer, 2003), pp. 383-401.

47   The *nouvelle théologie* and its approach to tradition receive attention in ch. 3, 'The Authority of the Community (of All the Saints): Towards a Postmodern Baptist Hermeneutic of Tradition'.

48   Fiddes, *Participating in God*; M.S. Medley, *Imago Trinitatis: Toward a Relational Understanding of Becoming Human* (Lanham, Md.: University Press of America, 2002); M.T. Marshall, *Joining the Dance: A Theology of the Spirit* (Valley Forge, Pa.: Judson Press, 2003). In the cited works by Medley and Marshall, the retrieval of perichoretic Trinitarianism is mediated by an engagement with feminist Trinitarian theologians such as Patricia Wilson-Kastner and Catherine Mowry LaCugna who make much constructive use of patristic perichoretic thought.

49   B. Harvey, *Another City: An Ecclesiological Primer for a Post-Christian World* (Harrisburg, Pa.: Trinity Press International, 1999); M.S. Medley, 'The Use of Theosis in Contemporary Baptist Theology' (unpublished paper presented to the annual meeting of the American Academy of Religion—Southeast Region, Atlanta, Georgia, 5-7 March 2004, and the joint annual meeting of the College Theology Society and

Thick Ecumenism

Seventh, catholic Baptist theologians are proponents of a thick ecumenism. A 'thin' ecumenism seeks to overcome difference through a too facile identification of lowest common denominator agreements between traditions. In contrast, a 'thick' ecumenism proceeds on the basis of a common commitment both to deep exploration of the ancient ecumenical tradition and to deep exploration of the particularities of the respective denominational traditions—an approach to ecumenical dialogue that Tarmo Toom, an Estonian Baptist with a doctorate from The Catholic University of America who teaches theology in the United States (John Leland Center for Theological Studies, Arlington, Virginia, USA), calls a 'diachronic ecumenism' that 'takes a deep look into the shared past of Christianity and finds there the basis for mutual understanding and appreciation'.[50] This is the sort of ecumenism exemplified by the Center for Catholic and Evangelical Theology and its journal *Pro Ecclesia*. The fourteen volumes of *Pro Ecclesia* published through 2005 contain articles authored by Toom, Williams, George, Harvey, Holmes, Thompson, Nigel Wright (Principal, Spurgeon's College, London, England), Ralph Wood (Baylor University, Waco, Texas, USA), Scott Moore (Baylor University, Waco, Texas, USA), and Roger Olson (George W. Truett Theological Seminary, Baylor University, Waco, Texas, USA), all of whom are Baptist theologians committed in some manner to this thick ecumenism that characterizes a catholic Baptist theology operating within the horizon of tradition.[51] Fiddes

National Association of Baptist Professors of Religion Region-at-Large, Washington, D.C., 3-6 June 2004).

50   T. Toom, 'Baptists on Justification: Can We Join the Joint Declaration on the Doctrine of Justification?' *ProEccl* 13.3 (Summer, 2004), p. 291, n. 7.

51   T. George, 'John Paul II: An Appreciation', *ProEccl* 14.3 (Summer, 2005), pp. 267-70; N.G. Wright, 'The Petrine Ministry: Baptist Reflections', *ProEccl* 13.4 (Fall, 2004), pp. 451-65; D.H. Williams, 'The Disintegration of Catholicism into Diffuse Inclusivism', *ProEccl* 12.4 (Fall, 2003), pp. 389-93; T. George, 'The Sacramentality of the Church: An Evangelical Baptist Perspective', *ProEccl* 12.3 (Summer, 2003), pp. 309-23; B. Harvey, 'Review Essay: M.B. Copenhaver, A.B. Robinson, and W.H. Willimon, *Good News in Exile*; M.J. Dawn, *A Royal 'Waste' of Time*; C. Van Gelder, ed., *Confident Witness-Changing World*; J.R. Wilson, *Living Faithfully in a Fragmented World*', *ProEccl* 10.4 (Fall, 2001), pp. 487-90; S.R. Holmes, 'The Justice of Hell and the Display of God's Glory in the Thought of Jonathan Edwards', *ProEccl* 9.4 (Fall, 2000), pp. 389-403; T. George, 'An Evangelical Reflection on Scripture and Tradition', *ProEccl* 9.2 (Spring, 2000), pp. 184-207; R.C. Wood, 'Review Essay: D.W. Fagerberg, *The Size of Chesterton's Catholicism*', *ProEccl* 9.2 (Spring, 2000), pp. 236-40; S.H. Moore, 'The End of Convenient Stereotypes: How the First Things and Baxter Controversies Inaugurate Extraordinary Politics', *ProEccl* 7 (Winter, 1998), pp. 17-47; R.E. Olson, 'Whales and Elephants: Both God's Creatures, but Can They Meet?

has explored at length the implications for Baptist faith and practice of an ecumenism that 'begins from the bottom up rather than top-down', has a 'vision of 'full communion' rather than 'one world church', and is open to 'the acceptance of diversity in the unity'.[52]

Not all Baptist theologians mentioned in connection with these seven identifying marks of a catholic Baptist theology would identify themselves with all seven marks, and there are doubtless other Baptist theologians unnamed herein who would gladly concur with all seven marks. Of the Baptist theologians in the United States with whose work I am familiar, Freeman, George, Harvey, Medley, Newman, Thompson, Williams, and Wood[53] most fully exemplify my description of catholic Baptist theologians (though some of them might wish to qualify such a categorization). Among British Baptists, one may easily discern the seven catholic Baptist marks in the writings of Colwell, Cross, Ellis, Fiddes, and Holmes. The work of these catholic Baptist theologians collectively maps out possible pathways towards the renewal of Baptist ecclesial life through a conscious retrieval of the catholic tradition that already belongs to Baptists as members of the body of Christ. Perhaps like the small circle of Oxford Tractarians who sought the renewal of the Church of England along similar lines in the nineteenth century, their influence also may yet extend far beyond their initial prospects of success.[54]

Towards Baptist Catholicity: Seeking a Place for Tradition in the Baptist Vision

Towards Baptist Catholicity is this theologian's effort to contribute to this encouraging trend in Baptist academic theology. The substance of the essays that constitute the chapters of this book had earlier incarnations as

---

Evangelicals and Liberals in Dialogue', *ProEccl* 4 (Spring, 1995), pp. 165-89; as well as the previously cited articles by Toom, 'Baptists on Justification', Harvey, 'Eucharistic Idiom of the Gospel', and Thompson, 'New Question in Baptist History.'

52   P.S. Fiddes, 'The Church's Ecumenical Calling: A Baptist Perspective', ch. 9 in *Tracks and Traces*, pp. 193-227.

53   Wood, whose scholarship focuses on the intersection of theology and literature, is not a systematic or constructive theologian proper. Nevertheless, the identifying marks of a catholic Baptist theology are in the background of Wood's books, articles, essays, and reviews exploring the theological dimensions of works of fiction by American and British authors and in the foreground of R.C. Wood, *Contending for the Faith: The Church's Engagement with Culture* (ICTT, 1; Waco, Tex.: Baylor University Press, 2003), esp. pp. 185-98.

54   The Oxford Movement as a possible paradigm for catholic Baptist renewal receives attention in ch. 10, '"What Keeps You from Becoming a Catholic?" A Personal Epilogue'.

addresses, journal articles, book chapters, and contributions to *Festschriften* presented and published during the period 2001-2006. Though they were initially conceived for various occasions, audiences, and readerships, in both their previous and present forms they are unified in the contention that the reconstruction of the Baptist vision in the wake of modernity's dissolution requires the retrieval of the ancient catholic tradition that forms Christian identity through liturgical rehearsal and embodied practice.

Any perspective on the role of tradition in Christian faith and practice is situated within a particular conception of the nature of Christian authority. Who or what authorizes a doctrine or a practice in the church? What are the proper functions of Scripture, tradition, reason, and experience (as the so-called 'Wesleyan Quadrilateral' identifies the major sources of Christian authority) in an economy of authority? What role does the church in its local, denominational, and universal expressions play in authorizing doctrine and practice? The Baptist vision has been shaped by distinctive ways of answering these questions. Chapter 2, 'Baptist Understandings of Theological Authority: A North American Perspective', accordingly provides a broad context for the proposals in this book by surveying the patterns of authority for faith and practice that are exemplified in Baptist confessions of faith and the writings of Baptist theologians, with special reference to North American expressions of Baptist life. Originally prepared for the North American phase of a five-year series of bilateral conversations between the Baptist World Alliance and the Anglican Consultative Council, the chapter places this case for the importance of tradition for the Baptist vision in the context of the ecumenical quest for a mutually recovered catholicity.

The Baptist denomination was born out of reactions against coercive structures of ecclesiastical authority that the earliest Baptists believed had stifled the Spirit and had restricted ecclesial communities from obeying the Spirit's voice they heard speaking in the Scriptures. The concepts of tradition that Baptists have typically rejected are linked to these formative traumatic experiences of oppression by ecclesiastical hierarchies that appealed to tradition as substantiating their authority. Chapter 3, 'The Authority of the Community (of All the Saints): Towards a Postmodern Baptist Hermeneutic of Tradition', therefore proposes an alternative conception of tradition and its relationship to Christian community that respects these aspects of Baptist origins while seeking to address the postmodern situation in which Baptists now find themselves.

Some Baptist readers may protest that the proposals in this book are asking Baptists to embrace something that is alien to the Baptist tradition. While they may be in tension with certain expressions of the Baptist vision that have prevailed in America in the nineteenth and twentieth centuries, these proposed perspectives on tradition have precedents in earlier patterns of Baptist faith and practice, especially during the first century of Baptist existence from the early 1600s to the early 1700s. Chapter 4, 'Baptist Confessions of Faith and the Patristic Tradition', explores the surprisingly rich continuity that early Baptist confessional documents maintained with pre-Reformation doctrinal catholicity.

Although the doctrine of the Trinity is one of the principal loci of Baptist confessional continuity with the pre-Reformation theological tradition, many modern Baptists have shown little interest in the connections between formal articulations of Trinitarian orthodoxy and the faith and practice of Baptist churches. Sometimes this indifference toward Trinitarian theology is rooted in the supposition that the patristic Trinitarian formulations were developments beyond the clear teaching of the Bible that obscured the richness of the biblical story by reducing it to rational propositions. Chapter 5, 'From Triadic Narrative to Narrating the Triune God: Towards a Baptist Appreciation of Trinitarian Catholicity', offers an alternative reading of the development of patristic Trinitarian theology that underscores its continuing relationship to biblical narrative and its liturgical rehearsal by the church.

The formation of Christians through the narration of biblical salvation history by the community at worship was the chief end and primary context for patristic biblical interpretation. Yet much post-Enlightenment biblical interpretation by Baptist Scripture scholars has become detached from this context and given insufficient attention to this end, and the teaching and preaching of the Bible in Baptist congregations has long been disconnected from the practice of reading the Bible along with the communion of saints that includes patristic and medieval expositors of Scripture along with Reformation-era and modern interpreters. Chapter 6, 'Hebrews in Patristic Perspective: Benefits of Catholicity for Baptist Biblical Interpretation', illustrates the utility of consulting ancient catholic biblical exegesis, in addition to modern critical commentaries, for helping Baptists towards a more fully ecclesial reading of Scripture, using the biblical book selected by a group of Baptists in the United States for their 2006 Annual Bible Study as the primary illustration of these benefits.

The next three chapters turn to the ecclesial and institutional settings in which a contemporary Baptist retrieval of pre-Reformation catholicity might take place. Thus far interest in a catholic Baptist programme of retrieval has been almost exclusively limited to academic theologians. The current state of affairs might lead some to regard this discussion as a curious phenomenon, interesting but ultimately of little consequence for the warp and woof of Baptist church life. Yet it may be that Baptist theologians teaching in seminaries, divinity schools, and universities are precisely the ones who have the greatest long-term potential for influencing Baptist congregations and their ministers towards Baptist catholicity through their exercise of the ecclesial teaching office to which they have been called. Those who teach in institutions of graduate/professional theological education are the ones charged with the responsibility for the theological formation of future Baptist ministers, and through them the doctrinal formation of members of Baptist congregations. Chapter 7, 'Hearing the Voice of the Community: Karl Barth's Conversation with the Fathers as a Paradigm for Baptist and Evangelical *Ressourcement*', looks to this Swiss Reformed theologian's career-long critical engagement with patristic theology as a possible model for Baptist theologians in mining the catholic tradition for the resources they need in their constructive theological work in, with, and for Baptist communities today.

Intentional engagement with the pre-Reformation catholic tradition in the form of classroom lectures, systematic theologies, and other theological publications is an ultimately insignificant intellectual exercise if it does not have an impact on what happens in the regular worship and teaching ministries of local Baptist churches, which is where the most significant theological formation of Baptist Christians takes place. Chapter 8, 'Praying and Believing: Retrieving the Patristic Interdependence of Worship and Theology', focuses on the weekly worship of Baptist congregations as the primary means by which Baptists regularly participate in and are formed by the Christian tradition.

Baptists throughout the world, but especially in the United States, have been prolific founders and generous supporters of institutions of Christian higher education. They have established not only seminaries and divinity schools for the graduate/professional training of ministers but also colleges and universities that provide undergraduate, graduate, and professional education in a wide variety of academic disciplines and professional fields. Baptist colleges and universities provide opportunities, far beyond what local churches are able to provide, for Baptist and non-Baptist students to enter into intensive intellectual engagement with the riches of the Christian tradition in connection with the study of the liberal arts and preparation for specific vocations. A lively debate is underway in the United States about the identity and mission of Christian colleges and universities, and Baptists have been increasingly active participants in this discussion. Chapter 9, 'Contesting Our Story: Catholicity and Communal Conflict in Baptist Higher Education', suggests ways in which the re-conceived place for tradition in the Baptist vision proposed in this book, in particular the recognition of the value of dissent about the tradition for the health of the tradition, can help Baptist institutions of higher education with ever more diverse faculties, student bodies, and constituencies to survive the conflicts that have sometimes ensued when such institutions have become more intentional about their Christian identities.

These proposals regarding tradition and Baptist catholicity emerge from tensions between my own experience of the Baptist tradition that has formed me in Christian faith and my hopes for the future of this tradition that still has so much to contribute to the broader body of Christ yet also has so much to learn from the rest of the 'one, holy, catholic, and apostolic church'. The final chapter, '"What Keeps You from Becoming a Catholic?" A Personal Epilogue', offers concluding reflections on this tension. This epilogue makes a case that working towards catholicity within the denominational communion of one's nurture and calling rather than seeking it in another communion is a matter of ecumenical responsibility. The epilogue also draws lessons from historical examples of catholic retrieval movements in other denominations that are, like Baptists, communions currently separated ecclesiastically from Rome and Constantinople but nonetheless called along with Rome and Constantinople to seek the realization of Jesus' prayer to the Father on behalf of the church: 'that they may be one, as we are one, I in them and you in me, that they may become completely one, so that the world may know that you have sent me and have loved them even as you have loved me' (John 17.22-23).

CHAPTER 2

Baptist Understandings of Theological Authority: A North American Perspective

'The apostles and the elders met together to consider this matter. After there had been much debate, Peter stood up and said to them, "My brothers, you know that in the early days God made a choice among you, that I should be the one through whom the Gentiles would hear the message of the good news and become believers. And God, who knows the human heart, testified to them by giving them the Holy Spirit, just as he did to us; and in cleansing their hearts by faith he made no distinction between them and us. Now therefore why are you putting God to the test by placing on the neck of the disciples a yoke *that neither our ancestors nor we have been able to bear?* On the contrary, we believe that we will be saved through the grace of the Lord Jesus, just as they will." *The whole assembly kept silence, and listened to Barnabas and Paul as they told of all the signs and wonders that God had done through them among the Gentiles.* After they finished speaking, James replied, "My brothers, listen to me. Simeon has related how God first looked favorably on the Gentiles, to take from among them a people for his name. *This agrees with the words of the prophets, as it is written...* Therefore *I have reached the decision* that we should not trouble those Gentiles who are turning to God, but we should write to them to abstain only from things polluted by idols and from fornication and from whatever has been strangled and from blood. For in every city, for generations past, Moses has had those who proclaim him, for he has been read aloud every Sabbath in the synagogues." Then the apostles and the elders, *with the consent of the whole church*, decided to choose men from among their members and to send them to Antioch with Paul and Barnabas. They sent Judas called Barsabbas, and Silas, leaders among the brothers, with the following letter... So they were sent off and went down to Antioch. When they *gathered the congregation together*, they delivered the letter. *When its members read it, they rejoiced at the exhortation.'* Acts 15.6-31 NRSV (emphasis added)*

When I was invited to prepare a paper on 'A Baptist Understanding of Authority' for the North American phase of the Anglican-Baptist International Conversations held at Acadia University, Wolfville, Nova Scotia, Canada, 10-12 September 2003, my first step in preparing for the task was to modify the title of that presentation (upon which the present chapter is based).[1] A literal construal of the topic would have rendered my task impossible, for there is not a singular Baptist understanding of authority, nor are there universally authoritative sources in the Baptist world to which one might look for expressions of such an understanding. Although Baptist historians have from time to time published collections of confessions of faith adopted by Baptist congregations and denominational bodies across the past four centuries,[2] such collections were intended to function as historical reference works rather than as handbooks of doctrinal standards comparable to those of other Protestant traditions,[3] e.g. the Lutheran *Book of Concord* or the *Book of Confessions* of the Presbyterian Church (USA).[4] One might offer instead 'A Baptist's Understanding of Authority', but the idiosyncrasies of an individual Baptist theologian's understanding of authority would have contributed little to the aims of the dialogue. Instead, that presentation and this chapter offer an overview of Baptist understandings of authority, plural, with special reference to the

---

1   This meeting followed five previous phases held in regions in which there is significant local contact between adherents to the Baptist and Anglican traditions: Norwich, England (for the European region) in 2000; Yangon, Myanmar (for the Asia/Pacific region) in 2001; Nairobi, Kenya (for the African region) in 2002; and Santiago, Chile (for the Latin American region) and Nassau, Bahamas (for the Caribbean region) in January 2003. The delegations to these theological conversations pursued the following mutual objectives: (1) 'To enable Anglicans/Baptists to learn from each other and to deepen understanding of relationships between our two communions in the light of their histories'; (2) 'To share with each other how we understand the Christian faith and to work toward a common confession of the Apostolic Faith'; (3) 'To identify issues of doctrine and the nature of the church to be explored further in possible future conversations'; and (4) 'To look for ways to cooperate in mission and community activities and increase our fellowship and common witness to the Gospel'. A final report of these conversations has now been published: Anglican Communion Office and Baptist World Alliance, *Conversations around the World 2000-2005: The Report of the International Conversations between the Anglican Communion and the Baptist World Alliance* (London: Anglican Communion Office, 2005).

2   E.g., E.B. Underhill, *Confessions of Faith and Other Public Documents Illustrative of the History of the Baptist Churches of England in the 17th Century* (London: Haddon Brothers, 1854); W.J. McGlothlin, *Baptist Confessions of Faith* (Philadelphia: American Baptist Publication Society, 1911); Lumpkin, *Baptist Confessions of Faith*; G.K. Parker, *Baptists in Europe: History and Confessions of Faith* (Nashville, Tenn.: Broadman Press, 1982).

3   This function of collections of Baptist confessions has been noted by, *inter alios*, W.L. Lumpkin, 'The Nature and Authority of Baptist Confessions of Faith', *RevExp* 76 (Winter, 1979), p. 18.

4   R. Kolb and T.J. Wengert, eds., *The Book of Concord: The Confessions of the Evangelical Lutheran Church*, trans. C.P. Arand (Minneapolis: Fortress Press, 2000); Presbyterian Church (USA), *The Constitution of the Presbyterian Church (USA): Part 1, Book of Confessions* (Louisville, Ky.: Office of the General Assembly, 1996).

Baptist context in North America. In what follows, the discussion of authority is limited to *theological* authority for Baptist faith and practice. Nevertheless, as doctrinal authority cannot be separated from its ecclesial locus, there will necessarily be some conceptual overlap with ecclesiastical authority. This survey begins by giving voice to basic convictions about authority held in common by most Baptists, but within the explanation of each common conviction the diversity that characterizes Baptist understandings of those convictions receives some attention. As sources for these understandings, confessions of faith adopted by various Baptist associational and denominational bodies provide the major indicators of common Baptist opinion. In addition to these confessional testimonies to Baptist perspectives on theological authority, references to recent and contemporary Baptist theologians from North America serve to indicate emerging trends in Baptist understandings of authority not yet reflected in more consensual confessional statements.

The Baptist Ecclesial Location of the Perspective

Before proceeding with this overview, a note about the background and context out of which these reflections on Baptist understandings of authority are offered is in order. I am a life-long Baptist—raised, baptized, and ordained as a minister in Baptist congregations in Texas affiliated with the Southern Baptist Convention (SBC), the largest Protestant denomination in North America with approximately 42,000 member congregations at present. The years of my undergraduate and graduate theological education (1986-1997) overlapped with a period during which the SBC was embroiled in a bitter political and theological struggle for control of its agencies and institutions, in particular its six official theological seminaries.[5] Beginning in 1979, well-organized campaigns by ultraconservative Southern Baptists (often called "fundamentalists" by their opponents) succeeded in electing candidates identified with their cause as president of the SBC at their annual conventions. As the president of the SBC appoints the members of committees charged with nominating the

---

5   See Leonard, *God's Last and Only Hope*; Ammerman, *Baptist Battles*; Morgan, *The New Crusades, the New Holy Land*; Hankins, *Uneasy in Babylon: Southern Baptist Conservatives and American Culture*. For a 'moderate' recounting of the conflict and the genesis of the Cooperative Baptist Fellowship and related institutions, see W.B. Shurden, ed., *The Struggle for the Soul of the SBC: Moderate Responses to the Fundamentalist Movement* (Macon, Ga.: Mercer University Press, 1993). Histories of the conflict written from the perspective of the ultraconservatives are J. Sutton, *The Baptist Reformation: The Conservative Resurgence in the Southern Baptist Convention* (Nashville, Tenn.: Broadman & Holman, 2000), and J. Hefley, *The Conservative Resurgence in the Southern Baptist Convention* (Hannibal, Mo.: Hannibal Books, 1991).

membership of the boards of trustees of all SBC institutions, by 1990 ultraconservative majorities controlled the boards of the seminaries and other institutions. In 1991 moderate to progressive Southern Baptists (often called "liberals" by their opponents), by then disenfranchised from leadership of the SBC and its institutions for the foreseeable future, formed the Cooperative Baptist Fellowship (CBF). Approximately 1,300 local congregations are currently affiliated with the CBF; many of these continue to maintain some degree of affiliation with the SBC as well. The CBF funds several institutions and agencies that provide the same sorts of denominational services and mission avenues formerly provided for these congregations by the SBC, but with much looser ties: a missions organization; a publishing house; a news service; an ethics center; and twelve new institutions of theological education, including university-related divinity schools, free-standing seminaries, and programs of Baptist studies in non-Baptist theological schools.[6] I teach systematic theology and ethics in one of these new CBF-related theological education institutions, the Campbell University Divinity School in Buies Creek, North Carolina. As a theologian identified with the CBF, I belong to an expression of Baptist life that has its origins in protest against the imposition of narrowed doctrinal parameters as criteria for denominational service. On the other hand, as a specialist in patristic theology whose thought has been significantly enriched by dialogue with the great thinkers of the formative period of Christian doctrine, I have a keen interest in helping Baptists to claim the post-biblical Christian tradition as their own. This chapter and this book as a whole reflect a tension that is at the heart of my own work as a Baptist theologian: between the Baptist tradition of dissent and liberty of conscience on the one hand and the Baptist indebtedness to post-New Testament and pre-Reformation doctrinal tradition on the other. This tension is not, however, an idiosyncratic, recent, and alien addition to

---

6   The following institutions of theological education have 'partner' relationships with the CBF: Baptist Seminary of Kentucky, Lexington, Kentucky; Baptist Theological Seminary at Richmond, Richmond, Virginia; Baptist House of Studies, Duke University Divinity School, Durham, North Carolina; Baptist Studies Program, Brite Divinity School, Texas Christian University, Fort Worth, Texas; Baptist Studies Program, Candler School of Theology, Emory University, Atlanta, Georgia; Campbell University Divinity School, Buies Creek, North Carolina; M. Christopher White School of Divinity, Gardner-Webb University, Boiling Springs, North Carolina; Central Baptist Theological Seminary, Kansas City, Kansas (a seminary of the American Baptist Churches, USA, since 1901, but newly affiliated also with the CBF); George W. Truett Theological Seminary, Baylor University, Waco, Texas; Logsdon School of Theology, Hardin-Simmons University, Abilene, Texas; McAfee School of Theology, Mercer University, Atlanta, Georgia; and Wake Forest University Divinity School, Winston-Salem, North Carolina.

historic Baptist identity, for the earliest Baptists took great pains to highlight their continued connections with the church in its catholicity.[7]

Ultimate Authority: The Triune God

In general, Baptists ascribe ultimate authority to the Triune God. Although Baptists in both England and North America have experienced occasional outbreaks of Unitarianism in the past, and although Baptist confessions have sometimes preferred the biblical language of Father, Son, and Spirit to explicitly Trinitarian language, in the main Baptists are Nicaeno-Constantinopolitan Trinitarians, even when they are not conscious of the historical origins of their Trinitarian faith.[8] With few exceptions, early Baptist confessions issued in the Netherlands and England begin not with statements about the authority of the Bible (and frequently lacked such statements) but rather with articles on the nature and attributes of the one God who is Father, Son, and Holy Spirit. It is not making too much of this ordering of confessional statements to discern in it the conviction that God is the ultimate authority for Christian faith and practice.[9] Confessions issued in North America during the nineteenth and twentieth centuries, however, have normally begun with an article on the inspiration and authority of the Scriptures. This shift does not indicate a reversal of ultimate authorities in North American Baptist thought. The initial placement of articles on the Scriptures in these more recent North American confessions may be attributed rather to two factors. First, the *Philadelphia Confession* of 1742, the earliest Baptist associational confession adopted in the American colonies, inherited this placement of the article on the Scriptures from the *Second London Confession* of 1677, which in turn was derived from the ordering of the *Westminster Confession* of 1647.[10] The widespread adoption of the *Philadelphia Confession* by local churches and associations throughout the colonies no doubt influenced the ordering of later American confessions. Second, during the nineteenth and twentieth

---

7   See ch. 4, 'Baptist Confessions of Faith and the Patristic Tradition'.

8   On the echoes of Nicaeno-Constantinopolitan Trinitarianism in early Baptist confessions of faith, see again ch. 4, 'Baptist Confessions of Faith and the Patristic Tradition'.

9   Cf. J.B. Pool, 'Christ, Conscience, Canon, Community: Web of Authority in the Baptist Vision', *PRSt* 24.4 (Winter, 1997), pp. 421-22.

10   For the *Second London Confession* and *Philadelphia Confession*, see W.L. Lumpkin, *Baptist Confessions of Faith*, rev. edn. (Valley Forge, Pa.: Judson Press, 1969), pp. 241-95 and 348-51; the English text of the *Westminster Confession* is printed in *The Creeds of Christendom with a History and Critical Notes*, 6th edn., ed. P. Schaff, rev. D.S. Schaff, vol. 3, *The Evangelical Protestant Creeds* [New York: Harper & Row, 1931; reprint, Grand Rapids, Mich.: Baker Book House, 1990], pp. 598-673 [page references are to reprint edition]).

centuries American Baptists began to respond to the challenges of historical-critical biblical studies and evolutionary theory, with some Baptist groups giving increased attention to the inspiration and authority of the Scriptures in their confessions. Even if these documents emphasize Scripture as the means by which God is known, those who have adopted and affirmed these confessions would agree that any legitimate source of religious authority derives from the God who is revealed in the person of Jesus Christ to whom the Spirit bears witness.

Derivative Authority: The Supremacy of the Scriptures

In general, Baptists identify Scripture as the supreme earthly source of authority. Many early Baptist confessions lacked articles on the Scriptures,[11] but they evidenced a radical biblicism in their copious prooftexting of confessional statements with parenthetical and marginal biblical references.[12] Most Baptist confessions adopted in North America have contained an article specifically addressing the inspiration and authority of the Scriptures. The *Philadelphia Confession* of 1742 contains a lengthy article on the Scriptures influenced by the *Westminster Confession* via the *Second London Confession*. The perspective of the *Philadelphia Confession* on the sufficiency of the Bible, illumined by the Spirit, as the authority for Christian faith and practice hints at a rejection of other possible sources of authority but allows for the adaptability of such things as the polity and worship of the church in light of reasoned reflection on social context.

> The whole Councel of God concerning all things necessary for his own Glory, Mans Salvation, Faith and Life, is either expressely set down or necessarily contained in the *Holy Scripture*; unto which nothing at any time is to be added, whether by new Revelation of the *Spirit*, or traditions of men. Nevertheless we acknowledge the inward illumination of the Spirit of God, to be necessary for the saving understanding of such things as are revealed in the Word, and that there are some circumstances concerning the worship of God, and the government of the Church common to humane actions and societies; which are to be ordered by the light of nature, and Christian prudence according to the general rules of the Word, which are always to be observed.[13]

---

11   J.L. Garrett, Jr., 'Sources of Authority in Baptist Thought', *BHH* 13 (1978), p. 42.

12   Cf. E.F. Tupper, 'Biblicism, Exclusivism, Triumphalism: The Travail of Baptist Identity', *PRSt* 29.4 (Winter, 2002), pp. 411-12.

13   Lumpkin, *Baptist Confessions of Faith*, pp. 250-51. These page references are actually to Lumpkin's printing of the text of the *Second London Confession*, as Lumpkin

The most widely influential article on the Scriptures in Baptist confessions issued in the United States is the article with which the *New Hampshire Confession* of 1833 begins.

> We believe [that] the Holy Bible was written by men divinely inspired, and is a perfect treasure of heavenly instruction; that it has God for its author, salvation for its end, and truth, without any mixture of error, for its matter; that it reveals the principles by which God will judge us; and therefore is, and shall remain to the end of the world, the true centre of Christian union, and the supreme standard by which all human conduct, creeds, and opinions should be tried.[14]

This article was incorporated in or adapted by confessions printed in numerous Baptist church manuals and issued by such Baptist bodies as the American Baptist Association, the General Association of Regular Baptists, and notably the SBC, which made the *New Hampshire Confession* the basis of the statement of the *Baptist Faith and Message* that the SBC adopted in 1925, revised in 1963, amended in 1998, and revised yet again in 2000. The next section of the chapter focuses on the articles on the Scriptures in the latter confessional statement partly because it represents the Baptist context out of which I come as a member of the CBF, but primarily because the successive modifications of the article on the Scriptures in the *Baptist Faith and Message* illustrate well the diversity that has characterized recent understandings of biblical authority in Baptist life in North America.

Divergent Understandings of Biblical Authority

From the formation of the SBC in 1845 until 1925, Southern Baptists did not have an officially adopted confession of faith. In 1924 the allegations of Texas pastor J. Frank Norris that Baptist educational institutions were teaching evolutionary theory motivated Convention messengers to charge a committee with drafting a confession of faith. Chaired by SBC president E. Y. Mullins (who was also the president of The Southern Baptist Theological Seminary in Louisville, Kentucky), the committee added only one word to the article on the Scriptures in the *New Hampshire Confession*. Whereas the *New Hampshire Confession* called the Bible 'the supreme standard by which all human conduct, creeds, and opinions should be tried', the 1925 *Baptist Faith and Message* qualified the 'opinions' as '*religious* opinions'.[15] This modification subtly limited the scope of biblical authority

---

only printed the two new articles of the *Philadelphia Confession* that were added to the *Second London Confession* in the section on the *Philadelphia Confession*.

14   Lumpkin, *Baptist Confessions of Faith*, pp. 361-62.

15   'The Memphis Articles of 1925: Report of Committee on Baptist Faith and Message', in *A Baptist Source Book*, ed. R.A. Baker (Nashville, Tenn.: Broadman Press, 1966), p. 201.

to matters of faith and practice—in other words, not scientific matters—and enabled both those who allowed for the possibility that evolution was the means by which God created human beings and those who opposed all forms of evolutionary theory to affirm the same statement on the authority of the Bible. It is significant that the convention declined to adopt a proposed anti-evolution amendment to the article on 'Man'.[16]

In 1961 Ralph Elliott, professor of Old Testament at Midwestern Baptist Theological Seminary (Kansas City, Missouri), published a book titled *The Message of Genesis* with Broadman Press, the Convention's publishing arm.[17] Controversy over the book's application of historical-critical methodologies to the interpretation of Genesis and some of Elliott's specific interpretive conclusions led messengers to the 1962 annual convention of the SBC in San Francisco to recommend that a committee chaired by SBC president Herschel Hobbs draft a new statement of faith that would provide guidelines for the agencies of the Convention. The resulting revision of the *Baptist Faith and Message*, approved by messengers to the 1963 Convention in Kansas City, Missouri, added a phrase and a sentence to the article on the Scriptures in the 1925 statement. The first addition asserted that the Bible 'is the record of God's revelation of Himself to man'.[18] This addition distinguished between the Bible and the revelation that preceded and resulted in the writing of Scripture, subtly allowing for interpretive approaches that reckoned seriously with the human dimensions of the biblical text. Such a distinction had been made decades earlier by Southern Baptist theologian W.T. Conner, who wrote in 1936 that 'Revelation preceded the Bible... The Bible is the product of revelation'.[19] The second addition, 'The criterion by which the Bible is to be interpreted is Jesus Christ',[20] permitted those who saw some moral and theological progression in God's revelation from the earliest layers of the Old Testament to God's definitive revelation in Jesus Christ to affirm the statement in good conscience. This revision seems to combine an affirmation of the

---

16   The proposed amendment read: 'We believe man came into the world by direct creation of God, and not by evolution. This creative act was separate and distinct from any other work of God and was not conditioned upon antecedent changes in previously created forms of life.' Lumpkin, *Baptist Confessions of Faith*, p. 391.

17   R.H. Elliott, *The Message of Genesis* (Nashville, Tenn.: Broadman Press, 1961). For an autobiographical perspective on the controversy engendered by this book, see R.H. Elliott, *The 'Genesis Controversy' and Continuity in Southern Baptist Chaos: A Eulogy for a Great Tradition* (Macon, Ga.: Mercer University Press, 1992).

18   'Baptist Faith and Message' (1963), article 1, in Lumpkin, *Baptist Confessions of Faith*, p. 393.

19   W.T. Conner, *Revelation and God: An Introduction to Christian Doctrine* (Nashville, Tenn.: Broadman Press, 1936), pp. 78-79.

20   'Baptist Faith and Message' (1963), article 1, in Lumpkin, *Baptist Confessions of Faith*, p. 393.

trustworthiness of the Bible with openness to the contributions of contemporary biblical and theological scholarship to its interpretation.

Following decades of theological controversy from which more conservative Southern Baptists emerged in control of denominational agencies, a revision of the article on the Scriptures in 2000 moved in a different direction from its predecessors in 1925 and 1963. The article alters the statement that the Bible 'is the *record* of God's revelation of Himself to man' to read that the Bible '*is* God's revelation of Himself to man' (emphasis added), thus equating the Bible, in its entirety, with revelation proper.[21] The final sentence added in the 1963 revision, 'The criterion by which the Bible is to be interpreted is Jesus Christ', is deleted and replaced with 'All Scripture is a testimony to Christ, who is Himself the focus of divine revelation.'[22] These most recent modifications reflect a shift in North America's largest Baptist group toward an understanding of biblical authority defined in terms of a theory of biblical inerrancy along the lines of the 1978 Chicago Statement on Biblical Inerrancy.[23] In the larger Baptist context in North America, many Baptists would affirm this understanding of the inspiration and authority of the Bible;[24] many Baptists would affirm standard historical-critical conclusions about the formation of the Bible and their usefulness for biblical interpretation;[25] and many other Baptists would view these battles as vestiges of a dying modernity and would prefer to move beyond them by focusing instead on the manner in which Scripture functions authoritatively for the Baptist communities that are gathered by its proclamation and study.[26] A focus on the authoritative function of Scripture in the life of the community implies a relationship between Scripture and other possible sources of authority to which members of the

---

21   Southern Baptist Convention, *The Baptist Faith and Message: A Statement Adopted by the Southern Baptist Convention June 14, 2000* (Nashville, Tenn.: LifeWay Christian Resources, 2000), article 1.

22   Southern Baptist Convention, *Baptist Faith and Message 2000*, article 1.

23   International Council on Biblical Inerrancy, 'Chicago Statement on Biblical Inerrancy', *JETS* 21 (December, 1978), pp. 289-96. This statement is now printed in bulletins of the official seminaries of the SBC along with the 2000 *Baptist Faith and Message* and other confessional documents. For various Southern Baptist perspectives on the appropriateness of this conceptualization of the nature of biblical inspiration and authority, alongside representative non-Baptist evangelical perspectives, see Conference on Biblical Inerrancy, *The Proceedings of the Conference on Biblical Inerrancy, 1987* (Nashville, Tenn.: Broadman Press, 1987).

24   E.g., L.R. Bush and T.J. Nettles, *Baptists and the Bible*, rev. edn. (Nashville, Tenn.: Broadman & Holman, 1999).

25   E.g., R.B. James, ed., *The Unfettered Word: Confronting the Authority-Inerrancy Question* (Macon, Ga.: Smyth & Helwys, 1994).

26   E.g., Broadway et al., 'Re-Envisioning Baptist Identity' (see appendix 1, 'Re-Envisioning Baptist Identity: A Manifesto for Baptist Communities in North America').

community may turn, consciously and unconsciously, when they interpret the Scriptures together.

Other Sources of Authority?

Confessions adopted by Baptists in North America have tended toward a *Sola Scriptura* understanding of authority in that they specify Scripture as the 'supreme authority' but do not explicitly identify other subordinate sources of authority.[27] This tendency is expressed in popular Baptist sentiment in the slogan 'no creed but the Bible'. The founding president of the Southern Baptist Convention referenced this axiom in 1845 to explain why the Convention had adopted no doctrinal statement,[28] but as the previous chapter noted, the slogan originated earlier in the Stone-Campbell Restorationist movement that later produced such denominations as the Disciples of Christ.[29] Underlying the frequent Baptist use of this slogan in American contexts is a widespread theoretical commitment to a *Sola Scriptura* perspective on authority, but like the Magisterial Reformers, the actual hermeneutical practice of Baptists might be better described as *Suprema Scriptura*. Baptist confessions, especially those adopted during the seventeenth century, contain numerous echoes of the doctrinal formulations of Nicaeno-Constantinoplitan Trinitarianism and Chalcedonian Christology, employing theological terminology with origins in the fourth century and later.[30] When Baptists affirm doctrinal formulations with patristic origins or embrace the authority of a biblical canon, they are at least unconsciously granting some degree of authority to tradition.

Several Baptist theologians are increasingly willing to speak of the Bible as the supreme authority for faith and practice, while explicitly admitting other subordinate sources to a pattern of religious authority. James Leo Garrett, Jr., (emeritus, Southwestern Baptist Theological Seminary, Fort Worth, Texas, USA) suggests that 'Baptists who emphasize the use of Baptist confessions of faith and who insist on a clearly articulated doctrine of the Trinity, often using terms easily traceable to the patristic age, would do well to affirm *suprema Scriptura*.'[31] Molly Marshall has invoked the categories of the so-called 'Wesleyan Quadrilateral', observing that Baptists have historically complemented the authority of the Bible with an

---

27   Garrett, 'Sources of Authority in Baptist Thought', p. 43.

28   'The Southern Baptist Convention, To the Brethren in the United States; To the Congregations Connected with the Respective Churches; and to All Candid Men', in *Proceedings of the Southern Baptist Convention 1845*, pp. 17-20.

29   Boring, *Disciples and the Bible*, p. 18.

30   See ch. 4, 'Baptist Confessions of Faith and the Patristic Tradition'.

31   J.L. Garrett, Jr., *Systematic Theology: Biblical, Historical, and Evangelical*, vol. 1 (Grand Rapids, Mich.: William B. Eerdmans, 1990), p. 181.

emphasis on religious experience, but she expresses the wish that Baptists 'would not only attend to scripture and experience, but also to reason and tradition' as contributing to 'our understanding of the character of God'.[32] As mentioned in chapter 1, Stanley Grenz outlined a threefold pattern of authoritative sources for theology: Scripture as 'theology's "norming norm"', tradition as 'theology's hermeneutical trajectory', and culture as 'theology's embedding context'.[33] Jeff Pool (Berea College, Berea, Kentucky, USA, formerly of Southwestern Baptist Theological Seminary), proposes that 'religious authority in the Baptist vision occurs as a web of dynamic interactions between the living God as disclosed in Jesus of Nazareth and attested by the Holy Spirit, the individual human's conscience and conduct, and the Christian community as the body of Christ'.[34] According to Pool, there is no hierarchical ordering of the sources that form this web. Rather, they intersect in dialectical relationship at seven principal junctures: the 'formative authority' of the Triune God, which is actualized only in conjunction with the other junctures in the web of authority; the 'transformative authority' of Christ and the conversion of human life; the 'conformative authority' of the Christian and the image of Christ; the 'informative authority' of the Holy Spirit, Christian understanding, and the canon of Scripture; the 'performative authority' of Christian conduct and

---

32   M.T. Marshall, 'Southern Baptist Theology Today: An Interview with Molly Marshall-Green', *TheolEd* 40 (Fall, 1989), pp. 25-26. An early Christian pattern of interfacing sources of authority not unlike the 'Wesleyan Quadrilateral' may be seen in the passage from Acts 15.6-31 that prefaces this chapter: in the phrases emphasized by italics, one may observe the function of Scripture, tradition, reason, and experience in the efforts of the Jerusalem apostolic conferees to discern as a community the mind of the Spirit on the ecclesial problems occasioned by the conversion of Gentiles to faith in Christ. While there has been a tendency in some recent expressions of American Methodism to treat the four sources, which were identified by modern Wesleyan scholars as components of a pattern of religious authority operative in the thought of John Wesley, as if they were equal sources of authority to be weighed in formulaic fashion when considering questions of faith and practice, Wesley himself never enumerated them as a 'quadrilateral', and Scripture was clearly his preeminent source of authority (see T.A. Campbell, 'The "Wesleyan Quadrilateral": The Story of a Modern Methodist Myth', in *Doctrine and Theology in the United Methodist Church*, ed. T.A. Langford [Nashville, Tenn.: Abingdon, 1991], pp. 154-61, and A.C. Outler, 'The Wesleyan Quadrilateral—in John Wesley', in *The Wesleyan Theological Heritage: Essays of Albert C. Outler*, ed. T.C. Oden and L.R. Longden [Grand Rapids, Mich.: Zondervan, 1991], pp. 21-37). For a more skeptical perspective on the propriety of a Baptist adoption of the 'Wesleyan Quadrilateral', see J.B. Green, 'Biblical Authority and Communities of Discourse', in *Baptists in the Balance: The Tension between Freedom and Responsibility*, ed. E.C. Goodwin (Valley Forge, Pa.: Judson Press, 1997), pp. 151-73, esp. 163-64.

33   Grenz and Franke, *Beyond Foundationalism*, pp. 57-166.

34   Pool, 'Christ, Conscience, Canon, Community', p. 417.

the imitation of Christ; the 'multiformative authority' of the Holy Spirit, the
priesthood of all Christians, and the congregation (an authority which
functions both locally and globally); and the 'interformative authority' of
the Christian and the universal priesthood.[35] These Baptist thinkers do not
agree on the precise shape a pattern of religious authority ought to take, but
they illustrate the growing recognition in Baptist theology that biblical
authority always exists and functions in relationship to other sources of
authority that inform the community's interpretation and practice of the
biblical story.

Baptists, Tradition, and Creeds

Several primarily younger Baptist theologians have urged their fellow
Baptists to acknowledge tradition in particular as a formal source of
authority. The contributions of Philip Thompson, Mark Medley, and D.H.
Williams highlighted in the previous chapter exemplify this trend among
Baptist academic theologians in North America.[36] Their work recognizes
that tradition is inescapable in its function as a source of authority for
anyone who seeks to make the Scriptures the norm for faith and practice.
Though Christians who prize the authority of the Bible are not always
aware of this function, they all read their authoritative Bible through the
lenses of the traditions that have been mediated to them by various
expressions of Christian community, with results both good and ill. These
tradition-retrieving Baptist theologians believe that becoming more
conscious of the inescapable role of tradition in Christian faith and practice
can help Baptists to distinguish between healthy and harmful sources of
tradition.

Some Baptist theologians in North America have called for Baptists to
give attention in particular to the role that creeds and confessions as
expressions of tradition might play in a larger pattern of theological
authority. Although Baptists have tended to claim explicitly only the Bible
as a formal source of authority, they have issued confessions of faith
detailing their distinctive understandings of the Bible with notable
frequency. While early English Baptists seem not to have distinguished
clearly between 'creeds' and 'confessions',[37] in North American Baptist life
there has been a tendency to reject the authority of the former and

---

35   Pool, 'Christ, Conscience, Canon, Community', pp. 425-43.

36   Thompson, 'Re-envisioning Baptist Identity', p. 302; Medley, 'Catholics,
Baptists, and the Normativity of Tradition', pp. 121, 126-28; Williams, *Retrieving the
Tradition and Renewing Evangelicalism*, pp. 101-31; Williams, *Evangelicals and
Tradition*.

37   For example, a group of General Baptist churches in England called their 1678
confession 'An Orthodox Creed' (Lumpkin, *Baptist Confessions of Faith*, pp. 295-334).

understand the latter only as descriptive of common Baptist opinion on matters of faith and practice. In the SBC there has been a shift from conceiving of confessions as 'guides for interpretation' and as 'having no authority over the individual conscience' (so the preambles of the 1925 and 1963 statements of the *Baptist Faith and Message*)[38] to the specifying of their role in the 2000 revision of the *Baptist Faith and Message* as 'instruments of doctrinal accountability'.[39] On the other hand, some among the 'disenfranchised moderates' in the context of these recent developments in the Southern Baptist Convention have proposed ways in which Baptists might reclaim the proper function of the ancient ecumenical creeds, even while rejecting coercive uses of more recent Baptist confessions. In addition to the proposals along these lines by Barry Harvey, Elizabeth Newman, and Timothy George mentioned in chapter 1,[40] Glenn Hinson (emeritus, The Southern Baptist Theological Seminary, Louisville, Kentucky, USA and Baptist Theological Seminary at Richmond, Virginia, USA, now teaching at the new Baptist Seminary of Kentucky, Lexington, Kentucky, USA), has proposed that Baptists might be helped toward an appropriation of the ancient creeds by understanding them as concise expressions of the covenant commitment made in baptism, learned in catechesis, and recalled in liturgy.[41] Some Baptists have in fact made liturgical use of the Apostles' Creed: during the inaugural meeting of the Baptist World Alliance at Exeter Hall in London in 1905 and again at the centennial Baptist World Congress in Birmingham, England, in 2005, participants recited the Apostles' Creed as a demonstration of the solidarity of the Baptist tradition with the larger Christian communion, and a hymnal and a book of worship produced in recent years for use in the Baptist Union of Great Britain each include the text of the Apostles' Creed and other texts from the ecumenical Christian liturgical tradition.[42] A few Baptist

---

38   Lumpkin, *Baptist Confessions of Faith*, p. 392.

39   Southern Baptist Convention, *Baptist Faith and Message 2000*, 'Preamble'.

40   Harvey, 'Doctrinally Speaking', pp. 56-57, n. 82; Harvey, 'Where, Then, Do We Stand?', pp. 359-80, esp. 371-79; Newman, 'The Priesthood of All Believers', p. 56, n. 32; Russell, 'Q&A with Timothy George', pp. 1G, 4G.

41   E.G. Hinson, 'The Nicene Creed Viewed from the Standpoint of the Evangelization of the Roman Empire', in *Faith to Creed: Ecumenical Perspectives on the Affirmation of the Apostolic Faith in the Fourth Century. Papers of the Faith to Creed Consultation Commission on Faith and Order NCCCUSA October 25-27, 1989— Waltham, Massachusetts*, ed. S.M. Heim (Grand Rapids, Mich.: William B. Eerdmans, 1991), pp. 117-28.

42   Psalms and Hymns Trust, *Baptist Praise and Worship* (Oxford: Oxford University Press, 1991) prints the Apostles' Creed on the inside cover of the hymnal and within as reading 424, and the book of worship published by the Baptist Union of Great Britain, *Gathering for Worship: Patterns and Prayers for the Community of Disciples*, ed. C.J. Ellis and M. Blyth (Norwich, England: Canterbury Press, 2005), includes the

congregations in the United States on occasion include corporate recitation of the ancient ecumenical creeds in their services of worship, but at present the practice is neither frequent in these few congregations nor widespread in Baptist life in North America.

Towards a Baptist Rethinking of Authority

Each class session of my introductory Christian Theology course at Campbell University Divinity School begins with a hymn, prayer, and corporate recitation of the Apostles' Creed during the first half of the course and the Nicaeno-Constantinopolitan Creed during the remainder of the term. At the end of a recent offering of the course, one of my Baptist students wrote on a final exam paper that one of the most significant things she had learned in the course was the theological importance of the liturgical use of the creed; another student wrote that he refused to participate in reciting the creed because he was Baptist, and 'Baptists don't believe in creeds'. I am confident that the latter student's perspective is more representative of the average Baptist layperson's attitude toward post-biblical tradition as a source of authority. Explicit Baptist recognition of sources of theological authority in addition to Scripture thus far exists almost exclusively in the context of academic theological discourse; extrabiblical sources of authority have yet to be referenced by Baptist confessions of faith in North America.[43] However, Baptist laypeople, even

---

Apostles' Creed in multiple suggested patterns for the celebration of baptism and other services of worship.

43   A major exception to this generalization from outside North America is the 1678 confession issued by General (i.e., non-Calvinistic) Baptists in England under the title *An Orthodox Creed*. Article 38 of the *Orthodox Creed* commends the reception and belief of the Nicene, (pseudo-) Athanasian, and Apostles' Creeds by Baptists, subordinating their authority to that of Scripture but regarding them as reliable summaries of biblical teaching: 'The three creeds, viz. Nicene creed, Athanasius' creed, and the Apostles creed, as they are commonly called, ought thoroughly to be received, and believed. For we believe, they may be proved, by most undoubted authority of holy scripture, and are necessary to be understood of all christians; and to be instructed in the knowledge of them, by the ministers of Christ, according to the analogy of faith, recorded in sacred scriptures, upon which these creeds are grounded, and catechistically opened, and expounded in all christian families, for the edification of young and old, which might be a means to prevent heresy in doctrine, and practice, these creeds containing all things in a brief manner, that are necessary to be known, fundamentally, in order to our salvation; to which end they may be considered, and better understood of all men, we have here printed them under their several titles as followeth...' (Lumpkin, *Baptist Confessions of Faith*, p. 326). The first two sentences of this article are taken from article 8 of the *Thirty-Nine Articles* of the Church of England. In addition, at least two recent European Baptist confessions of faith likewise make positive reference to the Apostles' Creed: the first paragraph of the confession adopted in 1977 by German-

if they are not conscious they are doing so, are in fact reading the Bible through the lenses of all sorts of tradition and forming opinions about numerous issues of faith and practice on the basis of what seems reasonable to them and what best accords with their own Christian experience. But if one asks typical Baptists why they believe their conviction on a particular matter of faith or practice is the right one, they will likely respond that this is what they understand the Bible to mean. That is how authority tends to function in typical North American Baptist understanding.

It is my conviction as a Baptist theologian that this typical Baptist understanding of theological authority must be amended if Baptists are to possess the theological resources they need for the reconstruction of Baptist life after the collapse of the modern worldview that has significantly shaped the development of the Baptist tradition during the past two centuries, especially in North America. In its functional reduction of theological authority to the encounter of the individual conscience with the biblical text, the stereotypical North American Baptist understanding of authority described above isolates Baptist individuals and congregations from the shared wisdom of the *communio sanctorum* that has sustained the church through two millennia, a recovery of which is necessary for the continued vitality of the Baptist expression of the Christian tradition in this postmodern age. There is potential, however, for a Baptist recovery of the authority of the *communio sanctorum* in an extension to the universal church (the existence of which is affirmed by mainstream Baptist ecclesiology, even if denied by 'Landmark' Baptists) of the Baptist ecclesiological principle that the local congregation as a community gathered under the Lordship of Christ possesses a certain derivative authority, subordinate to the Scriptures, for the ordering of its faith and practice. The universal church is the larger community of all the saints through all the ages that also possesses a derivative authority, subordinate to the Scriptures, to which Baptists and members of any other denominational tradition must listen as they seek to think and act Christianly. Curtis Freeman has expressed a similar hope that Baptists might come to think of themselves as 'catholic baptists':

> The key to appropriating our heritage in a truly apostolic faith is learning to locate ourselves within the full history of the church—past and present—with all its richness and diversity. Through the display of this story over the centuries we find continuity with the apostolic. In this story we meet a host of faithful witnesses: martyrs and confessors, desert mothers and church fathers, scholastics

---

speaking Baptist unions in Germany, Austria, and Switzerland 'presupposes the Apostles' Creed as a common confession of Christendom' (Parker, *Baptists in Europe*, p. 57), and the initial paragraph of the confession approved by the Swedish-Speaking Baptist Union of Finland in 1979 'accepts the Apostolic Creed as the comprehensive creed for the union' (Parker, *Baptists in Europe*, p. 111).

and mystics, reformers and radicals, puritans and pietists. These and more are our spiritual heritage, too. They are the fount through which the apostolic spring flows. When baptists become ecumenical enough to reclaim the whole Christian story as our heritage, we shall surely stand in the waters of that glad river (Ps 46.4) where John and Jesus stood until that day when we shall gather with the saints before that river glorious whose crystal tide flows by the throne of God and the Lamb (Rev 22.1).[44]

As Baptists learn to appropriate this apostolic heritage en route to becoming 'catholic baptists', they may well find that claiming 'no creed but the Bible' is no longer an adequate expression of their understanding of theological authority. The next chapter of *Towards Baptist Catholicity* seeks a more suitable Baptist theological hermeneutic by bringing the Baptist tradition of communal dissent into dialogue with various contemporary perspectives on tradition that have the potential to make room for the distinctive ecclesial and theological gifts the Baptist tradition has to offer to the larger catholic tradition and thus may encourage Baptists in turn to make room for the ecclesial and theological gifts of the church in its catholicity.

---

44   Freeman, 'A Confession for Catholic Baptists', p. 94. Freeman's spelling of 'baptist' with a lower-case "b" again reflects the usage of McClendon, *Systematic Theology*, vol. 1, *Ethics*, pp. 17-35.

CHAPTER 3

The Authority of the Community (of All the Saints): Towards a Postmodern Baptist Hermeneutic of Tradition

'Tradition without history has homogenized all the stages of development into one statically defined truth; history without tradition has produced a historicism that relativized the development of Christian doctrine in such a way as to make the distinction between authentic growth and cancerous aberration seem completely arbitrary....The history of Christian doctrine is the most effective means available of exposing the artificial theories of continuity that have often assumed normative status in the churches, and at the same time it is an avenue into the authentic continuity of Christian believing, teaching, and confessing. Tradition is the living faith of the dead; traditionalism is the dead faith of the living.' *Jaroslav Pelikan*[1]

'So then, brothers and sisters, stand firm and hold fast to the traditions that you were taught by us, either by word of mouth or by our letter.' *1 Thessalonians 2.15 NRSV*

For many contemporary Baptists in the United States, the slogan 'no creed but the Bible' which Baptists have appropriated from the Stone-Campbell 'Restoration' movement expresses what these Baptists believe to be the essential principle of a distinctively Baptist theology: the Bible is the only sufficient rule for faith and practice, and therefore any post-biblical theological development is superfluous, theologically suspect, and possesses no authority for Christians today. If such a radical *Sola Scriptura* hermeneutic is indeed an inviolable rule of Baptist theological method, then the only authentically Baptist hermeneutic of tradition is a rejection of tradition as a source of Christian authority.

Contemporary forms of Baptist anti-traditionalism have their roots in the Enlightenment conviction that traditional understandings of the world—

---

1   J. Pelikan, *The Christian Tradition: A History of the Development of Doctrine*, vol. 1, *The Emergence of the Catholic Tradition (100-600)* (Chicago: University of Chicago Press, 1971), p. 9.

religious and otherwise—are inadequate in light of modern knowledge and tend to limit the progress of humanity. Some versions of postmodern thought radicalize this characteristic of modernity, viewing all forms of tradition as inherently oppressive. If postmodernity were monolithic in this estimate of tradition, a postmodern hermeneutic of tradition would likewise be necessarily negative.

The crafting of a hermeneutic of tradition that is both consciously addressed to the postmodern situation and faithfully Baptist is a viable project, however, for two reasons. First, there are constructive streams of postmodern thought that do have a place for tradition. Some of these will receive attention later in this chapter. Second, the collapse of modernity raises serious questions about the continued viability of certain perspectives commonly identified as Baptist theological distinctives, including the Baptist aversion to tradition as a source of authority, which may very well prove to be inseparable from the modern milieu in which they developed.[2] The reconstruction of Baptist life after modernity may therefore require a Baptist formulation of a postmodern hermeneutic of tradition. Such an undertaking will require a re-evaluation of the Baptist 'tradition' of antagonism or indifference toward tradition, critical dialogue with non-Baptist projects in the postmodern retrieval of tradition, and creative consideration of the positive contributions self-consciously Baptist communities still have to make to Christianity in a postmodern world even while recovering the riches of the pre-modern, pre-Baptist tradition.

The Hermeneutics of Suspicion and Baptist Suspicion of Tradition

Most a-traditional Baptists—including such theologically diverse exemplars of this disconnectedness from the catholic tradition as 'Landmarkers'[3] and champions of radically individualistic interpretations of 'soul competency'—would be shocked to discover how similar their

---

2   On the relationship between modernity and the development of Baptist life and thought, see T. Maddox, 'Revisioning Baptist Principles: A Ricoeurian Postmodern Investigation' (PhD thesis, The Southern Baptist Theological Seminary, 1997), pp. 1-21, and the previously cited articles by Freeman: 'Can Baptist Theology Be Revisioned?', 'A New Perspective on Baptist Identity', and 'E.Y. Mullins and the Siren Songs of Modernity'.

3   'Landmarkers' are Baptists in the tradition of J.M. Pendleton, *An Old Landmark Re-set* (Nashville, Tenn.: South-Western Publishing House, 1859), and J.R. Graves, *Old Landmarksim: What Is It?* (Memphis, Tenn.: Baptist Book House, 1880), who contended that Baptist local churches are the only true New Testament churches and that these have existed in unbroken succession since the first Christian century. See J.E. Tull, *High-Church Baptists in the South: The Origin, Nature, and Influence of Landmarkism*, ed. M. Ashcraft (Macon, Ga.: Mercer University Press, 2000).

hermeneutic of tradition is to radically secular expressions of postmodern deconstructionism. The label 'hermeneutics of suspicion' has been applied to interpretive theories that are deeply distrustful of the ability of human consciousness, and especially its expression in language, to represent reality.[4] Karl Marx (1818-83), Friedrich Nietzsche (1844-1900), and Sigmund Freud (1856-1939) anticipated the extreme pessimism over the meaningfulness of language that characterizes the deconstructionist thought of Jacques Derrida (1930-2004), Michel Foucault (1926-84), Richard Rorty (1931-), and, among Christian theologians who have appropriated this perspective, Mark C. Taylor (1945-) and Don Cupitt (1934-). For deconstructionists, language is a socially conditioned construct that is inseparable from its context, can appeal to no universal rationality to adjudicate its putative correspondence to reality, is incapable of conveying meaning in any objective sense, and (following Foucault) inevitably asserts power over both what it describes and those to whom it is directed. The primary task of deconstructionist hermeneutics is accordingly to expose the illegitimacy of the claim of any interpretation (with interpretation understood to be inherent both in the articulating of a text, written or otherwise, and in the subsequent act of interpreting it) to have yielded objective meaning. Neither the biblical text nor post-biblical Christian tradition is exempt from such deconstruction by both non-Christian and Christian practitioners of the hermeneutics of suspicion.

While most Baptists would rightly resist any deconstructive assault on the meaningfulness and authoritative status of Scripture, many of the same Baptists are just as distrustful of the post-New Testament early Christian tradition as are deconstructionist readers of this tradition. The common Baptist suspicion of tradition, however, is not postmodern in origin but rather owes at least as much to Enlightenment 'antagonism to all tradition'[5] as it does to the peculiar path of development some streams of Baptist life took from the Radical Reformation. In the era of the end of modernity, several Baptist voices have been calling attention to the pervasive and injurious impact of Enlightenment perspectives on twentieth-century Baptist faith and practice as well as to the need for a 're-envisioning' of

---

4   See, e.g., P. Ricoeur, *Freud and Philosophy: An Essay on Interpretation* (New Haven, Conn.: Yale University Press, 1970). It should be pointed out that Ricoeur does not view the 'hermeneutics of suspicion' as necessarily negative but rather as a first step toward the constructive retrieval of traditional narratives and symbols. This moment of constructive retrieval in Ricoeur is considered later in this chapter.

5   A. MacIntye, *Whose Justice? Which Rationality?* (Notre Dame, Ind.: University of Notre Dame Press, 1988), p. 10.

Baptist identity at the dawning of the twenty-first century.[6] Meanwhile, Baptist patristics specialist D.H. Williams has identified other sources of the Baptist suspicion of tradition in some of the unique features of Free Church and Baptist historiography. In *Retrieving the Tradition and Renewing Evangelicalism: A Primer for Suspicious Protestants*, he challenges Free Church Christianity's tendentious reading of church history through the lenses of a "fall paradigm" in which Constantine's embrace of Christianity leads to its corruption, a state of affairs which is overcome only by the sixteenth-century Reformation—or, in a particularly idiosyncratic Baptist reading of church history that continues to influence Baptist ecclesiologies in the United States (especially in the South), the "fall" is countered by the preservation of an unbroken succession of non-Catholic "true churches" from which modern-day Baptists descend.[7] Williams points out that this paradigm not only misrepresents the development of patristic Christianity but also misappropriates some of the rhetoric of the Reformers, whose reforming programmes were undergirded not only by a return to the Scriptures but also by a rigorous retrieval of theological perspectives and liturgical practices from the fourth and fifth centuries C.E. Although no serious Baptist historian today holds to a theory of Baptist successionism, the enduring legacies of J.M. Carroll's *The Trail of Blood* are reflected in the constitutions and by-laws of many Baptist associations, especially in the Southwestern United States, that still prohibit the seating of messengers from churches that accept persons baptized by 'alien immersion' for church membership and from churches that do not practice 'closed communion', and also in the reluctance of some Baptist communions to enter into ecumenical alliances. The a-traditional legacy of that sort of historiographical apology for Baptist faith and practice is evident in a pastoral conversation recounted by Williams in his prologue: 'I once was informed with kindly intentions by a deacon of the first church I pastored that the study of the early creeds and councils is something Catholics or Episcopalians do, but true Christians need only uphold the complete authority of the Bible and the empowering of the Holy Spirit in a personal way.'[8]

---

6   See especially Broadway, Freeman, Harvey, McClendon, Newman, and Thompson, 'Re-Envisioning Baptist Identity: A Manifesto for Baptist Communities in North America', reprinted here as appendix 1.

7   Williams, *Retrieving the Tradition and Renewing Evangelicalism*, pp. 101-31.

8   Williams, *Retrieving the Tradition and Renewing Evangelicalism*, p. 1.

Reevaluating the A-Traditional Baptist 'Tradition'

This Baptist 'tradition' of antipathy toward tradition must be reevaluated in light of two considerations to which Baptists have not given sufficient attention: the inseparability of the biblical documents and the canon to which they belong from tradition, and the disparity between the Baptist profession of *Sola Scriptura* and the reality of Baptist hermeneutical practice. The first consideration challenges the polarization of Scripture and tradition on historical grounds, while the second consideration calls for an honest and critical awareness of what Baptists actually do when they interpret Scripture and think theologically.

It cannot be denied that the texts that comprise Scripture are the product of traditioning processes within ancient Jewish and early Christian communities. In the case of the Hebrew Scriptures, several centuries of oral tradition in communal/liturgical settings frequently preceded the preservation of the tradition in written texts. Both 'liberal'[9] and 'conservative'[10] approaches to form criticism of the New Testament gospels have highlighted the contributions of communal traditioning processes to the canonical form of the Jesus tradition. The Apostle Paul provided evidence for the existence of these processes in his use of technical rabbinical terms for the reception and transmission of tradition in accounting for his own sources of the Jesus tradition he communicated to the Christian community in Corinth in 1 Cor. 11.23 and 15.3.[11]

Unless one expands the concept of biblical inspiration to include not only the production of the biblical documents but also their canonization in late fourth-century episcopal synods, it must be conceded that the canon of Scripture is the product of the same sort of consensual development of tradition in the post-New Testament period that also produced the *regula fidei* ('rule of faith') reflected in the conciliar creeds. If a Baptist accepts

---

9   E.g., M. Dibelius, *Die Formgeschichte des Evangeliums*, 2d edn. (Tübingen: J.C.B. Mohr, 1933) [ET, *From Tradition to Gospel*, trans. B.L. Woolf (New York: Charles Scribner's Sons, 1934)]; R. Bultmann, *Die Geschichte der synoptischen Tradition*, 3d edn. (Göttingen: Vandenhoeck und Ruprecht, 1958) [ET, *History of the Synoptic Tradition*, trans. J. Marsh (New York: Harper and Row, 1963)].

10   E.g., H. Riesenfeld, *The Gospel Tradition and its Beginnings: A Study in the Limits of 'Formgeschichte'* (London: A.R. Mowbray, 1957); B. Gerhardsson, *Memory and Manuscript: Oral Tradition and Written Transmission in Rabbinic Judaism and Early Christianity* (ASNU, 22; Lund: C.W.K. Gleerup, 1964); idem, *The Origins of the Gospel Traditions* (Philadelphia: Fortress Press, 1979); R. Riesner, *Jesus als Lehrer: Eine Untersuchung zum Ursprung der Evangelien-Überlieferung* (WUNT^2, 7; Tübingen: J.C.B. Mohr, 1981).

11   On the significance of this language for traditioning processes in primitive Christianity, see E.E. Ellis, *The Making of the New Testament Documents* (BIS, 39; Leiden: Brill, 1999), pp. 53-59.

the canon of Scripture as the only authoritative rule for faith and practice and accords that status to no other ancient Jewish or early Christian writings, then she has accepted the authority of at least one post-biblical doctrinal tradition.

Acceptance of the canon is certainly not the only instance in which the actual hermeneutical practice of most Baptists gives evidence that Scripture is being read through doctrinal lenses ground in patristic Christianity, the sixteenth-century Reformation, or later developments in the Baptist tradition(s). Many Baptists, though perhaps not consciously dependent on Nicaeno-Constantinopolitan trinitarian or Chalcedonian christological formulations,[12] would nevertheless oppose theological proposals that seem not to regard Father, Son, and Holy Spirit as consubstantial, coequal, and coeternal, or that appear not to affirm the full divinity and full humanity of Jesus Christ—but only on the basis of what they believe to be self-evident in Scripture. Although the raw material for the later doctrine of the Trinity is present in Scripture,[13] the fully developed doctrine would hardly have been self-evident to the earliest interpreters of the New Testament. Many Baptists would also regard paedobaptism, for example, as an erroneous doctrine not on the basis of a conscious appeal to a Baptist doctrinal tradition but rather because they believe it to be an unbiblical practice, even though it is the Baptist doctrinal tradition in which they are steeped that has influenced them toward this reading of Scripture. The result of this disparity between the conscious Baptist hermeneutical principle of a radicalized *Sola Scriptura* and the reality of an unconscious Baptist reading of Scripture through the lenses of all sorts of tradition is a confusion of the teachings of Scripture with what one believes the Scriptures to teach (on unconsciously traditional grounds), leaving many Baptists ill-equipped for wrestling with the intra-canonical tensions of the Bible and unable to appreciate the developmental nature of doctrine.

As Baptists came to grips with modernity, the consciously negative hermeneutic of tradition represented by such slogans as 'no creed but the Bible' served well the theological agenda of both fundamentalism and liberalism. By uncritically reading their beliefs into the text of the inerrant Bible, Baptist fundamentalists forged a two-edged 'sword of the Lord' which they wielded against both the traditions of Rome and the innovations of the unbelieving liberals. Through the use of historical-critical methods of interpretation, Baptists of more liberal inclinations were better able to

---

12   Many seventeenth-century Baptist confessional documents, however, contain clear echoes of these patristic doctrinal formulations, which are addressed in ch. 4, 'Baptist Confessions of Faith and the Patristic Tradition'.

13   See A.W. Wainwright, *The Trinity in the New Testament* (London: S.P.C.K., 1962).

distinguish between what the biblical texts in their original contexts actually said and what had become traditional ways of interpreting those texts. Without a place for post-biblical tradition in their hermeneutic, however, they were free to jettison traditional interpretations of Scripture while remaining true to their allegiance to 'no creed but the Bible'.

The legacies of these modern Baptist appropriations and transformations of the Reformation hermeneutical principle *Sola Scriptura* (actually *Suprema Scriptura* in the practice of the Reformers) are still very much with contemporary Baptists. Might a place for tradition in Baptist theological method, perhaps in the form of the broad outlines of the consensual development of the early Christians' rule of faith in light of which they read the Scriptures, have prevented the extreme theological polarization of Baptist life in the latter half of the twentieth century? One can only speculate about Baptists, but Roman Catholic biblical scholarship during the same period may illustrate some of the benefits of a having a place for tradition, even if it is not a form of tradition Baptists could easily adopt. In 1943 Pope Pius XII issued the encyclical letter *Divino Afflante Spiritu*, which in the face of warnings from within the Church of grave dangers associated with the historical-critical interpretation of Scripture actually urged Catholic biblical scholars to embrace the tools of modern critical scholarship while also continuing in the tradition of the theological exegesis of the patristic interpreters.[14] The dogmatic constitution *Dei Verbum* issued in 1965 during the Second Vatican Council likewise provides generous room for the historical investigation of Scripture and distinguishes between the perspectives of Scripture in its historical context and the later developments of tradition.[15] The document produced by the Pontifical Biblical Commission on *The Interpretation of the Bible in the Church* and accepted by Pope John Paul II in 1993 continues in this tradition and is marked by careful attention to recent developments in biblical studies, literary theory, and philosophical hermeneutics as well as to the ecclesial context and traditional norms of interpretation.[16] I

14 Pius XII, *Divino Afflante Spiritu*, in *AAS* 35 (Rome: 1943), pp. 297-326; ET in *Rome and the Study of Scripture: A Collection of Papal Enactments on the Study of Holy Scripture Together with the Decisions of the Biblical Commission*, 5th edn., ed. C.J. Louis (St. Meinrad, Ind.: 1953), pp. 79-107. On the influence of *Divino Afflante Spiritu* on Catholic biblical scholarship, see R.B. Robinson, *Roman Catholic Exegesis Since Divino Afflante Spiritu: Hermeneutical Implications* (SBLDS, 111; Decatur, Ga.: Scholars Press, 1988).

15 'Dogmatic Constitution on Divine Revelation' (Vatican II, *Dei Verbum*, 18 November 1965), in *Vatican Council II: The Conciliar and Post Conciliar Documents*, rev. edn., ed. A. Flannery (Northport, N.Y.: Costello Publishing, 1992), pp. 750-65.

16 Pontifical Biblical Commission, *The Interpretation of the Bible in the Church* (Washington, D.C.: United States Catholic Conference, 1993).

experienced the health of this stream of confessional scholarship as a student in Fr. Joseph Fitzmyer's seminar on Paul's Epistle to the Romans at The Catholic University of America in 1995. Fr. Fitzmyer was free to lead us in examining the manner in which Paul interacts with material from different redactional strata of the Pentateuch and in comparing the theologies of Romans and the deutero-Pauline epistles, while remaining a faithful Roman Catholic whose scholarly ministry as a Jesuit priest is in good ecclesiastical standing. Southern Baptist practitioners of critical biblical scholarship during the same period have not fared as well ecclesiastically.[17] A new hermeneutic of tradition may provide both 'conservative' and 'moderate' to 'progressive' Baptists with needed help in emerging from the devastation wrought by the modern 'battle for the Bible' into constructive engagement with the postmodern world.

Paradigms for Postmodern Retrieval of Tradition: Some Non-Baptist Dialogue Partners

Although Williams has argued well the need for Baptists to embrace the ancient Christian tradition as their own, he does not offer a strategy for incorporating this tradition into specifically Baptist faith and practice. In crafting one, Baptists cannot simply tack tradition on to Scripture as an additional source of authority. One of the providential theological vocations of Baptists may have been to call the larger Christian community to fidelity to the Bible as the earliest and normative layer of the tradition, especially in situations in which some development of the tradition stands in need of critique and correction by Scripture. Any Baptist appropriation of tradition in a pattern of authority will need to be faithful to the distinctive theological and ecclesial gifts Baptists have to offer to the communion of saints. But as Baptists lack a tradition of tradition, they will need to engage in dialogue with other serious proposals for retrieving early Christian tradition in a postmodern context. The possible dialogue partners suggested below are by no means inclusive of all contemporary theological projects in the retrieval

---

17   In the course of the theological-political controversy in the Southern Baptist Convention, the personal positions of theological educators on historical-critical conclusions about the date, authorship, and literary composition of the books of the Bible seemed to be a litmus test for the soundness of their theology, with acceptance of these conclusions indicating theological liberalism and repudiation of these conclusions being regarded as evidence of an orthodox theology. Contra such assumptions, theological orthodoxy can indeed go hand-in-hand with rigorous historical-critical study of the Scriptures. A robustly orthodox theology of creation and incarnation ought to warrant historical investigation of the formation of the Scriptures, while a rejection of such studies and their conclusions may be a symptom of a theology of biblical inspiration that is analogous to Docetism in Christology.

of tradition, and they reflect the idiosyncrasies of this theologian's reading and inclinations. They are introduced here so that Baptist theological students, pastors, and other ministers will hopefully become interested in further reading and learning from some of these resources that may be of assistance to them in developing a Baptist hermeneutic of tradition for a postmodern context.

Thomas Oden: Postmodern Paleo-Orthodoxy

The current theological programme of Thomas C. Oden (1931-), a Methodist theologian serving as the Henry Annson Buttz Professor of Theology and Ethics in the Theological School of Drew University Madison, New Jersey, USA, is unquestionably the most prominent contemporary North American effort to retrieve ancient Christian tradition for the renewal of postmodern Christianity. Many pastors possess on the shelves of their studies the initial volumes in the aggressively marketed *Ancient Christian Commentary on Scripture* edited by Oden.[18] Oden's association with this project is the latest outgrowth of the personal theological reorientation announced in his 1979 book *Agenda for Theology: Recovering Christian Roots.*[19] After his earlier interests in theological anthropology in dialogue with modern psychological theory and various then-contemporary theological movements, Oden became dissatisfied with the adequacy of modern theology for the critical engagement of modern culture and turned to 'classical Christian thinking' as a corrective.[20] Subsequent projects such as his three-volume systematic theology (1987-94),[21] the volumes in the *Classical Pastoral Care* series (1987-1994),[22] and the *Ancient Christian Commentary on Scripture* (1998-) are attempts to gain a fresh hearing of 'paleo-orthodox' perspectives on Christian faith and

---

18   T.C. Oden, ed., *The Ancient Christian Commentary on Scripture* (Downers Grove, Ill.: InterVarsity Press, 1998-). For an introduction to the use of more extensive print and electronic resources for the contemporary recovery of patristic biblical interpretation, see S.R. Harmon, 'A Note on the Critical Use of *Instrumenta* for the Retrieval of Patristic Biblical Exegesis', *JECS* 11.1 (Spring, 2003), pp. 95-107.

19   T.C. Oden, *Agenda for Theology: Recovering Christian Roots* (San Francisco: Harper & Row, 1979).

20   Oden recounted these developments in 'Then and Now: The Recovery of Patristic Wisdom', *ChrCent* 107 (12 December 1990), pp. 1164-1168.

21   T.C. Oden, *The Living God* (San Francisco: Harper & Row, 1987); *The Word of Life* (San Francisco: Harper & Row, 1992); *Life in the Spirit* (San Francisco: Harper & Row, 1994).

22   T.C. Oden, *Classical Pastoral Care*, 4 vols. (Grand Rapids, Mich.: Baker Books, 1987-94).

practice by summarizing and anthologizing the sources of classical Christian tradition.

What sort of paradigm does Oden offer for retrieving this tradition? Oden refers readers of his systematic theology to a 'pyramid of sources', with the Scriptures serving as the wide base of the pyramid and modern theologians occupying the narrow apex of the pyramid. After Scripture, pride of place goes to patristic interpreters of Scripture—especially the four Eastern (Athanasius, Basil of Caesarea, Gregory of Nazianzus, John Chrysostom) and four Western (Ambrose, Augustine, Jerome, Gregory the Great) 'Doctors of the Church', but also including others of great influence in this period such as Origen (at points not regarded as unorthodox[23]), Gregory of Nyssa, John of Damascus, Hilary of Poitiers, and Leo the Great.[24] Next are medieval theologians such as Thomas Aquinas and Reformers such as Luther and Calvin who are regarded as having faithfully appropriated and transmitted the ancient doctrinal consensus. Fewer modern sources are noted, 'not because they are inferior but because they have had less time to affect the consensus';[25] a glance at the indices reveals an attraction to Barth among more recent theologians. Within these post-biblical sources, conciliar creedal and confessional documents are weighted more heavily than the writings of individual theologians.[26]

Oden has performed a valuable service to the church (especially in its evangelical and mainline Protestant expressions) by recalling to its attention the common heritage that preceded the modern fragmentation of Christianity. However, there are difficulties with both Oden's construal of the classical sources to be retrieved and his strategy for contemporary retrieval. The constant references to 'consensus' in ancient Christian teaching leave the impression that the shaping of the theology now regarded as 'classic' was far more easy and unanimous than it actually was. He seems to assume the degree of continuity in orthodox Christian teaching sought by Vincent of Lérins in the so-called 'Vincentian Canon' outlining the criteria of authoritative tradition: *quod ubique, quod semper, quod ab omnibus creditum est*—'that which everywhere, always, by all has been believed'.[27] That many positions cherished as classical by large numbers of Christians do not pass this threefold test of ecumenicity, antiquity, and consent is illustrated by Vincent's own use of these criteria to show that the

---

23   Oden, *Word of Life*, p. xx.
24   Oden, *Word of Life*, p. xvii.
25   Oden, *Word of Life*, p. xv.
26   Oden, *Word of Life*, p. xvii.
27   Vincent of Lérins *Commonitorium* 2.1-3 (G. Rauschen and P.B. Albers, eds., *Florilegium Patristicum*, vol. 5, *Vincentii Lerinensis Commonitoria*, ed. G. Rauschen [Bonn: P. Hanstein, 1906], p. 12; ET, NPNF[2] 11:132).

position of Augustine (one of the four Western Doctors!) on predestination had not been believed everywhere, always, or by all.[28] There are, of course, numerous concepts essential to the Christian faith, such as the location of salvation in Jesus Christ, which easily meet Vincent's criteria. Yet Oden's quest for universality in classical Christian thinking ironically approaches being the same sort of modern enterprise as classical liberalism's attempt to discern the universally applicable and timeless essence of Christianity. A perspective on the tradition that constructively engages the postmodern situation must also appreciate the particularity and heterogeneity of the developing tradition. Although Oden is self-consciously retrieving tradition for a postmodern context, his work does not give enough attention to postmodern thought, some constructive expressions of which would actually substantiate the need for a recovery of tradition and might facilitate the goals of his project through their appreciation for premodern hermeneutics and the value of communal tradition. A postmodern hermeneutic of tradition should embrace both dialogue with the tradition and dialogue with the culture.[29] Oden's project helps the church with the first of those twin tasks. One may have to look elsewhere for help with the contextual utilization of tradition in a critical and constructive manner.[30]

Karl Barth: Beginning with the Community of Faith

Although the theological career of Karl Barth (1886-1968) predates the widespread awareness of a transition from modernity to postmodernity, Barth may very well be the first postmodern theologian.[31] His work was a

---

28   Oden is himself willing to reevaluate later developments in the tradition in light of its earliest layers, as evidenced by his continued affirmation of the ordination of women for pastoral ministry well into his turn toward tradition: T.C. Oden, *Requiem: A Lament in Three Movements* (Nashville: Abingdon Press, 1995), p. 17.

29   Dialogue with the culture, it should be noted, must proceed on the basis of a firm rooting in the Christian tradition. The Christian theologian may not assume a stance of detached objectivity between the tradition and the culture, but neither may the Christian theologian do theology within the tradition but detached from the culture. Tillich's correlational theology, for example, properly proceeded from thorough grounding in the tradition to correlative dialogue with the concerns of existentialist thought.

30   Among the thinkers treated in this chapter, L. Boff and C.M. LaCugna are particularly sensitive in their attention to the cultural contexts in which their theologies are situated.

31   Some of the parallels (and differences) between Barth's thought and more recent constructive Christian postmodern thought are explored by M.I. Wallace, *The Second Naiveté: Barth, Ricoeur, and the New Yale Theology*, 2d edn. (SABH, 6; Macon, Ga.: Mercer University Press, 1995).

reaction against the modern theological programmes of nineteenth-century theology, and his refusal to ground Christian theology in anything other than the self-disclosure of God in Jesus Christ has much in common with the nonfoundationalism of postmodern thought.[32]

An under-appreciated facet of Barth's critique of modern theology is his retrieval of tradition in the service of this critique. The influence of a rigorous study of Anselm on Barth's theological methodology (*fides quaerens intellectum*, 'faith seeking understanding') is well known, as is his extensive interaction with and dependence upon Calvin, Luther, and classic Reformed and Lutheran confessional documents. Barth's 'Neo-Orthodoxy' is more than a return to the centrality of the Word and a rediscovery of the theology of the Reformation, however. Like the Reformers,[33] Barth was a student of the church fathers and carefully considered patristic perspectives in forming the theology articulated in the *Church Dogmatics*, and among the medieval theologians he engaged in extended, constructive dialogue with Thomas Aquinas as well as with Anselm. Barth's thoroughgoing retrieval of the dogmatic tradition of the church in its catholicity as an unavoidable task of theological reflection is one of the major features that distinguish his thought from that of other neoorthodox theologians.

But what sort of authority does tradition possess for Barth? True to the Scripture principle of the Reformation, he ascribes 'absolute and material authority' only to 'Holy Scripture as the Word of God'; nevertheless, under the authority of Scripture there is 'an indirect and relative formal authority' in the church.[34] Since this authority exists only in subordination to the Word of God, it is exercised in the 'humility which consists...in the incompleteness of its own knowing and acting and speaking which that involves, in the openness to reformation through the Word of God which

---

32   *CD* I/1, p. xiii. On the complexities of the relationship of Barth's thought to modernity and postmodernity, see G. Ward, 'Barth, Modernity, and Postmodernity', in *The Cambridge Companion to Karl Barth*, ed. J.B. Webster (Cambridge: Cambridge University Press, 2000), pp. 274-95.

33   See the following essays in I. Backus, ed., *The Reception of the Church Fathers in the West: From the Carolingians to the Maurists*, 2 vols. (Leiden: E.J. Brill, 1997): M. Schulze, 'Martin Luther and the Church Fathers', vol. 2, pp. 573-626; I. Backus, 'Ulrich Zwingli, Martin Bucer and the Church Fathers', vol. 2, pp. 627-60; J. van Oort, 'John Calvin and the Church Fathers', vol. 2, pp. 661-700; and the literature cited therein. On the theological significance of the fathers for the early Lutheran tradition, see also A. Merkt, *Das patristische Prinzip: Eine Studie zur theologischen Bedeutung der Kirchenväter* (SVC, 58; Leiden: Brill, 2001), pp. 121-53.

34   *CD* I/2, p. 538. Cf. the definition of Christian doctrine offered by Pelikan, *The Christian Tradition*, vol. 1, *The Emergence of the Catholic Tradition*, p. 1: 'What the church of Jesus Christ believes, teaches, and confesses on the basis of the word of God.'

constantly confronts it in Holy Scripture'.[35] This authority is therefore not a body of authoritative propositions faithfully transmitted from one generation to the next by the church but rather is the church itself, in all its fallibility, as the community gathered in subordination to the Word of God, and thus the community to whose confession one must listen as a theologian who participates in the 'debate about a right faith which goes on in the Church'[36] (and for Barth, all believers are theologians[37]).

Perhaps no Protestant theologian has been more faithful than Barth in subordinating theological reflection to the Word of God while carefully listening to the confession of the church in doing so. Baptists will readily identify with his radical subordination of all possible sources of authority for Christian faith to the Word of God as encountered in Scripture. They may also find attractive his understanding of tradition as the community's confession of faith, which is fallible, debatable, and open to reformulation, yet cannot be avoided by those who do theology in, with, and for this community. Baptists would certainly do well to emulate Barth's practice of doing theology in dialogue with all those who have contributed to the doctrinal tradition of the church across the ages and across denominational traditions.[38] Barth's engagement of the patristic theological tradition as a possible model for a Baptist retrieval of tradition receives more focused attention in chapter 7 of this book.

La Nouvelle Théologie: Renewal through Ressourcement

While Barth was calling Protestantism to renewed attention to the tradition of the church's reception of the Word, a group of Roman Catholic theologians in Europe advanced a similar programme for the renewal of Catholicism. Centered in France and led by Henri de Lubac (1896-1991), Jean Daniélou (1905-1974), Yves Congar (1904-1995), and Hans Urs von

---

35   *CD* I/2, p. 586.

36   Barth, *CD* I/2, p. 589.

37   K. Barth, 'Theology', in *God in Action: Theological Addresses*, trans. E.G. Homrighausen and K.J. Ernst (Edinburgh: T & T Clark, 1937), p. 57: 'But the problem of theology, as the purity of the Church's task, is set before the *whole* Church. In the Church there are really no non-theologians. The concept "laymen" is one of the worst concepts in religious terminology, a concept that should be eliminated from the Christian vocabulary'.

38   Although frequently more descriptive than constructive in approach, the two-volume *Systematic Theology* of Baptist theologian J.L. Garrett, Jr. approximates (on a smaller scale) the historical and ecumenical breadth of *CD* in its choice of dialogue partners (*Systematic Theology: Biblical, Historical, and Evangelical*, 2 vols. [Grand Rapids, Mich.: William B. Eerdmans, 1990-1995; 2nd edn., North Richland Hills, Tex.: BIBAL Press, 2000-2001].

Balthasar (1905-1988), among others, the movement now identified as the *nouvelle théologie* emphasized the need for *ressourcement*, the retrieval of the ancient (especially patristic) sources of the Christian tradition, as a prerequisite for *aggiornamento*, the updating of the tradition with reference to the contemporary situation. Although the Second Vatican Council is popularly interpreted in terms of the *aggiornamento* emphasis, the work of the Council was deeply rooted in the emphasis of the *nouvelle théologie* on *ressourcement* as a means toward the revitalization of twentieth-century Catholicism. The theologians of the *nouvelle théologie* approached this goal by combining energetic historical scholarship in the form of critical editions of patristic texts and studies of patristic theology with constructive dialogue with the major philosophical movements of the twentieth century.[39]

Baptists who are coming to grips with the limitations of historical-critical biblical exegesis in a postmodern context and are beginning to appreciate the polyvalence or 'surplus of meaning' inherent in biblical texts should give consideration to de Lubac's proposals in *Medieval Exegesis: The Four Senses of Scripture*, his attempt to revitalize Catholic biblical scholarship as a thoroughly theological endeavor through a reconsideration of the hermeneutics of late patristic and medieval Christianity.[40] The many studies of the thought of Gregory of Nyssa by Daniélou and von Balthasar are worthy exemplars for finding resources for contemporary theology in the early tradition, and Congar's ecclesiological works demonstrate how these resources may help a tradition-enriched theology to become more rather than less open to the contemporary world.[41] As the *nouvelle théologie* had in mind the modern rather than postmodern world, however, contemporary Baptists will need to move beyond its engagement with

---

39   For more extensive introduction to the *nouvelle théologie*, see F. Kerr, 'French Theology: Yves Congar and Henri de Lubac', in *The Modern Theologians: An Introduction to Christian Theology in the Twentieth Century*, 2d edn., ed. D.F. Ford (Cambridge, Mass.: Blackwell, 1997), pp. 105-17; M. D'Ambrosio, 'Ressourcement Theology, Aggiornamento, and the Hermeneutics of Tradition', *Communio* 18 (Winter, 1991), pp. 530-55; J.F. Kobler, 'On D'Ambrosio and Ressourcement Theology', *Communio* 19 (Summer, 1992), pp. 321-25.

40   H. de Lubac, *Exégèse médiéval: Les quatres sens de l'Écriture*, 2 vols. (Paris: Aubier, 1959); ET, *Medieval Exegesis*, 2 vols. (Grand Rapids: William B. Eerdmans, 1998).

41   E.g., J. Daniélou, *From Glory to Glory: Texts from Gregory of Nyssa's Mystical Writings*, trans. and ed. H. Musurillo (New York: Charles Scribner's Sons, 1961; reprint, Crestwood, N.Y.: St. Vladimir's Seminary Press, 1995); H.U. von Balthasar, *Presence and Thought: An Essay on the Religious Philosophy of Gregory of Nyssa*, trans. M. Sebanc (San Francisco: Ignatius Press, 1995); Y. Congar, *Divided Christendom: A Catholic Study of the Problem of Reunion*, trans. M.A. Bousfield (London: G. Bles, 1939).

modern thought and seek out additional dialogue partners with self-consciously postmodern perspectives on tradition.

Alasdair MacIntyre: Tradition, Community, and Rationality

Though a moral philosopher rather than theologian, the thought of Alasdair MacIntyre (1929-) is of great relevance for Christian experiments in the postmodern retrieval of tradition. In *After Virtue: A Study in Moral Theory*, a seminal work for contemporary narrative/character ethics, MacIntyre defines 'a living tradition' as 'an historically extended, socially embodied argument, and an argument precisely in part about the goods which constitute that tradition'.[42] This understanding of tradition as an argument-driven, ongoing communal narrative that provides the community with 'a grasp of those future possibilities which the past has made available to the present'[43] has a number of advantages over more static concepts of tradition. First, tradition as an ongoing narrative is not an idealized past to be recovered in the present but rather the story apart from which one can neither understand the present nor be truly open to the future completion of the story. Second, the construal of tradition as argument (cf. Barth's 'debate about a right faith which goes on in the Church'[44]) includes all persons who, though perhaps differing from majority perspectives in the community, are nevertheless committed to being a part of the community and contribute to its welfare through their constructive dissension. Internal conflict is then essential to tradition, for tradition is not merely a corpus of conclusions reached in a series of arguments but rather is the argument itself, which cannot be separated from any conclusions that issue from it. Third, the social embodiedness of tradition prevents tradition from becoming reduced to a body of authoritative propositions with which the individual thinker may interact. In MacIntyre's proposal, one may live out of a tradition only as a person whose identity is received from the story of the community to which one belongs and to which one may contribute by joining the argument about the story and its implications.

In the later book *Whose Justice? Which Rationality?* MacIntyre counters the Enlightenment notion of a universal rationality to which anyone can appeal and by which anyone can be persuaded with an alternative understanding of the nature of rationality: rationality is always the

---

42   A. MacIntyre, *After Virtue: A Study in Moral Theory*, 2nd edn. (Notre Dame, Ind.: University of Notre Dame Press, 1984), p. 222.

43   MacIntyre, *After Virtue*, p. 223.

44   *CD* I/2, p. 589.

rationality of a particular tradition.[45] Consequently, there is no rationality that can transcend the particularities of multiple traditions of rationality and judge the rightness of the rationality of any particular tradition. While one could object that this conception of traditioned rationality falls prey to a complete relativism, there is in this understanding an internal objectivity within a particular tradition that grows out of its 'historically extended, socially embodied argument...about the goods which constitute that tradition'.[46] Although there can be no objective comparison of traditions (for that would require something that does not exist, a rationality untouched by tradition), a tradition may make internal progress through encounter with another tradition.[47] Yet as the rationalities of different traditions function as different languages that cannot simply be translated into each other, this encounter may only take place through the learning of a 'second first language'.[48]

In light of their own tradition as dissenters, Baptists may find a place for themselves in MacIntyre's portrayal of the communal and argumentative character of tradition (a possibility to which this chapter will return).[49] His proposal for the growth of a tradition through bilinguality may also prove useful for the crafting of a viable Baptist hermeneutic of tradition. Since Baptists lack a tradition steeped in the conscious appropriation of tradition, they might do well to adopt as a 'second first language' (or more accurately in this case, a second dialect of the first language) the Christian traditions that consciously live in continuity with the catholic tradition: Roman Catholicism, Eastern Orthodoxy, and Anglicanism. One may not simply evaluate these more robust hermeneutics of tradition as a dispassionate external observer. One must try them on for size and live with their particularities of worship, spirituality, and doctrine before they can make significant contributions to the rethinking of a Baptist hermeneutic of tradition. Oden's retrieval project might be best appreciated along these lines as an experiment in helping Christians whose first-language tradition is one steeped in modernity to learn 'classical Christian thinking' as a second first-language tradition.

---

45   A. MacIntyre, *Whose Justice? Which Rationality?* (Notre Dame, Ind.: University of Notre Dame Press, 1988), pp. 7-11.

46   MacIntyre, *After Virtue*, p. 222.

47   MacIntyre, *Whose Justice?*, ch. 18, "The Rationality of Traditions" (passim).

48   MacIntyre, *Whose Justice?*, pp. 387-88.

49   For another Baptist appreciation of this aspect of MacIntyre's characterization of a 'living tradition', see J.R. Wilson, *Living Faithfully in a Fragmented World: Lessons for the Church from MacIntyre's After Virtue* (CMMC; Harrisburg, Pa.: Trinity Press International, 1997), pp. 45-67, esp. 59-61.

Paul Ricoeur: Tradition in the Second Naïveté

The hermeneutical theory of French philosopher Paul Ricoeur (1913-2005) likewise makes room for critique of a tradition by those who yet embrace the tradition. In *The Symbolism of Evil* and other works,[50] Ricoeur describes and advocates a hermeneutical journey that moves from a precritical 'first naïvité' through a moment of critical explanation to a postcritical 'second naïvité'.[51] In the 'first naïvité', which may be associated with both the outlook of the premodern world and the early stages of a contemporary person's hermeneutical development, one interprets language (or a thing, event, text, or work of art—or a tradition) literally, i.e., as meaning what it seems to mean upon initial encounter. Although Ricoeur develops his hermeneutical theory in response to the despair of meaning wrought by interpretive theory in the tradition of the 'masters of suspicion', he still maintains the necessity of passing through a critical approach to interpretation in which one suspects that there may be more to be understood than is evident in the initial, literal interpretation. But this hermeneutic of suspicion must ultimately yield to a 'second naïvité', a willingness once again to be addressed by the meaning-rich text, the meaning of which cannot be exhausted by critical interpretation: 'Beyond the desert of criticism, we wish to be called again.'[52]

Ricoeur applies this 'hermeneutics of suspicion and retrieval'[53] explicitly to the 'text' of tradition in an article evaluating the hermeneutical perspectives of Hans-Georg Gadamer and Jürgen Habermas as they apply to ethical theory and its relationship to culture.[54] For Ricoeur, ethical

---

50   P. Ricoeur, *The Symbolism of Evil*, trans. Emerson Buchanan (Boston: Beacon Press, 1967), pp. 347-57; *Interpretation Theory: Discourse and the Surplus of Meaning* (Fort Worth: Texas Christian University Press, 1976), pp. 71-88; 'The Model of the Text: Meaningful Action Considered as a Text', in *Hermeneutics and the Human Sciences: Essays on Language, Action, and Interpretation*, ed. J.B. Thompson (Cambridge: Cambridge University Press, 1981), pp. 131-44.

51   D.R. Stiver provides an accessible explanation of Ricoeur's 'threefold hermeneutical arc' in 'A Hermeneutical Arc', ch. 2 in *Theology after Ricoeur: New Directions in Hermeneutical Theology* (Louisville, Ky.: Westminster John Knox Press, 2001), pp. 56-78. Stiver is a Baptist theologian who has creatively embraced Ricoeur as a valuable dialogue partner for those doing theology in a postmodern context.

52   Ricoeur, *Symbolism of Evil*, p. 349.

53   This is the characterization of Ricoeur's hermeneutical theory in A.C. Thiselton, *New Horizons in Hermeneutics: The Theory and Practice of Transforming Biblical Reading* (Grand Rapids, Mich.: Zondervan, 1992), pp. 344-78.

54   P. Ricoeur, 'Ethics and Culture: Habermas and Gadamer in Dialogue', *PhilTod* 17 (1973), pp. 153-65, cited in J.C.K. Goh, *Christian Tradition Today: A Postliberal Vision of Church and World* (LTPM, 28; Louvain: Peeters Press, 2000), pp. 37-39.

ideologies cannot be critiqued as pure ideas, for they arise within the tradition of a culture. Critique therefore requires a retrieval of the tradition, but the tradition cannot simply be repristinated. One must seek an 'ethical distance' from the tradition so that the tradition makes 'even our doubt and our contestation...possible'[55] en route to the reinterpretation and appropriation of the tradition.

The combination of a radicalized *Sola Scriptura* hermeneutic with Enlightenment individualistic rationalism has made modern Baptists prone to evaluate theological positions vis-à-vis Scripture as pure ideas, disengaged from the tradition of theological argumentation that gave birth to the ideas. Baptists will be better equipped for doing theology if they learn to stand consciously in the Christian theological tradition with both a critical eye toward it and a willingness to receive its address to them in the 'second naïvité'.

John Milbank, Catherine Pickstock, and Company: Radical Orthodoxy

Perhaps the most thoroughly constructive response to the end of modernity in contemporary theology is the 'radical orthodoxy' proposed by John Milbank (1952-) and Catherine Pickstock, among other largely British and mainly Cambridge-connected theologians. Milbank, Pickstock, and Graham Ward (1955-) explain the term by which their programme has become labeled in the introduction to a collection of essays by proponents of radical orthodoxy:

> In what sense *orthodox* and in what sense *radical*? Orthodox in the most straightforward sense of commitment to credal Christianity and the exemplarity of its patristic matrix. But orthodox also in the more specific sense of reaffirming a richer and more coherent Christianity which was gradually lost sight of after the late Middle Ages. In this way the designation 'orthodox' here transcends confessional boundaries, since both Protestant biblicism and post-tridentine Catholic positivist authoritarianism are seen as aberrant results of theological distortions already dominant even before the early modern period....Radical, first of all, in the sense of a return to patristic and medieval roots, and especially to the Augustinian vision of all knowledge as divine illumination...second, in the sense of seeking to deploy this recovered vision systematically to criticise modern society, culture, politics, art, science and philosophy with an unprecedented boldness...in yet a third sense of realising that via such engagements we *do* have also to rethink the tradition.[56]

---

55   Ricoeur, "Ethics and Culture," p. 165.
56   J. Milbank, C. Pickstock, and G. Ward, eds., *Radical Orthodoxy: A New Theology* (London: Routledge, 1999), p. 2.

The theological framework for this postmodern turn to tradition is the 'participatory philosophy' of Plato as it is reinterpreted by the Christian doctrine of the Incarnation.[57] This effort to recover premodern modes of thinking is a response to problematic aspects of contemporary thought without and within the church. On the one hand, radical orthodoxy responds to the rejection of metanarrative in nihilistic forms of postmodern thought with an unapologetic embrace of traditional Christian theology as *the* metanarrative that interprets all other narratives.[58] On the other hand, radical orthodoxy is critical of the appeal of both liberal and conservative streams of Christian theology to foundations for theological discourse external to the Christian metanarrative. By 'undercutting some of the contrasts between theological liberals and conservatives'[59] in dispensing with these external foundations, the proposals of radical orthodoxy may offer pathways beyond the liberal-conservative polarities bequeathed by modernity.

As Baptists are among the most radical representatives of the 'Protestant biblicism' judged 'aberrant' in light of the earlier orthodox tradition, they may find radical orthodoxy's approach to the retrieval of tradition difficult to swallow. Nevertheless, this particular movement towards tradition offers some promising possibilities for ecumenical dialogue via a reexamination of the tradition common to all Christian denominations, for a more thoroughgoing critique of contemporary culture by a mind that is more consistently Christian because it is grounded in the tradition of Christian thinking, and for creativity in rethinking the tradition in light of the unique challenges of the postmodern world.[60] Pickstock's work on the ultimately liturgical nature of language and all of life may help Baptists towards a recovery of liturgy as the primary locus of tradition.[61]

---

57   Milbank et al., eds., *Radical Orthodoxy*, pp. 3-4.

58   G. Hyman, *The Predicament of Postmodern Theology: Radical Orthodoxy or Nihilist Textualism?* (Louisville, Ky.: Westminster John Knox Press, 2001), pp. 3-4.

59   Milbank et al., eds., *Radical Orthodoxy*, p. 4.

60   M.S. Medley has noted a number of parallels between 'radical orthodoxy' and the Baptist/Free Church theological project of Stanley Grenz and John Franke (M.S. Medley, review of S.J. Grenz and J.R. Franke, *Beyond Foundationalism: Shaping Theology in a Postmodern Context* [Louisville, Ky.: Westminster John Knox Press, 2000], in *IJST* 4.1 (March, 2002), pp. 83-90.

61   C. Pickstock, *After Writing: On the Liturgical Consummation of Philosophy* (CCT; Oxford: Blackwell, 1998).

Leonardo Boff and Catherine Mowry LaCugna: Traditional Resources for Liberation

Although liberation and feminist theologies are certainly critical of the oppressive and patriarchal aspects of the Christian tradition, liberation theologian Leonardo Boff (1938-) and feminist theologian Catherine Mowry LaCugna (1952-1997), both Roman Catholics, exemplify the ways in which a retrieval of tradition can yield useful resources for theologies of liberation. At the core of the thought of both Boff and LaCugna is a creative recovery of classical Trinitarian theology in the Cappadocian tradition, especially the mature perichoretic Trinitarianism of John of Damascus.[62]

In *Trinity and Society*, Boff challenges the hierarchical abuse of power in church and society on the basis of a thoroughly social Trinitarianism. Both a-Trinitarian forms of monotheism and monarchical (i.e., hierarchical or subordinationistic) forms of Trinitarianism pose political dangers in that they 'can justify totalitarianism and the concentration of power in one person's hands, in politics and in religion'.[63] A perichoretic model of intra-Trinitarian relations—one in which Father, Son, and Spirit equally share divine status, power, and action through the 'mutual indwelling', 'interpenetration', or 'dance' of the three persons—makes egalitarian, inclusive communion rather than hierarchy the divine basis for the transformation of ecclesial and political life.[64]

In *God for Us: The Trinity and Christian Life*, LaCugna joins Boff and fellow feminist theologian Patricia Wilson-Kastner (1944-)[65] in teasing out the liberative potential of Trinitarian *perichoresis*. But whereas Boff and Wilson-Kastner make the perichoretic Trinitarian relations a model for

---

62   *Perichōrēsis* in Christian theological usage was originally employed in the fourth century with reference to the mutual interpenetration or coinherence of the divine and human natures of the person of Christ (e.g., Gregory of Nazianzus *Oration* 38.13 [ET, NPNF² 7:349]. In the sixth century pseudo-Cyril (*On the Trinity* 10) applied it to the mutual interpenetration or coinherence of the three persons of the Trinity, a concept anticipated in the fourth century by the Cappadocian Fathers and developed more fully early in the eighth century by John of Damascus to safeguard Eastern trinitarian theology against both tritheism and monarchianism (e.g., *On the Orthodox Faith* 1.14 [ET, NPNF² 9:17]). In this perichoretic understanding of intra-Trinitarian relations, each person of the Trinity fully shares in the being and work of the other persons and thus makes manifest the divine unity (cf. John 10.38—'the Father is in me and I am in the Father' [NRSV]). On the patristic use of *perichōrēsis*, see G.W.H. Lampe, *A Patristic Greek Lexicon* (Oxford: Clarendon Press, 1961), s.v. '*perichōrēsis, hē*'.

63   L. Boff, *Trinity and Society*, trans. P. Burns (TLS; Maryknoll, N.Y.: Orbis Books, 1988), p. 20.

64   Boff, *Trinity and Society*, pp. 137-54.

65   See P. Wilson-Kastner, *Faith, Feminism, and the Christ* (Philadelphia: Fortress Press, 1983).

human relations, LaCugna highlights the divine openness toward the inclusion of humanity in the perichoretic 'dance' suggested by the doctrine, which then becomes a model for the partnership of all persons, divine and human.[66]

Boff and LaCugna illustrate the potential of the retrieval of tradition for providing resources for creative theological reflection that address the contemporary concerns of church and society. It is of special interest to Baptists to note that Boff and LaCugna as Catholic theologians are able to draw on one aspect of the tradition (perichoretic Trinitarianism) in order to call into question other problematic developments in the tradition that were emerging during the same period (hierachical ecclesiologies, political theories, and anthropologies). The retrieval of tradition does not have to be an uncritical return to past doctrines and practices. Baptists will also be especially interested in the similarities of the perichoretic ecclesiologies proposed by Boff and LaCugna to Free Church patterns of polity.[67]

Geoffrey Wainwright: The Liturgical Locus of Tradition

Duke Divinity School theologian Geoffrey Wainwright (1939-) would likely not identify himself as a postmodern theologian.[68] Yet his thought does address the place of tradition in theology and the means of its retrieval in a manner that is highly relevant to both postmodern and Baptist concerns. Whereas modern theology tended to be rooted in and concerned with the realm of universal ideas, postmodern theology is interested in particularity and in the practices associated with ideas. At a popular level, many self-consciously postmodern Christians are manifesting a renewed interest in the Christian practice of worship as a primary expression of its particularity. At the same time, no dimension of Baptist theology, modern or postmodern, is more underdeveloped than a Baptist theology of

---

66   C.M. LaCugna, *God for Us: The Trinity and Christian Life* (New York: HarperCollins, 1991), pp. 269-78. LaCugna serves as a fruitful dialogue partner for Baptist theologian M.S. Medley in ch. 2 of his book *Imago Trinitatis*, pp. 19-68.

67   E.g., Boff, *Trinity and Society*, pp. 152-54; cf. J. Moltmann, *The Trinity and the Kingdom: The Doctrine of God*, trans. M. Kohl (Minneapolis: Fortress Press, 1993), p. 202, where Moltmann links these concepts to presbyterial and synodal (as opposed to episcopal) patterns of polity, with 'leadership based on brotherly advice'.

68   Wainwright's approach to doing theology does have much in common with postmodern approaches, however, especially in his refusal to provide an epistemological justification for theology and in his conviction that theology must remain an 'open system'. See G. Wainwright, *Doxology: The Praise of God in Worship, Doctrine, and Life. A Systematic Theology* (New York: Oxford University Press, 1980), pp. 1-3, 435-38.

worship.[69] Wainwright, a Methodist of British origin with an appreciation for aspects of the Baptist tradition, offers a theology rooted in the tradition of the church's liturgical practices in *Doxology: The Praise of God in Worship, Doctrine, and Life* and other works.[70]

Wainwright finds the proper locus of tradition not in texts or a body of propositional truths but in the worship of the Christian community:

> It is the Christian community that transmits the vision which the theologian, as an individual human being, has seen and believed. As a believer, the theologian is committed to serving the Christian community in the transmission and spread of the vision among humanity. *Worship* is the place in which that vision has come to a sharp focus, a concentrated expression, and it is here that the vision has often been found to be at its most appealing. The theologian's thinking therefore properly draws on the worship of the Christian community and is in duty bound to contribute to it. The specific task of the theologian lies in the realm of *doctrine*. He is aiming at a coherent intellectual expression of the Christian vision. He should examine the liturgy from that angle, both in order to learn from it and in order to propose to the worshipping community any corrections or improvements which he judges necessary.[71]

The substance of tradition is then the 'Christian vision', which is liturgically transmitted primarily via Scripture (understood as an essentially liturgical book in both origin and subsequent function in the church), creeds (understood as 'summary confession of faith and as hermeneutical grids through which believers interpret both the ample witness of Scripture and the church and also their own religious stance'), and hymns.[72] At the core of Wainwright's project is the ancient Latin formula *lex orandi, lex credendi*—'the law of praying is the law of believing'[73]—which may

---

69   When I wrote in a previous version of this chapter 'Although there is presently no Baptist liturgical theology of the magnitude of Wainwright's project, much encouraging work is being done to rectify this deficiency' (S.R. Harmon, 'The Authority of the Community [of All the Saints]: Toward a Postmodern Baptist Hermeneutic of Tradition', *RevExp* 100.4 [Fall, 2003], pp. 618-19, n. 68), I could cite as examples of this 'encouraging work' only a handful of journal articles and essays. Since then this significant lacuna in published Baptist theology has been filled splendidly by Ellis, *Gathering*.

70   This approach is also evident in G. Wainwright, *Eucharist and Eschatology* (New York: Oxford University Press, 1978), and G. Wainwright, *For Our Salvation: Two Approaches to the Work of Christ* (Grand Rapids, Mich.: William B. Eerdmans, 1997).

71   Wainwright, *Doxology*, p. 3.

72   Wainwright, *Doxology*, pp. 4, 6-7, 149-283.

73   The influential formula seems to have originated with Prosper of Aquitaine (d. after 455) in a treatise formerly attributed to Celestine I, the *Capitula* or *Praeteritorum*

legitimately be interpreted by reversing the two participles so that it is understood to mean that 'worship influences doctrine, and doctrine worship'.[74]

Baptist theology has indeed influenced Baptist worship, but largely through subtraction in light of a radical biblicism: worship practices in the Church of England or other bodies that were deemed to be without biblical precedent were rejected, and in their place the reading and preaching of the Word and (later) the singing of hymns became the principal means of the transmission of the Christian vision. The eventual result was that apart from the singing of hymns of pre-Baptist and non-Baptist origin, Baptist worship has largely become divorced from the liturgically-situated tradition of the church in its catholicity. In order to incorporate the *lex orandi, lex credendi* principle into postmodern Baptist theological reflection, Baptists may need first to explore other Christian worship traditions in which the principle has long been practiced and carefully seek appropriate ways to incorporate the best of the riches of the ecumenical liturgical tradition into their own worship. Chapter 8 of this book suggests some specific patterns and practices that Baptists might retrieve from the liturgical tradition of the church in its catholicity and so become more intentional about their worship as a principal bearer of the doctrinal tradition that forms Christians in their faith and practice.

George Lindbeck and the 'New Yale Theology': Tradition as Communal Narrative

The movement in contemporary North American theology that most nearly approaches being a parallel to Barth and European neoorthodoxy is what has been variously labeled 'postliberalism', 'narrative theology', and 'the New Yale Theology'.[75] Though the movement's coalescence is traceable to the call of George Lindbeck (1923-) for a 'postliberal theology' in the concluding chapter of his 1984 book *The Nature of Doctrine*,[76] other

---

Sedis Apostolicae episcoporum auctoritates, de gratia Dei et libero voluntatis arbitrio 8; (ET, 'Official Pronouncements of the Apostolic See on Divine Grace and Free Will' [ACW, 32], p. 183): *lex supplicandi statuat legem credendi*, 'Let the rule of prayer lay down the rule of faith'. In context, Prosper invokes this principle in an argument against semi-Pelagianism: the fact that during the liturgy Christian pastors throughout the world always pray that God may bring people to faith provides traditional grounds for attributing the entirety of the human experience of salvation to God's gracious work.

74   Wainwright, *Doxology*, p. 218.

75   For a brief introduction to postliberal theology, see W.C. Placher, 'Postliberal Theology', in *The Modern Theologians*, pp. 343-56.

76   G.A. Lindbeck, *The Nature of Doctrine: Religion and Theology in a Postliberal Age* (Louisville, Ky.: Westminster John Knox Press, 1984), pp. 112-38.

scholars associated with Yale Divinity School in the 1970s and later also contributed to the formation of an approach to theology that has a much more spacious place for tradition than did the liberal theologies that dominated the American theological scene during much of the twentieth century. Hans Frei (1922-1988) both mediated the influence of Barth to the movement and called to its attention the importance of narrative for Christian theology, Brevard Childs (1923-) and David Kelsey (1932-) insisted that biblical authority must be sought in the traditional function given to the Scriptures by the community of faith that created and canonized them, and Paul Holmer (1916-2004) drew from the linguistic philosophy of Ludwig Wittgenstein (1889-1951) to argue that the meaningfulness of theological expressions is tied to the traditional rules by which these expressions are articulated and understood in the communities from which they arise.[77]

Lindbeck, a Lutheran theologian whose work in ecumenical theology has been motivated by his observation of the proceedings of the Second Vatican Council as a representative of the Lutheran World Federation, advocates a 'cultural-linguistic' or 'rule' theory of the function of doctrine as more conducive to ecumenical dialogue than the conservative and liberal approaches to doctrine spawned by modernity. The *propositional* approach to doctrine, common in conservative theologies but also found elsewhere on the theological spectrum, 'emphasizes the cognitive aspects of religion and stresses the ways in which church doctrines function as informative propositions or truth claims about objective realities'.[78] The *experiential-expressive* approach, characteristic of liberal theologies in the tradition of F.D.E. Schleiermacher, 'interprets doctrines as noninformative and nondiscursive symbols of inner feelings, attitudes, or existential orientations'.[79] Lindbeck's *cultural-linguistic* (or *regulative* or *rule*) approach maintains that 'the function of church doctrines that becomes most prominent…is their use, not as expressive symbols or truth claims, but as communally authoritative rules of discourse, attitude, and action'.[80] In other words, just as grammar governs the meaningfulness of language, so doctrine governs whether a given idea or practice possesses meaningfulness

---

77   E.g., H. Frei, *The Eclipse of Biblical Narrative: A Study in Eighteenth and Nineteenth Century Hermeneutics* (New Haven: Yale University Press, 1974); B.S. Childs, *The New Testament as Canon: An Introduction* (Philadelphia: Fortress Press, 1984); D.H. Kelsey, *The Uses of Scripture in Recent Theology* (Philadelphia: Fortress Press, 1975); P.L. Holmer, *The Grammar of Faith* (San Francisco: Harper & Row, 1978).

78   Lindbeck, *Nature of Doctrine*, p. 16.

79   Lindbeck, *Nature of Doctrine*, p. 16.

80   Lindbeck, *Nature of Doctrine*, p. 18.

as a Christian idea or practice. Theology then must be done in, with, and for a particular community that has a certain tradition, primarily narrative in form, which regulates the community's thinking and acting.[81]

But for which community, and on the basis of which narrative, does doctrine function in this manner? Certain ideas and practices make sense within the Baptist telling of the Christian narrative but not in the Roman Catholic version of the narrative, for example, and vice-versa. If a Baptist hermeneutic of tradition borrows from Lindbeck's call to be faithful to the particularity of the community's traditional story without widening the scope of that community beyond the boundaries of Baptist communities, the resulting theologies and practices will be extremely idiosyncratic and possibly even sub-Christian in light of the intertwining of the Baptist story with the narratives generated by the modern world. A postmodern Baptist hermeneutic of tradition will need to rethink the narrow ecclesiologies that have contributed to the typical Baptist's ignorance of (and thus failure to be formed by) the traditional narratives common to the larger Christian community.

A Postmodern Baptist Hermeneutic of Tradition

A hermeneutic of tradition that responds constructively to the postmodern condition must seek alternatives to static, propositional understandings of tradition, be open to premodern expressions of tradition as resources for the revitalization of faith and practice in a more authentically Christian direction, and give attention to the relationship between tradition and the community which has produced it and for which it has some normative function. A Baptist hermeneutic of tradition will maintain a place for the ecclesial distinctiveness of Baptist communities while becoming more open to the traditional resources of the larger Christian community. I offer to my fellow Baptists the following brief expression of a postmodern Baptist hermeneutic of tradition in the hope that it might fulfill these conditions and play some small role in fostering a constructive dialogue among Baptist ministers, students, teachers, and laypersons about a new place for tradition in the Baptist vision.

The Normative Function of Tradition: The Authority of the Community (of All the Saints)

While it is true that Christ and the Scriptures that bear witness to him have always been the preeminent sources of authority for Baptist faith and practice, Baptists have also ascribed a derivative authority to the local

---

81   Lindbeck, *Nature of Doctrine*, pp. 120-22.

church as a covenant community gathered around the proclamation of the Word of God under the Lordship of Christ. Baptists have been averse to granting this authority to local, regional, national, or international associational bodies beyond the local church, but in many cases some Baptist groups have unwisely shunned participation in interdenominational partnerships and dialogues, even though bodies such as the National Council of Churches and World Council of Churches exercise no authority over member denominations and churches. This aversion of many Baptists to ecumenical involvement is symptomatic of an underlying conviction that since Baptists are thought to have recovered (or for those influenced by Landmarkism, preserved faithfully throughout all of Christian history) the New Testament pattern of faith and practice, a Baptist congregation needs no sources of authority or resources for renewal beyond the Bible and the illumination of the Holy Spirit.

The ancient Christian confession of belief in the *communio sanctorum*, the communion of saints, may suggest ways in which Baptists may affirm their connection to the larger Christian community to which they belong, and thus to its tradition, without yielding the distinctiveness or authority of their own communities. The Latin phrase, which originated in Gaul at the end of the fourth century and in the following century began appearing in the predecessors of the received text of the Apostles' Creed, is capable of multiple translations and interpretations: (1) with *sanctorum* taken as neuter, a sharing 'of holy things', i.e., participation in the sacraments; or (2) with *sanctorum* as masculine, (a) a 'fellowship [consisting] of holy persons', (b) a 'fellowship with holy persons' in the sense of the martyrs and saints [distinguished from ordinary Christians], or (c) a 'fellowship with holy persons' in the sense of all believers, both living and deceased.[82] The latter interpretation is the more traditional and most common of the options, and would include Baptists along with all other Christians of all ages in one real, living, and continuous community under the Lordship of Christ.

Any Baptist who self-consciously engages in theological reflection must do so first as part of the communion of saints (cf. Barth) and then as a Baptist who is a member of the communion of saints. This communion possesses an authority under the Lordship of Christ as the community that in every age has confessed its faith on the basis of the biblical story of God's saving acts, has retold this story in worship, and thus has shaped, clarified, and applied the tradition in every age so that no Christian can read Scripture except through lenses ground in earlier ages. Because this traditioning community is not limited to a superior class of recognized

---

82   J.N.D. Kelly, *Early Christian Creeds*, 2d edn. (New York: David McKay Co., 1960), pp. 388-91.

saints but includes all Christians from all ages, its authority is not limited to the writings of 'doctors of the church' or the creeds and canons of ecumenical councils or any other body of orthodox propositions, but rather resides in the community as a whole and therefore in every denominational branch thereof.[83] The traditioning community to which the Baptist theologian must listen includes not only the Separatist-Anabaptist-Anglican-Roman Catholic-early catholic (patristic) genealogy from which Baptists descend, but also Eastern Orthodox, Pentecostal, and other traditions of Christian community that have branched differently from this line of descent. As the stories of all Christian traditions constitute the traditional resources available to contemporary Baptist communities, ministers responsible for the theological formation of Baptists will need to become more diligent students of church history and better observers of the contemporary church in all its wonderfully varied expressions in order to help their congregations benefit from the location of the authority of tradition in the communion of the saints.[84]

The Vehicle of Tradition: The Story of the Community

If tradition in this paradigm is the authority of the community composed of all the saints, how can the diversity this entails have some normative function? Lindbeck's cultural-linguistic or regulative theory of doctrine is helpful at this point. The 'grammar' that makes certain ideas and practices identifiable and meaningful as Christian 'language' is the traditional story of the communion of the saints. Since this story is told in rich particularity by the canonical scriptures, wherever the Bible is read, proclaimed, taught, and practiced in community, there the tradition of the community that formed and was formed by these scriptures is present and functions as a normative authority for the church, even when it fosters significant diversity in faith and practice. For many Baptists, the proclamation of the Word is the irreducible minimum of worship, and even when this is the only thing that takes place in worship, the authority of the community of all

---

83   Such an inclusive location of communal tradition does not exclude, however, the identification of some sources of traditional authority within the communion of saints as possessing greater degrees of authority than other sources. This problem receives some attention in ch. 7, 'Hearing the Voice of the Community: Karl Barth's Conversation with the Fathers as a Paradigm for Baptist and Evangelical *Ressourcement*'.

84   Holmes, *Listening to the Past*, pp. 18-36, also extends the authority of the tradition-bearing community to the communion of the saints, in which 'the doctors are not dead and gone, but living and active, and members together of the same body of Christ to which we belong' (p. 30).

the saints is made present—minimally so, but present nonetheless. This normative function of communal tradition will be enhanced, however, if the story is also made present through the confession of the ancient creeds (understood as concise narrative summaries of the biblical story that in turn reinforce the traditional shape of that story),[85] the singing of hymns from the whole of the Christian tradition, and the tangible enactment of the story in water, bread, and wine (cf. Wainwright). Baptists have traditionally prized the gospel story as declared in the Spirit-enabled preaching of the Word and personal testimony as the means by which people encounter the living Christ.[86] The spiritual formation of Baptists through the internalization and embodiment of the gospel story may be enhanced by drawing upon the liturgical tradition of the larger Christian community in planning services of worship that maximize the community's exposure to the story that regulates its life.[87]

The Critical Function of Tradition: The Argument of the Community

As Baptists have a distinctive place in the history of the church as dissenters, a Baptist hermeneutic of tradition must allow for dissent within the tradition—not as a good in itself, but as a state of affairs that is necessitated by the current failures of the church to embody the unity that is an eschatological mark of the church. Dissent can be a step toward unity only if pursued as a conversation that requires contestation because of the present participation of the church in the fallen nature of humanity en route to the eschatological realization of the unity of the church. Baptists who have been traditioned as dissenters may need to be reminded from time to time of the eschatology of this temporal contestation, but their traditioning in dissent can also help them appreciate the critical function of tradition as the argument of the community and may help them find their place within this argument.

---

85   On the narrative shape and function of the ancient creeds, see P.M. Blowers, 'The *Regula Fidei* and the Narrative Character of Early Christian Faith', *ProEccl* 6 (Spring, 1997): 199-228.

86   This understanding of the place of the gospel story in Baptist faith and practice is evident in F.L. Mauldin, *The Classic Baptist Heritage of Personal Truth: The Truth as It Is in Jesus* (Franklin, Tenn.: Providence House Publishers, 1999).

87   J.W. McClendon, Jr. offers a Baptist proposal for incorporating into worship the stories of Christians from all ages and denominations who have embodied the Christian story in exemplary ways in the appendix 'Christian Worship and the Saints' in *Biography as Theology: How Life Stories Can Remake Today's Theology* (Philadelphia: Trinity Press International, 1974), pp. 172-84.

Whenever my divinity students have read the document 'Re-Envisioning Baptist Identity: A Manifesto for Baptist Communities in North America',[88] which gives significant attention to a re-envisioning of the authority of the community in Baptist life, some of them have invariably responded with questions along these lines: 'Where would a Martin Luther have a place in this vision?' 'Doesn't this ignore the Baptist tradition of dissent?' 'What if the community studying the Scriptures together is a fundamentalist one?' Some published responses from other Baptist theologians have expressed similar concerns about whether the 'Manifesto' allows a sufficient place for critique of the tradition of the community and dissent from it.[89] In response to these critiques, it should be pointed out that the co-authors of the 'Manifesto' are in fact dissenters themselves—dissenters from the hegemony of particular modern interpretations of the Baptist tradition that they believe are shaped more by later American expressions of radical individualism than by the earliest expressions of the Baptist vision of Christian community in the seventeenth century.[90] The 'Manifesto' explicitly rejects authoritarianism in the community, but its case for the authority of the community and its tradition could be supplemented by affirming more explicitly the indispensability of the dissenter for the communal argument that constitutes, drives, and clarifies the tradition of the community (cf. MacIntyre).[91]

This means that even the heretic and the schismatic belong in some sense to the tradition.[92] By definition, one must first be a Christian in order

---

88   See appendix 1, 'Re-Envisioning Baptist Identity: A Manifesto for Baptist Communities in North America'.

89   E.g., Shurden, 'The Baptist Identity and the Baptist *Manifesto*', pp. 321-40; Jones, 'Re-Visioning Baptist Identity from a Theocentric Perspective', pp. 35-57.

90   See P.E. Thompson, '"As It Was in the Beginning"(?): The Myth of Changelessness in Baptist Life and Belief', in *Recycling the Past or Researching History?*, pp. 184-206.

91   This conceptualization of a dissent that contributes to the health of the community's tradition is implicit in the 'Manifesto': 'We thus affirm an open and orderly process whereby faithful communities deliberate together over the Scriptures with sisters and brothers of the faith, excluding no light from any source. When all exercise their gifts and callings, when every voice is heard and weighed, when no one is silenced or privileged, the Spirit leads communities to read wisely and to practice faithfully the direction of the gospel (1 Cor. 14.26-29).'

92   Cf. Holmes, *Listening to the Past*, p. 35: 'Heresy, however dangerous and wrong it may be judged, and however much it should result in a breach of communion, is still clearly a part of the Christian tradition, albeit a part that has been judged inadequate and wrong, and not something foreign.' There are hints in this direction in T.W. Tilley, *Inventing Catholic Tradition* (Maryknoll, N.Y.: Orbis Books, 2000), pp. 136-39, but he leaves this notion undeveloped. For a Baptist engagement with Tilley's

to be a heretic or a schismatic. The ecclesiology of Augustine regarded the
Donatist schismatics as members of the catholic Christian community, even
if separated from it.[93] The ancient conciliar doctrinal formulations bear the
stamp of the contributions of heretics, even though their positions did not
carry the day: Nicaea requires Arius, Constantinople requires Eunomius,
and Chalcedon requires Eutyches and Nestorius. The community can bear
doctrinal controversy in the form of disagreement over 'the goods which
constitute that tradition'[94] and in fact benefits from the contributions of
theological disagreement to the ongoing clarification of the tradition.[95] But
the community cannot bear heresy in the sense suggested by the earliest
Christian usage of the term: a heresy is a *hairesis*, a 'choice' of heterodox
'opinion' leading to 'division',[96] whenever a dissenter is so insistent that a
self-determined viewpoint be recognized as authoritative teaching within
the church that it divides the community. Although patristic scholarship has
suggested that some of their teachings were misunderstood by some of their
orthodox opponents (especially in the case of Nestorius), and in spite of the
undeniable mistreatment of heretics by some of their orthodox opponents
and their imperial supporters, and in the face of an understandable Baptist
inclination to sympathize with the ecclesiastical outcasts of Christian
history, it must be acknowledged that ancient arch-heretics such as Arius,
Eunomius, Eutyches, and Nestorius were heretics in this latter sense of the
heresy that the community cannot bear. For the sake of its tradition,
however, the community does need dissenters who are committed to
advancing the good of the community and who do so through their dissent,
even when their 'side' of the argument is not in the majority.

The hermeneutic of tradition proposed herein does not yet adequately
address the theological criteria by which a dissenting perspective might be
considered heretical. Work remains to be done on a 'hermeneutic of heresy'

---

proposals for a contemporary Catholic theology of tradition, see Medley, 'Catholics,
Baptists, and the Normativity of Tradition'.

93   Augustine *De Baptismo contra Donatistas* 1.5; 1.10; 6.30-34 (NPNF[1] 4:414-
15, 417-18, 493-95). The ancient Christian authors with whom Augustine interacts in
this treatise exemplify the wide diversity of viewpoints on the spiritual status of heretics
that existed in early catholic Christianity.

94   MacIntyre, *After Virtue*, p. 222.

95   Cf. Paul's recognition of the temporal necessity of the recognition and
contestation of *hairesis* in the community in light of the noetic limitations of the earthly
church in 1 Cor. 11.19: 'Indeed, there have to be factions (*haireseis*) among you, for
only so will it become clear who among you are genuine (*hoi dokimoi*)'.

96   Cf. the interrelationship between these semantic domains of *hairesis* in early
Christian usage in H. Schlier, '*haireomai, hairesis*' in *Theological Dictionary of the
New Testament*, ed. G. Kittel, trans. G.W. Bromiley (Grand Rapids, Mich.: William B.
Eerdmans, 1964), vol. 1, pp. 180-85.

that corresponds to this hermeneutic of tradition. While this task is beyond the scope of this chapter, I suggest here that a teaching might be considered destructively heretical if the narrative it references or presupposes is so significantly different from the Christian narrative that it is really another story altogether. For example, Docetism qualifies as a censurable heresy because its story is of a god who shuns materiality, saving at the greatest possible distance from humanity and refusing to enter into the created order and the experience of suffering that pervades this present order. This is an altogether different story from the church's narrative of the God who pronounces creation 'good' and who in Jesus Christ assumes human flesh and suffers 'for us and for our salvation'. It might be objected that certain understandings of the classical divine attribute of 'impassibility' might seem to differ from this subplot of the story as well. In response to this possible objection to this narrative criterion of heresy, I grant that impassibility is a dimension of the tradition that needs to be critically re-examined in light of the normativity of Scripture and the historical development of the tradition, yet such a critical re-examination may discover that the patristic advocates of impassibility had a rather different problem in mind than the quite legitimate concerns of moderate advocates of theopassianism and that the fathers nuanced their concept of impassibility in such a way that God does indeed have a positive personal solidarity with human suffering as the God who has a qualitatively different relationship to suffering than humans have and who consequently is able to help them in the midst of their suffering.[97] A necessary corollary of any 'hermeneutic of heresy' is an ethic of polemics, as the treatment of heretics throughout the tradition has not exemplified the most thoroughly Christian practices of Christian community.

Many Baptists will disagree with these suggestions about the function that tradition might have in Baptist theology in a postmodern milieu. Such dissent is welcome, for it is the stuff of which the tradition is made. If any objectors are concerned that an explicit place for the catholic tradition in Baptist theological method would embrace something alien to the Baptist tradition, however, their concerns are addressed in part by the next chapter, which finds in early Baptist confessions of faith a surprisingly robust sense of catholic theological identity.

---

97   See P.L. Gavrilyuk, *The Suffering of the Impassible God: The Dialectics of Patristic Thought* (OECS; New York: Oxford University Press, 2004).

CHAPTER 4

Baptist Confessions of Faith and the Patristic Tradition

'In the first place, it is a *duty* which we owe both to the Catholic Church and to our own, to take our reformed confessions in the most Catholic sense they will admit.' *John Henry Newman*[1]

'Most biblicistic Protestants…adhere in practice to postbiblical trinitarianism: they do not deny what the Nicene Creed teaches, but they ignore the creed itself and act as if its teachings were self-evidently Scriptural.' *George A. Lindbeck*[2]

When a colleague in another school of my university learned that this project was exploring connections between Baptist confessions of faith and the patristic tradition, he asked with some surprise, 'Are there any?' His was a logical question, for one might reasonably suppose that the confessional documents of a people who have sometimes claimed to have 'no creed but the Bible' would betray little evidence of regard for post-biblical councils and creeds. A retired colleague, a church historian, responded with a wink, 'You're not going to trace a "trail of blood" back through the Donatists, are you?', alluding to the peculiar historiographical arguments of 'Landmark' Baptists for a Baptist organic continuity with ancient Christianity via a succession of non-catholic sects such as the Montanists, Donatists, and other groups through the ages not in communion with the 'false' Catholic Church.[3] Yes, there are indeed significant connections between Baptist confessions of faith and the patristic tradition, but no, one does not have to resort to pushing Baptist origins back sixteen centuries through a disreputable genealogy in order to demonstrate such connections. This chapter proposes three historical theses about the vestiges of the patristic tradition that are discernable in previous Baptist confessions

---

1   J.H. Newman, 'Remarks on Certain Passages in the Thirty-Nine Articles', *Tracts for the Times* 90 (London: J.G.F. & J. Rivington, 1841), p. 80.

2   Lindbeck, *Nature of Doctrine*, p. 74.

3   See J.M. Carroll, *The Trail of Blood* (Lexington, Ky.: American Baptist Pub. Co., 1931).

of faith and concludes with three constructive proposals for more intentional interaction with the patristic tradition in any future confessions of faith that Baptist communities may have occasion to draft and adopt in response to new ecclesial circumstances.

Vestiges of the Patristic Tradition in Baptist Confessions

A chronological reading of major confessions of faith issued by Baptist individuals, congregations, associations, and denominational bodies with an eye open for theological language and concepts that cannot be explained by a pure a-traditional radical biblicism, but instead evidence the mediation of language and concepts that are traceable to post-New Testament patristic Christianity, suggests the following summary conclusions regarding the relationship between Baptist confessions of faith and the patristic tradition.

First Historical Thesis

The first historical thesis concerns the theological categories within which Baptist confessions have evidenced a concern for doctrinal continuity with patristic Christianity. *Continuities between the patristic tradition and Baptist confessions are found primarily in echoes of Nicaeno-Constantinopolitan Trinitarianism and Chalcedonian Christology.* There is of course much broad theological agreement between Baptist confessions and the formative Christian thought of the patristic period, but language that is identifiably patristic in origin appears almost exclusively in confessional statements about the Triune God or the person of Christ.

Some confessions are Trinitarian without employing phraseology that is necessarily patristic in origin. The *Declaration of Faith of English People Remaining at Amsterdam in Holland* of 1611, the *Midland Association Confession* of 1655, and the *Standard Confession* of 1660 simply cite the Johannine Comma (the latter confession does so by quotation sans citation).

That there are THREE which beare record in heaven, the FATHER, the WORD, and the SPIRIT; and these THREE are one GOD, in all equalitie, 1 Jno. 5.7; Phil. 2.5, 6.[4]

That this infinite Being is set forth to be the Father, the Word, and the Holy Spirit; and these three agree in one. 1 John v.7.[5]

---

4   'Declaration of Faith of English People Remaining at Amsterdam in Holland', in Lumpkin, *Baptist Confessions of Faith*, p. 117.

5   'Midland Association Confession', article 2, in Lumpkin, *Baptist Confessions of Faith*, p. 198.

That there are three that bear record in Heaven, the Father, the Word, the holy Spirit, and these three are one.[6]

While the 'Johannine Comma' would eventually cease to be a viable biblical prooftext for Trinitarian doctrine on text-critical grounds, it certainly belonged to the biblical text then utilized by the Baptists who drafted these confessions and thus enabled them to confess the doctrine via biblical language. *The Faith and Practice of Thirty Congregations* of 1651 marshals multiple biblical texts in addition to the 'Johannine Comma' that show the oneness of the three divine persons in the economy of salvation (though here the 'Word' is the word of God the Father, which is one with the Son and the Spirit).

That God's Word, Son, or Spirit, are one, 1 *Ioh.* 5.7. *Jude* 1. *Heb.* 10. 29. *Rom.* 15. 16. God and his Word are one; *Ioh.* 1. 1. The Word quickneth, *Psal.* 119. 50. The Son quickeneth, *Eph.* 2. 1. And the spirit quickneth, Ioh. 6. 63. So they are one. God giveth Gifts, and the Son doth the same, also the holy Ghost, So they are one. *Iam.* 1. 17. *Eph.* 4. 10, 11. *Acts* 2. 38. 1. *Thes.* 1. 5. *Ioh.* 6.44. *Io.* 14. 6. *Eph.* 1. 18. 1 *Cor.* 12. 3. *Math.* 10. 40. *Gal.* 3. 2.[7]

The *New Hampshire Confession* of 1833 and its descendants, the successive revisions of the *Baptist Faith and Message* adopted by the Southern Baptist Convention in 1925, 1963, and 2000, affirm God's self-revelation as Father, Son, and Spirit without more explicit statements about the immanent Trinity.

[We believe] That there is one, and only one, living and true God...revealed under the personal and relative distinctions of the Father, the Son, and the Holy Spirit; equal in every divine perfection, and executing distinct but harmonious offices in the great work of redemption.[8]

The *Baptist Faith and Message* (1925) incorporated the essence of the article on God from the *New Hampshire Confession*, with slight revisions that hint at the patristic theological categories of 'nature' and 'essence' or 'being'.

---

6   'Standard Confession', article 7, in Lumpkin, *Baptist Confessions of Faith*, p. 227.

7   'The Faith and Practice of Thirty Congregations', article 20, in Lumpkin, *Baptist Confessions of Faith*, p. 178.

8   'New Hampshire Confession', article 2, in Lumpkin, *Baptist Confessions of Faith*, p. 362.

> There is one and only one living and true God...He is revealed to us as Father,
> Son and Holy Spirit, each with distinct personal attributes, but without division of
> nature, essence or being.[9]

The latter clause does give some attention to the immanent relations of the
Trinity. The 1963 revision of the *Baptist Faith and Message* again only
slightly modified the wording of the Trinitarian statement ('The eternal
God reveals Himself to us as Father, Son, and Holy Spirit, with distinct
personal attributes, but without division of nature, essence, or being') and
added sub-articles on 'God the Father', 'God the Son', and 'God the Holy
Spirit'.[10] The most recent revision of the *Baptist Faith and Message* (2000)
inserts the word 'triune' ('The eternal triune God reveals Himself to us as
Father, Son, and Holy Spirit, with distinct personal attributes, but without
division of nature, essence, or being'), subtly moving beyond the reticence
of the *New Hampshire Confession* and the previous versions of the *Baptist
Faith and Message* to make explicit affirmations regarding the immanent
Trinity.[11]

Just as the Trinitarian affirmations of these Baptist confessions of faith
tended to be consistent with the classical formulations of Nicaeno-
Constantinopolitan Trinitarian faith while utilizing biblical rather than
patristic language to express these basic doctrinal convictions, so also the
Christological articles of many confessions are consistent with Chalcedon
without dependence on its language, preferring biblical expressions instead.
Nevertheless, a number of Baptist confessions did employ Trinitarian and
Christological formulations from the ancient creeds.

John Smyth's *Short Confession of Faith in XX Articles* of 1609 refers in
article 6 to Jesus Christ as 'true God and true man...taking to himself, in
addition, the true and pure nature of a man, out of a rational soul, and
existing in a true human body'.[12] This does not stray far from the anti-
Apollinarian language of the Chalcedonian symbol.[13] The next article of

---

9   'Baptist Faith and Message" (1925), article 2, in R.A. Baker, *A Baptist Source
Book with Particular Reference to Southern Baptists* (Nashville, Tenn.: Broadman
Press, 1966), p. 201.

10   'Baptist Faith and Message' (1963), article 2, in Lumpkin, *Baptist Confessions
of Faith*, pp. 393-94.

11   *The Baptist Faith and Message: A Statement Adopted by the Southern Baptist
Convention June 14, 2000* (Nashville, Tenn.: LifeWay Christian Resources, 2000),
article 2.

12   'Short Confession of Faith in XX Articles by John Smyth', article 6, in
Lumpkin, *Baptist Confessions of Faith*, p. 100.

13   H. Denzinger and A. Schönmetzer, eds., *Enchiridion Symbolorum:
definitionum et declarationum de rebus fidei et morum*, 36th edn. (Freiburg: Herder,

Smyth's *Short Confession* is essentially an expansion of the second article of the Apostles' Creed with additional affirmations about the life of Christ between birth and passion, emphasizing his humanity.

> That *Jesus Christ*, as pertaining to the flesh, *was conceived by the Holy Spirit in the womb of the Virgin Mary*, afterwards *was born*, circumcised, baptized, tempted; also that he hungered, thirsted, ate, drank, increased both in stature and in knowledge; he was wearied, he slept, at last *was crucified, dead, buried, he rose again, ascended into heaven*; and that to himself as only King, Priest, and Prophet of the church, all power both in heaven and earth is given (emphasis added—parallels to the Apostles' Creed in italics).[14]

The *Declaration of Faith of English People Remaining at Amsterdam* (1611) uses the term 'subsistence', a common English translation of *hypostasis*, for the persons of the Trinity,[15] and echoes Chalcedon in the language of its confession of the two natures of Christ.[16]

1976), § 301 [hereinafter *DS*]: '*theon alēthōs, kai anthrōpon alēthōs ton auton ek psychēs logikēs kai sōmatos*'.

14 'Short Confession of Faith in XX Articles by John Smyth', article 7, in Lumpkin, *Baptist Confessions of Faith*, p. 100.

15 This usage of 'subsistence' also appears in the *Second London Confession*, along with much additional classical language for the immanent Trinitarian relations: 'In this divine and infinite Being there are three subsistences, the Father the Word (or Son) and Holy Spirit, of one substance, power, and Eternity, each having the whole Divine Essence, yet the Essence undivided, the Father is of none neither begotten nor proceeding, the Son is Eternally begotten of the Father, the holy Spirit proceeding from the Father and the Son, all infinite, without beginning, therefore but one God, who is not to be divided in nature and Being; but distinguished by several peculiar, relative properties, and personal relations; which doctrine of the Trinity is the foundation of all our Communion with God, and comfortable dependence on him' ('Second London Confession', ch. 2, in Lumpkin, *Baptist Confessions of Faith*, p. 253). While this statement is almost wholly derived from the corresponding article in the *Westminster Confession*, the latter confession referred to the three 'persons'; thus 'subsistences' belongs to the redaction of this material in the *Second London Confession*. The significance of this use of confessional source material is addressed under the second historical thesis in the next subsection of this chapter.

16 Echoes of the Chalcedonian two-natures Christology also appear in the Christological statements of the Particular Baptist *Somerset Confession* of 1656 ('WE believe that Jesus Christ is truly God...and truly man, of the seed of David' ['Somerset Confession', article 13, in Lumpkin, *Baptist Confessions of Faith*, p. 206]) and the General Baptist document *The Unity of the Churches* of 1704 ('We do believe, that there is but one Lord Jesus Christ, the second Person in the Trinity, and the only begotten Son of God; and that he did, in the fulness of time, take to himself our nature, in the womb of the blessed Virgin Mary, of whom, in respect of the flesh, he was made; and so is true

That IESVS CHRIST, the Sonne off GOD the second Person, or subsistence in the Trinity, in the Fulness off time was manifested in the Flesh, being the seed off David, and off the Isralits, according to the Flesh. Roman. 1.3 and 8.5. the Sonne off Marie the Virgine, made of hir substance, Gal. 4.4. By the power off the HOLIE GHOST overshadowing hir, Luk. 1.35. and being thus true Man was like vnto us in all thing, son onely excepted. Heb. 4.15. being one person in two distinct natures, TRVE GOD, and TRVE MAN.[17]

Pneumatological portions of some of these Trinitarian articles also reflect classical credal language. In particular, the Constantinopolitan affirmation of the procession of the Spirit within the Godhead, in its expanded Western form with the *Filioque* clause,[18] appears in *Propositions and Conclusions Concerning True Christian Religion* of 1612-1614,[19] the *First London Confession* of 1644,[20] the *Second London Confession* of 1677,[21] and the *Orthodox Creed* of 1678.[22]

God, and true Man, our Immanuel' ['The Unity of the Churches', in Lumpkin, *Baptist Confessions of Faith*, p. 340]).

17   'A Declaration of Faith of English People Remaining at Amsterdam in Holland', article 8, in Lumpkin, *Baptist Confessions of Faith*, p. 119.

18   The affirmation of the procession of the Spirit from the Father ('*to ek tou patros ekporeuomenon*', *DS* § 150) in the creed of the Council of Constantinople in 381 was altered in Latin translation with the insertion of '*Filioque*' in this phrase in the version of the creed professed by the Third Council of Toledo in 589 ('*qui ex Patre Filioque procedit*', *DS* § 470).

19   'Propositions and Conclusions Concerning True Christian Religion', article 52, in Lumpkin, *Baptist Confessions of Faith*, p. 133: 'That the Holy Ghost proceedeth from the Father and the Son (John xiv. 26, and xvi. 7)'. This confession foreshadows in article 5 the tendency of several later confessions to eschew propositions about the nature of God apart from what may be known about God as God relates to humanity in the economy of salvation: 'That these terms, Father, Son, and Holy Spirit, do not teach God's substance, but only the hinder parts of God: that which may be known of God' (Lumpkin, *Baptist Confessions of Faith*, p. 125).

20   'The London Confession, 1644', article 2, in Lumpkin, *Baptist Confessions of Faith*, pp. 156-57: 'In this God-head, there is the Father, the Sonne, and the Spirit; being every one of them one and the same God; and therefore not divided, but distinguished one from another by their severall properties; the Father being from himselfe, the Sonne of the Father from everlasting, the holy Spirit proceeding from the Father and the Sonne.'

21   'Second London Confession', ch. 2.3, in Lumpkin, *Baptist Confessions of Faith*, p. 253: '...the Father is of none neither begotten nor proceeding, the Son is Eternally begotten of the Father, the holy Spirit proceeding from the Father and the Son'.

22   'The "Orthodox Creed"', article 3, in Lumpkin, *Baptist Confessions of Faith*, p. 299: 'The father is of none, neither begotten nor proceeding; the son is eternally begotten of the father; the holy ghost is of the father, and the son, proceeding.'

Although continuity with the patristic tradition is evident almost exclusively in these Trinitarian and Christological formulations, there are instances of clear continuity with the patristic tradition beyond those doctrinal loci. The *Second London Confession* calls the church 'Catholick or universal',[23] and the *Orthodox Creed* confesses faith in 'one holy catholick church',[24] the language of the Nicaeno-Constantinopolitan Creed minus the fourth ('apostolic') of the *notae ecclesiae*.[25] The most explicit and thoroughgoing referencing of the patristic tradition among Baptist confessions of faith takes place in the *Orthodox Creed*, which reproduces of the Apostles', Nicene, and (pseudo-) Athanasian Creeds and encourages Baptists to receive and believe them.[26]

Second Historical Thesis

This feature of the *Orthodox Creed* leads to a second historical thesis. *Continuities between the patristic tradition and Baptist confessions are not necessarily attributable to a conscious engagement with the patristic tradition as a source of religious authority or resource for theological reflection; rather, these continuities were retained from the ecclesiastical bodies out of which the confessing Baptist communities came or by which they were influenced.* While one aim of this book is to advocate an intentional retrieval of the patristic tradition by contemporary Baptist and Free Church communities, the clear echoes of the patristic tradition present in early Baptist confessions are not evidence of a similarly intentional programme in the seventeenth century (although they may serve as precedents to which a concern for Baptist catholicity may appeal and can help subvert common modern Baptist assumptions about 'the Baptist tradition'). The commendation of 'the three creeds' in article 38 of the *Orthodox Creed* illustrates this thesis.

> The three creeds, viz. Nicene creed, Athanasius's creed, and the Apostles [sic] creed, as they are commonly called, ought thoroughly to be received, and believed. For we believe, they may be proved, by most undoubted authority of holy scripture, and are necessary to be understood of all christians; and to be instructed in the knowledge of them, by the ministers of Christ, according to the analogy of faith, recorded in the sacred scriptures, upon which these creeds are

---

23   'Second London Confession', ch. 26.1, in Lumpkin, *Baptist Confessions of Faith*, p. 285.
24   'The "Orthodox Creed"', article 29, in Lumpkin, *Baptist Confessions of Faith*, p. 318.
25   *DS* § 150: '...*eis mian hagian, katholikēn kai apostolikēn ekklēsian*'.
26   'The "Orthodox Creed"', article 38, in Lumpkin, *Baptist Confessions of Faith*, p. 326.

grounded, and catechistically opened, and expounded in all christian families, for the edification of young and old, which might be a means to prevent heresy in doctrine, and practice, these creeds containing all things in a brief manner, that are necessary to be known, fundamentally, in order to our salvation; to which end they may be considered, and better understood of all men, we have here printed them under their several titles as followeth.[27]

The language of the first portion of this article is lifted almost verbatim from article 8 of the *Thirty-Nine Articles of Religion of the Church of England*.[28] Likewise, when the *Second London Confession*[29] and the *Orthodox Creed*[30] call the church 'catholic', they are indebted to chapter 25 of the *Westminster Confession of Faith* (1647), which served as the model for the articles on the church in both confessions.[31] Also derived from the *Westminster Confession* are the echoes of the Nicaeno-Constantinopolitan Creed and the Chalcedonian definition in the Trinitarian and Christological portions of the *Second London Confession*,[32] the *Orthodox Creed*,[33] and the

---

27   'The "Orthodox Creed"', article 38, in Lumpkin, *Baptist Confessions of Faith*, p. 326.

28   'The three Credes, Nicene Crede, Athanasian Crede, and that whiche is commonlye called the Apostles' Crede, ought throughlye to be receaued and beleued: for they may be proued by moste certayne warrauntes of holye scripture' (text of the English edition of 1571, in *The Creeds of Christendom with a History and Critical Notes*, 6th edn., ed. P. Schaff, rev. D.S. Shaff, vol. 3, *The Evangelical Protestant Creeds* [New York: Harper & Row, 1931; reprint, Grand Rapids, Mich.: Baker Book House, 1990], p. 492).

29   'Second London Confession', ch. 26.1, in Lumpkin, *Baptist Confessions of Faith*, p. 285: 'The Catholick or universal Church, which (with respect to internal work of the Spirit, and truth of grace) may be called invisible, consists of the whole number of the Elect, that have been, are, or shall be gathered into one, under Christ the head thereof; and is the spouse, the body, the fulness of him that filleth all in all.'

30   'The "Orthodox Creed"', article 29, in Lumpkin, *Baptist Confessions of Faith*, p. 318: 'There is one holy catholick church, consisting of, or made up of the whole number of the elect, that have been, are, or shall be gathered, in one body under Christ, the only head thereof; which church is gathered by special grace, and the powerful and internal work of the spirit; and are effectually united unto Christ their head, and can never fall away.'

31   'Westminster Confession of Faith', ch. 25, in Schaff, *Creeds of Christendom*, vol. 3, p. 657: 'The catholic or universal Church, which is invisible, consists of the whole number of the elect, that have been, are, or shall be gathered into one, under Christ the head thereof; and is the spouse, the body, the fullness of him that filleth all in all'.

32   Cf. 'Second London Confession', ch. 2.3 and ch. 8.1-7, in Lumpkin, *Baptist Confessions of Faith*, pp. 253 and 260-62, with 'Westminster Confession of Faith', chs. 2 and 8, in Schaff, *Creeds of Christendom*, vol. 3, pp. 606-07 and 619-20.

Philadelphia Confession's appropriation of the *Second London Confession*.[34] In the case of John Smyth's *Confession*, the use of Chalcedonian language is attributable to his theological education at Cambridge and his previous ministry in the Church of England.[35] One should not rule out the possibility of Mennonite precedent for Smyth's echoes of classical Christian doctrine, however, for similar points of contact with the patristic tradition appear in some of the Anabaptist confessions.[36] One in particular, Peter Ridemann's *Rechenschaft* of 1540, was prefaced by the Apostles' Creed.[37]

The affirmation of patristic perspectives on the doctrines of the Trinity and the person of Christ by Baptist confessions demonstrates that Baptists have tended to read the Bible through lenses ground in the fourth and fifth centuries. However, their spectacles were fitted for them by Anglican, Reformed, and possibly Anabaptist opticians. This is not to minimize the significance of what Philip Thompson has identified as 'a catholic spirit among early Baptists',[38] but rather to identify the lines of transmission by which the early Baptists received this spirit. Despite their radical biblicism, they did not easily depart from the hermeneutical pre-understanding they inherited or appropriated from other ecclesiastical bodies, an understanding that is ultimately traceable to the patristic tradition. Thus, as Thompson argues, 'the early Baptists...believed themselves to be speaking from

---

33   Cf. 'The "Orthodox Creed"', articles 3-7, in Lumpkin, *Baptist Confessions of Faith*, p. 299-301, with 'Westminster Confession of Faith', chs. 2 and 8, in Schaff, *Creeds of Christendom*, vol. 3, pp. 606-07 and 619-20.

34   The *Philadelphia Confession* added to the *Second London Confession* only two articles, one on the singing of psalms and hymns (ch. 23) and one on the imposition of hands (ch. 31). See Lumpkin, *Baptist Confessions of Faith*, pp. 348-53.

35   Smyth's writings give evidence of a fair degree of familiarity with patristic sources, although he explicitly cited the church fathers only for polemical purposes. See M.A. Smith, 'The Early English Baptists and the Church Fathers' (PhD thesis, The Southern Baptist Theological Seminary, 1982), pp. 8-24.

36   E.g., the *Waterland Confession* of Hans de Ries and Lubbert Gerrits (1580) contains the following echoes of patristic formulations: article 1, 'We believe...that there is one God...Creator and Preserver of heaven and earth, of things visible and invisible' (Lumpkin, *Baptist Confessions of Faith*, p. 44); article 3, 'The Father...begat his Son from eternity, before all creatures...The Holy Spirit is God's power, might or virtue, proceeding from the Father and the Son. These three are neither divided nor distinguished in respect of nature, essence, or essential attributes'. (Lumpkin, *Baptist Confessions of Faith*, p. 45); article 8, 'Jesus is...true God and true man' (Lumpkin, *Baptist Confessions of Faith*, p. 48).

37   'Ridemann's *Rechenschaft*, 1540', in Lumpkin, *Baptist Confessions of Faith*, p. 38.

38   Thompson, 'A New Question in Baptist History', pp. 51-72.

within a tradition larger than any single communion'.[39] Their confessions established their continuity with this larger tradition as well as their distinctive place within it. This function of early Baptist confessions of faith provides precedent within the Baptist tradition for a contemporary catholic Baptist retrieval of the patristic tradition.

Third Historical Thesis

A third historical thesis concerns the diachronic development of Baptist confessions of faith in the extent to which they demonstrate an affinity with the patristic theological tradition. *Continuities between the patristic tradition and Baptist confessions are most evident in confessions issued during the first century of Baptist existence, the seventeenth century.* This was not true of all confessions produced during the period, but John Smyth's *Confession* of 1609 and the *Orthodox Creed* of 1678 mark the beginning and end of the most explicit interactions with the patristic tradition in Baptist confessions (although the *Philadelphia Confession* extended the patristic features of the *Second London Confession* to another century and a new continent). Confessions adopted after the seventeenth century, especially those adopted by Baptists in America, shied away from patristic formulations in favor of more biblical terminology. In the case of the doctrine of the Trinity, whereas the creeds and their echoes in earlier Baptist confessions were largely concerned with the immanent relationships of the divine persons, the later confessions tended to emphasize the persons of the Godhead as known in God's activity of self-revelation or in the economy of salvation. For example, the *New Hampshire Confession* affirms faith in 'one...living and true God' who is 'revealed under the personal and relative distinctions of the Father, the Son, and the Holy Spirit'.[40] Such an approach is not unprecedented in the earlier confessions: the *Propositions and Conclusions Concerning True Christian Religion* of 1612-1614 taught '[t]hat these terms, Father, Son, and Holy Spirit, do not teach God's substance, but only the hinder parts of God: that which may be known of God'.[41] Similar radical biblicist perspectives became more prominent while echoes of the patristic tradition all but vanished in subsequent centuries.

What accounts for this phenomenon? A 1982 doctoral dissertation by Michael Smith under the direction of Baptist patristic historian E. Glenn Hinson examined the use of the church fathers in Baptist writers from John

---

39   Thompson, 'A New Question in Baptist History', p. 71.

40   'New Hampshire Confession', article 2, in Lumpkin, *Baptist Confessions of Faith*, p. 362.

41   'Propositions and Conclusions Concerning True Christian Religion', article 5, in Lumpkin, *Baptist Confessions of Faith*, p. 125.

Smyth to Joseph Hooke. Smith found many appeals to patristic texts in the ecclesiological polemics of these writers, but he also identified a precipitous decline in Baptist use of the fathers toward the end of the seventeenth century, with a complete absence of interaction with the fathers after 1701. Smith attributes this trend primarily to the 1689 Act of Toleration: after this alteration in their relationship to the larger social order, Baptists no longer had to justify the ecclesial legitimacy of their separate existence to those who valued continuity with ancient Christian tradition.[42]

Smith's thesis makes sense for interaction with the patristic tradition in early Baptist theological literature in general, but two additional factors may be involved where the confessions are concerned. First, the decline in credal terminology in Baptist confessions coincides with the intellectual upheaval of the Enlightenment. Even those who did not embrace the anti-supernaturalism of the Enlightenment worldview experienced some attraction to its anti-traditionalism. That Baptist confessions became less traditional in their wording during this time is hardly surprising. Second, the radical individualism of the American soil in which the Baptist tradition took root and flourished during the next two centuries had little room for ancient doctrinal norms that might limit the freedom of the individual conscience. Confessions that expressed doctrine simply by means of biblical texts and biblical terminology allowed individuals to interpret those texts according to the dictates of their consciences.

Constructive Proposals for Interaction with the Patristic Tradition in Future Baptist Confessions

The reconstruction of Baptist life after the collapse of the modern milieu with which later developments of the Baptist tradition became entwined will require fresh attention to two formative periods for Baptist Christian faith and practice: not only the period of Baptist origins in the seventeenth century but also the patristic period, which is formative and in some manner normative for the larger Christian tradition. Toward that end, this chapter makes the following constructive proposals for more intentional interaction with the patristic tradition in any future attempts to confess the faith of Baptist communities.

First Constructive Proposal

The first proposal addresses the implications of future Baptist confessions of faith for the ecumenical catholicity of the church. *Any new Baptist*

---

42   Smith, 'The Early English Baptists and the Church Fathers', p. 146.

confession of faith should be conceived as a Baptist exposition of the Nicaeno-Constantinopolitan Creed, sans the Filioque clause. Just as the great Baptist confessions of the seventeenth century established both the continuity of Baptist communities with the larger Christian tradition and the distinctiveness of Baptist faith and practice within this larger tradition, so a contemporary Baptist confession must express what Baptists share with other Christians as well as what makes Baptists unique. The faith of the Nicaeno-Constantinopolitan Creed is professed by Roman Catholicism, Eastern Orthodoxy, and many Protestant denominations. It has also functioned as the foundational text for the Faith and Order discussions in the World Council of Churches. Embracing the Nicaeno-Constantinopolitan Creed as the framework for a new Baptist confession would demonstrate Baptist continuity with historic Christianity and as well as Baptist solidarity with contemporary non-Baptist Christianity.[43] Expositions of the statements of the Creed would serve both to emphasize the doctrines that Baptists share in common with all other orthodox Christians and to express the distinctively Baptist position on some doctrines. With regard to the latter purpose served by a Baptist exposition of the Creed, for example, an explanation of what a Baptist means when she professes to believe in 'one holy, catholic, and apostolic church' would serve as the starting point for a summary of Baptist ecclesiological distinctives, but in as catholic a sense as the realities of the Baptist tradition will admit.[44] Omission of the *Filioque* clause in such a document would be both ecumenically necessary and, as Jürgen Moltmann has argued, theologically beneficial.[45]

In addition to establishing continuity with the larger Christian tradition and distinctiveness within it, the confessional pattern proposed here would help guard against the temptation towards doctrinal minimalism that would surely be encountered in any attempt to craft a new confession of faith by moderate Baptists in the United States who were disenfranchised in the

---

43   M.E. Boring, *Disciples and the Bible*, pp. 429-30, has expressed a similar hope for a recovery of the use of ancient ecumenical creeds by Disciples of Christ churches as a means of strengthening their connections with the universal church.

44   An example of the kind of endeavor envisioned here, though from an ecumenical rather than specific denominational perspective, is provided by the World Council of Churches, *Confessing the One Faith: An Ecumenical Explication of the Apostolic Faith as it is Confessed in the Nicene-Constantinopolitan Creed (381)*, Faith and Order Paper No. 153 (Geneva: WCC Publications, 1991).

45   Moltmann, *The Trinity and the Kingdom*, pp. 178-90. For one Baptist theologian's perspective on the implications of the Protestant positions on the theological propriety of the *Filioque* taken by Moltmann on the one hand and Karl Barth on the other, see W. McWilliams, 'Why All the Fuss about *Filioque*? Karl Barth and Jürgen Moltmann on the Procession of the Spirit', *PRSt* 22.2 (Summer, 1995), pp. 167-81.

recent denominational controversy in the Southern Baptist Convention. Yet at the same time, the Nicaeno-Constantinopolitan Creed is potentially more inclusive of diverse theological positions than most more-detailed Baptist confessions have been. The Nicaeno-Constantinopolitan Creed addresses neither the nature of biblical inspiration nor the gender of clergy (to name examples of matters of faith and practice bitterly contested among some Baptists in the United States), nor does this creed require that one follow its example in the use of gendered God-language (to name an example of a divisive issue among mainline Protestants in general in the United States).[46] A confession of this pattern might also prove to be of particular value for Baptist dialogue with representatives of Eastern Orthodoxy, who have not always been convinced that their Baptist neighbors in Eastern Europe represent the faith confessed in the Creed.

Second Constructive Proposal

A second proposal responds to the common modern Baptist assumption that Baptists are 'non-credal', an assumption that would undoubtedly prevent many Baptists from seriously considering the possibility of basing a future Baptist confession of faith on the Nicaeno-Constantinopolitan Creed or engaging in other forms of intentional retrieval of the patristic tradition by Baptist communities in the confessing of their faith. *Such intentional appropriation of the patristic tradition will require a Baptist re-envisioning of the nature and function of creeds.* If many Baptists rightly reject a credalism in which creeds or confessions of faith are imposed as

---

46   On the issues raised by the presence of masculine language for God in the Nicaeno-Constantinopolitan Creed from the perspective of this contemporary discussion, see E.R. Geitz, *Gender and the Nicene Creed* (Harrisburg, Pa.: Morehouse Publishing, 1995). That some of those who contributed to the crafting of the patristic creeds were not insensitive to the theological concerns noted by feminist theologians is evident in Gregory of Nyssa's insistence that since God transcends the human categories of gender, 'Father' and 'Mother' are interchangeable with reference to God (Gregory of Nyssa *hom. in Cant.* 7, in *Gregorii Nysseni: In Canticum Canticorum*, ed. H. Langerbeck [Leiden: E.J. Brill, 1960], GNO 6:212.14-213.2). Gregory did not apply this conclusion about the import of gendered God-language through any alteration of the language of the liturgy, however, and it may be that contemporary efforts to make the language of worship more gender-inclusive will avoid certain theological and practical difficulties if they follow Gregory's example of explanation and supplementation rather than the replacement of the language of the Lord's Prayer, the Creed, the baptismal formula, and other traditional liturgical texts with gender-neutral or feminine language.

'instruments of doctrinal accountability',[47] how may they nevertheless arrive at a healthy respect for the creeds of the ancient church as the heritage of Baptists along with all other Christians? Glenn Hinson has proposed that Baptists may be helped toward an appreciation of the tradition represented by the Nicaeno-Constantinopolitan Creed through an understanding of the ancient creeds as concise expressions of the covenant commitment made in baptism, learned in catechesis, and recalled in liturgy.[48] I wish to supplement this helpful proposal by suggesting that Baptists might also conceive of the creeds as concise narrative rehearsals of salvation-history.[49] In an earlier generation British novelist Dorothy L. Sayers, whose non-fiction theological writings are beginning to be appreciated by American evangelicals,[50] similarly advocated a fresh hearing of Christian doctrine as story and creeds as summaries of the plot of that story.

> The Christian faith is the most exciting drama that ever staggered the imagination of man—and the dogma *is* the drama. That drama is summarized quite clearly in the creeds of the Church, and if we think it dull it is because we either have never really read those amazing documents, or have recited them so often and so mechanically as to have lost all sense of their meaning....So that is the outline of the official story—the tale of the time when God was the under-dog and got beaten, when He submitted to conditions He has laid down and became a man like the men He had made, and the men He had made broke Him and killed Him. This is the dogma we find so dull—this terrifying drama of which God is the victim and hero. If this is dull, then what, in Heaven's name, is worthy to be called exciting?[51]

This is not a novel understanding of the nature and function of the ancient creeds, for they were already understood as summaries of the story and teachings of the Bible during the period of their origin, as evidenced by the following quotation from Cyril of Jerusalem (d. 387):

---

47   The phrase is from the preface to the 2000 revision of the *Baptist Faith and Message*, where it is employed with reference to the interpretation of the function of Baptist confessions of faith by the framers of the 2000 revision.

48   Hinson, 'The Nicene Creed Viewed from the Standpoint of the Evangelization of the Roman Empire', pp. 117-28.

49   This suggestion reflects the influence of the 'narrative theology' movement, especially the aspects of the thought of George Lindbeck explored in the previous chapter of this book.

50   See L.K. Simmons, *Creed without Chaos: Exploring Theology in the Writings of Dorothy L. Sayers* (Grand Rapids, Mich.: Baker Academic, 2005).

51   D.L. Sayers, 'The Greatest Drama Ever Staged Is the Official Creed of Christendom', ch. in *Creed or Chaos?* (New York: Harcourt, Brace and Co., 1949), pp. 3-5.

> For not according to [human] pleasure have the articles of faith been composed, but the most important points collected from the Scriptures make up one complete teaching of the faith. And just as the mustard seed in a small grain contains in embryo many future branches, so also the creed embraces in a few words all the religious knowledge in both the Old and the New Testament.[52]

Disciples of Christ historian and patristics specialist Paul Blowers has highlighted the pervasively narrative shape of patristic theology in general and in particular the narrative function of the *regula fidei* at the core of patristic theology.[53] Baptists, whose worship and witness from their beginnings has emphasized the telling of the Gospel story in proclamation and personal testimony, can appreciate this function of the ancient creeds.

A Baptist confession conceived as an exposition of the Creed would flesh out the plot of this narrative summary with a Baptist spin on the story. One point at which Baptists might wish to flesh out the plot is the second article of the Creed. As Glen Stassen pointed out during his Presidential Address at the 2000 Annual Meeting of the National Association of Baptist Professors of Religion, there are serious Christological lacunae in the Creed's exclusive focus on birth, death, and resurrection as the soteriologically significant events in the life of Christ.[54] Those who place a high premium on personal commitment to Jesus as Lord may be inclined to identify other dimensions of the life of Christ that ought to be confessed in the covenant commitment expressed in the Creed, as did John Smyth in his *Confession*.

Recognition of the predominately biblical sources of the language of the creeds would also help Baptists receive them as summaries of the biblical story. Although the use of biblical language is sometimes identified as a characteristic of confessions that distinguishes them from creeds,[55] those

---

52   Cyril of Jerusalem *Catecheses* 5.12 (*The Works of Saint Cyril of Jerusalem*, trans. L.P. McCauley and A.A. Stephenson [FC, 61; Washington, D.C.: The Catholic University of America Press, 1969], vol. 1, p. 146).

53   Blowers, 'The *Regula Fidei* and the Narrative Character of Early Christian Faith', pp. 199-228.

54   G.H. Stassen, 'Baptist Identity for a New Millennium' (unpublished presidential address, National Association of Baptist Professors of Religion annual meeting, Nashville, Tennessee, November 18, 2000). This deficiency was also noted by Dietrich Bonhoeffer, who in a draft of a catechesis prepared as a theological student at the University of Berlin expressed his belief that 'the Apostle's Creed lacked enough references to Jesus' life on earth' (E. Bethge, *Dietrich Bonhoeffer: A Biography*, rev. edn., trans. E. Mosbacher [Minneapolis: Fortress Press, 2000], p. 89 [quoted material is Bethge's summary]).

55   E.g., J.B. Pool, '"Sacred Mandates of Conscience": A Criteriology of Credalism for Theological Method Among Baptists', *PRSt* 23.4 (Winter, 1996), p. 368.

who crafted the creeds were very reluctant to employ non-biblical language. When they did so, as in the Nicene use of *homoousios*, it was only in an effort to clarify the meaning of the biblical text. Baptist confessions actually have employed a much higher percentage of non-biblical language than did the ancient creeds.

Third Constructive Proposal

The third proposal is a focused expression of one of the primary concerns of this book as a whole. *Such intentional appropriation of the patristic tradition will also require a re-envisioning of the place of tradition in Baptist theology.* Baptists have traditionally claimed only the Bible as their authority for faith and practice, yet their acceptance of this Bible as authoritative also involves the acceptance of the post-biblical tradition that fixed the canon of Scripture. As the Baptist confessions of faith examined in this chapter demonstrate, early Baptists also accepted the authority of doctrines that are not necessarily self-evident in Scripture but were the outcome of centuries-long processes of doctrinal development during the patristic period. Honest reflection on the disparity between the Baptist profession of a pure *Sola Scriptura* hermeneutic and the reality of Baptist hermeneutical practice, in which matters of faith and practice are adjudicated on the basis of a reading of the Scriptures within the matrix of a consideration of other sources of religious authority (i.e., a *Suprema Scriptura* hermeneutic), is the point of departure for the necessary re-envisioning of the relationship of tradition to Scripture and other sources of authority in the Baptist vision.[56]

Baptists have expressed continuity with the patristic tradition in many of their historic confessions of faith. Baptist vitality in a postmodern age may well depend on the willingness of Baptists to recover this continuity in the present and future confessing of their faith. The next chapter of this book turns to the doctrine of the Trinity as an important doctrinal focus for a recovery of catholicity in Baptist theology, highlighting the essentially

---

56   Non-sequential readers of the chapters of this book will find an attempt at this sort of re-envisioning of the place of tradition in Baptist theological method in ch. 3, 'The Authority of the Community (of All the Saints): Towards a Postmodern Baptist Hermeneutic of Tradition'.

biblical and narrative core features of the development of patristic Trinitarian theology as means of helping Bible-believing and Gospel story-telling Baptists to appreciate the centrality of this doctrine for their worship, work, and witness.

CHAPTER 5

From Triadic Narrative to Narrating the Triune God: Towards a Baptist Appreciation of Trinitarian Catholicity

'The only option for Christian theology...is to be trinitarian.' *Catherine Mowry Lacugna*[1]

'[M]ost Baptists are Unitarians that simply have not yet gotten around to denying the Trinity.' *Curtis W. Freeman*[2]

Postliberal narrative theology rightly insists that story rather than doctrinal proposition is the primary language of Christian theology. This conception of the nature of doctrine, however, could suggest that early Christian doctrinal development was a movement away from an original narrative faith that was progressively supplanted by a system of doctrinal propositions as Christian thought accommodated itself to Hellenistic philosophy during the patristic period. The development of Trinitarian theology might seem to substantiate such a perspective, for the early church's narration of the saving acts of the God of Abraham, Isaac, and Jacob which the church had experienced in the risen Christ and the outpoured and indwelling Spirit was increasingly qualified in the fourth century and beyond by formulas defining the proper understandings of essence, person, and relation in the Trinity—a movement from the triadic narration of the economy of the saving acts of God to propositional speculation about the immanent Trinity. A more carefully nuanced account of the development of patristic Trinitarian theology, however, would need to recognize the continued priority of narrative in the liturgy and catechesis of the church during and after the period of the hammering out of the church's doctrine of the Trinity. Properly understood, propositions such as 'one substance, three persons' or 'co-eternal, co-equal, consubstantial'

---

1   LaCugna, *God for Us*, p. 3.
2   C.W. Freeman, 'God in Three Persons: Baptist Unitarianism and the Trinity', *PRSt* 33.3 (Fall, 2006; forthcoming).

functioned as condensed narratives, stories-in-a-nutshell intended to summarize and clarify rather than replace the story handed over to catechumens and rehearsed in worship. Patristic Trinitarian development was thus not as much a movement from a triadic narrative to a propositional explanation of the Trinity as it was a development from the rehearsal of a triadic narrative to the narration of a mature theological characterization of the Triune God that was not yet disconnected from the economy of salvation.

Given the rather checkered history of the doctrine of the Trinity in Baptist faith and practice, it is especially important for Baptists to take notice of this pattern in the post-biblical development of the doctrine. As Curtis Freeman has observed, the biblicism of Baptists has sometimes joined forces with rationalism to make modern Baptists deeply suspicious of doctrines that seem to them to have received their formulation from a later ecclesiastical hierarchy rather than from the Bible itself.[3] Samuel Mansell, an anti-Trinitarian British Baptist pastor of the late eighteenth century cited by Freeman, exemplified an extreme form of this tendency in his rejoinder to a Trinitarian opponent: 'your method is to call all who differ from you, graceless, empty fools; and men fallen into damnable errors—and declare all damned who live and die rejecting your Popish tenet of Three Co-Equal Gods in one Godhead—though you have not one line of truth in all the Bible, as your authority so saying'.[4] Many contemporary Baptists likewise may be inclined to look with suspicion on the mature patristic doctrine of the Trinity as a 'Popish tenet', unless they can appreciate its inseparable connections to the Bible itself and its narration of the economy of salvation. A story recounted by Fisher Humphreys (Beeson Divinity School, Samford University, Birmingham, Alabama, USA) provides evidence of this inclination among more recent Baptists in the United States.

> Many years ago when I was lecturing on the doctrine of the Trinity in one of my classes at New Orleans Baptist Theological Seminary, a student told the class about an experience he had while serving as pastor of one of the small Baptist churches in south Louisiana. One Sunday he preached a sermon about the Trinity. Afterwards one of his deacons asked him privately and with great sincerity, 'Preacher, why are you talking to us about that Roman Catholic stuff?'[5]

---

3   See Freeman, 'God in Three Persons'.

4   S. Mansell, *A Second Address to Mr. Huntington* (London: J. Parsons, 1797), pp. v-vi, cited by Freeman, 'God in Three Persons'.

5   F. Humphreys, review of C.E. Braaten and R.W. Jenson, eds., *The Catholicity of the Reformation*, A. Dulles, *The Catholicity of the Church*, and G. Weigel, *Soul of the World: Notes on the Future of Public Catholicism*, in *PRSt* 26.1 (Spring, 1999), p. 95.

The early Christian movement from triadic narrative to narrating the Triune God may best be appreciated by beginning neither with the fourth-century conciliar debates nor with the third-century controversies over monarchianism but rather by starting in an unlikely place: the seven letters written by Ignatius of Antioch en route to his martyrdom early in the second century and only a very few years beyond the close of the period of Christian history to which most Baptists have looked as the normative expression of Christian faith and practice, the first-century New Testament era. The first major portion of this chapter will explore Ignatius' reception of antecedent triadic traditions in order to supply the context for the remainder of the chapter, a survey of the major episodes in the early church's ongoing efforts to address the tensions and difficulties already inherent in the triadic narration of the economy of salvation by the Ignatian correspondence and the New Testament traditions echoed in these letters.

The Economic Legacy of the Triadic Narrative: Ignatius of Antioch

The seven authentic letters of Ignatius of Antioch[6] are scarcely considered classic Trinitarian texts. The triadic formula appears only in *Magn.* 13.1-2, and only two other passages link all three divine persons together in the same context (*Eph.* 9.1, 18.2). Yet these and other Ignatian texts that relate the Son to the Father and the Spirit to the Son do suggest an incipient Trinitarianism that manifests a broad continuity with the New Testament and an essential compatibility with the fully developed Trinitarian theology of the late patristic period. The place of this incipient Trinitarianism in the development of patristic Trinitarian theology is best appreciated against the backdrop of antecedent written, oral, and/or liturgical traditions with which Ignatius may have had contact. These traditions, reflected in the documents

---

6   Letters attributed to Ignatius of Antioch have circulated in three recensions: a short recension, preserved only in Syriac, containing abridged versions of the letters to the Ephesians, the Romans, and Polycarp along with a paragraph from the letter to the Trallians; a middle recension consisting of the seven letters to the Ephesians, Magnesians, Trallians, Romans, Philadelphians, Smyrnaeans, and Polycarp attested by Eusebius of Caesarea *Hist. eccl.* 3.36.5-11; and a long recension containing expanded versions of the seven letters of the middle recension as well as six additional letters—one to Ignatius from a Mary of Cassobola, and others from Ignatius to Mary of Cassobola, the Tarsians, the Antiochenes, Hero, and the Philippians. The modern consensus on the genuineness of the seven letters of the middle recension was established in the late nineteenth century through the investigations of T. Zahn and J.B. Lightfoot and has been maintained by the majority of more recent Ignatian scholars (W.R. Schoedel, *Ignatius of Antioch: A Commentary on the Letters of Ignatius of Antioch* [Hermeneia; Philadelphia: Fortress Press, 1985], pp. 3-7).

that came to comprise the New Testament, mediated to Ignatius a triadic economic narrative that was itself already incipiently Trinitarian.

The Trinity in the New Testament Traditions

Studies of Ignatius' relationship to the New Testament documents have identified three trajectories of early Christian tradition with which Ignatius had probable contact: (1) the Pauline tradition represented chiefly by 1 Corinthians; (2) the Antiochene tradition represented by the 'M'-material in Matthew—the portions of Matthew that belong to neither the double (=Q) nor triple (=Markan) synoptic traditions; and (3) the Johannine tradition mediated to Ignatius via a common theological milieu rather than a written gospel.[7] These points of contact do not coincide directly with the explicitly

---

7   Committee of the Oxford Society of Historical Theology, *The New Testament in the Apostolic Fathers* (Oxford: Clarendon Press, 1905), pp. 67, 69, 71-72, 79, 83; W.J. Burghardt, 'Did Saint Ignatius of Antioch Know the Fourth Gospel?' *TS* 1 (1940), pp. 7-15; C. Maurer, *Ignatius von Antiochien und das Johannesevangelium* (ATANT, 18; Zürich: Zwingli-Verlag, 1949), pp. 25-43 and 92-93; É. Massaux, *Influence de l'Évangile de saint Matthieu sur la littérature chrétienne avant saint Irénée* (Leuven: University Press, 1950); ET, *The Influence of the Gospel of Saint Matthew on Christian Literature before Saint Irenaeus*, vol. 1, *The First Ecclesiastical Writers*, trans. N.J. Belval and S. Hecht, ed. A.J. Bellinzoni (NGS, 5; Macon, Ga.: Mercer University Press, 1990), pp. 86-96; H. Köster, *Synoptische Überlieferung bei den apostolischen Vätern* (TU, 17; Berlin: Akademie-Verlag, 1957), pp. 24-61; H. Rathke, *Ignatius von Antiochien und die Paulusbriefe* (TU, 99; Berlin: Akademie-Verlag, 1967), pp. 39, 41-47, 64-66, 98-99; J.S. Sibinga, 'Ignatius and Matthew', *NovT* 8 (1966), pp. 263-83; R. Bauckham, 'The Study of Gospel Traditions Outside the Canonical Gospels: Problems and Prospects', in *Gospel Perspectives*, vol. 5., *The Jesus Tradition Outside the Gospels*, ed. D. Wenham (Sheffield: JSOT Press, 1984), p. 398. These investigations of the connections between Ignatius and New Testament traditions suggest the following conclusions. First, the circumstances of Ignatius' journey toward martyrdom were probably such that he had no written New Testament documents before him in the process of writing his letters. This would account for the almost complete lack of direct quotations combined with the large number of literary parallels (cf. L.E. Wright, *Alterations of the Words of Jesus As Quoted in the Literature of the Second Century* [HHM, 25; Cambridge: Harvard University Press, 1952], pp. 41-42). Second, Ignatius was intimately acquainted with 1 Corinthians. While Ignatius also probably knew Ephesians and possibly 1 and 2 Timothy, the frequency of the echoes of 1 Corinthians suggests that this epistle was an especially formative traditional source for Ignatius' thought. Third, Ignatius was particularly influenced by the M-tradition, likely in the form of the continuing oral tradition of the church of Antioch a few decades after the writing of Matthew (so Sibinga and Bauckham). This would account for the differences in wording between Ignatius and the Matthean parallels. If Antioch may be identified as the provenance of Matthew's gospel, in particular of the M-source, then it is probable

triadic passages in Ignatius, but the broadly Trinitarian narration of salvation history by Ignatius was nonetheless influenced by the manner in which these three streams of tradition construed the relationships between Father, Son, and Spirit in that narrative. Although there is not a full-fledged doctrine of the Trinity in the New Testament, Arthur Wainwright rightly observed that 'the problem of the Trinity was being raised and answered in New Testament times, and had its roots in the worship, experience, and thought of first-century Christianity.'[8] The raising and answering of this problem in 1 Corinthians, the M-material of Matthew, and John is the specific background for Ignatius' echoes of the triadic narrative.

For Paul in 1 Corinthians, the Trinitarian problem was primarily Christological. Some passages implicitly identify Christ with God the Father. In 1 Cor. 1.8, the Old Testament 'Day of the Lord' (*yôm YHWH*) becomes 'the day of the Lord Jesus Christ'.[9] The prayer *marana tha* ('Our Lord, come!') addressed to Christ in 1 Cor. 16.22 had been addressed to Yahweh in the Qumran literature.[10] On the other hand, this identification of the Son with the Father also suggests an element of distinction between the two. Christ is 'the power of God and the wisdom of God' in 1 Cor. 1.24. Distinction is also present in the dyadic confession in 1 Cor. 8.6, in which the Father is the source and the Son is the intermediate agent of creation. An eschatological subjection of the Son to the Father is suggested by 1 Cor. 15.24-28, where the Son 'hands over the kingdom to God the Father' (v. 24), and 'will also be subjected to the one who put all things in subjection

---

that the Matthean traditions directly influenced Ignatius. Fourth, it is less likely that Ignatius was influenced directly by a written Gospel of John, but in light of the conceptual parallels between Ignatius and John it is probable that they shared a common theological milieu (see J.H. Charlesworth and R.A. Culpepper, 'The Odes of Solomon and the Gospel of John', *CBQ* 35 [1973], pp. 298-322, esp. 314-15, where the authors point to conceptual parallels between the letters of Ignatius, the Qumran scrolls, the *Odes of Solomon*, and the Johannine literature; cf. C. Trevett, *A Study of Ignatius of Antioch in Syria and Asia* [Lewiston, N.Y.: Edwin Mellen, 1992], p. 24). H.J. Bardsley, 'The Testimony of Ignatius and Polycarp to the Writings of St. John', *JTS* 14 (1913), pp. 207-220, provides a concise comparison of the theologies of Ignatius and the Johannine writings.

8   Wainwright, *The Trinity in the New Testament*, p. vii.

9   D.B. Capes, *Old Testament Yahweh Texts in Paul's Christology* (WUNT^2, 47; Tübingen: J.C.B. Mohr [Paul Siebeck], 1992), pp. 83-84. The same phenomenon also occurs in 2 Cor. 1.14; 1 Thess. 5.2; 2 Thess. 2.2; Phil. 1.6; 1.10; 2.16 (p. 86, n. 190).

10   Capes, *Old Testament Yahweh Texts*, pp. 43-47; J.A. Fitzmeyer, 'The Semitic Background of the New Testament *Kyrios*-Title', ch. in *A Wandering Aramean: Collected Aramaic Essays* (SBLMS, 25; Missoula, Mont.: Scholars Press, 1979), pp. 124-25; M. Black, 'The Christological Use of the Old Testament in the New Testament', *NTS* 18 (1971), p. 11.

under him, so that God may be all in all' (v. 28). The relationship of the
Spirit to the other two persons is not as developed as that of the Son to the
Father. There are frequent references to the Spirit as 'the Spirit of God' (1
Cor. 2.11; 2.14; 3.16; 6.11; 7.40; 12.3). The Spirit is also 'from God' (*ek
tou theou*, 1 Cor. 2.12; *apo theou*, 1 Cor. 6.19), the agent of God's
revelation (1 Cor. 2.10), and the distributor of divine gifts (1 Cor. 12.4-11).
Nowhere in 1 Corinthians or elsewhere does Paul identify the Spirit as God
or direct worship to the Spirit.[11] However, the Spirit is clearly linked with
the Father and the Son in the divine economy in 1 Cor. 12.4-6: 'Now there
are varieties of gifts, but the same Spirit; and there are varieties of services,
but the same Lord; and there are varieties of activities, but it is the same
God who activates all of them in everyone.'

The only triadic passage in the M-material is the tripartite baptismal
formula of Matt. 28.19 which, according to Wainwright, 'more than any
other saying of the New Testament...suggests the growth of a Trinitarian
doctrine.'[12] It is highly unlikely that this saying is an *ipsissimum verbum* of
Jesus. As an M-saying, it is part of the latest redactional stage of Matthew.
In addition, in the Acts of the Apostles baptism is consistently in the name
of Jesus, rather than a bipartite or tripartite formula, and Paul refers to
baptism into Christ or Christ Jesus.[13] If the Matthean evangelist has shaped
this saying and if Antioch was Matthew's geographical provenance, then
Matt. 28.19 probably reflects the development of the liturgical tradition of
the church of Antioch only a few decades before Ignatius was bishop
there.[14]

While no triadic formulae proper occur in the Gospel of John,
Wainwright notes that 'the threefold pattern is more prominent there than in
any other part of the New Testament'.[15] Again, most of the relevant
material is Christological. At the outset of the Gospel, John makes a clear

---

11   A possible exception is 2 Cor. 3.17: 'Now the Lord is the Spirit'. However,
Wainwright, *Trinity in the New Testament*, pp. 226-27, who is not averse to the
possibility of an ascription of divinity to the Spirit this early, nevertheless concludes that
the juxtaposition of this phrase with 'the Spirit of the Lord' in the same verse nuances
the statement by distinguishing between the Spirit and the Lord.

12   Wainwright, *Trinity in the New Testament*, p. 237.

13   Wainwright, *Trinity in the New Testament*, p. 239.

14   These historical conclusions about the shaping of this dominical saying should
not be allowed to minimize the theological authority of the canonical form of the saying
for the Trinitarian faith of the church. Even though the Trinitarian formula may have
been adapted to the baptismal practice of the church at Antioch by Matthean redaction,
the church must receive these words as the divine authorization of the Trinitarian
baptismal formula—as the patristic church did in fact receive them in privileging the
Matthean formula over the formula in Acts in its liturgies.

15   Wainwright, *Trinity in the New Testament*, p. 243.

identification of Jesus with God: Christ as the *logos* 'was God' (John 1.1). Behind the seven 'I am' sayings (John 6.35; 8.12; 10.7; 10.11; 11.25; 14.6; 15.1) may be an implicit identification of Jesus with Yahweh, the *egō eimi ho ōn* of Exod. 3.14 (LXX).[16] Jesus explicitly identifies himself with God the Father in John 10.30: 'The Father and I are one.' The exclamation of Thomas in John 20.28, 'My Lord and my God!', also identifies the Son with the Father. Again, there is also a distinction between the Father and the Son, seen especially in the frequent references to the Father-Son relationship. Jesus says that 'the Father is greater than I' (John 14.28) and that the Father has sent him (John 3.17; 6.57; 8.42; 11.42; 17.3; 17.8; 20.21). Distinction and identification are juxtaposed in John 1.1: 'the Word was with God', yet 'the Word was God'. Like Paul, John neither calls the Spirit God nor ascribes worship to the Spirit, but the Gospel does link the activity of the Spirit with the actions of both the Father and the Son. The Spirit is the gift of the Father (John 14.16-17), and the Father sends the Spirit in the name of the Son (John 16.26). The Son also is the sender of the *paraklētos* (John 16.17). There are five triadic passages in which Father, Son, and Spirit are mentioned together: the testimony of John the Baptist that the one on whom the Spirit descends is the Son of God in John 1:32-34, the references to the sending/coming of the Spirit in the farewell discourse (John 14.16-26, 15.26, and 16.13-15), and the 'Johannine Pentecost' passage in John 20.21-22. While these passages are not formulaic, they do indicate that the Johannine community regarded God the Father, Jesus, and the Holy Spirit to be linked together in the economy of God's salvific dealings with humanity.

The Trinity in the Ignatian Correspondence

As was the case in 1 Corinthians, M, and John, the overwhelming majority of the texts of Trinitarian significance in Ignatius are concerned with the relationship between the Father and the Son. These references fall into two distinct categories that reflect a Christological tension in the thought of Ignatius: those that identify Christ as God, and those that imply a distinction between the Father and the Son.

Ignatius explicitly applies the designation 'God' to Christ in a number of passages. In the inscription to *Ephesians*, the church is united and elected *en thelēmati tou patros kai Iēsou Christou, tou theou hēmōn*, 'by the will of the Father and of Jesus Christ, our God'.[17] Here the bracket force of the

16   So, *inter alios*, E.M. Sidebottom, *The Christ of the Fourth Gospel in the Light of First-Century Thought* (London: S.P.C.K., 1961), pp. 43-44.
17   All English translations of Ignatius, unless otherwise noted, are from B.D. Ehrman, ed. and trans., *The Apostolic Fathers* (LCL, 24; Cambridge: Harvard

first instance of the definite article *tou* implies the unity of *patros* and *Iēsou Christou*, and *tou theou hēmōn* stands in apposition with *Iēsou Christou*. Ignatius repeats this designation of Christ as 'our God' in *Eph.* 15.3, where he is 'our God in us'. The title 'our God Jesus Christ' appears four times (*Eph.* 18.2, *Rom.* inscr., *Rom.* 3.3, *Pol.* 8.3), and in two other passages 'God' is in apposition to 'Jesus Christ' (*Trall.* 7.1, *Smyrn.* 1.1).

The most striking texts identifying Christ with God occur in connection with references to the sufferings of Christ. Ignatius' Ephesian recipients have rekindled the work they share with him 'by the blood of God' according to *Eph.* 1.1, and in *Rom.* 6.3 Ignatius begs to be allowed to be 'an imitator of the suffering of my God'. In both of these passages, the latter of which is crucial for Ignatius' theology of martyrdom, 'God' is clearly intended to refer to Christ. If read through the lenses of subsequent Christological developments, this language would be deemed dangerously inadequate. Such a radical identification of Christ with God could be seen as compatible with modalistic monarchianism, and the implicit attribution of the sufferings of the cross to God would have incurred the opposition of the later opponents of theopassianism. There is nothing inherently heterodox about these expressions, however, when they are read in the context of the comparatively undeveloped theology of the early second century. Similar terminology appears in Clement of Rome,[18] and two and one-half centuries later no less an orthodox figure than Gregory of Nazianzus also used comparable language.[19] In light of the probable connections with the Johannine theological milieu, these statements could be seen as a radicalization of the clear identification of Jesus with the Father in the Gospel of John. The point of this intensification of the Christology of the late first century is that no one less than God is the source of the salvation present in the crucified Christ.[20]

Other passages maintain a distinction between God the Father and Christ the Son. This is implicit in the stereotypical dyadic formulae that occur in the inscriptions and farewell greetings of the letters,[21] possibly in imitation

---

University Press, 2003), vol. 1, pp. 218-321. This is also the edition followed here for the Greek text.

18   J.B. Lightfoot (*The Apostolic Fathers: Clement, Ignatius, and Polycarp*, 2nd edn., pt. 2, *Ignatius and Polycarp* [London: Macmillan, 1889, 1890; reprint, Peabody, Mass.: Hendrickson, 1989], vol. 2, p. 30, citing *1 Clem.* 2.1 in Codex Alexandrinus, where the antecedent of *ta pathēmata autou* is *theou* (the other extant Greek MS, Codex Constantinopolitanus, reads *Christou*).

19   D.F. Winslow, 'The Idea of Redemption in the Epistles of St. Ignatius of Antioch', *GOTR* 11 (1965), pp. 120-21, citing Greg. Naz. *Oration* 45.19, 22, 28-29.

20   Winslow, 'Idea of Redemption', p. 121.

21   So J.N.D. Kelly, *Early Christian Doctrines*, rev. edn. (San Francisco: Harper & Row, 1978), p. 93.

of similar Pauline formulae.[22] Ignatius greets the Magnesian believers 'in God the Father and in Jesus Christ' (*Magn.* inscr.). The same formula also occurs in the farewell of *Eph.* 21.2. The letter to the Philadelphians is addressed to 'the church of God the Father and of the Lord Jesus Christ that is in Philadelphia of Asia' (*Phild.* inscr.). Polycarp 'has God the Father and the Lord Jesus Christ as his bishop' (*Pol.* inscr.; more literally, 'is being bishoped by...' [*episkopēmenō hypo*]). Similar dyadic formulae are found also in *Trall.* 1.1, *Rom.* inscr., *Phild.* 1.1, 3.2, and *Smyrn.* inscr.

Passages indentifying Jesus Christ as the Son of the Father also suggest that Ignatius clearly distinguished between the Father and the Son. Such texts include *Eph.* 2.1, *Magn.* 3.1, *Trall.* inscr., *Rom.* inscr., and *Smyrn.* 1.1. While a case could be made for dependence on similar Johannine texts, the affirmation that Jesus is the Son of the Father is so foundational for the Christology of the New Testament that it is impossible to single out John as Ignatius' influence. These passages simply echo a pervasive element of the faith of the first-century church.

Ignatius also calls attention to the subordination of the Son to the Father during the earthly ministry of Jesus. The Son's dependence on and subjection to the Father is the paradigm for the church's dependence on and subjection to its bishops and presbyters in *Magn.* 7.1, *Magn.* 13.2, and *Phild.* 7.2. Christ also plays a somewhat subordinate functional role as intermediary and instrumental agent in other aspects of Ignatius' portrayal of the divine economy. In a call to unity in *Eph.* 4.2, Ignatius exhorts his readers to sing 'in one voice through Jesus Christ to the Father' (cf. *Rom.* 2.2). The inscription of *Magnesians* is addressed to 'the one [i.e., the church] that has been blessed by the gracious gift of God the Father in Christ Jesus our Savior'. Believers bear the 'stamp (*charaktēra*) of God the Father...through Jesus Christ' (*Magn.* 5.2), are resurrected by the Father 'in Christ Jesus' (*Trall.* 9.2), and have their prayers fulfilled by the Father 'in Jesus Christ' (*Trall.* 13.3). *Phild.* 9.1 pictures Jesus, 'the high priest', as the 'door of the Father, through which Abraham and Isaac and Jacob and the prophets and the apostles and the church enter'. That Ignatius did not confuse the Son and the Father is also evident in two passages depicting Christ as the revealer of the Father, *Magn.* 8.2 and *Rom.* 8.2.

Although these passages do suggest a degree of subordination in the relationship of the Son to the Father in the thought of Ignatius, this feature of Ignatian Christology cannot be compared to later forms of heretical subordinationism that extrapolate economic subordination into the eternal, immanent Godhead. Rather, when read in light of the antecedent New Testament traditions, these passages merely continue the Johannine tendency toward economic subordination. As in the Gospel of John, texts

---

22   Cf. Rathke, *Ignatius und die Paulusbriefe*, pp. 41-47.

subordinating the Son to the Father in the economy of salvation serve to balance those passages in which Christ is radically identified with God with little or no qualification.

Ignatius relates the Spirit and the Son in only two passages. Both of these texts focus on the functional role of the Holy Spirit in the divine economy. In *Magn.* 9.2, Ignatius calls attention to the role of the Spirit in revealing the Son to the Old Testament prophets, who were Jesus' disciples 'in the Spirit'. According to the inscription to *Philadelphians*, the Holy Spirit is the agent of Jesus Christ in providing leadership for the church: bishops, presbyters, and deacons are 'appointed in accordance with the mind of Jesus Christ' and 'securely set in place by his Holy Spirit'. In both of these passages, Ignatius portrays the Spirit as subordinate to the Son. In this, however, he does not go beyond the pneumatology of the Gospel of John, in which the Spirit 'will not speak on his own' (John 16.13).

There is one instance of the triadic formula proper in Ignatius: in *Magn.* 13.1, he wishes that the Magnesian believers may prosper 'in the Son and the Father and in the Spirit'. Ignatius may be dependent on the tradition reflected in the triadic baptismal formula in Matt. 28.19, even though the ordering of persons differs. While a modified, expanded triadic formula does appear in 2 Cor. 13.14, Ignatius probably was not familiar with that epistle and his language is more similar to that of Matthew than to 2 Corinthians. Apart from Ignatius, the triadic formula occurs in the sub-apostolic literature only in *1 Clem.* 58.2 and *Did.* 7.1-2.[23] The language of the *1 Clement* text is even more dissimilar to the language of Ignatius than that of the Pauline formula, and the *Didache* passage is clearly dependent on the Matthean baptismal formula. In light of the connections with M, Ignatius as well may have been loosely dependent on the liturgical tradition of the church of Antioch, specifically its tripartite baptismal formula reflected in Matt. 28.19, for his lone triadic formula. This is certainly not to suggest that the tripartite formula was an Antiochene innovation; its use surely must have been much more widespread in light of the interdependence of multiple 'apostolic missions' in the late first century.[24] It is nevertheless interesting to note that the term *trias* was first applied to the Godhead in extant early Christian literature by Theophilus of Antioch (c. 180).[25] The tradition of the church of Antioch in the first two centuries

---

23   Noted by V. Corwin, *St. Ignatius and Christianity at Antioch* (New Haven: Yale University Press, 1960), p. 142, n. 36.

24   See Ellis, *Making of the New Testament Documents*.

25   Theophilus of Antioch *Ad Autolycum* 2.15. However, one should not ascribe to this use of *trias* a fully-formed Trinitarianism, as D.S. Wallace-Hadrill, *Christian Antioch: A Study of Early Christian Thought in the East* (Cambridge: Cambridge University Press, 1982), p. 69, observes: 'Despite his distinction of being the first

may therefore have been characterized by an emerging Trinitarian consciousness. Perhaps just as 'it was in Antioch that the disciples were first called "Christians"' (Acts 11.26), so it may also have been in Antioch that God was first called 'Trinity'.

In two other passages, Ignatius expands the triadic formula by narrating some aspect of the divine persons' participation in the economy of salvation. In *Eph.* 18.2, the Spirit is the divine agent in the conception of Jesus in accordance with the economy or dispensation of God.

The passage that most explicitly articulates the manner in which Ignatius conceived of relationships within the Godhead is *Eph.* 9.1, where Ignatius describes the Ephesian believers with a metaphor reminiscent of Paul's temple motif in the Corinthian correspondence (1 Cor. 3.16-17; 6.19; 2 Cor. 6.16): 'You are stones of the Father's temple, being prepared for the building of God the Father...carried up to the heights by the crane of Jesus Christ, which is the cross, using as a cable the Holy Spirit'. Within this metaphor, functional distinctions are made in the soteriological roles of Father, Son, and Spirit. God the Father is both the source and the goal of the new temple constructed of believers, the cross of Jesus Christ is the instrument of redemption, and the Holy Spirit makes the cross efficacious for the believer.[26] It is possible that Ignatius was conceptually dependent not only on the Pauline image of the body of Christ as the new temple but also on the functional expansion of the triadic formula in 1 Cor. 12.4-6, where as in Ignatius there is a differentiation in soteriological function between Father, Son, and Spirit, yet they share in the one work of salvation.

The first-century Pauline, Antiochene, and Johannine narrations of salvation history in incipiently Trinitarian terms therefore intersected in the account of the economy of salvation expressed in the Ignatian correspondence. The Pauline tradition as found in 1 Corinthians contributed a rich functional development of the simple triadic formula. The Antiochene tradition reflected in the M-material of Matthew provided an ongoing liturgical stimulus to Trinitarian thought in the church of Antioch through its tripartite baptismal formula. The Johannine tradition contributed to a theological context conducive to Trinitarian reflection with its more radical identification of the Son with the Father, its differentiation between the Father and the Son, and its emphasis on the participation of all three persons in the divine economy. Viewed against the backdrop of these

---

Christian writer known to use the term Trinity, it is hard to regard Theophilus as a Trinitarian at all. His God is rather a Unity with ill-defined offshoots or personified qualities.'

26   This interpretation of the role of the Spirit in the metaphor is suggested by C.C. Richardson, *The Christianity of Ignatius of Antioch* (New York: Columbia University Press, 1935), p. 46.

antecedent traditions, Ignatius' references to relationships between Father, Son, and Spirit are in continuity with the tributaries out of which they flow: both the New Testament tradition and Ignatius identify the Son and the Spirit with God the Father, distinguish these persons from one another, and narrate salvation history as a triadic story of the three persons' joint participation in the divine work of saving human beings. Ignatius' primary contribution to the development of patristic Trinitarian theology in the early second century was his much more radical identification of Christ with God, especially his identification of the sufferings of Christ as 'the sufferings of my God'. These features of Ignatius' characterization of the divine economy left un-raised and unanswered several questions that would later occasion successive episodes in the church's ongoing struggle to tell faithfully its story of the God experienced in the risen Christ and the indwelling Spirit. In what sense is Christ identified with God? What does this identification mean for the church's inheritance of a monotheistic faith in the one God of Abraham, Isaac, and Jacob? What are the implications of the subordination of the Son in the divine economy for this identification? What place does the Spirit have in this conception of one God with personal distinctions? If there are three personal distinctions, what is the nature of the respective intra-Trinitarian relationships? The patristic church hammered out the doctrine of the Trinity as we know it today in response to these questions, seeking in each episode to render a true account of the triadic narrative it had received from the apostles and their successors.

Narrating the Triune God: Ecclesial Shaping of the Story

The remainder of this chapter surveys the development of patristic Trinitarian theology from the second century through Augustine of Hippo in the West and John of Damascus in the East, but it is far from a complete overview of this development. Others have extensively and ably provided that elsewhere, and there is no need to duplicate their efforts here.[27] Instead this is a selective account of the ecclesial needs that occasioned the various stages in the development of the doctrine of the Trinity, highlighting the significance of these episodes for the church's narration of its Trinitarian

---

27   E.g., B. Studer, *Trinity and Incarnation: The Faith of the Early Church*, trans. M. Westerhoff, ed. A. Louth (Collegeville, Minn.: Liturgical Press, 1993); R.P.C. Hanson, *The Search for the Christian Doctrine of God: The Arian Controversy 318-381* (Edinburgh: T. & T. Clark, 1988); R.M. Grant, *The Early Christian Doctrine of God* (Charlottesville: University Press of Virginia, 1966); G.L. Prestige, *God in Patristic Thought* (London: S.P.C.K., 1936); and of course the relevant sections of standard introductions to early doctrinal development: e.g., Pelikan, *Christian Tradition*, vol. 1, pp. 172-225; Kelly, *Early Christian Doctrines*, pp. 83-137, 223-79.

faith and the inseparability of the doctrinal propositions that emerge from these episodes from the first-order narrative that they summarize, condense, and clarify.

Explaining the Narrative to Outsiders: The Greek Apologists

In the middle of the second century, the church increasingly encountered questions about its peculiar story of God that distinguished Christian faith from other accounts of the divine in the Mediterranean world of late antiquity. With the parting of the ways between synagogue and church now well advanced, the church continued to face Jewish charges that it had abandoned the faith of the *Shema* (Deut. 6.4-6) for polytheism. On the other hand, the Roman persecutors of the church and critics of its faith accused Christians of atheism—i.e., of disavowing the pantheon. Second-century Christian thinkers such as Aristides, Justin Martyr, Tatian, Athenagoras, and Theophilus of Antioch, collectively known as the Apologists, addressed defenses against these charges to the educated citizens and leaders of the Roman world. In these 'apologies', they explained the coherence of the Christian account of God in terms of elements of Greek philosophy that had influenced both Hellenistic Judaism and Roman Stoicism. These explanations were highly influential for later developments in the church's struggle to narrate their faith rightly, owing both to the help these explanations provided for conceiving of real personal distinctions within the one God and to the limitations of these conceptions in accounting for the unity of God and the relationship of the Spirit to the other two persons.

Justin Martyr exemplifies well this episode in Trinitarian development, as in his two *Apologies* and his *Dialogue with Trypho the Jew* he offered an account of the Christian story of God that responded extensively to both Greco-Roman and Jewish objections to this story. In response to the Jewish objections, Justin argued not only that what Christians believe about Christ was anticipated by the Hebrew Scriptures but also these writings conceive of the wisdom and word of God as being both distinct from the Father and yet of the Father's very being, just as a word that remains in the mind and the word that is spoken are distinguishable and yet are one, and just as a fire that kindles another fire is both two fires and one and the same fire.[28] To the Greco-Roman objections about atheism, Justin replied that the Christian concept of Christ as the word, the *logos* of God, was already familiar to the Stoics, whose concept of the *logos* distinguished between an 'immanent word', the *logos endiathētos*, and an 'expressed Word', the *logos prophorikos*. By identifying the incarnate Christ with the *logos*

---

28   E.g, Justin Martyr *Dialogus cum Tryphone Judaeo* 61, 128 (ET, ANF 1:227-28, 264).

prophorikos, Justin attempted to show how Christians could believe in one God yet worship the incarnate Christ—Christ could be both eternally united with God as the *logos endiathetos* and yet manifest in time and space as the *logos prophorikos*.[29] These attempts to explain the Christian story to outsiders focused on the relationship of Christ to the one God, and accordingly Justin gave little attention to the Spirit. Nevertheless, Justin testified to the ongoing importance of the triadic narrative for Christian liturgy in his descriptions of the manner in which Christians celebrate baptism and the Eucharist and offer prayer in Sunday worship: all these acts of worship invoke or are directed toward Father, Son, and Spirit.[30]

Problematic Versions of the Narrative: Monarchianism and Its Opponents

The Apologists' efforts to communicate the intelligibility of the Christian story of God were helpful for explaining how a plurality of persons was not inconsistent with monotheism and how belief in the incarnation was not incompatible with belief in a transcendent God, but their Logos Christology also left lingering concerns about the essential unity of God. Several third-century Christian thinkers thus sought to re-emphasize the "monarchy" of God—the oneness (Greek *monos*, 'sole' or 'single') of the authority and power (Greek *arche*) of the Godhead. Two different strategies for safeguarding the divine monarchy emerged during this period. 'Dynamic monarchianism', as historians of Christian thought have labeled this first approach, located the fullness of divinity only in the person of God the Father. This account of God was triadic and could appeal to the biblical economy of salvation for support, but it preserved the oneness of God by ranking the Son among the creatures of God and attributing the Son's divinity to his adoption by the Father. Paul of Samosata, bishop of Antioch until 268, exemplified this strategy.[31] Its reading of the divine economy in subordinationistic or hierarchical terms would continue to be an attractive reading of the triadic narrative in the next century, even though fourth-century Arian subordinationists would disavow adoptionism. A second strategy, 'modalistic monarchianism', was likewise an account of God that took the triadic structure of the economy of salvation seriously, but it

---

29   E.g., Justin Martyr *1 Apologia* 5, 61 (ET, ANF 1:164, 183); *2 Apologia* 10 (ET, ANF 1:191-92); *Dialogus cum Tryphone Judaeo* 62 (ET, ANF 1:228). It was Theophilus of Antioch, however, who employed this terminology most consistently and systematically (Kelly, *Early Christian Doctrines*, p. 99)

30   Justin Martyr *1 Apologia* 61, 65-67 (ET, ANF 1:183, 185-86).

31   Eusebius of Caesarea *Historia Ecclesiastica* 7.29-30 (ET, *Eusebius: The Ecclesiastical History*, trans. J.E.L. Oulton [LCL, 265; Cambridge, Mass.: Harvard University Press, 1932], vol. 2, pp. 213-27).

safeguarded the oneness of God by denying any real personal distinctions between Father, Son, and Spirit, who were regarded as three operations or modes of the one God. The Greek word for 'person', *prosōpon*, could refer either to a 'face' or 'appearance', or to a 'person' who has a face or appearance; modalists such as Noetus of Smyrna (fl. late second century) and Sabellius (fl. early third century) understood the personhood of Father, Son, and Spirit in the former sense, so that they are three different ways in which the one God is made manifest in salvation history.[32] Consequently the later Greek fathers would make other lexical choices for terminology that designated the individual personhood of Father, Son, and Spirit.

Among other anti-heretical writers of the third century, Tertullian (d. c. 225) recognized the dangers inherent in these approaches to reconciling the triadic narrative and the oneness of God. Tertullian contended that modalism in particular rendered impossible the interplay of Father, Son, and Spirit upon which the economy of salvation depends, famously arguing that Praxeas (whom many have identified with Noetus) had through his teachings 'put to flight the Paraclete, and he crucified the Father'.[33] Tertullian's efforts to do justice both to the essential oneness of God and to the threeness of God in the biblical story and the threefold rule of faith that summarized it yielded terminology that became definitive for the Latin Christian West: *trinitas* as the name for the Godhead and *tres personae, una substantia,* 'one substance, three persons', as the formula that concisely summarized this clarification of the triadic narrative.[34] It may be that Tertullian's experience with Montanism contributed to his advances beyond the second-century apologists in giving more attention to the genuine personhood of the Spirit and thus offering a more fully Trinitarian account of God.[35]

In the Greek Alexandrian tradition during the same period, Origen (d. 254) developed a Trinitarian theology that not only avoided the difficulties of both dynamic and modalistic monarchianism but also addressed some of the problematic implications of the apologists' Logos Christology. Whereas Justin and the apologists could be read as suggesting that the 'expressed Word' became that at a point in time, so that God was the solitary Father until the expression of the Word introduced a distinction of persons into the Godhead, Origen understood the expressed relationship of the Word to the

---

32 Hippolytus *Contra Haeresin Noeti* (ET, ANF 5:223-31); Hippolytus *The Refutation of All Heresies* 9.13 (ET, ANF 5:148); Epiphanius *Panarion Adversus LXXX Haereses* 57 (ET, *The Panarion of Epiphanius of Salamis*, 2 vols., trans. F. Williams [NHS, 35-36; Leiden: E.J. Brill, 1987-1994]).

33 Tertullian *Adversus Praxean* 1 (ET, ANF 3: 597-98).

34 Tertullian *Adversus Praxean* 2-3 (ET, ANF 3: 598-99).

35 So Pelikan, *Christian Tradition*, vol. 1, p. 105.

Father, the relationship of 'being begotten' in the language of the Johannine Prologue, to be an eternal relationship, without beginning: the word is eternally generated, 'eternally begotten of the Father'—Origen's posthumous contribution to the Creed of the Council of Nicaea in 325.[36] Contra modalism, Origen maintained that the Father, Son, and Spirit differed from one another in *hypostasis*, 'individual subsistence', with the three *hypostaseis* eternally constituting God's being.[37] Origen's Trinitarian account of God was both expansive enough and subtle enough in the tension it maintained between an eternal equality of Father, Son, and Spirit as the one God and a temporal subordination in their respective roles in the economy of salvation that both the subordinationists and their opponents in the next major chapter of the church's debate about the most appropriate way to tell the divine story could appeal to this or that aspect of Origen's theology as precedents for their positions. Yet the emergence of Trinitarian orthodoxy in the fourth century was indebted to Origen's advances beyond other attempts to clarify the triadic narrative in light of various challenges in the second and third centuries.

Contesting the Plot: The Arian Controversy

A local church theological conflict in Alexandria that rapidly embroiled the rest of the Greek-speaking Christian world in doctrinal controversy early in the fourth century set the stage for a crucial turning point in the church's movement from an unsophisticated triadic narrative to a more carefully qualified narration of the story of the Triune God. Around 319, an Alexandrian presbyter (parish priest) named Arius became a controversial figure as word spread about some distinctive features of his teachings about the relationship between God the Father and Christ the Son. According to Arius' opponents—whose charges seem to be substantiated by Arius' few remaining writings—Arius taught something like the following summary: only the Father exists from eternity and does not owe his origin to another; the pre-existence of the Logos means that he came into being before the creation of the world, but he was nonetheless created and therefore had a beginning, (thus the accusation that Arius taught that 'there was [a time] when the Son was not'); the divine power manifest in the incarnate Christ was not the full divine power that belongs only to the Father, but rather that of a lesser category of divinity; and the incarnate Christ was neither fully

---

36   Origen *De Principiis* 1.2.4 (ET, *Origen: On First Principles*, trans. G.W. Butterworth [Gloucester, Mass.: Peter Smith, 1973], pp. 17-18).
37   Origen *Commentarii in Iohannem* 2.10.75 (ET, *Origen: Commentary on the Gospel According to John, Books 1-10*, trans. R.E. Heine [FC, 80; Washington, D.C.: The Catholic University of America Press, 1989], p. 114).

human nor fully divine, but partially both.[38] For these points, but especially for the non-eternality of the Logos and the essential subordination of the Logos to God the Father, Arius and his sympathizers could appeal to a literal interpretation of passages of Scripture referring to the begetting of the Son or his subordination to the will of the Father and a selective appropriation of Origen that jettisoned the doctrine of the eternal generation of the Son but magnified the aspects of Origen's thought that took seriously the Son's subordination in the economy of salvation.

A series of ecclesiastical responses to Arius began with his bishop, Alexander of Alexandria (d. 328), who likewise could claim Origen as a theological precedent. With Origen, Alexander insisted that the Johannine reference to the 'begetting' of the Son must be understood in terms of eternal generation, and thus not literally as a birth that happened at a point in time. Alexander agreed with Arius that only the Father is unoriginate, but disputed Arius' temporal understanding of the origin of the Son, as it is impossible for God to be without the Logos of God.[39] Alexander reluctantly convened a regional synod that examined and exiled Arius in 321, but that hardly halted what was by then a church-wide controversy. To make a long, complex, and intriguing story sufficiently short for the present purposes, a flurry of correspondence and the convening of additional regional synods eventuated in the call of Constantine for the first ecumenical council at Nicaea in 325, which anathematized Arius and his teachings and upheld the position of Alexander on the eternal generation of the Son and the doctrine elaborated by his then-deacon Athanasius (d. 373) of the *homoousios*, the consubstantiality of the Father and the Son, which implied also their co-eternality and co-equality. Although the debate at Nicaea has been caricatured as a moment when the fate of Christendom hung on a conflict over an iota-subscript (*homoousios* vs. *homoiousios*, 'similar substance'), this was no quibbling over mere words. At stake was the integrity of the very plot of the Christian story: it is either a story of a God who does not personally save but delegates the work of salvation to that which is less than the fullness of God, or it is a story of a God who is fully present in the saving work of the incarnate Son and the indwelling Spirit. Rowan Williams has insisted that the patristic church's decision for the latter way of narrating salvation history was salutary for the church in ways that the former version of the story's plot could never have been, for 'only Nicaea

---

38   English translations of letters by Arius addressed to Eusebius of Nicomedia and Alexander of Alexandria appear in W.G. Rusch, trans. and ed., *The Trinitarian Controversy* (SEChrTh; Philadelphia: Fortress Press, 1980), pp. 29-32.

39   Alexander of Alexandria *Letter to Alexander of Thessalonica* 15-23 (ET, Rusch, *Trinitarian Controversy*, pp. 35-37).

can actually do justice to...the self-sacrificing vulnerability of God'.[40] Nicaea did not immediately put an end to Arian tendencies, and understandings of the triadic narrative in terms of an essentially subordinated Godhead persisted into the late fourth century, resulting in the next major episode in the church's shaping of the story of the Triune God.[41]

Refining Liturgical Narration: The Pneumatomachian Controversy

While the first stage of the Arian controversy had focused on the relationship of the Son to the divinity of the Father, resulting in a detailed second article of the creed adopted at Nicaea with a third article that simply stated 'We believe in the Holy Spirit', a second stage of the controversy in the late fourth century concerned the place of the Holy Spirit in the Godhead and specifically the propriety of making the Spirit an object of the worship already directed toward the Father and the Son in the church's liturgy. By the fourth century the standard form of the triadic doxology was 'Glory to the Father, through the Son, in the Holy Spirit', a doxology rooted in the economy of salvation.[42] In the wake of the Council of Nicaea, however, many local liturgies began to guard against Arianism by emphasizing the equality of the three persons with the doxological form 'Glory to the Father and to the Son and to the Holy Spirit', with the implication that the three are equal in divinity, since only God may be worshipped.[43] Sometime in the early 370s Basil of Caesarea (d. 379) adopted for similar polemical reasons the doxology 'Glory to the Father,

---

40   R. Williams, *Arius: Heresy and Tradition*, rev. edn. (Grand Rapids, Mich.: William B. Eerdmans, 2002), p. 22. Although Williams believes the Nicene Fathers would themselves have rejected the notion of 'the self-sacrificing vulnerability of God' outright, Gavrilyuk in *Suffering of the Impassible God* compellingly contends that an opposition of patristic impassibility and modern affirmations of the suffering of God is a false dichotomy: unqualified expressions of both positions are problematic, and more carefully qualified expressions of both positions seek a positive relation of God to human suffering that offers not only encouragement to sufferers of God's solidarity with them but also a paradigm for divinely empowered triumph over suffering and the passions by those who belong to Christ.

41   Nicene orthodoxy was recognized as such even more gradually in the West: see D.H. Williams, *Ambrose of Milan and the End of the Nicene-Arian Conflicts* (OECS; New York: Oxford University Press, 1995).

42   Basil of Caesarea *De Spiritu Sancto* 58 (ET, *St. Basil the Great: On the Holy Spirit*, trans. D. Anderson [Crestwood, N.Y.: St. Vladimir's Seminary Press, 1980], p. 90).

43   J.A. Jungmann, *The Place of Christ in Liturgical Prayer*, 2nd rev. edn. (Staten Island, N.Y.: Alba House, 1965), pp. 175-90.

with (*meta*) the Son, together with (*syn*) the Holy Spirit',[44] drawing the ire of the neo-Arian Pneumatomachians, 'Spirit-fighters', who opposed any ascription of full divinity to the Holy Spirit and among other arguments appealed to the authority of the traditional liturgical formula with its Scripturally-based economic emphasis ('through' and 'in'). Basil countered in his treatise *On the Holy Spirit* that on the one hand, the liturgy is flexible rather than fixed and is not always drawn directly from the Bible, and on the other hand, there were already multiple precedents for making all three persons the recipients of worship in the doxologies of other local and regional liturgies.[45] Furthermore, the Caesarean formula did not direct worship to the Spirit as an isolated divine person but only as a member of the Trinity, '*together with*' the other two persons.[46] Nevertheless, as in Scripture it is the work of the Spirit to do for humanity what only God can do, it is not inappropriate to glorify the Spirit as God.[47]

To abbreviate a long and interesting story once again, a second ecumenical council meeting at Constantinople in 381 decided in the direction of Basil's theologically motivated liturgical revisions. The third article of the Creed of the Council of Nicaea was now expanded to apply to the Spirit the same relationship to the divinity of the Father and the Son that Nicaea had defined as the relationship of the Son to the divinity of the Father, underscoring the Spirit's actions in the divine story: 'the giver of life, who proceeds from the Father...who has spoken through the prophets', and by implication the Spirit's work in the church, baptism and forgiveness, resurrection, and the life to come in the remainder of the third article. In addition, along with the Father and the Son 'he is to be worshipped and glorified'. With the Nicaeno-Constantinopolitan Creed, the essential points that the church has come to associate with the doctrine of the Trinity were firmly in place. Although the emphasis of the doctrine was beginning to shift from an affirmation of the triadic shape of the divine economy to a focus on the immanent Trinity, God as God has been from eternity prior to and apart from the economy of creation and redemption, the shift was necessary for ensuring the integrity of the story the church told about the

---

44   Basil of Caesarea *De Spiritu Sancto* 3 (ET, *On the Holy Spirit*, trans. Anderson, p. 17). After mentioning this form of the doxology, Basil continues, 'and at other times we use "Glory to the Father *through* the Son *in* the Holy Spirit"', thus incorporating both economic and immanent forms of the doxology in the services he led.

45   Basil of Caesarea *De Spiritu Sancto* 71-74 (ET, *On the Holy Spirit*, trans. Anderson, pp. 106-112).

46   Basil of Caesarea *De Spiritu Sancto* 48 (ET, *On the Holy Spirit*, trans. Anderson, pp. 75-76).

47   Basil of Caesarea *De Spiritu Sancto* 49 (ET, *On the Holy Spirit*, trans. Anderson, pp. 76-78).

Triune God in its worship. The Arians and Pneumatomachians had extrapolated the subordination of the economy into the immanent Trinity and consequently narrated an economy in which a hierarchical God delegates creation and redemption to lesser divinities in the hierarchy. The defenders of Nicaeno-Constantinopolitan orthodoxy discerned in the economic narrative an inner logic that led to their portrayal of the immanent God as a Trinity of consubstantial, co-eternal, and co-equal persons. This characterization of the immanent God then enabled orthodox Christian worship to tell the story of the economy in such a way that the fullness of the Godhead is maximally involved in every action in salvation history—a story that the Arians and Pneumatomachians could not tell with equal effect because of the inherent limitations of their doctrine of God.

Character Development: The Clarification of Trinitarian Relations

Although subsequent conciliar deliberations in the next century moved beyond matters of Trinitarian theology proper to consider lingering questions about Christology, individual patristic theologians after Constantinople made important contributions to Trinitarian thought in their efforts to characterize the intra-Trinitarian relationships so as to avoid falling prey to tritheism on the one hand and modalism on the other. In the East, the Cappadocian Fathers—Gregory of Nazianzus (d. 390) and Gregory of Nyssa (d. c. 395) in addition to the latter's older brother of Basil of Caesarea—explained the unity of God in terms of the common divine *ousia*, 'essence', that the three persons share. The divine *ousia* is known only in the mutual relationships of the *hypostaseis*, 'individual subsistences' (the Cappadocian term for the 'persons'), which are differentiated by their unique relations to the other persons.[48] Although there is debate among Cappadocian scholars regarding the extent to which the Cappadocians proposed a fully social analogy for the Trinity in which God is a society of persons sharing a common divine nature,[49] at the very least they painted a thoroughly relational portrait of the Triune God from which more recent Trinitarian theologians would draw much inspiration. In continuity with the Cappadocian theology of Trinitarian relations, John of

---

48   E.g., Gregory of Nyssa *Ad Ablabium quod non sint tres dii* (ET, 'Answer to Ablabius', trans. C. Richardson, in *Christology of the Later Fathers*, ed. E. Hardy (LCC, 3; Philadelphia: Westminster Press, 1954), pp. 256-67; Gregory of Nyssa *Contra Eunomium* 2.2 (ET, NPNF² 5:101-103).

49   S. Coakley, '"Persons" in the "Social" Doctrine of the Trinity: A Critique of Current Analytic Discussion', in *The Trinity: An International Symposium on the Trinity*, ed. S.T. Davis, D. Kendall, and G. O'Collins (New York: Oxford University Press, 1999), pp. 123-44.

Damascus (d. c. 749) later synthesized the prior development of Eastern patristic Trinitarian thought and added to it the concept of *perichōrēsis*, the interpenetration or mutual indwelling of the three persons in the being and actions of one another.[50] Rooted in the biblical text of John 17.21-23 ('As you, Father, are in me and I am in you, may they also be in us'), the periochoretic Trinitarianism of John of Damascus was a relational understanding of God that made room for human participation in the divine life and work.

In the West, Augustine of Hippo (d. 430) likewise characterized God in relational terms. Although his psychological analogies for the Trinity suggest a location of the *imago trinitatis* in the individual human being,[51] Augustine's basic ideas about the relationships between Father, Son, and Spirit point in the direction of a relational or social location of the image of the Triune God in human beings, even though Augustine himself did not make such an application. According to another Augustinian analogy that exegeted the biblical proposition that 'God is love' (1 John 4.8), the Father is one who loves, the Son is the recipient of the Father's love, and the Spirit is their mutual love that processes from their relationship.[52] This explanation of the intra-Trinitarian relations supplied the theology that later led to the insertion of the *Filoque* into the Latin text of the Nicaeno-Constantinoplitan Creed at the Third Council of Toledo in 589 that would become so problematic for ecumenical relationships between East and West, and it also seemed to suggest a radically subordinated role for the Spirit. Its more positive contributions were extended and improved, however, in the Middle Ages by Richard of St. Victor (d. 1173), who modified Augustine's lover-beloved-mutual love analogy in arguing that love as an attribute of God is best explained by relations among three persons if God is to be love prior to the creation of a world to love: one who loves, one who is loved, and another with whom to share that love.[53] The Cappadocians, John of Damascus, and the Augustinian tradition aided the church in more fully developing the character of the Triune God in the story it rehearses in its worship so that this account 'shall manifest God as One yet not alone; but in its care to avoid the error of making Him lonely it shall not fall into the error of denying His unity', as Hilary of Poitiers (d. c. 367) urged.[54]

---

50   John of Damascus *De Fide Orthodoxa* 8 (ET, NPNF[2] 9:6-11).

51   Augustine of Hippo *De Trinitate* 10 (ET, NPNF[1] 3:134-43).

52   Augustine of Hippo *De Trinitate* 15.27-28 (ET, NPNF[1] 3:215-16).

53   Richard of St. Victor *De Trinitate* 3.14-15 (ET, 'Book Three of the Trinity', in *Richard of St. Victor: The Twelve Patriarchs, The Mystical Ark, Book Three of the Trinity*, trans. G.A. Zinn [CWS; New York: Paulist Press, 1979], pp. 387-89).

54   Hilary of Poitiers *De Trinitate* 7.8 (ET, NPNF[2] 9:121).

An appreciation of the relationship between the development of Trinitarian theology during the patristic period and the church's efforts to tell the biblical story faithfully in its worship and witness can help Baptists reclaim the centrality of the doctrine of the Trinity for their own faith and practice. Far from being an unbiblical, 'Popish' doctrine, the patristic doctrine of the Trinity developed from the inner logic of the triadic narrative handed over by the apostolic church through the New Testament documents and the rule of faith that summarized this story and provided the key to its interpretation.[55] When the church in ecumenical councils—or through its principal theologians who sought to interpret the faith of the church in, with, and for the church—defined more precisely what it meant to experience and worship the one God as Father, Son, and Holy Spirit, this second-order theological reflection did not eclipse but rather enhanced the first-order narration of salvation history that forms the identity of the faithful. The Nicaeno-Constantinopolitan version of the story and its take on the principal character, the Triune God, is arguably more effective in telling the story of God and God's relationship to the world and in helping people to find their place within this story than any other early Christian version of the story. A renewed attention to Trinitarian catholicity—along with catholicity in biblical interpretation, the focus of the next chapter, from which dimension of catholicity the catholic doctrine of the Trinity is inseparable—will thus enable Baptists even more compellingly 'to tell the old, old story of Jesus and His love'.[56]

---

55   On the centrality of first-order narrative in early Christian theology, see Blowers, 'The *Regula Fidei* and the Narrative Character of Early Christian Faith', pp. 199-228.

56   'I Love to Tell the Story', hymn 572 in *The Baptist Hymnal*, ed. W.L. Forbis (Nashville, Tenn.: Convention Press, 1991).

CHAPTER 6

Hebrews in Patristic Perspective: Benefits of Catholicity for Baptist Biblical Interpretation

'Not only Catholic and orthodox theologians, but even such Protestant thinkers as Barth, Pannenberg, André Benoît vie with one another in insisting that the theologian, in his reflection on the Scriptures, cannot ignore the Fathers. In view of their declarations, one would even be inclined to revive St. Jerome's celebrated expression cited by Vatican II as follows: ignorance of the Fathers is ignorance of the Scriptures and of Christ.' *Bertrand de Margerie*[1]

The past couple of decades have witnessed a remarkable surge of interest among both scholars and clergy in the biblical interpretation of the church fathers (and occasionally mothers[2]), the early Christian writers of the second through eighth centuries.[3] This interest is rooted in six major developments since the middle of the twentieth century. First, in the 1943 encyclical *Divino Afflante Spiritu* Pope Pius XII strongly encouraged Roman Catholic Scripture scholars towards the study of patristic biblical interpretation in conjunction with the use of modern historical-critical

---

1   B. de Margerie, *An Introduction to the History of Exegesis*, vol. 1, *The Greek Fathers*, trans. L. Maluf (Petersham, Mass.: Saint Bede's Publications, 1993), p. 2. The original expression from the prologue to Jerome's *Commentary on Isaiah* (*PL* 24:17) as quoted in *Dei Verbum* 25 is 'Ignorance of the Scriptures is ignorance of Christ' ('Dogmatic Constitution on Divine Revelation', in *Vatican II: The Conciliar and Post Conciliar Documents*, rev. edn., ed. A. Flannery [Northport, N.Y.: Costello Publishing, 1992], p. 764).

2   Selections from the small but nonetheless significant body of writings by early Christian women are anthologized in English translation in A. Oden, ed., *In Her Words: Women's Writings in the History of Christian Thought* (Nashville: Abingdon, 1994), pp. 17-83.

3   While it is common to identify the fifth century as the end of the patristic period in the West, with the career of Augustine of Hippo (d. 430) seen as its culmination, in the East the age of the fathers really extends to John of Damascus (d. c. 749). For the present purposes, the second through eighth centuries are defined as the patristic period in order to be inclusive of the Eastern developments.

methodologies.[4] Second, the *nouvelle théologie* movement in mid-twentieth-century Roman Catholic theology that preceded the Second Vatican Council sought a renewal of the Roman Catholic Church through retrieval of the classical sources of the Christian faith.[5] Third, in 1969 a major scholarly conference in Strasbourg, France on 'The Bible in the Fathers' focused international attention on the importance of patristic biblical interpretation and the need for ongoing research in that area.[6] The years that followed this conference saw a dramatic increase in the annual number of published studies of various aspects of patristic biblical interpretation. Fourth, the cross-fertilization Christian and Jewish scholarship since the Second World War has produced a significant body of scholarly literature comparing Jewish and Christian readings of their common sacred text, the Hebrew Bible, in the period of late antiquity.[7] Fifth, a postmodern consciousness of the limitations of historical-critical methodologies (i.e., 'diachronic' methodologies) for biblical interpretation has emerged among many theological educators and ministers. While some postmodern interpreters of the Bible have attempted to move beyond these limitations through various literary methodologies that focus on the narrative world within the text and the interaction between reader and text (i.e., 'synchronic' methodologies), others have sought aid from pre-modern readings of Scripture and in some cases have found these to be remarkably aware of the narrative dimensions of the text and its capacity to communicate multiple layers of meaning. Representative of the latter quest to recover patristic biblical exegesis as a resource for the contemporary church in its reading of the Bible are two commentary series that survey and anthologize the patristic interpretation of specific portions of Scripture: *The Ancient Christian Commentary on Scripture*, edited by Thomas Oden

---

4   Pius XII, *Divino Afflante Spiritu*, in *AAS* 35 (1943), pp. 297-326. Robinson, *Roman Catholic Exegesis Since Divino Afflante Spiritu*, has documented the influence of this encyclical on subsequent Roman Catholic biblical scholarship.

5   See Kerr, 'French Theology: Yves Congar and Henri de Lubac'; D'Ambrosio, 'Ressourcement Theology, Aggiornamento, and the Hermeneutics of Tradition'; Kobler, 'On D'Ambrosio and Ressourcement Theology'. De Lubac in particular contributed to a renewed appreciation for the continuing relevance of patristic perspectives on the interpretation of Scripture in *Exégèse medieval* (ET, *Medieval Exegesis*).

6   A. Benoit and P. Prigent, eds., *La Bible et les Pères: Colloque de Strasbourg (1er-3 Octobre 1969)* (Paris: Presses Universitaires de France, 1971); A. Benoit, P. Prigent, K. Aland, J. Duplancy, and B. Fischer, 'Pour un inventaire général de citations patristiques de la Bible Grecque: Appel et propositions aux Patrologues et aux Biblistes', *Greg* 51 (1970), pp. 561-65.

7   E.g, J. Frishman and L. Van Rompay, eds., *The Book of Genesis in Jewish and Oriental Christian Interpretation: A Collection of Essays* (Louvian: Peeters, 1997).

and published by InterVarsity Press, and *The Church's Bible*, edited by Robert Wilken and published by William B. Eerdmans.[8] These projects also exemplify a sixth factor that is both a contributor to and a consequence of the recent interest in patristic biblical interpretation: the production of a growing number of tools that enable the contemporary interpreter to gain access to patristic perspectives on Scripture much more easily than at any other time in Christian history, including the period when patristic commentaries and homilies on Scripture were first written and disseminated.[9]

Patristic exegesis of the New Testament Epistle to the Hebrews—the biblical book selected for the 2006 Annual Bible Study promoted by Smyth & Helwys Publishing, an independent publishing house that serves many congregations affiliated with the Cooperative Baptist Fellowship in the United States—has received focused attention as a result of this new

---

8   T.C. Oden, ed., *Ancient Christian Commentary on Scripture*; R.L. Wilken, ed., *The Church's Bible* (Grand Rapids: William B. Eerdmans, 2003-). The following volumes of *The Ancient Christian Commentary on Scripture* have been published or are scheduled for publication through 2007: *Genesis 1-11* (ed. A. Louth); *Genesis 12-50* (ed. M. Sheridan); *Exodus, Leviticus, Numbers, Deuteronomy* (ed. J. Lienhard); *Joshua, Judges, Ruth, 1-2 Samuel* (ed. J.R. Franke); *Job* (ed. M. Simonetti and M. Conti); *Proverbs, Ecclesiastes, Song of Solomon* (ed. J.R. Wright); *Isaiah 1-39* (ed. S.A. McKinion); *Isaiah 40-66* (ed. M.W. Elliott); *The Twelve Prophets* (ed. A. Ferreiro); *Matthew 1-13* (ed. M. Simonetti); *Matthew 14-28* (ed. M. Simonetti); *Mark* (ed. T.C. Oden and C. Hall); *Luke* (ed. A. Just); *John 1-10* (ed. J.C. Elowsky); *John 11-21* (ed. J.C. Elowsky); *Acts* (ed. F. Martin); *Romans* (ed. G. Bray); *1-2 Corinthians* (ed. G. Bray); *Galatians, Ephesians, Philippians* (ed. M.J. Edwards); *Colossians, 1-2 Thessalonians, 1-2 Timothy, Titus, Philemon* (ed. P. Gorday); *Hebrews* (ed. E.M. Heen and P.D.W. Krey); *James, 1-2 Peter, 1-3 John, Jude* (ed. G. Bray); and *Revelation* (ed. W.C. Weinrich). Additional volumes planned for the series are *1-2 Kings, 1-2 Chronicles, Ezra, Nehemiah, Esther*; *Psalms 1-50*; *Psalms 51-150*; *Jeremiah, Lamentations*; *Ezekiel, Daniel*; and *Apocrypha*. For a critical analysis of the limitations of the *Ancient Christian Commentary on Scripture* project, see R.D. Young's review of the initial volumes of the series, 'Texts Have Consequences', *FT* 91 (March, 1999), pp. 40-43; but see also the rejoinders of Oden and C. Hall in *FT* 94 (June/July, 1999), pp. 2-7. *The Church's Bible* has published two volumes to date: *The Song of Songs* (ed. R.A. Norris, Jr.) and *1 Corinthians* (ed. J.L. Kovacs). These latter volumes contain much more substantial continuous excerpts from patristic homilies and commentaries than do the volumes of the *Ancient Christian Commentary*.

9   This listing of contributing factors to contemporary interest in patristic exegesis is adapted from Harmon, 'Note on the Critical Use of *Instrumenta*', pp. 95-97. In its entirety (pp. 95-107), this article surveys the print and electronic tools available for locating and retrieving references to specific biblical passages in patristic literature, addresses the merits and limitations of these resources, and illustrates the critical use of these tools by using Matt. 13.52 as a test case.

interest in the patristic interpretation of the Bible. Patristic interpretation of Hebrews is the subject of a major monograph,[10] several journal articles and essays,[11] and a new volume of *The Ancient Christian Commentary on Scripture*.[12] Yet the awareness most Baptist seminary and divinity school graduates have of patristic perspectives on Hebrews is limited to a mention in New Testament survey courses of Origen's opinion on the authorship of Hebrews that 'who wrote the epistle, only God knows'.[13] This chapter on the patristic interpretation of Hebrews has two goals. First, it seeks to acquaint Baptist pastors and other ministers who may have occasion to preach and teach from Hebrews more fully with the place of the epistle among the homilies and commentaries on Scripture written during the patristic period, the contributions of Hebrews to the development of patristic theology, and the resources that are available for consulting the

---

10   R.A. Greer, *The Captain of Our Salvation: A Study in the Patristic Exegesis of Hebrews* (BGBE, 15; Tübingen: J.C.B. Mohr [Paul Siebeck], 1973).

11   Following are some of the more significant studies published in as journal articles or essays in multiauthor works, with those in English appearing first: H.E. Symonds, 'The Heavenly Sacrifice in the Greek Fathers', in *StudPat*, vol. 8, ed. F.L. Cross (TU, 93; Berlin: Akademie-Verlag, 1966), pp. 280-85; F.M. Young, 'Christological Ideas in the Greek Commentaries on the Epistle to the Hebrews', *JTS* n.s. 20 (April, 1969), pp. 150-63; P.M. Parvis, 'The *Commentary on Hebrews* and the *Contra Theodorum* of Cyril of Alexandria', *JTS* n.s. 26 (October, 1975), pp. 415-19; G.L. Cockerill, 'Heb 1:1-14, *1 Clem.* 36:1-6 and the High Priest Title', *JBL* 97.3 (September, 1978), pp. 437-40; P. Garnet, 'Hebrews 2:9: χάριτι or χωρίς?', in *StudPat* 18.1, *Historica-Theologica-Gnostica-Biblica*, ed. E.A. Livingstone (Kalamazoo, Mich.: Cistercian Publications, 1985), pp. 321-25; P. Bright, 'The Epistle to the Hebrews in Origen's Christology', in *Origeniana Sexta: Origène et la Bible/Origen and the Bible*, ed. G. Dorival and A. le Boulluec (BETL, 118; Leuven: Leuven University Press, 1995), pp. 559-65; J.M. Hallman, 'The Communication of Idioms in Theodoret's *Commentary on Hebrews*', in *In Dominico Eloquio/In Lordly Eloquence: Essays on Patristic Exegesis in Honor of Robert L. Wilken*, ed. P.M. Blowers et al. (Grand Rapids, Mich.: William B. Eerdmans, 2002), pp. 369-79; A.-M. La Bonnardière, 'L'épître aux Hébreux dans l'œuvre de saint Augustin', *RÉAug* 3 (1957), pp. 137-62; J.-C. Dhôtel, 'La "sanctification" du Christ d'après *Hébreux*, II, 11: Interprétations des Pères et des Scholastiques médiévaux', *RSR* 47 (1959), pp. 515-43; B. Quinot, 'L'influence de l'Épître aux Hébreux dans la notion augustinienne du vrai sacrifice', *RÉAug* 8 (1962), pp. 129-68; A. Vanhoye, 'Esprit éternel et feu du sacrifice en He 9,14', *Bib* 64.2 (1983), pp. 263-74; D. Gonnet, 'L'Utilisation Christologique de l'Épître aux Hébreux dans les *Oarationes contra Arianos* d'Athanase d'Alexandrie', in *StudPat* 32, ed. E.A. Livingstone (Leuven: Peeters Press, 1997), pp. 19-24.

12   E.M. Heen and P.D.W. Krey, eds., *Hebrews* (ACCS.NT, 10; Downers Grove, Ill.: InterVarsity Press, 2005).

13   This comment is from a passage in Origen's no longer-extant *Homilies on Hebrews* preserved in Eusebius of Caesarea *Ecclesiastical History* 6.25.13-14.

fathers' interpretation of specific passages from Hebrews. Second, this chapter illustrates through the specific case of Hebrews the potential benefits for Baptist biblical interpretation that may result when Baptist ministers develop a concern for hearing the church in its catholicity when they search and proclaim the Scriptures as a member of this larger communion of Bible readers.[14]

Patristic Homilies and Commentaries on Hebrews

Hebrews is comparatively well represented among the patristic commentaries and homily cycles devoted to the exposition of the New Testament epistles. There are eleven known commentaries or collections of homilies from this period that treat Hebrews comprehensively (or twelve, if one counts a commentary of questionable authenticity). The earliest of these is a fragment of the *Homilies on the Epistle to the Hebrews* by Origen (d. 254).[15] The earliest extant complete commentary is the *Commentary on the Epistle to the Hebrews* by Ephrem the Syrian (d. 373), written originally in Syriac but preserved only in Armenian translation.[16] Several important commentaries and collected homilies on Hebrews from the late fourth through sixth centuries exist only in fragments, some of which are found in 'catenae', late patristic anthologies of exegetical excerpts from earlier commentators. These include lost works by Didymus the Blind (d. 398), Severian of Gabala (fl. c. 400), Theodore of Mopsuestia (d. 428), Cyril of Alexandria (d. 444), Gennadius of Constantinople (d. 471), and Oecumenius (fl. sixth cent.).[17] There are at least three extant complete

---

14   Cf. the article by C.J. Scalise, 'Patristic Biblical Interpretation and Postmodern Baptist Identity', *RevExp* 101.4 (Fall, 2004), pp. 615-28, which similarly argues that an appreciation for the patristic church's reading of Scripture in light of the rule of faith and in the context of the liturgy would yield significant benefits for the construction of Baptist and evangelical identity in a postmodern context.

15   Origen *Fragmenta in Epistulam ad Hebraeos homiliae* (PG 14:1308-09).

16   Ephrem the Syrian *Commentary on the Epistle to the Hebrews* (in Armenian), in *Srboyn Ep`remi matenagrut`iwnk`* (Venetik, Armenia: Tparani Srboyn Ghazaru, 1836), vol. 3.

17   Didymus the Blind *Fragmenta in epistulam ad Hebraeos (in catenis)*, in *Pauluskommentare aus der griechischen Kirche: aus Katenenhandschriften gesammelt und herausgegeben*, 2d edn., ed. K. Staab (NTAbh, 15; Münster: Aschendorff, 1984), pp. 83-112; Severian of Gabala *Fragmenta in epistulam ad Hebraeos (in catenis)*, in *Pauluskommentare aus der griechischen Kirche*, ed. Staab, pp. 213-351; Theodore of Mopsuestia *Fragmenta in epistulam ad Hebraeos (in catenis)*, in *Pauluskommentare aus der griechischen Kirche*, ed. Staab, pp. 113-212; Cyril of Alexandria *Fragmenta in epistulam ad Hebraeos* (PG 74:953-1005); Gennadius of Constantinople *Fragmenta in epistulam ad Hebraeos* (PG 85:1664-65; on this fragment see also S.J. Voicu,

commentaries and homily cycles in addition to the commentary by Ephrem the Syrian: the *Homilies on the Epistle to the Hebrews* by John Chrysostom (d. 407), the *Interpretation of the Epistle to the Hebrews* by Theodoret of Cyrus (d. c. 466), and the *Exposition of the Epistle to the Hebrews* by Cassiodorus (d. c. 580).[18] A *Commentary on the Epistle to the Hebrews* is attributed to John of Damascus (d. c. 749), but the genuineness of this attribution has been questioned.[19] In addition to these eleven (or twelve) known comprehensive treatments of Hebrews in the patristic period, there are single homilies on specific passages from Hebrews that are not part of larger collections. These include homilies on Heb. 1.3 by Gregory the Illuminator (d. c. 328), on Heb. 3.1 by Nestorius (d. c. 451), and on Heb. 11.38 and 13.17 by Caesarius of Arles (d. 543).[20] Apart from the excerpts translated in the volume on Hebrews in the *Ancient Commentary on Scripture*, the only complete patristic commentaries and homilies on Hebrews currently available in English translation are those by John Chrysostom and Theodoret of Cyrus.[21]

The most influential patristic treatment of Hebrews is the collection of homilies by John Chrysostom, the earliest and most extensive Greek commentary on the epistle to survive in its entirety. The collection was translated into Latin by the sixth century and was foundational for subsequent late patristic and medieval Latin commentaries. Late medieval, Byzantine, and Reformation theologians drew more extensively on Chrysostom than on any other patristic interpreter of Hebrews. The editors of the *Ancient Christian Commentary on Scripture* volume on Hebrews accordingly chose Chrysostom's homilies as the basis for the commentary.[22]

'Gennadio di Costantinopoli: La trasmissione del frammento *In Hebr* 9, 2-5', *OCP* 84 [1982], pp. 435-37); Oecumenius *Commentarii in epistolam ad Hebraeos*, in *Pauluskommentare aus der griechischen Kirche*, ed. Staab, pp. 462-69.

18   John Chrysostom *In epistulam ad Hebraeos argumentum et homiliae1-34* (PG 63:13-236); Theodoret of Cyrus *Interpretatio in epistulam ad Hebraeos* (PG 82:673-785); Cassiodorus *Expositio epistulae ad Hebraeos* (PL 68:685-794).

19   John of Damascus (?) *Commentarii in epistolam ad Hebraeos* (PG 95:929-97).

20   H.J. Sieben, *Kirchenväterhomilien zum Neuen Testament: Ein Reperorium der Textausgaben und Übersetzungen, mit einem Anhang der Kirchenväterkommentare* (InstrPat, 22; The Hague: Martin Nijhoff International, 1991), pp. 174-78.

21   John Chrysostom *Homilies on the Epistle to the Hebrews* (NPNF[1] 14:363-522); Theodoret of Cyrus 'Interpretation of Hebrews', in *Theodoret of Cyrus: Commentary on the Letters of St. Paul*, trans. and ed. R.C. Hill (Brookline, Mass.: Holy Cross Orthodox Press, 2001), vol. 2, pp. 136-207.

22   Heen and Krey, eds., *Hebrews*, pp. xx-xxi.

Of the patristic commentaries and homilies on Hebrews, only the commentary by Cassiodorus and the single homilies by Caesarius of Arles are from the Western, Latin patristic tradition. What accounts for the Eastern, Greek predominance of commentaries and homilies on Hebrews? It is true that in the patristic period there are generally more Greek than Latin commentaries and homilies on any biblical book. In the case of Hebrews, however, the Christological controversies of the late fourth and fifth centuries provided an additional theological impetus for the production of commentaries on Hebrews in the Eastern church. These controversies were primarily Eastern in geographical provenance and Greek and Syriac in language; they did not embroil the Latin West in controversy as intensely as in the East. The portrait of Christ as the divine and human Son of God painted by the epistle made Hebrews a logical scriptural battleground for these Christological controversies, just as the soteriological controversies between the Augustinian and Pelagian camps in the West contributed to a flowering of late patristic commentaries and homilies on Romans in Latin.

The Place of Hebrews in the Development of Patristic Theology

Hebrews thus not only served as a biblical text from which the fathers preached but also played a significant role in the development of patristic theology, especially under the rubric of Christology. As Rowan Greer's study of the patristic exegesis of Hebrews demonstrated, there was a distinctive Alexandrian exegesis of Hebrews that corresponded to the Alexandrian approach to Christology, and there was a distinctive Antiochene exegesis of Hebrews that corresponded to the Antiochene approach to Christology.[23] Much has been made of the difference between the hermeneutics of the respective schools, with the Alexandrians emphasizing an allegorical interpretation and the Antiochenes insisting on the literal sense of the text, but studies of patristic exegesis are increasingly making clear that these hermeneutical contrasts are overdrawn. The Alexandrians valued the literal sense of the text, and the Antiochenes found significance in deeper layers of meaning beyond the literal. The finely nuanced distinctions between and within these exegetical and Christological schools of thought are exceedingly complex, and adequate explanation of them is well beyond the scope of the present section of this article. Nevertheless, one may make the following broad generalizations about Alexandrian and Antiochene Christology.

---

23   Greer, *Captain of Our Salvation*, pp. 1-6 and 356-59.

Alexandrian Christology

The Alexandrians tended to emphasize the oneness of Christ, with the divinity and humanity of Christ constituting one being in which the divine *Logos* is joined to human flesh. Since this perspective emphasized the unity of the nature of Christ, which received its primary identity from the divine *Logos*, the proponents of this perspective came to be known as 'Monophysites', from the Greek *monos*, 'one', and *physis*, 'nature'. Apollinaris of Laodicea (d. c. 390) was the most extreme representative of this position, teaching that Christ had a human body and soul, but that the human spirit was replaced by the divine *Logos*. The teaching of Cyril of Alexandria, though also emphasizing the singularity of the nature of Christ, was more congruent with what became Christological orthodoxy following the Council of Chalcedon (451).

Antiochene Christology

The Antiochenes, on the other hand, emphasized the distinction between divine and human natures in Christ, with both natures maintaining their own unique identities and attributes. Whereas the Alexandrians envisioned a union of the divine *Logos* and human flesh, for the Antiochenes it is crucial that the divine *Logos* be joined not to human flesh in general but to a human being in particular. Since this perspective emphasized the distinction between the two natures, its proponents came to be known as 'Dyophysites', from the Greek *dyo*, 'two', and *physis*, 'nature'. Nestorius was the most extreme representative of this position, allegedly maintaining that the incarnation joined together not only two natures but also two persons, divine and human, each with its own distinct identity. The teaching of John Chrysostom, and to lesser degrees Theodore of Mopsuestia and Theodoret of Cyrus, was more consistent with the Christology endorsed by Chalcedon.

Hebrews 2.10-18 and the Suffering of Christ

Theologians of each party in the controversy appealed to Hebrews as biblical support for their positions, and the positions of their respective opponents required them to explain certain features of Hebrews to which their opponents could appeal for support. Nestorius, for example, could argue that Hebrews made a clear distinction between the identities associated with the two natures: the 'reflection of God's glory and the exact imprint of God's very being' (Heb. 1.3) as the nature of the divine Word is distinguished from the human nature of 'the pioneer of salvation' (Heb. 2.10) and 'merciful and faithful high priest' (Heb. 2.17).[24] Both Nestorius and more mainstream Antiochenes could therefore easily maintain the impassibility of God, a perspective on the divine nature they shared in common with the Alexandrians and patristic theology in general, by identifying these sufferings with the human nature of Christ. Thus Chrysostom explains Heb. 2.10 in this fashion: '"He himself was tested by what he suffered"—this is altogether low, and mean, and unworthy of God....God is incapable of suffering. But he describes here what belongs to the Incarnation, as if he had said, "Even the very flesh of Christ suffered many terrible things"'.[25]

While the proper concern of a 'theology after Auschwitz', as Jürgen Moltmann's *The Crucified God* has been called,[26] has been to affirm God's positive relationship to the experience of suffering, the reception of such theologies (and their basic affirmations indeed ought to be received) has also reinforced—and perhaps helped to create—a caricature of the patristic emphasis on the impassibility of God: the fathers denied that God could suffer, and since the fathers were obviously wrong about this, their theologies of divine impassibility should be dismissed as irrelevant for contemporary theology. To regard the fathers' perspectives on God's relationship to suffering as the result of the ignorance and barbarism of the ancients as this caricature seems to suggest, however, is to fall prey to a modern chronological snobbery that cannot be sustained in the postmodern situation, and to attribute the patristic affirmation of impassibility simply to the Hellenizing of an original Hebraic belief in a passionate God is to distort the development of patristic thought on the basis of assumptions that historians are beginning to contend are untenable. The historical arguments of most modern advocates of theopassianism are dependent on historical theologian Adolf von Harnack's interpretation of patristic doctrinal development as the replacement of an original ethical gospel with a Hellenistic philosophical theology.[27] According to this influential theory of

---

24   Williams, *Captain of Our Salvation*, p. 353.

25   John Chrysostom *Homilies on the Epistle to the Hebrews* 5 (NPNF[1] 14:389).

26   J. Moltmann, *Der gekreuzigte Gott: Das Kreuz Christi als Grund und Kritik christlicher Theologie* (Munich: Chr. Kaiser Verlag, 1972); ET, *The Crucified God: The Cross of Christ as the Foundation and Criticism of Christian Theology*, trans. R.A. Wilson and J. Bowden (Minneapolis: Fortress Press, 1993).

27   See especially A. von Harnack, *Lehrbuch der Dogmengeschichte*, 3 vols. in 2 (Freiburg im Breisgau: J.C.B. Mohr, 1886-90) [ET, *History of Dogma*, trans. N. Buchanan, 7 vols. in 4 (New York: Dover Publications, 1961)]; and *Das Wesen des Christentums: sechzehn Vorlesungen vor Studierenden aller Facultäten im Wintersemester 1899/1900 an der Universität Berlin gehalten* (Leipzig: Hinrichs, 1908) [ET, *What Is Christianity?*, trans. T.B. Saunders (New York: Harper, 1957)].

doctrinal development, the church fathers, influenced by the Stoic ideal of *apatheia*, 'passionlessness', reasoned that a perfect God could not share in the human imperfection of being subject to suffering and the power of the passions and so made impassibility a fundamental divine attribute. Paul L. Gavrilyuk sets forth a convincing argument against this 'theory of theology's fall into Hellenistic philosophy' in his recent book *The Suffering of the Impassible God: The Dialectics of Patristic Thought*, in which he makes the case that an opposition of patristic impassibility and modern affirmations of the suffering of God is a false dichotomy. Unqualified expressions of both positions are problematic, and more carefully qualified expressions of both positions seek a positive relation of God to human suffering that not only offers the encouragement to sufferers that God has solidarity with them in their suffering but also provides them with a paradigm for a divinely empowered triumph over suffering and the passions by those who belong to Christ.[28]

Such carefully qualified expressions of God's relationship to suffering in the incarnation of Christ are found in both Antiochene and Alexandrian interpretations of Heb 2.10-18. Early Christian theologians of both schools maintained the impassibility of God, yet they did so as part of a paradox in which the impassible God is passible as the incarnate Word, who is both the subject and the object of the perfection through suffering mentioned in Heb. 2.10: 'It was fitting that God, for whom and through whom all things exist, in bringing many children to glory, should make the pioneer of their salvation perfect through sufferings'. While 'God' is the subject that makes the pioneer of salvation perfect through suffering in the NRSV translation of v. 10, in the Greek text the subject is the more ambiguous masculine third personal pronoun. Theodore of Mopsuestia of the Antiochene school of Christology and biblical interpretation specifies the pronoun's referent as the Word, the second person of the Trinity, who makes perfect through suffering the human to whom the Word is joined in the incarnation.[29] Thus in the economy of salvation God as the incarnate Word is both impassible and passible, both the one who perfects through suffering and the one who is made perfect through suffering. In this way the Word incarnate is 'able to help those who are being tested' (v. 18)—objectively by sharing flesh and blood and becoming subject to death in order to destroy death's sway over those who suffer and free them from its fear (vv. 14-15) and subjectively both by identifying with them as a fellow sufferer whose showing of mercy is grounded in the experience of suffering (v. 17) and by providing a paradigm for impassible suffering by followers of Christ themselves. The

---

28   Gavrilyuk, *Suffering of the Impassible God.*

29   Theodore of Mopsuestia *Fragmenta in epistulam ad Hebraeos* (PG 66:9571; ET in Greer, *Captain of Our Salvation*, p. 236).

Alexandrian theologian and exegete Cyril of Alexandria held that believers could share in the impassible passion of Christ whenever they suffered, for through the Holy Spirit they have access to the qualitatively different relation to suffering that God has.[30] In patristic perspective, then, God suffers impassibly—entering into suffering without being overcome by it—and so may those who belong to God, follow the Word incarnate, and share in God's Spirit. The patristic interpretation of Hebrews shaped these convictions regarding Christology and its relationship to the attributes of the divine nature, and these convictions in turn shaped the patristic interpretation of Hebrews as these early theologians turned to the text of Hebrews for theological guidance and polemical support in the midst of the Christological controversies.[31]

Patristic Resources for Teaching and Preaching Hebrews Today

The minister who preaches or teaches from Hebrews and wishes to have access to the perspectives of the earliest interpreters of the epistle will want to purchase the recently published volume on Hebrews in *The Ancient Christian Commentary on Scripture*. In addition to this resource, one may also want to consult the two full-length patristic commentaries/homilies on Hebrews that are currently available in English translation, as in their entirety they provide a better sense of the nature of patristic preaching and biblical interpretation than do the excerpts anthologized in the volume in *The Ancient Christian Commentary on Scripture*. John Chrysostom's *Homilies on the Epistle to the Hebrews* are included in volume 14 of the *Nicene and Post-Nicene Fathers*, First Series, published in a relatively inexpensive reprint edition by Hendrickson Publishers. As this series is now in the public domain in terms of copyright law, it is also available on the Internet.[32] Robert C. Hill's 2001 translation of Theodoret of Cyrus' *Interpretation of the Epistle to the Hebrews* is available in an inexpensive paperback edition from Holy Cross Orthodox Press.

How may these ancient resources assist those who preach or teach from Hebrews today? One may not simply read a patristic homily or commentary on Hebrews and then reproduce these interpretations and applications of

---

30   Regarding this aspect of Cyril's Christology, see J.W. Smith, 'Suffering Impassibly: Christ's Passion in Cyril of Alexandria's Soteriology', *ProEccl* 11.4 (Fall, 2002), pp. 463-83.

31   Some material in the preceding three paragraphs is adapted from S.R. Harmon, 'Between Text and Sermon: Hebrews 2:10-18', *Int* 59.4 (October, 2005), pp. 404-406.

32   Available online, for example, on the Christian Classics Ethereal Library site at www.ccel.org.

Scripture, for their context is not ours. Nevertheless, these earliest attempts to make sense of Hebrews serve as important reminders that the questions we have when we read Hebrews may be more narrowly related to our own denominational and historical context than to the broader concerns of the church's catholic tradition of exegesis. This chapter cannot exhaustively survey the contributions that a knowledge of patristic perspectives on Hebrews may make to contemporary preaching and teaching, but a specific example serves to illustrate the benefits of consulting *The Ancient Christian Commentary on Scripture* or the commentaries and homilies by John Chrysostom and Theodoret of Cyrus when preparing a sermon or teaching session based on a passage from the epistle.

Hebrews 6.1-8 and Apostasy

If Baptist ministers were to be surveyed and asked to identify the ten most problematic interpretive difficulties in the New Testament, they would likely place Heb. 6.1-8 and its mention of 'apostasy' near the top of that list. This passage has served as a major interpretive battleground in the larger tensions between two theological poles that have been present in the Baptist tradition since its seventeenth-century origins. The earliest General Baptists, more Arminian in their theological orientation, confessed on the basis of Hebrews the real possibility of apostasy, with eternal consequences, for those who belong to Christ.

> That men may fall away from the grace off GOD, Heb. 12.15, and from the truth, which they have received & acknowledged, Chap. 10.26. after they have taisted off the heavenly gift, and were made pertakers off the HOLY GHOST, and have taisted off the good word off GOD, & off the powers off the world to come. Chap. 6,4 5.[33]

The earliest Particular Baptists, more Calvinist in their theological orientation, confessed a contrary perspective.

> Those who have this pretious faith wrought in them by the Spirit, can never finally nor totally fall away; and though many stormes and floods do arise and beat against them, yet they shall never be able to take them off that foundation and rock which by faith they are fastened upon, but shall be kept by the power of God to salvation.[34]

---

33   'A Declaration of Faith of English People Remaining at Amsterdam in Holland' (1611), article 7, in Lumpkin, *Baptist Confessions of Faith*, p. 118.

34   'The [First] London Confession, 1644', article 23, in Lumpkin, *Baptist Confessions of Faith*, p. 163.

The tension and cross-fertilization between these two streams of the Baptist tradition ultimately resulted in many Baptists in the United States adopting aspects of both Calvinism and Arminianism, with not a few Baptists in the United States—especially the southern United States—becoming for all practical purposes 'fifth-point Calvinists', meaning that while they may have grave doubts about unconditional election, limited atonement, total depravity, and irresistible grace, they cling tenaciously to the fifth point of Calvinism as defined by the Synod of Dordrecht (1618-19): the perseverance of the saints (or as popularly expressed with less theological propriety, 'once saved, always saved'). As the result of their denominational heritage, then, many Baptists come to the text of Hebrews 6 with the question, 'Is this saying that a person, once saved, can lose his or her salvation?'

One discovers upon consulting patristic homilies and commentaries on Hebrews 6 that Christians in the patristic era brought a rather different, but not entirely unrelated, theological and practical concern to their reading of that passage. They were asking two primary questions of the text. First, is it possible for someone who has fallen into sin after baptism to repent and experience forgiveness? Second, if a person who has fallen into sin after baptism does repent, may that person be re-baptized? Early in Western, Latin-speaking Christianity, Heb. 6.4 was understood as teaching that it is impossible to repent from serious post-baptismal sins. Subsequent patristic exegesis of that text concurred that baptism was unrepeatable, but it tended to hold forth the possibility of repentance and restoration following a post-baptismal return to sin.[35] Theodoret of Cyrus exemplifies these interpretive perspectives in his comments on the insistence of Heb. 6.4-6 that 'it is impossible to restore again to repentance those who have once been enlightened, and have tasted the heavenly gift, and have shared in the Holy Spirit, and have tasted the goodness of the word of God and the power of the age to come, and then have fallen away, since on their own they are crucifying again the Son of God and are holding him up to contempt.'

> It is out of the question, he is saying, for those who have approached all-holy baptism, shared in the grace of the divine Spirit and received the type of the eternal goods to make their approach again and be granted another baptism. This is no different, in fact, from fixing the Son of God to the cross again and besmirching him again with the dishonor already shown. As he in his own case endured the passion once, we too likewise ought to share the passion with him once. We are buried with him in baptism, and we rise with him; so it is not possible for us to enjoy the gift of baptism again....Our former self was crucified with him in baptism by receiving the type of death. By 'goodness of the Word of God' he meant the promise of good things; 'powers of the age to come' is the

---

35   Heen and Krey, eds., *Hebrews*, p. 83.

term he used of baptism and the grace of the Spirit: through them it is possible to attain the promised goods. Now, the apostle said this to teach the believers from Jews not to think all-holy baptism is like the Jewish baptisms: they did not wash away sins, but cleansed the body of apparent defilement—hence they were applied many times and frequently. This baptism of ours, on the contrary, is one only, for the reason that it involves the type of the saving passion and resurrection and prefigures for us the resurrection to come. The followers of Novatian use these words to contest the truth, failing to understand that the divine apostle, far from prohibiting the remedies of repentance, set the limit for divine baptism.[36]

The reference to 'the followers of Novatian' and their appeal to this text as biblical support for their denial of reconciliation to the *lapsi*, the 'lapsed' who had denied their faith during persecution, suggests that Heb. 6.4-6 had been a common locus for controversy over baptism, post-baptismal sin, and restoration since at least the middle of the third century.

Ephrem the Syrian likewise denies the possibility of a second baptism on the same grounds argued by Theodoret but specifies a post-baptismal remedy that extends the benefits initiated by the unrepeatable first baptism.

After the apostle said these words and discouraged them from sinning and being in want of propitiation, he changed his tone and encouraged them, as if to say, 'If there is no second baptism to purify you, your deeds and charity are to be an eternal baptism for you.' Though', he says, 'we speak thus' and close the door of mercy before the just ones lest they may sin, nevertheless the door of mercy is open for penitents. 'God is not so unjust as to overlook your work', that is, your gift, 'and the love' which you have for the saints and the poor who are in Jerusalem.[37]

Although it may seem that Ephrem argues that human works earn forgiveness of post-baptismal sin, his point is that those who repent and once again embrace the Christian way of life may once again enjoy the forgiveness that they experienced in their rite of initiation into the church. Along the same lines Ambrose of Milan, assuming the Pauline authorship of Hebrews, asks about the possibility that the text meant that post-baptismal sins could not be forgiven, 'Could Paul teach in opposition to his own act? He had at Corinth forgiven sin through penance; how could he himself speak against his own decision?'[38] Ambrose's reply to this rhetorical objection both affirmed the possibility of repentance for post-

---

36   Theodoret of Cyrus *Interpretatio in epistulam ad Hebraeos* (PG 82:716; ET in Hill, trans. and ed., *Theodoret of Cyrus*, vol. 2, pp. 159-60; quoted in Heen and Krey, eds., *Hebrews*, p. 84).

37   Ephrem the Syrian *Commentary on the Epistle to the Hebrews*, ET in Heen and Krey, eds., *Hebrews*, p. 85.

38   Ambrose of Milan *Concerning Repentance* 2.2.7 (NPNF[2] 10:345).

baptismal sins and rejected the repetition of baptism for those who turn from post-baptismal sins and return to Christ.

> It was right first of all to remove our anxiety, and to let us know that even after baptism, if any sinned their sins could be forgiven them, lest a false belief in a reiterated baptism should lead astray those who were destitute of all hope of forgiveness. And secondly, it was right to set forth in a well-reasoned arguments that baptism is not to be repeated....So, then, that which he says in this Epistle to the Hebrews, that it is impossible for those who have fallen to be 'renewed unto repentance, crucifying again the Son of God, and putting him to open shame', must be considered as having reference to baptism, wherein we crucify the Son of God in ourselves, that the world may be by him crucified for us....But Christ was crucified once, and died to sin once, and so there is but one, not several baptisms...And indeed I might say also to any one who thought that this passage spoke of repentance, that things which are impossible with men are possible with God; and God is able whensoever he wills to forgive us our sins, even those which we think cannot be forgiven....it seemed impossible that sins should be forgiven through repentance, but Christ gave this power to his apostles, which has been transmitted to the priestly office. That, then, has become possible which was impossible. But, by a true reasoning, he convinces us that the reiteration by anyone of the sacrament of baptism is not permitted.[39]

Severian of Gabala, Photius, and John Chrysostom joined Theodoret, Ephrem, and Ambrose in voicing the common patristic conviction that, as not only Heb. 6.4-6 but also Eph. 4.5 suggested, there is only 'one baptism', an unrepeatable act, but also offering listeners and readers hope in the God who is able to forgive anything.[40]

Awareness of these features of the patristic interpretation of Hebrews 6 may help the minister to put questions about apostasy and the loss of one's salvation in perspective. The passage is not so much about the loss of salvation or the impossibility of forgiveness after straying from the faith as it is about the impossibility of doing again that which Christ has already done by virtue of the believer's union with Christ's crucifixion and resurrection in baptism. One may return to Christ, his way, and his church, but such a return is not a new conversion and does not call for a new baptism; it is a return to this already-performed work in the believer's life. It is not necessary to concur with all the exegetical rationales by which the

---

39   Ambrose of Milan *Concerning Repentance* 2.2.7-12 (NPNF[2] 10:345-46).

40   Severian of Gabala *Fragmenta in epistulam ad Hebraeos* 6.6, in *Pauluskommentare aus der griechischen Kirche*, ed. Staab, p. 349 (ET in Heen and Krey, eds., *Hebrews*, p. 85); Photius *Fragmenta in epistulam ad Hebraeos* 6.6, in *Pauluskommentare aus der griechischen Kirche*, ed. Staab, p. 646 (ET in Heen and Krey, eds., *Hebrews*, p. 85); John Chrysostom *Homilies on the Epistle to the Hebrews* 9 (NPNF[1] 14:411).

fathers arrived at these conclusions from the biblical text in order to find in them a helpful way beyond the interpretive impasses imposed on the text by the legacies of a sixteenth-century intramural debate within the Reformed tradition. At the very least, the ancient Christian consensus on the unrepeatability of baptism ought to give Baptist congregations pause before quickly requiring those whose infant baptism in another Christian communion was joined with subsequent faith to be re-baptized when joining a Baptist congregation or before quickly agreeing to the request to be re-baptized of those who have previously been baptized with believer's baptism but now believe they have truly come to faith for the first time.[41] There is indeed one baptism practiced by the church in its catholicity—a baptism that includes both 'believer's baptism' as a baptismal practice most appropriate to New Testament-like experiences of adult conversion and infant baptism as a baptismal practice most appropriate to the experience of being nurtured from infancy toward faith by family and congregation—and this one baptism belongs at the beginning of one's journey of faith rather than at multiple subsequent points along that journey.[42]

---

41   Cf. Holmes, *Listening to the Past*, pp. 108-21, who as a Baptist theologian exploring patristic resources for ecumenical dialogue between Baptist and non-Baptist communions over the issue of baptism offers a similar perspective on the relationship of Baptist congregations to the 'one baptism' that belongs to the church in its catholicity, while also counseling ministerial sensitivity in respecting the consciences of individuals who wish to be baptized again: 'This might involve Baptists, for the sake of charity, choosing not to query the baptismal status of those who have undergone infant baptism. Equally, it might involve others accepting the conscientious decision to seek rebaptism of one they consider baptised, and the conscientious decision of certain ministers to perform the rite' (p. 120).

42   Colwell, *Promise and Presence*, pp. 109-34, offers a thorough treatment of these issues that addresses some problematic ecclesiological implications of 'open membership' policies in churches of the Baptist Union of Great Britain (and is also applicable to similar 'open membership' policies of some Baptist congregations in the United States). While such policies might initially seem to hold forth much ecumenical promise, they may actually create more serious ecumenical difficulties by implicitly disregarding the importance of baptism. To accept a candidate for membership in a Baptist congregation who was baptized as an infant in another Christian communion on the basis of his or her profession of Christian faith alone while shrinking from affirming the validity of that baptism is to imply that baptism is not a condition for church membership at all. The remedy for these difficulties is not to discard 'open membership' policies in favor of a reversion to 'closed membership', but rather to amend 'open membership' policies so that they join baptism and faith as prerequisites for membership and are 'open' in the sense that they explicitly recognize the validity of infant baptism as a practice of Christian initiation when it is joined with subsequent faith. Baptist congregations that adopt this envisioned form of a more ecclesiologically sound 'open membership' policy would still practice only 'believer's baptism' as their sole form of

Patristic Exegesis and Baptist Proclamation of Hebrews

These glimpses of the role patristic interpretation of Hebrews has played in the formation of early Christian theology and of the insights that may be gained from consulting these perspectives when preaching and teaching on Hebrews are by no means exhaustive. They are provided here as appetizers intended to interest Baptist ministers in the main courses to follow if they consult the Hebrews volume of *The Ancient Christian Commentary on Scripture* and the English translations of the works of John Chrysostom and Theodoret of Cyrus on Hebrews. In light of the function of Hebrews in the development of patristic Christology, preaching a series of sermons from Hebrews (an opportunity for such a series is presented by Year B of the *Revised Common Lectionary*—the lectionary most often used by Baptist ministers in the United States who follow the Christian year in their preaching—with semi-continuous Epistle lessons from Hebrews 1-10 from Proper 27 through Proper 33, and with lessons from chapters 11-13 resuming in Year C, Proper 19 through Proper 22) or teaching an annual Bible study on the epistle provides the minister with an excellent opportunity for giving attention to Christology and its implications not only for Christian thinking but also for the living of the Christian life. As Rowan Greer concluded in his study of the place of Hebrews in the ancient Christological controversies, it is not at all inappropriate, but rather advisable and salutary, to use classical Christian doctrines such as Christology as reading glasses whenever one studies the Scriptures, for their lenses help bring the larger connections of specific biblical texts into focus.

> May it not be the case that we, like the Fathers, are obliged to take our theologies and, while revering the text and respecting its autonomy, use them boldly in our exegesis? Hebrews tells us that Christ is the brightness of God's glory and the Captain of our salvation, but we must use our theology if we are to give any satisfactory account of what this means.[43]

The Christology confessed by most Christians, the two-natures Christology of Chalcedon, did not come to full expression straight out of the biblical text. But if it is true to the biblical text and makes better sense of it than any

---

baptismal practice, and should also develop a meaningful rite of congregational covenant commitment on the part of parents and congregation on the occasion of the birth of a child to parents who are members of that congregation and who pledge to nurture their child toward Christian faith (along with ways of publicly recognizing 'steps toward faith' made by children of various ages as they appropriate this nurture for themselves, while deferring baptism until the completion of a rigorous course of pre-baptismal catechesis sometime in the early to middle teenage years).

43   Greer, *Captain of Our Salvation*, pp. 358-59.

alternative Christology, then it will bear the test of using it 'boldly in our exegesis'. Does the minister have a Chalcedonian Christology? Then he or she should follow the lead of the fathers by reading Hebrews through Chalcedonian lenses and using the text of Hebrews to help the congregation understand what it means for Jesus Christ to be both fully human and fully divine, the two natures united in one person who is the 'pioneer of their salvation' and their 'merciful and faithful high priest', and why such ideas have implications for the everyday living of the Christian life. Patristic perspectives on Hebrews are interesting in their own right, but they are valuable for the life of the church today only if they help make clear such implications for contemporary faith and practice.

Baptist ministers who proclaim and teach the Scriptures in local congregations will read the Scriptures along with the catholic community of biblical interpreters as an integral component of their preparation for preaching and teaching only if their most influential guides in interpretation, their seminary or divinity school professors of the Old and New Testaments, have helped them appreciate the benefits of considering such ecclesial readings of the Bible along with the insights offered by modern commentators during the years of their formal theological education for ministry. As this also holds true for the prospect of the doing of theology in conversation with the church in its catholicity by Baptist parish ministers, the next chapter primarily addresses Baptist academic theologians, who through their ministries of teaching and writing theology have the opportunity to influence Baptist ministers, and ultimately the Baptist churches they serve, towards Baptist catholicity.

CHAPTER 7

Hearing the Voice of the Community: Karl Barth's Conversation with the Fathers as a Paradigm for Baptist and Evangelical *Ressourcement*

'[I]f tradition is "an extension of the franchise" by "giving votes to the most obscure of all classes, our ancestors", then the history of tradition requires that we listen to the choruses and not only to the soloists—nor only to the virtuosi among the soloists.' *Jaroslav Pelikan, echoing G.K. Chesterton*[1]

A noteworthy feature of several recent theological projects that might be broadly categorized as 'evangelical'[2] is the attention they are giving to retrieval of the patristic theological tradition. Much evangelical Protestantism has so strongly emphasized a radicalized version of the *Sola Scriptura* hermeneutic of the Reformation that many who identify themselves as evangelicals seem to assume that they can easily make sense of the Bible and apply its teachings to the contemporary situation without the aid of reading glasses ground by the classical Christian theological tradition. Yet evangelical voices such as Baptist patristics specialist D.H. Williams and mainline Protestant theologians Thomas Oden and Robert Jenson, among others, are now encouraging the church to find needed

---

1   J. Pelikan, *The Vindication of Tradition* (New Haven: Yale University Press, 1984), p. 17; quotation is from G.K. Chesterton, *Orthodoxy* (Garden City, N.Y.: Image Books, 1959), p. 48.

2   In this chapter the term 'evangelical' is employed as a descriptor of Protestant Christians whose application of the Scripture principle of the Reformation has tended to minimize the importance of tradition in their hermeneutic. This usage includes both those who are not Baptists proper but are 'baptists' from the broader Free Church tradition according to the usage of McClendon (*Systematic Theology*, vol. 1, *Ethics*, pp. 17-35) and those who identify themselves as 'evangelicals' within other non-Free Church mainline Protestant denominations, while also recognizing the historiographical problems associated with an unqualified application of the term to Baptists (for various perspectives on this question, see J.L. Garrett, Jr., E.G. Hinson, and J.E. Tull, *Are Southern Baptists "Evangelicals"?* [Macon, Ga.: Mercer University Press, 1983]).

resources for vitality in a postmodern world by recovering the ancient tradition to which all Christians are heirs.[3]

One may find precedents for such a tradition-rooted program of renewal in the *nouvelle théologie* movement in twentieth-century European Roman Catholicism introduced in chapter 3 of this book. The theologians of the *nouvelle théologie* called for the work of *ressourcement*, the 'retrieval' of the ancient sources of the Christian tradition, as the necessary precursor to the subsequent task of *aggiornamento*, 'updating' the tradition in relationship to the contemporary situation. Towards these ends, the proponents of the *nouvelle théologie* engaged in much meticulous historical scholarship, producing critical editions of patristic texts and publishing numerous studies of patristic theology, but they also brought these traditional sources into dialogue with the intellectual currents of the twentieth century. Their emphasis on retrieval as a means to the revitalization of Catholicism in the mid-twentieth century has much in common with contemporary evangelical efforts to renew Protestantism by re-introducing it to its patristic roots.

While evangelical theology in general and Baptist theology in particular will profit greatly from an engagement with the theologians of the *nouvelle théologie*, there is a precedent and paradigm for Baptist and evangelical patristic *ressourcement* much closer to home in the theology of Karl Barth, whose third way beyond liberal and fundamentalist versions of modernism provided a theological haven for many Baptist theologians in North America during the second half of the twentieth century[4] and whose later theology of baptism as expounded in the fragmentary final part-volume of the *Church Dogmatics* provided unexpected encouragement to the Baptist position.[5] One of the main features of Barth's thought that distinguishes him from his Protestant contemporaries, including some of his early allies among the dialectical theologians, is his insistence on beginning with the community of faith and hearing the church's confession of faith as it comes

---

3   Williams, *Retrieving the Tradition and Renewing Evangelicalism*; Oden, *Agenda for Theology*, and his three-volume systematic theology *The Living God, The Word of Life*, and *Life in the Spirit*; R.W. Jenson, *Systematic Theology*, 2 vols. (New York: Oxford University Press, 1997-99). Retrieval of the ancient tradition of the undivided church is also central to the Catholic-Evangelical ecumenical programme reflected in Jenson's work with the Center for Catholic and Evangelical Theology and its journal *Pro Ecclesia*.

4   Many Baptist theologians of the era shared this experience, but it is exemplified well in print by B. Ramm, *After Fundamentalism: The Future of Evangelical Theology* (San Francisco: Harper & Row, 1983).

5   *CD* IV/4.

to him from other members of the church.[6] Barth articulates this communal understanding of the locus and function of tradition early in the section on 'Authority under the Word' in the *Church Dogmatics*:

> But it is obvious that before I myself make a confession I must myself have heard the confession of the Church, i.e., the confession of the rest of the Church. In my hearing and receiving of the Word of God I cannot separate myself from the Church to which it is addressed. I cannot thrust myself into the debate about a right faith which goes on in the Church without first having listened....If I am to confess my faith generally with the whole Church and in that confession be certain that my faith is the right faith, then I must begin with the community of faith and therefore hear the Church's confession of faith as it comes to me from other members of the Church. And for that very reason I recognise an authority, a superiority in the Church: namely, that the confession of others who were before me in the Church and are beside me in the Church is superior to my confession if this really is an accounting and responding in relation to my hearing and receiving of the Word of God, if it really is my confession as that of a member of the body of Christ.[7]

The contributions of Anselm, Luther, Calvin, and classic Protestant confessions to this 'hearing' of the church's confession are well known. What has not yet fully received the attention it deserves is Barth's sustained listening to patristic theology en route to developing his own theses about the church's teaching. The few published studies that have addressed this topic have focused either on Barth's appropriation of Nicaeno-Constantinopolitan and Chalcedonian perspectives or on his rejection of

---

6   G. Dorrien, *The Barthian Revolt in Modern Theology: Theology without Weapons* (Louisville, Ky.: Westminster John Knox, 2000), p. 2, observes that Barth 'drank more deeply from the well of Protestant orthodoxy than any of his counterparts, a fact that ultimately set him apart from most of them', but this observation could easily be extended to include Barth's deep drinking from the whole of the Christian tradition—patristic and medieval as well as Reformation and post-Reformation sources.

7   Barth *CD* I/2, p. 589. As early as the Göttingen lectures in dogmatics, Barth had insisted that 'no one reads the Bible directly', that 'we all read it through spectacles, whether we like it or not', and that these spectacles are properly supplied by the 'historical, relative, and formal' authority that resides in the church: 'Scripture cannot come to us as God's Word without there being an authoritative canon and text, fathers, dogma, and a teaching office' (K. Barth, *The Göttingen Dogmatics: Instruction in the Christian Religion*, ed. H. Reiffen, trans. G.W. Bromiley [Grand Rapids, Mich.: William B. Eerdmans, 1991], pp. 229 and 245). B.L. McCormack, *Karl Barth's Critically Realistic Dialectical Theology: Its Genesis and Development 1909-1936* (Oxford: Oxford University Press, 1997), pp. 346-50, provides a helpful exposition of Barth's developing understanding of a relative authority by which the church mediates the Word of God and the formation of an 'ecclesial hermeneutic' during the Göttingen period.

anything approaching a natural theology in the thought of the fathers.[8]
These studies have not given sufficient attention to Barth as a critical reader
of patristic texts in his own right, nor has Barth's patristic retrieval been
explored as a possible paradigm for the utilization of patristic theology in
constructive theology today. The remainder of this chapter first offers
biographical evidence of Barth's serious career-long interest in the early
church fathers as theological dialogue partners before setting forth several
observations on the overall shape of Barth's interaction with patristic
authors and texts in the *Church Dogmatics* and then concluding with
reflections on the possibilities of this interaction as a paradigm for a
contemporary Baptist and evangelical engagement with patristic theology.

Biographical Evidence of Barth's Interest in the Fathers

Connections with the early church fathers function as a sort of inclusio
framing Barth's earthly existence. In 1881, five years before Karl's birth,
his father Johann Friedrich ('Fritz') Barth was awarded his *Doktor der
Theologie* for a dissertation on Tertullian's interpretation of Paul.[9] The eve
of Karl's death found him writing a lecture for a forum of Catholic and
Reformed Christians in Zürich in which he was emphasizing the need for
the church to listen to its 'fathers' who in God are living voices.[10] In
between, Barth's theological education and later preparations for lecturing
and writing on dogmatics reveal a much more than passing interest in
patristics. As a theological student, he spent the 1906-1907 *Wintersemester*
in Berlin, where he principally devoted himself to the lectures of Adolf von
Harnack on the development of early Christian doctrine.[11] The following
year Barth submitted his qualifying dissertation for the *Magister* degree at
the University of Bern, a work of 194 pages on 'The Descent of Christ to

---

8   For an extensive treatment of Barth's interaction with patristic theology that
focuses primarily on his retrieval of Nicaeno-Constantinopolitan Trinitarianism and
Chalcedonian Christology, see E.P. Meijering, *Von den Kirchenvätern zu Karl Barth:
Das altkirchliche Dogma in der 'Kirchlichen Dogmatik'* (Amsterdam: J.C. Gieben,
1993). Others who have given attention to Barth's dialogue with patristic theology
include T.F. Torrance, 'Karl Barth and Patristic Theology', in *Theology Beyond
Christendom: Essays on the Centenary of the Birth of Karl Barth, May 10, 1886*, ed. J.
Thompson (Allison Park, Pa.: Pickwick Publications, 1986), pp. 215-39; A.H.
Armstrong, 'Karl Barth, the Fathers of the Church, and "Natural Theology"', *JTS* n.s.
46.1 (April, 1995), pp. 191-93; and G. Hunsinger, 'Karl Barth's Christology: Its Basic
Chalcedonian Character', in *Cambridge Companion to Karl Barth*, pp. 127-42.
9   E. Busch, *Karl Barth: His Life from Letters and Autobiographical Texts*, trans.
J. Bowden (Grand Rapids, Mich.: William B. Eerdmans, 1994), p. 1.
10   Busch, *Karl Barth*, pp. 497-98.
11   Busch, *Karl Barth*, pp. 38-40.

Hell in the First Three Centuries'.[12] Though he was acquiring the tools for patristic research, Barth was not yet ready to hear patristic voices as having something relevant to contribute to theological reflection in the present. In one of his early sermons as an assistant pastor in Geneva (1909-1911), Barth expressed his aversion to the Christ 'presented by the Chalcedonian Definition to the ancient Church', saying, 'I will gladly concede that if Jesus were like this I would not be interested in him'.[13]

A decade later, the commentary on Romans completely ignored the patristic exegetical tradition: therein is only a single, indirect reference to Augustine (though it should be granted that the commentary's polemical purposes naturally steered Barth toward other sorts of dialogue partners).[14] When the invitation to join the theological faculty in Göttingen eventually resulted in the opportunity to begin a cycle of lectures in dogmatic theology in the *Sommersemester* of 1924, Barth became convinced that his preparations must include a close reading of the major dogmatic works of the early church fathers.[15] In a circular letter sent to Eduard Thurneysen and other friends dated March 4, 1924, Barth mentioned the 'preliminary studies' for the lectures in dogmatics in which he had been engaged during the vacation between semesters: the apologies of Justin Martyr and Aristides, the *Octavius* of Minucius Felix, Origen's *Contra Celsum*, Tertullian, Athenagoras, the *Catechetical Oration* of Gregory of Nyssa, and Augustine's *Enchiridion*.[16] After listing these he exclaims, 'Wenn ich nur schneller Latein und Griechisch lesen könnte!' ('If only I could read Latin and Greek more quickly!')—a lament which suggests that at the very least Barth consulted the Greek and Latin texts and did not rely only on German translations. The authors and treatises Barth mentions were at that time readily available in German translation in the *Bibliothek der Kirchenväter* series, with the exception of Peter Koetschau's translation of *Contra Celsum*, which did not appear until 1926-27. These volumes doubtless would have been available to Barth in the Göttingen library, the vastness of

---

12   Busch, *Karl Barth*, p. 43.

13   Busch, *Karl Barth*, p. 54. Busch includes this statement in the context of several quotations from sermons dated 1910-11.

14   K. Barth, *Der Römerbrief*, 5th edn. (Münich: Chr. Kaiser Verlag, 1929), 'Register', pp. 526-28.

15   Busch, *Karl Barth*, p. 154.

16   E. Thurneysen, ed., *Karl Barth—Eduard Thurneysen Briefwechsel*, vol. 2, *1921-1930*, Karl Barth-Gesamtausgabe, vol. 5, *Briefe* (Zürich: Theologischer Verlag, 1974), p. 236; ET, J.D. Smart, ed. and trans., *Revolutionary Theology in the Making: Barth-Thurneysen Correspondence, 1914-1925* (Richmond, Va.: John Knox Press, 1964), pp. 175-76 (the ET ends the excerpt after the reference to Augustine's *Enchiridion*, while the original continues, 'Wenn ich nur schneller Latein und Griechisch lesen könnte!').

which had awed him with the immensity of the academic task he had undertaken in accepting the Göttingen professorship.[17] Since in the later *Church Dogmatics* he quoted only from the Greek and Latin texts of the fathers, it is likely that Barth read at least some of these texts from original language editions.

These 'preliminary studies' in patristic dogmatic treatises do not seem to have made identifiable contributions to this initial *Dogmatics*. In the *Göttingen Dogmatics* Barth did not refer at all to the aforementioned works of Aristides, Minucius Felix, Athenagoras, or Gregory of Nyssa.[18] The published form of these lectures from 1924-1926 contains only a single reference to Justin Martyr's *1 Apology*, one to Tertullian's *Apologeticum*, and one to Origen's *Contra Celsum*. Though there are thirty-two references to Augustine, none is to the *Enchiridion*.[19] Perhaps the reason for the relative silence of these sources in the *Göttingen Dogmatics* is Barth's frustration with his grasp of the 'strange new world' he encountered in the church fathers: in the circular letter of March 1924 he went on to say that what he encountered there was of 'ambiguous greatness and great

---

17   K. Barth to E. Thurneysen, 6 November 1921, in Thurneysen, ed., *Barth-Thurneysen Briefwechsel*, vol. 2, p. 6; referenced in McCormack, *Barth's Critically Realistic Dialectical Theology*, pp. 294-95.

18   There is a single reference to Gregory of Nyssa, but it is a general reference to Gregory from a secondary source and not a citation of the *Catechetical Oration* (K. Barth, *Unterricht in der christlichen Religion*, vol. 3, *Die Lehre von der Versöhnung/Die Lehre von der Erlösung (1925/1926)*, ed. H. Stoevesandt, Karl Barth-Gesamtausgabe, pt. 2, vol. 13 [Zürich: Theologischer Verlag, 2003], p. 83). In the prolegomena volume of the *Christian Dogmatics*—the publication of the initial cycle of lectures in dogmatics at Münster discontinued in published form in favor of beginning a dogmatics afresh with the *Church Dogmatics* in Bonn—Barth did cite the *Catechetical Oration* eight times, anticipating a more extensive conversation with Nyssene theology in the *Church Dogmatics* (K. Barth, *Die christliche Dogmatik im Entwurf*, vol. 1, *Die Lehre vom Worte Gottes: Prolegomena zur christlichen Dogmatik (1927)*, ed. G. Sauter, Karl Barth-Gesamtausgabe, pt. 2, vol. 7 [Zürich: Theologischer Verlag, 1982], 'Register II. Namen', pp. 605-13).

19   K. Barth, *Unterricht in der christlichen Religion*, vol. 1, *Prolegomena (1924)*, ed. H. Reiffen, Karl Barth-Gesamtausgabe pt. 2, vol. 9 (Zürich: Theologischer Verlag, 1985), 'Register II. Namen', pp. 384-87; vol. 2, *Die Lehre von Gott/Die Lehre vom Menschen (1924/1925)*, ed. H. Stoevesandt, Karl Barth-Gesamtausgabe, pt. 2, vol. 10 (Zürich: Theologischer Verlag, 1990), 'Register II. Namen', pp. 449-53; vol. 3, *Die Lehre von der Versöhnung/Die Lehre von der Erlösung (1925/1926)*, ed. H. Stoevesandt, Karl Barth-Gesamtausgabe, pt. 2, vol. 13 (Zürich: Theologischer Verlag, 2003), 'Register II. Namen'. As the currently available ET of the *Göttingen Dogmatics* translates only the first volume and one third of the second volume of the three volumes of that cycle of lectures in the *Gesamtausgabe*, its 'Index of Names' (pp. 483-86) yields only partial information for these purposes.

ambiguity', 'very new' and 'full of instruction' for him, but lamenting that he needed 'infinitely more time' to consider these things.[20] What these preparatory forays into patristic texts did provide was a basic familiarity with these resources that drew Barth back into dialogue with them during the work on the *Church Dogmatics* from 1929 onward, for in the *Church Dogmatics* he did make notable use of the specific treatises mentioned in the 1924 letter. Within the *Church Dogmatics* are seven references to the apologies of Justin Martyr, two to Aristides, four to Minucius Felix, thirty-eight to Tertullian (though Barth did not specify which works of Tertullian he read in 1924, the best inference from the letter is the *Apologeticum*, which Barth cited four times out of these thirty-eight references[21]), three to Athenagoras, fourteen to Gregory of Nyssa's *Catechetical Oration*, and numerous references to Augustine's *Enchiridion* among the 204 total references to Augustine. A more complete overview of the patristic presence in the *Church Dogmatics* follows in the next major section of the chapter.

Barth underwent a much more extensive immersion in patristic studies during a sabbatical leave in the *Sommersemester* of 1929 granted by the University of Münster in reward for his declining of an invitation to join the faculty at Bern. He spent the leave at the Bergli, a retreat home owned by friends Rudolph and Gerty Pestalozzi in Switzerland, working on an 'intensive reading of Augustine and also of Luther',[22] the fruit of which is reflected in the sheer number of references to both Augustine (204) and Luther (317) in the *Church Dogmatics*.[23] Barth's assistant Charlotte von Kirschbaum joined Barth at the Bergli and worked with him on this material throughout the sabbatical. It is not claiming too much for von Kirschbaum's contributions to suggest that she ought to be regarded as co-author of the 'fine print sections' of the *Dogmatics* in which the documentation of Barth's interaction with Augustine and the rest of the Fathers appears, if one understands co-authorship to include some degree of shared responsibility for research, outlining, occasional drafting, and editing. The style that emerges in the published form of the fine print sections, however, is arguably that of Barth, and other assistants who performed similar duties for Barth have sought to dispel rumors that these sections were essentially authored by von Kirschbaum but published under

---

20   Thurneysen, ed., *Barth-Thurneysen Briefwechsel*, vol. 2, p. 236.

21   McCormack, *Barth's Critically Realistic Dialectical Theology*, p. 334, reads the letter's mention of Tertullian in context as a reference to the *Apologeticum*.

22   Busch, *Karl Barth*, p. 184.

23   *CD: Index Volume with Aids for the Preacher*, ed. Bromiley and Torrance, pp. 185-205.

Barth's name.[24] Nevertheless, von Kirschbaum did do much spadework in the primary texts. In the early years of her assistantship to Barth, she studied Latin in order to read patristic, medieval, and Reformation texts,[25] and for these small-print note sections in the *Dogmatics* she gathered and arranged the primary and secondary texts with which Barth would interact and probably made preliminary sketches of some notes and possibly occasional inserts into the manuscript which Barth would not see until he corrected the page-proofs.[26] When one thinks of Barth as a reader of patristic texts, then, one ought to conceive of this as a collaborative reading of the fathers that is partly dependent on von Kirschbaum's own patristic scholarship (with the exception of the final fragmentary part-volume of volume IV of the *Church Dogmatics*, for which Eberhard Busch had assumed von Kirschbaum's former duties and in which, it is worth noting, there are comparatively few patristic references).

A pair of anecdotes illustrates Barth's interest in acquiring patristic texts for his own library. On a 1929 tour of Italy with his friends the Pestalozzis and von Kirschbaum during the summer sabbatical, Barth noticed and purchased a five-volume edition of the works of Ambrose of Milan in a street market. As Barth later wrote of the trip, 'From then on Ambrose took his firm and often somewhat disruptive place in the back of the car, so that Lollo [von Kirschbaum] can be said to have entered Rome between at least two church fathers'.[27] Presumably Barth was the other 'church father'. Paul Lehmann recalls coming to Bonn as a student in the early 1930s and making an appointment to meet Barth. When invited into Barth's study, Lehmann took note of the volumes of the Migne *Patrologia Graeca et*

---

24   S. Selinger, *Charlotte von Kirschbaum and Karl Barth: A Study in Biography and the History of Theology* (PSSLRE; University Park, Pa.: Pennsylvania State University Press, 1998), p. 77, referencing personal communications with Hinrich Stoevesandt and Eberhard Busch.

25   According to a letter from Barth at the Bergli to Thurneysen dated 29 April 1929, during this Bergli sabbatical Barth and von Kirschbaum periodically took breaks from their morning studies of Augustine and afternoon studies of Luther in order to study Latin and English together (Thurneysen, ed., *Barth-Thurneysen Briefwechsel*, vol. 2, p. 660), and two letters from Barth to Thurneysen during the subsequent *Wintersemester* in Münster mention thrice-weekly Latin lessons with a tutor taken along with Barth's daughter Franziska by von Kirschbaum 'um dereinst auch Reformatoren und Kirchenväter im Grundtext zur Kenntnis nehmen zu können' (Thurneysen, ed., *Barth-Thurneysen Briefwechsel*, vol. 2, pp. 688-89 and 705).

26   Selinger, *Charlotte von Kirschbaum and Karl Barth*, pp. 61 and 75-78; see also R. Köbler, *In the Shadow of Karl Barth: Charlotte von Kirschbaum*, trans. K. Crim (Louisville, Ky.: Westminster/John Knox, 1989), pp. 58-60.

27   Busch, *Karl Barth*, p. 186, citing K. Barth, 'Italienische Eilreise', unpublished manuscript account of the Italy trip.

Latina among other books lining Barth's shelves and commented on this as a contrast with the studies of Lehmann's professors at Union Theological Seminary. Barth's reply was to ask, '*What* do American theologians read, then?'[28]

The Shape of Patristic Retrieval in the *Church Dogmatics*

There is ample evidence in the *Church Dogmatics* that, contrary to John Yocum's assertion that 'Barth's explicit reliance on patristic sources is limited',[29] Barth was indeed a theologian who read extensively in Migne and other sources of patristic literature. The following six summary observations describe the overall shape of Barth's retrieval of patristic texts in the *Dogmatics*.

Patristic Conversation Partners

First, some statistical observations: The name register in the index volume to the *Church Dogmatics* includes a total of 686 references to eighty individual patristic authors.[30] Of these, seven qualify as Barth's major patristic dialogue partners (number of references in parentheses): Augustine (204), Irenaeus (44), Tertullian (38), Athanasius (34), Origen (26), John of Damascus (19), and Gregory of Nyssa (18). Eleven other patristic figures are cited between ten and fifteen times: Cyril of Jerusalem (15), Ignatius of Antioch (15), Pseudo-Dionysius the Areopagite (14), Justin Martyr (14), Basil of Caesarea (13), Gregory of Nazianzus (12), John Chyrsostom (11), Cyprian (11), Eusebius of Caesarea (10), Gregory the Great (10), and Marcion (10, if one counts general references to Marcion's teachings). Thirteen are referenced between five and nine times: Hilary of Poitiers (9), Ambrose of Milan (8), Jerome (8), Clement of Alexandria (7), Arius (6), Cyril of Alexandria (6), Nestorius (6), Pelagius (6), Vincent of Lérins (6), the *Shepherd of Hermas* (5), Hippolytus (5), Lactantius (5), and Theophilus of Antioch (5). References to forty-nine other ancient Christian writers, personages, or texts of anonymous or pseudonymous authorship appear from one to four times in the *Dogmatics*.[31] Some of the following observations will identify patterns in Barth's use of these sources.

---

28   P. Lehmann, 'The Ant and the Emperor', in *How Karl Barth Changed My Mind*, ed. D.K. McKim (Grand Rapids, Mich.: William B. Eerdmans, 1986), p. 38.

29   J. Yocum, 'What's Interesting about Karl Barth? Barth as Polemical and Descriptive Theologian', *IJST* 4.1 (March, 2002), p. 43, n. 56.

30   *CD: Index Volume*, pp. 185-205.

31   (Number of references in parentheses) Athenagoras (4), Epiphanius (4), Minucius Felix (4), Paul of Samosata (4), Aristides (3), *Epistle of (Pseudo-) Barnabas*

Augustine of Hippo

Second, it is obvious from these statistics that Augustine is Barth's patristic dialogue partner nonpareil. Almost thirty percent of the references to individual patristic authors are to Augustine. One might be inclined to attribute the Augustinian dominance of Barth's patristic interaction to his intensive study of Augustine in 1929, but there are more significant theological factors behind the frequency of reference to Augustine. On the one hand, Barth's chief dialogue partners among the Reformers whose perspectives on many matters Barth sought to retrieve and reinterpret in the *Church Dogmatics*, Luther and Calvin in particular, were themselves heavily indebted to Augustine. A fresh consideration of their contributions required a close reading of their Augustinian roots. On the other hand, Barth had earlier discerned in Augustine's emphasis on the inherence of divine grace in the *imago dei* the beginnings of a trajectory that ran through the medieval scholastic concept of the *analogia entis* to Schleiermacher's anthropocentrism.[32] Barth does of course employ Augustine to illustrate the ancient roots of theological directions that Barth himself affirms,[33] but

---

(3), Clement of Rome (3), Fulgentius of Ruspe (3), Melito of Sardis (3), Sabellius (3), Benedict of Nursia (2), Boethius (2), *Clementine Homilies* (2), *Didache* (2), Didymus of Alexandria (2), *Epistle to Diognetus* (2), Ephraem the Syrian (2), Eunomius (2), Eutyches (2), Isidore of Seville (2), Leo the Great (2), Macedonius of Constantinople (2), Novatian (2), Anthony (1), Apelles (1), Apollinaris of Laodicea (1), Arnobius (1), Artemon (1), Pseudo-Augustine (1), Celestine I (1), *2 Clement* (1), Dionysius of Rome (1), Eusebius of Emesa (1), Gennadius (1), Gregory of Elvira (1), Honorius I (1), *Protoevangelium of James* (1), Leo III (1), Macarius the Great (1), Marius Victorinus (1), Noetus of Smyrna (1), Papias of Hierapolis (1), Peter Chrysologus (1), Photius (1), Praxeas (1), Priscillian (1), Rufinus (1), Tatian (1), and Valentinus (1).

32   Barth traced these connections in a lecture in Elberfeld, Germany on 9 October 1929 titled 'Zur Lehre vom Heiligen Geist'; ET, *The Holy Spirit and the Christian Life: The Theological Basis of Ethics*, trans. R.B. Hoyle (Louisville, Ky.: Westminster John Knox, 1993), pp. 3-6; cf. the comments of Torrance, 'Karl Barth and Patristic Theology', p. 217. Following his summer of studies in Augustine and Luther and three weeks prior to the Elberfeld lecture, Barth wrote to Paul Althaus with reference to his rejection of certain directions in the thought of Emmanuel Hirsch, 'The extremely angry antithesis in which I find myself precisely in relation to his theology has once again become clear to me in a very lively way, remarkably through my preoccupation with Augustine. I believe that as long as we do not root Augustinianism completely out of the doctrine of grace, we will never have a Protestant theology' (K. Barth to P. Althaus, 14 September 1929, copy in Karl Barth-Arichiv, Basel; cited and translated by McCormack, *Barth's Critically Realistic Dialectical Theology*, p. 390).

33   E.g., *CD* III/1, pp. 8-10, where Barth opposes the tendency of Schleiermacher's followers to root knowledge of God as creator of the world in the religious self-consciousness of the 'absolute feeling of dependence' with Augustine's emphasis on the truth of God that God speaks through creation.

Barth's engagement of Augustine and the Augustinian tradition also turns polemical when he finds it necessary either to reject a concept of Augustine that in Barth's view had influenced the subsequent tradition in problematic directions or to offer an alternative reading of some aspect of Augustine's thought in contradistinction to what he viewed as a wrong-headed use of Augustinian concepts in later theology.[34] The positive imprint of Barth's sustained conversation with Augustine is principally seen in Barth's understanding of the intra-trinitarian relations. His defense of the *Filioque*, for example, proceeds from his interaction with Augustine just as naturally as the original insertion of *Filioque* into the Creed at the Third Council of Toledo in 589 did from the Western consolidation of the Augustinian tradition in the sixth century.[35]

Eastern Conversation Partners

Third, although the overwhelming number of references to Augustine might initially suggest that Barth's dialogue with the fathers is one-sidedly Western, closer examination demonstrates that this is not actually the case. Of Barth's seventeen most frequent patristic dialogue partners exclusive of Augustine—those cited between ten and forty-four times—thirteen are eastern fathers: Irenaeus (who was eastern in language and theological orientation though serving as bishop in the West), Athanasius, Origen, John of Damascus, Gregory of Nyssa, Cyril of Jerusalem, Ignatius of Antioch, Pseudo-Dionysius the Areopagite, Justin Martyr, Basil of Caesarea, Gregory of Nazianzus, John Chyrsostom, and Eusebius of Caesarea. The four Western exceptions are Tertullian, Cyprian, Gregory the Great, and Marcion; these are reduced to three if one eliminates the general references to the heretical positions of Marcion from the tally. Furthermore, the most explicit patristic contributions to the expression of Barth's theology are in the main Greek rather than Latin:[36] for example, Barth's championing of the Athanasian insistence on the unity of God's act and God's being[37] and his rejection of the Latin teaching that the Son of God assumed neutral human nature, unaffected by sin, in favor of the Greek perspective in which

---

34   E.g., *CD* I/1, pp. 239-40 and 45-46, where Barth first traces the *analogia entis* to Augustinian theology and rejects it but then points to hints in the direction of an *analogia fidei* elsewhere in Augustine.

35   *CD* I/1, pp. 473-87.

36   Torrance, 'Karl Barth and Patristic Theology', p. 219.

37   *CD* II/1, pp. 257-321. Barth does not cite Athanasius in this particular context, but as noted by Torrance, 'Karl Barth and Patristic Theology', pp. 223-24, Barth seems to have gleaned this insight from his interaction with Athanasius.

Christ takes fallen human nature upon himself in order to redeem and purify it.[38]

Communal Expressions of Patristic Theology

Fourth, a focus only on Barth's interaction with individual patristic authors would ignore the second most frequent and arguably most significant source of this interaction with the patristic tradition: the councils and creeds of the patristic age. There are eighty-seven references to patristic creeds and councils, bringing the total number of patristic references in the *Dogmatics* to 773. I suggest that these additional references ought to be considered a single source for two reasons. First, Barth invariably cites these from the Denzinger *Enchiridion Symbolorum*.[39] Though its contents certainly derive from separate sources, Barth repeatedly turned to this standard compendium of Catholic conciliar theology whenever he needed to consult the consensual teaching of the church during the patristic period. Second, Barth's theological methodology emphasized the indispensability of hearing the confession of the rest of the church before articulating dogma as an individual theologian.[40] This understanding of the place of the community in Christian confession meant that he accorded conciliar expressions of theology a status that surpassed that of the writings of individual theologians.[41] If one must attach specific patristic labels to the shape of Barth's thought, his theology is Nicaeno-Constantinopolitan and Chalcedonian in character rather than, say, Augustinian or Athanasian or Cappadocian.

---

38   E.g., *CD* IV/2, pp. 92-95; Torrance, 'Karl Barth and Patristic Theology', pp. 229-31. It should be noted that although patristic influence is undeniable in these aspects of Barth's thought, he does not directly link them with patristic citations in those immediate contexts. It is only in this sense that Yocum's claim that 'Barth's explicit reliance on patristic sources is limited' (Yocum, 'What's Interesting about Karl Barth?', p. 43, n. 56) has some basis in the textual evidence of Barth's engagement of patristic theology in the *Church Dogmatics*.

39   Barth's references correspond to the section numbering of the fourteenth/fifteenth edition: H. Denzinger, C. Bannwart, and J.B. Umberg, eds., *Enchiridion Symbolorum: Definitionum et declarationum de rebus fidei et morum*, 14th and 15th edn. (Freiburg im Breisgau: Herder, 1922).

40   *CD* I/2, pp. 585-660.

41   As early as the *Göttingen Dogmatics*, Barth had specified 'general ecclesiastical doctrinal decisions' as a particular locus of authority in the church. See McCormack, *Barth's Critically Realistic Dialectical Theology*, p. 347, citing Barth, *Unterricht in der christlichen Religion*, p. 279; ET *Göttingen Dogmatics*, p. 229.

Doctrinal Loci of the Conversation

Fifth, Barth's patristic retrieval is not evenly distributed throughout the doctrinal loci of the *Dogmatics*. The richest concentration of patristic references is in the two part-volumes of volume I, *The Doctrine of the Word of God*, with 378 references—almost half of the total patristic references in the *Dogmatics*. In contrast, the two part-volumes of volume II, *The Doctrine of God*, contain 125 references; the four part-volumes of the much-lengthier volume III, *The Doctrine of Creation*, have 156 references; and in the four part-volumes of volume IV, *The Doctrine of Reconciliation*, there are 115 patristic references. This pattern of distribution reflects the agenda of Barth's prolegomena volume: expounding the revelatory significance of the doctrines of the Trinity and the Incarnation would hardly have been possible apart from a careful consideration of patristic perspectives. In addition, the polemic against natural theology called for a tracing of its modern incarnations back to their ancient precedents as well as the exploration of alternative patterns in the ancient sources. As E.P. Meijering has noted, Barth's clear disagreements with the Fathers usually have to do with indications of a 'natural theology' in their thought.[42] The contesting of these disagreements thus also contributed to the lopsided patristic presence in volume I.

Agenda of the Conversation

Sixth, Barth did not go looking for prooftexts in the fathers to support his positions. Patristic references are sometimes notably absent in contexts in which there is a patristic precedent for Barth's own perspective. For example, Barth rejects the Origenist version of a dogmatic universalism as a denial of divine and human freedom, although the logic of Barth's doctrine of election points in the direction of universal salvation.[43] Yet Barth does not mention Gregory of Nyssa's understanding of a universal *apokatastasis* or restoration, even though Gregory's concept, like Barth's doctrine of election and unlike Origen's concept of *apokatastasis*, has ample room for both divine and human freedom and assumes a more orthodox protology that does not posit the preexistence of souls which fall

---

42   Meijering, *Von den Kirchenvätern zu Karl Barth*, pp. 10, 32, 48, 164-70, 304, 391, and 431. A.H. Armstrong explores this conclusion of Meijering's study in 'Karl Barth, the Fathers of the Church, and "Natural Theology"', pp. 191-95.

43   Barth mentions and rejects the scholastic Origenist concept of a necessary universal *apokatastasis* in *CD* II/2, pp. 295, 417, 422, and 476. Barth's rationale for rejecting such a dogmatic universalism is that if God must save humanity and humanity must be saved, then neither God nor humanity would be free (*CD* II/2, pp. 417-23).

into materiality, [44] and even though in other connections Barth made liberal use of the *Catechetical Oration* (thirteen references), within which is one of Gregory's clearest expressions of this distinctive concept, yet without mentioning this feature of the treatise.[45] Barth thus read the fathers not to ransack them for support but rather to listen to the doctrinal tradition of the church in its catholicity, a tradition that had the capacity to shape his perspectives and yet with which he had the freedom to disagree in light of a fresh hearing of the Word of God in Scripture.

Barthian Possibilities for Baptist and Evangelical Retrieval of Patristic Theology

A major motivation for the contemporary interest in retrieval of the early Christian theological tradition is the need for constructive ecclesial responses to the dissolution of modernity.[46] As it is not anachronistic to suggest that Barth was the first major postmodern theologian, and since a key component of Barth's efforts to move beyond modernity was his turn to the premodern tradition, and because this turn occurred within a Reformed ecclesial tradition that had been involved in a centuries-long process of disengagement from the pre-Reformation tradition, certain features of Barth's retrieval of the fathers serve well as paradigms for future Baptist and evangelical engagements of patristic theology.

Returning Ad Fontes

Contemporary theologians would do well to emulate the rigor of Barth's return to the sources of the pre-Reformation tradition in doing constructive

---

44   For recent explorations of this theme in the thought of Gregory of Nyssa, see M. Ludlow, *Universal Salvation: Eschatology in the Thought of Gregory of Nyssa and Karl Rahner* (OTM; Oxford: Oxford University Press, 2000), pp. 1-111 and 237-77, and S.R. Harmon, *Every Knee Should Bow: Biblical Rationales for Universal Salvation in Early Christian Thought* (Lanham, Md.: University Press of America, 2003), pp. 83-123.

45   Barth cites Gregory of Nyssa's *Catechetical Oration* (*Or. cat.*) in the following passages of the *Church Dogmatics*: *CD* I/1, p. 276 (*Or. cat.*); *CD* I/1, p. 411 (*Or. cat.* 14, 19); *CD* I/1, p. 413 (*Or. cat.* 8); *CD* I/2, p. 31 (*Or. cat.* 24); *CD* I/2, p. 38 (*Or. cat.* 24); *CD* I/2, p. 126 (*Or. cat.* 11); *CD* I/2, p. 153 (*Or. cat.* 15f); *CD* I/2, p. 169 (*Or. cat.* 10); *CD* II/1, p. 222 (*Or. cat.* 1); *CD* II/1, p. 333 (*Or. cat.* 20); *CD* III/1, p. 44 (*Or. cat.* 8); *CD* IV/1, p. 180 (*Or. cat.* 26); and *CD* IV/1, p. 192 (*Or. cat.* 24). Gregory clearly affirms the restoration of all rational creatures to their 'original state' in *Or. cat.* 26, though not in the portion of that chapter referenced by Barth in *CD* IV/1, p. 180.

46   E.g., Williams, *Retrieving the Tradition and Renewing Evangelicalism*, pp. 11-13; Oden, 'Then and Now', pp. 1164-68.

theology. A classical pre-university education and the orientation of theology toward historical *Wissenschaft* in Barth's university studies had prepared him for consulting the Greek and Latin texts of the Migne *Patrologia* rather than relying solely on the conveniently available German translations of the *Bibliothek der Kirchenväter*.[47] Some recent North American Baptist and evangelical authors of systematic theologies, however, have tended to content themselves with citing the nineteenth-century English translations of the *Ante-Nicene Fathers* and *Nicene and Post-Nicene Fathers* series[48] and sometimes seem to have limited their citations of patristic texts largely to those contained therein.[49] While those English translations may be more readily available to North American theologians and their readers, many of them have been superseded by more

---

47   F.X. Reithmayr and V. Thalhofer, eds., *Bibliothek der Kirchenväter* (Kempten: J. Kösel, 1860-88); O. Bardenhewer, T. Schermann, and C. Weyman, eds., *Bibliothek der Kirchenväter*, 2nd edn. (Kempten and Munich: J Kösel, 1911-); O. Bardenhewer, J. Zellinger, and J. Martin, eds., *Bibliothek der Kirchenväter*, 2nd series (Munich: J. Kösel, 1932-). On the other hand, the *Church Dogmatics* offers no evidence that Barth sought out superior critical texts that by Barth's days as a student and professor had superseded Migne, e.g. *Die griechischen christlichen Schriftsteller der ersten drei Jahrhunderte* (Leipzig: Hinrichs'sche Buchhandlung, 1897-) or *Corpus Scriptorum Ecclesiasticorum Latinorum* (Vienna: C. Geroldi, 1866-).

48   A. Roberts and J. Donaldson, eds., *Ante-Nicene Fathers*, 10 vols. (Buffalo, N.Y.: Christian Literature, 1885-1896); P. Schaff, ed., *Nicene and Post-Nicene Fathers*, First Series, 14 vols. (New York: Christian Literature, 1886-89); P. Schaff and H. Wace, eds., *Nicene and Post-Nicene Fathers*, Second Series, 14 vols. (New York: Christian Literature, 1890-98). These series have been regularly reprinted by William B. Eerdmans and most recently by Hendrickson; owing to the expiration of their copyright, they are now also widely available on the Internet (e.g. in the Christian Classics Ethereal Library, available online at www.ccel.org).

49   This tendency may be observed, e.g., in S.J. Grenz, *Theology for the Community of God* (Grand Rapids, Mich.: William B. Eerdmans, 2000), and *The Social God and the Relational Self: A Trinitarian Theology of the Imago Dei*, The Matrix of Christian Theology, vol. 1 (Louisville, Ky.: Westminster John Knox, 2001), though Grenz did on rare occasions venture beyond the *Ante-Nicene Fathers* and *Nicene and Post-Nicene Fathers* for a text only available elsewhere, as in the case of the more recently discovered *Demonstration of the Apostolic Preaching* of Irenaeus, which Grenz, *Social God and the Relational Self*, p. 146, n. 26, cites from J.P. Smith, trans., *St. Irenaeus: Proof of the Apostolic Preaching* (ACW, 16; New York: Newman Press, 1978). On the other hand, the wide availability of the older English translations does make it possible for readers with limited access to large libraries with comprehensive holdings of the more recent translations to consult the larger context of theologians' citations of patristic literature. One solution, though not implemented in the present book, might be to include references both to the most widely available translation and to the best or most recent translation of a cited treatise, whenever possible.

recent translations,[50] and in any case they are only a representative selection from the vastly larger corpus of patristic literature, much of which remains to be translated into English.

Collaborating in the Conversation

As products of a theological academy that has become much more rigidly compartmentalized into disciplinary specializations than in Barth's era, few contemporary systematic theologians—especially those formed in Baptist and evangelical communities—will possess the requisite expertise for a more thoroughgoing retrieval of patristic texts in their constructive theological work. In light of these limitations, the collaborative nature of Barth's patristic retrieval suggests a workable paradigm for Baptist and evangelical patristic *ressourcement*. Just as Barth's dialogue with patristic theology depended on the historical research of von Kirschbaum and others, so constructive theologians today may utilize the available handbooks and bibliographical guides to the primary and secondary literature in patristic studies[51] and would do well to cultivate relationships with the rapidly growing number of church historians and historical theologians who are specializing in patristics. Only through such collaboration—and the best theology is always a thoroughly communal enterprise—will Baptist and evangelical systematic theology move beyond the customary references to this or that church father as a representative of a particular early doctrinal position.

Discerning the Voice of the Community

As Barth recognized, however, all patristic literature is not of equal value for the theologian's hearing of 'the Church's confession of faith as it comes...from other members of the Church'.[52] He rightly privileged the

---

50   E.g., the translations in the following series: Ancient Christian Writers (New York: Newman Press, 1946-); The Fathers of the Church (Washington, D.C.: The Catholic University of America Press, 1947-); Oxford Early Christian Texts (Oxford: Clarendon Press, 1970-); Eastern Christian Texts in Translation (Leuven: Peeters Press, 1997-); Popular Patristics Series (Crestwood, N.Y.: St. Vladimir's Seminary Press).

51   E.g., B. Altaner and A. Stuiber, *Patrologie: Leben, Schriften und Lehre der Kirchenväter*, 8th edn. (Freiburg im Breisgau: Herder, 1978); J. Quasten, *Patrology*, 4 vols. [vol. 4 edited by A. Di Berardino] (Westminster, Md.: Christian Classics, 1990-91); F.M. Young, *From Nicaea to Chalcedon: A Guide to the Literature and Its Background* (Philadelphia: Fortress Press, 1983); F.M. Young, L. Ayres, and A. Louth, eds., *The Cambridge History of Early Christian Literature* (Cambridge: Cambridge University Press, 2004).

52   *CD* I/2, p. 589.

communal expressions of theology that emerged from the early councils and the catechetically-oriented comprehensive dogmatic treatises in which individual patristic theologians sought to give voice to that which the community taught. While some theory-driven scholarship might view the conciliar creeds as the efforts of an elite hierarchy to repress the belief and behavior of the common people 'from above', Jaroslav Pelikan makes a compelling case for John Henry Newman's earlier contention that the ancient creeds represent 'The Orthodoxy of the Body of the Faithful' by which the common people influenced and on occasion held the hierarchy accountable 'from below'.[53] In light of this grassroots communal dimension of the patristic conciliar doctrinal formulations, Barth's extensive engagement with the Denzinger *Enchiridion Symbolorum* may be interpreted as a crucial means of Barth's conversation with the confession of the whole church, in the membership of which Barth believed 'there are really no non-theologians'.[54]

Barth also privileged as patristic conversation partners those fathers and those treatises which attempted to set forth Christian doctrine more comprehensively for the primary purpose of catechetical instruction. This selectivity reflects a distinction between two legitimate aspects of the dogmatic task: 'regular dogmatics', by which Barth meant 'an enquiry into dogma which aims at the completeness appropriate to the special task of the school, of theological instruction' that may in turn provide 'guidance to independent dogmatic work, *and not just the imparting of the specific results of the work of a specific teacher*', and 'irregular dogmatics', by which Barth meant 'the enquiry into dogma in which there is no primary thought of the task of the school...and thus no primary concern for the completeness mentioned above', but which is also important for the church as 'free discussion of the problems that arise for Church proclamation from the standpoint of the question of dogma'.[55] In the first part-volume of the prolegomena to the *Church Dogmatics*, Barth identified Origen's *On First Principles*, Gregory of Nyssa's *Catechetical Oration*, Cyril of Jerusalem's *Catecheses*, Augustine's *Enchiridion*, and John of Damascus' *On the Orthodox Faith* as patristic examples of 'regular dogmatics', and it was to these specific treatises and their authors that Barth tended to gravitate in his

---

53 J. Pelikan, *Credo: Historical and Theological Guide to Creeds and Confessions of Faith in the Christian Tradition* (New Haven: Yale University Press, 2003), pp. 336-68. Pelikan's reference is to J.H. Newman, 'The Orthodoxy of the Body of the Faithful During the Supremacy of Arianism', an essay originally published in *The Rambler* in 1859 and later reprinted in an appendix to J.H. Newman, *The Arians of the Fourth Century*, 4th edn. (London: Longmans, Green, and Co., 1876), pp. 445-68.

54 Barth, 'Theology', in *God in Action*, p. 57.

55 *CD* I/1, pp. 275-77 (emphasis added).

conversations with the fathers.[56] By focusing on their role as interpreters of the teaching of the community rather than their role as individual speculative theologians, Barth was able to retrieve from the fathers the most fruitful traditional sources for a *church* dogmatics, an ecclesial reading of the Word of God in Scripture rooted in and undergirding the community's worship, formation, and witness.

Baptist Systematic Theology and Patristic Retrieval

The voice of the community present in patristic credal and conciliar documents and in the fathers' efforts to interpret and transmit that voice in their catechetical treatises is not easily heard in modern systematic theologies produced by Baptist theologians. In many of these, the engagement of conversational partners tends to function not as a conversation of the theologian with the community and its hearing of the Word of God as reflected in its confession and catechesis but rather as a conversation between an individual theologian interpreting an unmediated biblical text and other individual theologians who likewise interpret an unmediated biblical text. A.H. Strong exemplified this tendency in his too-rigid distinction between systematic theology and dogmatic theology.

> Dogmatic theology is, in its strict usage, the systematizing of the doctrines as expressed in the symbols of the church, together with the grounding of these in the Scriptures, and the exhibition, so far as may be, of their rational necessity. Systematic Theology begins, on the other hand, not with the symbols, but with the Scriptures. It asks first, not what the church has believed, but what is the truth of God's revealed word.[57]

In keeping with this understanding of the task of systematic theology and its relationship to the voice of the community in the creeds, councils, and catechetical teaching of the church, the systematic theologies not only by Strong (1907) but also by William Newton Clarke (1898), E.Y. Mullins (1917), and W.T. Conner (1924) made little place for these expressions of the church's 'hearing and receiving of the Word of God'.[58] In varying degrees the more recent systematic theologies of Dale Moody (1981), James Leo Garrett, Jr. (1990-95, 1st edn.), James Wm. McClendon, Jr.

---

56   *CD* I/1, p. 276.

57   A.H. Strong, *Systematic Theology: A Compendium*, 3 vols. in 1 (Valley Forge, Pa.: Judson Press, 1907), pp. 41-42.

58   W.N. Clarke, *An Outline of Christian Theology* (New York: Charles Scribner's Sons, 1898); E.Y. Mullins, *The Christian Religion in Its Doctrinal Expression* (Philadelphia: Judson Press, 1917); W.T. Conner, *A System of Christian Doctrine* (Nashville: Sunday School Board of the Southern Baptist Convention, 1924).

(1986-2000), and Stanley Grenz (1994) have conversed more extensively with these voices of the community.[59] Yet present and future generations of Baptist theologians would benefit from a more intentional adoption of Barth's approach to the discernment of the voice of the community in its confessional and catechetical literature and principal teachers as a paradigm for their own selection and engagement of dialogue partners. Otherwise, as Pelikan has warned with a slightly different application in mind, they may run 'the danger of exaggerating the significance of the idiosyncratic thought of individual theologians at the expense of the common faith of the church'.[60]

Listening Eastwards and Westwards

While Augustine's voice dominated among the individual patristic dialogue partners Barth engaged in conversation, the retrieval of this voice in particular was perhaps a necessary facet of Barth's engagement of the Reformation and its Catholic context. As Reinhard Hütter notes, a dialectical engagement of the Reformers and Catholicism was already a formal feature of the Göttingen cycle of lectures in dogmatics, but the engagement of Catholicism became an experiential one only in Barth's move to Münster, a predominantly Catholic city where the Catholic theological faculty in the university was much older and larger than the Protestant theological faculty, which was founded only ten years before Barth joined it.[61] Since Barth utilized the sabbatical granted by the university near the end of his time in Münster for an intensive study of Augustine and Luther, it is likely that it was the encounter with Catholicism there that pushed him to engage Augustine more intentionally. Baptist and

---

59   D. Moody, *The Word of Truth: A Summary of Christian Doctrine Based on Biblical Revelation* (Grand Rapids, Mich.: William B. Eerdmans, 1981); Garrett, *Systematic Theology: Biblical, Historical, and Evangelical*, 2 vols. (1990-1995; 2nd edn., 2000-2001); McClendon, *Systematic Theology*, 3 vols. (1986-2000); Grenz, *Theology for the Community of God* (1994).

60   Pelikan, *Christian Tradition*, vol. 1, p. 3. In context, Pelikan is guarding against a confusion of the history of doctrine with the more general history of theology or the history of Christian thought.

61   R. Hütter, 'Karl Barth's Dialectical Catholicity: *Sic et Non*', ch. 5 in R. Hütter, *Bound to Be Free: Evangelical Catholic Engagements in Ecclesiology, Ethics, and Ecumenism* (Grand Rapids, Mich.: William B. Eerdmans, 2004), pp. 80-81 and 242-45, nn. 7-12; see also Busch, *Karl Barth*, pp. 177-89 on the Münster encounter with Catholicism. Similar experiential encounters with Catholicism were also significant for the theological development of the Baptist theologian James Wm. McClendon, Jr., who taught at the University of San Francisco 1966-69 and served as a visiting professor at the University of Notre Dame 1976-77.

evangelical theologians entering into ecumenical conversation with Roman Catholicism and the denominational descendants of the Magisterial Reformation will similarly need to involve Augustine in this conversation. But they should also follow the example of Barth's equally extensive conversation with the Eastern fathers, which kept Barth's patristic retrieval from being one-sidedly Western. Barth's work predated the late twentieth-century emergence of Eastern Orthodoxy as a major contributor to international ecumenical Christianity, but contemporary Baptist and evangelical theologians cannot ignore this tradition and its roots in Greek and oriental patristic thought. Occasional conflict between Orthodox Christians and Baptists in post-Soviet Eastern Europe should underscore for Baptist theologians in particular the importance of retrieving for Baptists the Eastern patristic heritage they ought to share in common with their Orthodox brothers and sisters.

Catholicity Beyond Trinitarian and Christological Orthodoxy

The location of the center of gravity in Barth's conversation with the fathers in the volumes of the *Church Dogmatics* dealing with the self-revelation of the Triune God may suggest a starting point for a Baptist and evangelical entry into patristic retrieval for constructive theology. As Trinitarian theology and Christology are the doctrinal rubrics under which mainstream Baptist and evangelical theology will already be in more direct continuity with patristic theological perspectives, it would be natural for theologians from these traditions to begin there in a conscious appropriation of the patristic tradition as their own heritage. But as it is precisely at the point most distant from the center of gravity in Barth's conversation with the fathers in the *Church Dogmatics*, ecclesiology, that Baptists and many evangelicals may find themselves most at odds with aspects of the patristic tradition and perhaps with other denominational traditions today, Baptist and evangelical theologians will need to choose a different path from Barth if they are to bring the totality of their theologies into dialogue with the fathers. More than two decades after the Lima document on *Baptism, Eucharist and Ministry* issued by the Faith and Order Commission of the World Council of Churches, many Baptist bodies worldwide have not responded to this crucial ecumenical proposal or have not received it in as welcoming a manner as might be desired,[62] nor has there been much Baptist

---

62   *Baptism, Eucharist and Ministry*, Faith and Order Paper No. 111 (Geneva: World Council of Churches, 1982). For published Baptist responses, see W.R. Estep, 'A Response to *Baptism, Eucharist and Ministry*: Faith and Order Paper No. 111', in W.H. Brackney and R.J. Burke, eds., *Faith, Life and Witness: The Papers of the Study and Research Division of the Baptist World Alliance 1986-1990* (Birmingham, Ala.:

interest in the more recent Princeton Proposal for Christian Unity.[63] If Baptists and evangelicals in the Free Church tradition are to be equipped for more significant participation in and more adequate responses to these and other ecumenical proposals, their theologians must begin to engage more comprehensively the ecclesiology and sacramental theology of the 'Great Tradition' of the undivided patristic church to which all denominational traditions today are heirs.

Listening Critically

Finally, Barth's engagement of patristic theology exemplifies a hermeneutic of tradition that remains sensitive to Baptist and evangelical concerns about traditionalism while also avoiding the hermeneutical naïveté of a radicalized *Sola Scriptura* that moves too easily from the ancient text straightway to contemporary theological construction. Though Baptist and evangelical rejections of tradition as a source of theological authority tend to characterize tradition primarily in terms of the more static sense of tradition as *traditia*, the 'things handed over'—creeds, conciliar canons, theological texts—that have accumulated throughout the history of the church as the products of the traditioning process, Barth understood the tradition of the church more in terms of *traditio*, 'a handing over', the dynamic process of traditioning that included both the formation of 'the Church's confession of faith as it comes to me from other members of the Church' and his own 'hearing and receiving of the Word of God' and

---

Samford University Press, 1990), pp. 2-16; M. Thurian, ed., *Churches Respond to Baptism, Eucharist and Ministry*, 6 vols. (Geneva: World Council of Churches, 1986-88); and *Baptism, Eucharist and Ministry 1982-1990: Report of the Process and the Responses*, Faith and Order Paper No. 149 (Geneva: World Council of Churches, 1990). A notable positive Baptist response to BEM came from the Myanmar (formerly Burma) Baptist Convention, which not only publicly affirmed the call of BEM to refrain from the re-baptism of those previously baptized as infants but also commended the document to the churches of the Convention to use as a study guide to help Baptists appreciate the theological significance of infant baptism in other communions (reported in Anglican Consultative Council and Baptist World Alliance, *Conversations Around the World 2000-2005*, pp. 50-51).

63   C.E. Braaten and R.W. Jenson, eds., *In One Body through the Cross: The Princeton Proposal for Christian Unity* (Grand Rapids, Mich.: William B. Eerdmans, 2003). Although there were no Baptists among the sixteen theologians and ecumenists selected by the Center for Catholic and Evangelical Theology to form the ecumenical study group that drafted and signed the Princeton Proposal, the program for a subsequent conference on the proposal at the University of Notre Dame in 2004 did announce a plenary paper delivered by Baptist theologian Timothy George on 'Papal Authority as Ecumenical Problem'.

'confession as a member of the body of Christ'.[64] Barth regarded this tradition as neither fixed nor infalliable, and he was free to take issue with various developments in the tradition—but only after first having heard fully the tradition handed over to him in and by the church. Barth's conversation with the fathers in the *Church Dogmatics* exemplifies moral philosopher Alasdair MacIntyre's characterization of a 'living tradition' as 'an historically extended, socially embodied argument, and an argument precisely in part about the goods which constitute that tradition'.[65] The best retrieval of the patristic tradition is not merely the replication of past patterns of faith and practice but rather the embodied appropriation and continuation of the argument about the goods of the Christian tradition extended to us by the saints who have gone before in the church. Barth could debate as well as defend patristic doctrinal formulations in his dialogue with the fathers. Baptists and others who have been deeply formed by the tradition of dissent may easily adopt this particular aspect of Barth's patristic retrieval. Indeed, it may be especially the contested character of Barth's conversation with the fathers that makes it a most suitable paradigm for a Baptist and evangelical *ressourcement* of patristic theology.

However salutary an intentional retrieval of the theological tradition of the church in its catholicity may be for Baptist constructive theology, such retrieval will remain a theoretical enterprise unless Baptist ministers formed by theological catholicity succeed in making the weekly worship of local Baptist congregations the primary context for the formation of worshippers by this tradition. The next chapter turns from the life of theologians in the Baptist academy to the life of Baptist congregations at worship and makes several concrete proposals for a more intentional Baptist integration of 'praying and believing', of worship and theology.

---

64   *CD* I/2, p. 589.
65   MacIntyre, *After Virtue*, p. 222.

CHAPTER 8

Praying and Believing: Retrieving the Patristic Interdependence of Worship and Theology

'From earth's wide bounds, from dawn to setting sun,
Through heaven's gates to God the three in one
They come, to sing the song on earth begun:
Alleluia! Alleluia!' *W.W. How*[1]

'Christian worship is a gathering of the church in the name of Jesus Christ and in the power of the Holy Spirit in order to meet God, through Scripture, prayer, proclamation and sacraments and to seek God's kingdom.' *Baptist Union of Great Britain, Gathering for Worship: Patterns and Prayers for the Community of Disciples*[2]

'It is a most invaluable part of that blessed "liberty wherewith Christ has made us free", that in his worship different forms and usages may without offence be allowed, provided the substance of the Faith be kept entire; and that, in every Church, what cannot be clearly determined to belong to Doctrine must be referred to Discipline; and therefore, by common consent and authority, may be altered, abridged, enlarged, amended, or otherwise disposed of, as may seem most convenient for the edification of the people, "according to the various exigency of times and occasions".' *The Book of Common Prayer of the Protestant Episcopal Church in the United States of America (1789)*[3]

One of my undergraduate college professors—a Baptist minister teaching in a Baptist college—frequently made the wry observation, 'Baptists are neither a thinking people nor a worshipping people.' Although I have since encountered many exceptions to both parts of that aphorism, I have become

---

1   'For All the Saints', hymn 478 in *Baptist Praise and Worship* (Oxford: Oxford University Press, 1991), stanza 7; text by W.W. How (altered), tune by R.V. Williams.

2   Baptist Union of Great Britain, *Gathering for Worship*, pp. xiv-xv.

3   'Preface' to *The Book of Common Prayer* (1789), printed in *The Book of Common Prayer and Administration of the Sacraments and Other Rites and Ceremonies of the Church, together with the Psalter or Psalms of David, according to the Use of the Episcopal Church* (New York: Oxford University Press, 1979), p. 9.

convinced that the latter deficiency has something to do with the former malady. There is indeed a connection between a Baptist lack of attention to some of the key liturgical practices by which the wider church has traditionally formed the minds of worshippers and a Baptist failure to cultivate the life of the Christian mind as a matter of devotion. A de facto a-liturgical approach to Christian discipleship among Baptists has fostered in many Baptists an unconsciously a-theological faith.

Baptists in the United States are in fact giving attention to worship today, but unfortunately much of that attention is focused on the widespread 'worship wars' that have broken out when local congregations have contemplated introducing contemporary music or 'seeker-sensitive' elements into their worship services. Some Baptist congregations have embraced 'contemporary worship', but this designation usually means simply that their services feature music of recent composition in popular styles. Baptist congregations that have resisted the use of contemporary music in their services tend to have one of the following two self-understandings of their worship. Some congregations describe their services as 'traditional worship', by which they mean not patterns of worship that have been handed over from one generation to another in the church for centuries but rather worship as the long-term members of the congregation remember it being done in the Baptist churches of their own experience. Some Baptist congregations, often historic downtown or university-bordering churches, practice what they call 'liturgical worship' (a redundancy inasmuch as all worship is *leitourgia*, 'service' to God), but frequently this means only that their services are more formal in tone, include music that is classical in composition or style, and feature ministers who wear robes. In such cases 'liturgy' is often little more than a veneer of formality and musical and intellectual sophistication applied to common Baptist patterns of worship. Other congregations have attempted mediation through 'blended worship', but invariably this means only that some of the music used in worship is recent in composition and popular in style, while some is earlier in composition and either classical in style or reflective of styles popular in previous generations. All of these positions in the current controversies over worship tend toward a myopic preoccupation with matters of superficial style that remains oblivious to more serious deficiencies in the substance of much Baptist worship—contemporary, traditional, liturgical, or blended. A pair of questions is not being adequately addressed in Baptist congregations in their debates over the style of their worship. First, how do the various acts of worship in a worship service contribute to the healthy theological formation of Christians? Second, what is the nature and content of the theology by which Christians are being formed in worship?

The ecclesial theologians of the patristic period, however, understood worship and theology as interdependent, inseparable practices. The greatest contribution that a Baptist retrieval of patristic Christianity may make to the renewal of contemporary Baptist life is not through the retrieval of specific patristic theological perspectives or practices per se (though such forms of retrieval may be salutary) but rather through the recovery of worship as the primary means by which people are formed in deeply Christian faith and practice, accompanied by the recovery of particular patterns and practices of worship that are patristic in origin yet have great potential for forming the contemporary faith of the church. After a fresh consideration of the manner in which worship and theology were interdependent in patristic Christianity and reflection on the extent to which this interdependence is already operative in Baptist worship, this chapter identifies specific theologically formative patterns and practices of worship that Baptists should consider retrieving from patristic Christianity and offers practical suggestions for the patient implementation of such patterns and practices in the weekly worship of Baptist congregations.

The Interdependence of Worship and Theology in Patristic Practice: A Narrative Interpretation

The patristic perspective on the proper relationship between worship and theology is concisely expressed by a pair of axioms from the writings of the church fathers. According to the fourth-century monastic theologian Evagrius of Pontus (345-399), 'If you are a theologian, you will pray truly; and if you pray truly, you will be a theologian'.[4] Evagrius here reflects the influence of his teacher Gregory of Nazianzus (c. 329-390), who during a resurgence of Arianism in the last half of the fourth century had discerned in Neo-Arian teaching a rationalistic approach to theology that was disconnected from the life of worship.[5] During a period of conflict in the early fifth-century Western church between adherents to the teachings of Augustine on the one hand and followers of Pelagius on the other concerning the relation of divine grace and the human will, Prosper of Aquitaine (c. 390-after 455) appealed to the church's liturgy as evidence against the position of the Semipelagians: the fact that in the liturgy

---

4   Evagrius of Pontus *Chapters on Prayer* 60 (ET, 'Chapters on Prayer', ch. 8 in R.E. Sinkewicz, trans. and ed., *Evagrius of Pontus: The Greek Ascetic Corpus. Translation, Introduction, and Commentary* [OECS; Oxford: Oxford University Press, 2003], p. 199.

5   Gregory of Nazianzus addresses these concerns in his *Theological Orations*, especially the first *Theological Oration* (*Oration* 27 in the complete collection of Gregory's *Orations*). ET, 'The Theological Orations', trans. C.G. Browne and J.E. Swallow, in *Christology of the Later Fathers*, ed. E.R. Hardy (LCC; Louisville: Westminster John Knox Press, 1954), pp. 128-214.

ministers throughout the Christian world entreat God to bring people to faith is evidence that the church has traditionally associated the experience of salvation with God's gracious initiative rather than human efforts to attain it. In making this argument, Prosper urged that one 'let the rule of prayer lay down the rule of faith' (*lex supplicandi statuat legem credendi*).[6] In the shortened formula *lex orandi, lex credendi* ('the rule of praying is the rule of believing'), Prosper's maxim has become influential for much subsequent reflection on the proper relationship between the doctrine and worship of the church. Worship is the norm for doctrine, and conversely doctrine norms worship.[7]

The classical example of the function of the *lex orandi, lex credendi* principle in patristic Christianity is the Pneumatomachian controversy addressed by the First Council of Constantinople (381). Led by Eustathius of Sebaste (c. 300-c. 380), the Pneumatomachians ('Spirit-fighters') denied that it was proper to name the Spirit as God, arguing partly from the precedent of early patterns of liturgy reflecting the economy of salvation that glorified 'the Father through the Son' (or after Nicaea I, 'and the Son') '*in* the Holy Spirit'. Their opponents such as Gregory of Nazianzus contended that the biblical description of the work of the Spirit is an account of the one work of salvation of the one God in which the three persons of the Trinity fully share. It is therefore theologically proper, they argued, to give directly to the Holy Spirit the same worship given to God the Father and, in accordance with Nicaea, God the Son. The second ecumenical council, Constantinople I (381), reflected this theological argument in the expanded third article of the creed associated with the council, the Nicaeno-Constantinopolitan Creed (commonly called the 'Nicene' Creed, though it is not the creed adopted by the Council of Nicaea): 'We believe in the Holy Spirit...who with the Father and the Son is worshipped and glorified'. This pneumatological position is subsequently incorporated into the liturgy, with various economic patterns of trinitarian doxology yielding to a version of the *Gloria Patri* rooted in the Nicaeno-Constantinopolitan perspective on the immanent Trinity: 'Glory be to the Father and to the Son and to the Holy Spirit', the version sung to this day even in many Baptist and other Free Church congregations.

Both parties in the Pneumatomachian controversy exemplify the close connections between worship and doctrine in patristic Christianity. In that case and in the aforementioned arguments of Prosper of Aquitaine against the Semipelagians, theologians with varying relationships to what comes to

---

6   Prosper of Aquitaine 'Official Pronouncements of the Apostolic See on Divine Grace and Free Will' 8, in *Defense of St. Augustine* (ACW, 32), p. 183.

7   Wainwright, *Doxology*, p. 218, understands the order of the participles *orandi* and *credendi* as reversible, so that 'worship influences doctrine, and doctrine worship'.

be recognized as orthodoxy appeal to a particular liturgical tradition as evidence for what they contend is a more traditional expression of a specific doctrinal position, and in the case of the Pneumatomachian controversy a particular doctrinal definition influences the development of the liturgy. An even more pervasive connection may be found between theology and worship in patristic Christianity if one understands the essence of ancient Christian worship as the participatory rehearsal of the story of the Triune God. Such an interpretation is both consistent with and augmented by the basic tenets of the narrative theology movement in recent British and American theology:[8] (1) the originary and essential language of Christian faith and practice is narrative rather than propositional in form; (2) the Christian narrative both shapes and is shaped by the Christian community; and (3) as persons become Christian, their stories are shaped by their identification with the Christian community and its narrative.[9] These features of a narrative account of Christian faith and practice are evident in the earliest description of Christian worship outside the New Testament in the *First Apology* of Justin Martyr (d. c. 165).

And on the day called Sunday, all who live in cities or in the country gather together to one place, and the memoirs of the apostles or the writings of the prophets are read, as long as time permits; then, when the reader has ceased, the president verbally instructs, and exhorts to the imitation of these good things. Then we all rise together and pray, and, as we before said, when our prayer is ended, bread and wine and water are brought, and the president in like manner offers prayers and thanksgivings, according to his ability, and the people assent, saying Amen; and there is a distribution to each, and a participation of that over which thanks have been given, and to those who are absent a portion is sent by the deacons. And they who are well to do, and willing, give what each thinks fit; and what is collected is deposited with the president, who succours the orphans

---

8   See, e.g., D. Ford, *Barth and God's Story: Biblical Narrative and the Theological Method of Karl Barth in the 'Church Dogmatics'* (SIHC, 27; Frankfurt: Peter Lang, 1981); Lindbeck, *Nature of Doctrine*; H. Frei, *Theology and Narrative: Selected Essays*, ed. G. Hunsinger and W.C. Placher (Oxford: Oxford University Press, 1993); S. Hauerwas and L.G. Jones, eds., *Why Narrative? Readings in Narrative Theology* (Grand Rapids, Mich.: William B. Eerdmans, 1989); G. Loughlin, *Telling God's Story: Bible, Church, and Narrative Theology* (Cambridge: Cambridge University Press, 1996). Although narrative theology has primarily developed within Anglo-American circles, there are exceptions to this generalization: e.g., J.B. Metz, 'A Short Apology of Narrative', in *Why Narrative?*, ed. Hauerwas and Jones, pp. 251-62.

9   This summary of the essential points of narrative theology is adapted from S.R. Harmon, '"Doctrines in the Form of a Story": Narrative Theology in Gregory of Nyssa's *Oratio Catechetica Magna*', in *Studia Patristica: Papers Presented at the Thirteenth International Conference on Patristic Studies held in Oxford, 2003*, ed. E.J. Yarnold and M. Wiles (Louvain: Peeters Publishers, forthcoming 2006).

and widows, and those who, through sickness or any other cause, are in want, and those who are in bonds, and the strangers sojourning among us, and in a word takes care of all who are in need. But Sunday is the day on which we all hold our common assembly, because it is the first day on which God, having wrought a change in the darkness and matter, made the world; and Jesus Christ our Saviour on the same day rose from the dead. For He was crucified on the day before that of Saturn (Saturday); and on the day after that of Saturn, which is the day of the Sun, having appeared to His apostles and disciples, He taught them these things, which we have submitted to you also for your consideration.[10]

All the acts of worship described by Justin in one way or another rehearse, enact, and invite participation in the story of God as disclosed in Jesus Christ. The overarching pattern of word and table, the basic framework for Sunday worship through the next two millennia, underscores the essential narrative character of early Christian worship in which the story is heard, touched, tasted, and embodied in various ways. The story of God's saving acts in Jesus Christ is made present through the reading of 'the memoirs of the apostles'—today's New Testament Scriptures—and connected to the larger story of the people of God, 'the writings of the prophets'—the Scriptures of our Old Testament. The exhortation 'to the imitation of these good things', a homily or sermon, invites worshippers to make the story their own and embody it. Corporate prayer simultaneously narrates salvation history through thanksgiving and leads believers to enter the story through their assent of 'Amen' to the president's voicing of their supplications. 'Participation' in the Eucharist is a tangible embrace of the story and an enactment of its communal dimensions; this communal story is also embodied in the diaconal extension of the Eucharist to those who are absent and in the collection for the care of those in need. The rationale for Sunday as the day of the common assembly links the story rehearsed in the assembly with the Hebrew creation narrative and with the new creation inaugurated by the resurrection of Jesus Christ. Sunday worship also places the story within the calendar, reinterpreting the progression of time in light of the Christian story.

Second-century Christians doubtless performed acts of worship not mentioned in Justin's brief summary, and in subsequent centuries additional forms of prayer, confessions of faith in the form of credal recitation, the various seasons of the full Christian calendar, and other liturgical practices joined the church's developing liturgical tradition. These developments retained the basic framework of word and table along with the essential narrative character of this framework and served in many cases to make the narrative substructure of the liturgy even more explicit. The careful and creative incorporation of patristic patterns and practices of liturgy into the

---

10   Justin Martyr *1 Apology* 67 (ET, ANF 1:185-68).

worship of the contemporary church can contribute to the church's renewal by helping the church to tell the Christian story more consistently, more thoroughly, and more effectively. As worshippers have the divine story imprinted upon their consciousness and find their place within this story week after week over a long period of time, they are formed in the faith and fitted for the practices that constitute the Christian life.

Rehearsal of the Divine Story in Typical Baptist Worship

Telling and entering into the Christian story in the context of worship is not alien to the Baptist experience of worship. Even though much Baptist worship has long been disconnected from some of these traditional means of making the divine story present in worship, a typical Baptist worship service also has an essential narrative character and includes various acts of worship that narrate salvation-history and invite people to make that story their own. The following generalizations about Baptist worship reflect my own experience of Baptist life in the Southern United States. But because they are based on three-and-a-half decades of conscious recollections of participation in Baptist worship services, membership in fourteen different Baptist congregations of various sizes and demographics, service as pastor of three rural congregations during my theological education and interim pastor of two congregations since becoming a theological educator, and hundreds of guest preaching and teaching experiences in a wide variety of Baptist congregations, these observations are likely to be broadly representative of Baptist life in this context.

The overarching structure of a typical Baptist worship service reflects the influence of two factors: a deeply entrenched anti-sacramentalism and revivalism. One manifestation of the anti-sacramental bent of Baptists in this context is an aversion to weekly communion. A common rationale offered for more infrequent celebrations of 'the Lord's Supper'—once a quarter or, less commonly, once a month—is a desire to maintain its special meaningfulness and keep it from becoming a meaningless routine through frequent repetition.[11] As a result, the standard Baptist worship service is not a service of word and table but rather a service of the word, which nonetheless is capable of a multifaceted telling of the Christian story in itself. Revivalism has also left its imprint upon Baptist worship, not only in the addition of an evangelistic invitation to a service of the word but also in a different sort of twofold division of the service: the 'music service' or 'song service' and the 'preaching service', a division that reflects the role of

---

11   Such rationales fail to convince, as those who offer them would likely deny emphatically that such regular acts of Baptist worship as the singing of hymns or the preaching of sermons lose their significance through weekly repetition.

revivalist musicians such as Ira Sankey (1840-1908) in leading those in attendance at evangelistic rallies in congregational singing as a preparation for hearing the evangelistic sermon. The emphasis on music in the first half of the service has unfortunately tended to reinforce an unconscious identification of worship with music, one result of which is that recent conflicts over worship in Baptist congregations have been essentially conflicts about musical style.[12] This musical portion of the service is nevertheless also capable of a multifaceted telling of the Christian story through the singing of hymns, choruses, solos, and choral anthems.

Within the overarching framework of a service of the word with its twofold division of the sung word and the preached word, there are numerous acts of worship performed Sunday after Sunday in Baptist worship services that have the function of rehearsing and reinforcing the Christian narrative. They include parallels to the acts of worship described by Justin Martyr: the act of gathering on Sunday, the reading of Scripture, a sermon, prayers, corporate responses (Justin's 'Amen' or other responses such as responsive readings/litanies and more informal responses invited by worship leaders such as 'good morning' or 'praise the Lord'), the Supper (when celebrated), and an offering. These acts point to a remarkable continuity between mid-second-century early Christian worship as described by Justin and typical Baptist worship two millennia later. In addition to these, typical Baptist worship services often include other liturgical acts that narrate salvation-history and invite worshippers to become a part of it. Many Baptist congregations will sing the 'Doxology' each Sunday in connection with the offering, underscoring the Trinitarian shape of the Christian story and making the offering a response to the work of the Triune God in creation and redemption. An opportunity to extend a greeting to fellow worshippers through handshakes, hugs, and informal conversation or through a formal invitation to extend a specific Christian greeting to one another reinforces the communal nature of the Christian story and, if properly explained, guards against participation in the divine story degenerating into a merely individual encounter with God (a constant threat in the American expression of Baptist life). An invitation to respond to the challenges of the sermon and to the beckoning of God in other aspects of the service reflects the cherished Baptist emphasis upon personal commitment and makes explicit the need for active appropriation of the Christian story in one's own life. Typical Baptist worship is thus already a bearer of doctrinal tradition in the form of the first-order telling of the story

---

12   The identification of music and worship in Baptist congregations is also reinforced through the tendency in Baptist institutions of theological education in the United States to assign the teaching of courses in worship to professors of church music.

of the Triune God via a variety of acts of worship that communicate this story.

Theologically Formative Patterns and Practices from Patristic Worship: Resources for Retrieval

The Baptist narration of the Christian story in the context of worship may be enhanced, however, through the retrieval of additional patterns and practices from the worship of the patristic church that are capable of bearing even thicker narrations of the story and of calling forth even deeper involvement in it and transformation by it in the experience of worshippers. These include observance of the full Christian year, the adoption of a common lectionary for the reading and proclamation of Scripture, movement toward services of word *and* table as the normal pattern for Sunday worship, corporate recitation of the ancient creeds, patristic forms of prayer that have particular value for their integration of doctrine and worship, confession of sin and declaration of pardon, the passing of the peace, telling the stories of exemplary saints, and even the occasional singing of hymns with texts of patristic composition. These additional patterns and acts of worship may be included in every single service of Sunday worship, even in a Baptist congregation. Over time, they would form Baptist worshippers theologically in a manner much more effective than any program of Christian education or discipleship that occurs outside the context of worship services.

Calendar

All Baptist congregations observe some sort of calendar in their worship. Though many Baptists may profess that they 'judge all days to be alike', in reality they do 'judge one day to be better than another' (Rom. 14.5) in the expectation they have for certain days and seasons of the year to be recognized in Baptist worship services. Some of these are the inheritance of the patristic church and its calendar. Easter was explicitly named as a regular feast of the church in the second century and was probably celebrated well before then, perhaps even in apostolic times, for the early controversies about its dating presuppose an origin of regular celebration in first-century Jewish Christianity prior to the parting of the ways between synagogue and church.[13] December 25 was celebrated as the Christmas feast the Nativity of Christ beginning in the fourth century in the West

---

13   P.G. Cobb, 'The History of the Christian Year', in *The Study of Liturgy*, rev. edn., ed. C. Jones, G. Wainwright, E. Yarnold, and P. Bradshaw (London: SPCK/New York: Oxford University Press, 1992), pp. 459-60.

and the fifth century in the East.[14] Other special dates on the calendar of a typical Baptist church reflect the official holidays of the secular calendar in the United States: New Year's Day, Valentine's Day, Mother's Day, Memorial Day, Father's Day, Independence Day, Labor Day, and Thanksgiving Day may all be expected to receive at least some attention in the Sunday service nearest those holidays. In some cases attention to these days in worship may even trump observance of significant feasts of the Christian calendar—the occasional coincidence of Trinity Sunday with Father's Day, with the latter celebrated and the former ignored, being a notable example.

If Baptist churches already observe a calendar without regarding such observances as unbiblical practices that hinder congregational freedom, and if they have already granted pride of place in this calendar to two Christian feasts of patristic origin, then they can certainly observe the Christian year in its fullness without protesting that such additional observances are 'un-Baptistic'. This Christian rendering of time begins with Advent (celebrated beginning in the sixth century), a four-week penitential season with an eschatological focus, anticipating the coming of Christ to our world in the present and in the second advent as well as anticipating the commemoration of his first advent at Christmas. Christmas is a two-week festival, with the 'twelve days of Christmas' beginning on 25 December and continuing through 5 January. Epiphany, a season of variable length depending on the date of Easter that begins on 6 January and extends to the beginning of Lent, was celebrated as a commemoration of the baptism of Christ beginning in the third century, but by the fourth century in the West it became also associated with the manifestation of Christ to the Gentiles in the persons of the Magi. Lent, a penitential season of forty days from Ash Wednesday to Easter, is first mentioned in the canons of the Council of Nicaea in 325. The culmination of Lent with the observances of Holy Week—Palm Sunday, Maundy Thursday, Good Friday, Holy Saturday, and the Paschal Vigil—likewise dates to the fourth century. Without Lent, and Holy Week in particular, the celebration of the resurrection on Easter Sunday communicates an overly-realized eschatology that neglects the proper connection of the hope of the resurrection to the cross as the primary paradigm for living the Christian life in the midst of the sufferings of life in its already-but-not-yet-redeemed condition between the advents.[15] Easter is not a single Sunday but a festal season of fifty days—a 'fifty-day long

---

14   F.L. Cross and E.A. Livingstone, eds., *The Oxford Dictionary of the Christian Church*, 2nd edn. (Oxford: Oxford University Press, 1974), s.v. 'Christmas'.

15   This Easter-sans-Lent pattern is exemplified by a Baptist college in the United States that for several years has celebrated the week *prior* to Easter Sunday as 'Resurrection Week' in campus chapel observances.

Sunday'—with the Ascension commemorated on the fortieth day.[16] Pentecost, celebrated on the fiftieth day (the eighth Sunday) after Easter, also dates to the fourth century as a recognized liturgical observance. Regular celebration of Pentecost and observance of the following Sunday, Trinity Sunday, would do much to strengthen the pneumatological and Trinitarian weaknesses in Baptist faith and practice. These Sundays mark a transition from a focus on the eschatological-Christological-soteriological-pneumatological aspects of the faith during the portion of the liturgical year that precedes them to an ecclesiological focus during the remainder of the liturgical year (referred to as Sundays after Pentecost, Sundays after Trinity, or ordinary time in different traditions).

Observing all the seasons of the Christian year places the weekly narration of the divine story within a larger narrative framework that leads worshippers year after year through the story of Christ and his church. The congregation's awareness of the progression of liturgical time will be heightened through the use of the traditional colors that since the twelfth century have come to correspond to the seasons of the Christian year, reinforcing the year's telling of the story with the sense of sight: purple for Advent and Lent; green for Epiphany and the Sundays after Pentecost; white during Christmas, on Easter, and on Trinity Sunday; and red on Palm Sunday, Good Friday, and Pentecost.[17]

Lectionary

Although Baptists have sometimes called themselves 'people of the Book', many Baptist congregations hear very little Scripture in the context of worship. A biblical text associated with the sermon may be read earlier in the service or as part of the sermon; typically this is a text chosen by the preacher. The result of such practices is that the congregation not only consumes a very meager diet of Scripture year after year but also appropriates a very narrow unofficial canon, read through the theological lenses of the pastor's own 'canon-within-the-canon'.

The patristic church began developing systematic cycles for the comprehensive reading of Scripture in worship that specified readings from the Psalms, Old Testament, Gospels, and other New Testament books during the fourth century. These lectionaries probably began as expansions of the Jewish lectionary cycles inherited by Jewish Christians and employed in their own worship, expanded to include Gospel readings and other New Testament texts. Use of such lectionaries had important

---

16   Cobb, 'History of the Christian Year', p. 463.
17   Cross and Livingstone, eds., *Oxford Dictionary of the Christian Church*, s.v. 'Colours, Liturgical'.

implications for the church's narration of its story in weekly worship. Contra Marcion and the Gnostics, the lectionary emphasized the continuity of the church's story with the story of Israel. The lectionary undergirded a canonical reading of Scripture in which specific texts derive their meaning from their relation to the larger story told by the whole canon, and the culmination of the weekly lections in the Gospel reading suggested a Christocentric hermeneutic for the reading of the larger story and its specific episodes in the texts for the day. As the early lectionaries eventually were linked to the seasons of the full liturgical year, the narration of the divine story through the reading of Scripture in worship became joined to the manner in which the Christian year unfolds the story of Christ and his church. Following the public reading of Scripture with the ancient words exchanged between reader and congregation, 'The word of the Lord/Thanks be to God' (or for Gospel readings, 'The Gospel of our Lord/Praise to you, Lord Christ'), provides worshippers with an opportunity to make a personal response to the invitation to make this story their own.

Some pastors may object to consistent use of the lectionary out of a fear that they will not have as much flexibility to address emerging needs in the world, community, or life of the congregation as they would if they chose their own texts. On the contrary, sticking to the readings of the *Revised Common Lectionary*[18] or other standard lectionary on the Sunday following events such as the 11 September 2001 terrorist attacks in the United States or the 26 December 2004 Southeast Asian tsunami can yield serendipitous connections between text and world that may reframe current events in light of the whole Christian story much more deeply than the surface connections between an event and the obvious text to which the minister gravitates for a sermon on such occasions. Preaching from a given week's Old Testament, Epistle, and Gospel readings pushes the preacher towards the coherence that is found only in the readings' relationship to the overarching biblical metanarrative, which fits worshippers with the lenses they need for seeing their world and themselves rightly. This kind of preaching will always be relevant.

Word and Table

The patristic pattern of word and table as the twofold structure of Sunday worship provides the ideal setting for a multifaceted, multi-sensory telling of the Christian story. The word as bearer of the Christian story has a sacrament-like quality in that human words, and in particular the human words of the Scriptures, become means by which the story of the Triune

---

18   Consultation on Common Texts, *The Revised Common Lectionary* (Nashville: Abingdon Press, 1992).

God becomes present as the Spirit breathes the Word of God through them. In turn, the sacrament of the Supper (and early Baptists did not shrink from calling it a sacrament[19]) has a word-like quality in that it is a tangible enactment of the story. In the Lord's Supper the bread and the cup become tangible means by which the story may be seen, held, and tasted as well as heard. Services of word and table also draw special attention to the Christocentricity and eschatological orientation of the story told in worship, as in the Supper worshippers 'proclaim the Lord's death until he comes' (1 Cor. 11.26).

It is no mere coincidence that the most severely truncated versions of the Christian narrative in Gnosticism also denied the material order as the sphere of God's redemptive work. Recovering the regular observance of word and table in worship may help Baptists not only to narrate the story of the Triune God more fully but in doing so may also help counter the Gnostic tendencies in American expressions of Baptist life noticed by observers such as Harold Bloom.[20] In the history of Christianity there exist two primary patterns of conceiving of God's relationship to the world and of ordering Christian faith and practice in light of this conception: sacramental Christianity and Christian Gnosticism. There are of course various places on a continuum between these two primary patterns. But the extent to which a particular Christian tradition is non-sacramental is the extent to which that tradition is ultimately Gnostic in the way it conceives of God's relationship to the world and orders its faith and practice accordingly. Weekly services of word and table will do much to help Baptists move towards the sacramental, and thus away from the Gnostic, on that continuum.

Creed

The ancient creeds known as the Apostles' Creed and the Nicaeno-Constantinopolitan ('Nicene') Creed had roots in earlier baptismal confessions and the *regula fidei* that in turn summarized the essence of the apostolic preaching in the form of condensed versions of the Christian narrative. By the fifth century the Nicaeno-Constantinopolitan Creed was recited in Eucharistic services. Eventually the Western church recited the

---

19   E.g., the *Orthodox Creed*, a 1678 General Baptist confession, refers to baptism and the Lord's Supper as 'the two sacraments' in article 27 (Lumpkin, *Baptist Confessions of Faith*, p. 317).

20   H. Bloom, *The American Religion: The Emergence of the Post-Christian Nation* (New York: Simon & Schuster, 1992), p. 22: 'Mormons and Southern Baptists call themselves Christians, but like most Americans they are closer to ancient Gnostics than to early Christians'; cf. also pp. 195-96, 202, 207, 209.

Apostles' Creed (which dates to the sixth century in its present form but has antecedents that date to the second century) in baptismal and non-Eucharistic services and the Nicaeno-Constantinopolitan Creed in services in which the Eucharist was celebrated, while the Eastern church recited the latter creed in all these contexts. Recital of the creed in worship rehearsed the story worshippers had confessed and made their own in baptism. The emphasis on the incarnational aspects of the story in the Nicaeno-Constantinopolitan Creed made it particularly well suited for recitation in Eucharistic services, as it connects the material elements of the Eucharist in which Christ is present in worship with the joining of divinity with materiality in the Incarnation in order to redeem the material order.

Not a few Baptists would consider recitation of the ancient creeds in a worship service to be contrary to traditional Baptist faith and practice. One reason Baptists tend to regard the creeds as 'un-Baptististic' is the oft-repeated slogan 'No creed but the Bible!' Many Baptists take this to be a concise declaration of historic Baptist identity. In 2009 Baptists will have existed for 400 years as an identifiable denomination, but as previous chapters have noted, it has only been during the past century and a half that some Baptists in the United States have echoed this slogan. Its origins are outside the Baptist movement proper in the work of Alexander Campbell (1788-1866), founder of the Disciples of Christ. Campbell's aversion was not to the ancient creeds per se—he frequently referenced them in his writings—but rather to the coercive use of more detailed Protestant confessions as tests of fellowship. Baptists are right to resist this coercive use of either creeds or confessions, but they would be wrong to let this legitimate concern keep them from experiencing the benefits of the proper uses of the creeds.

The Apostles' Creed and Nicaeno-Constantinopolitan Creed are properly used as expressions of worship. They are not lists of doctrinal propositions to which people are compelled to give assent; they are summaries of the biblical story of the Triune God, drawn from the language of the Bible itself. The creeds function as the Christian 'pledge of allegiance', for they declare the story to which Christians committed themselves in baptism. Reciting the creeds thus regularly renews the baptismal pledges of worshippers. Reciting the creeds invites worshippers to locate afresh their individual stories within the larger divine story that is made present in worship, for credal recitation is a form of 'symbolic' participation not only in the story of the Triune God but also in the very life of the Triune God that the story references and rehearses, a function suggested by the use of *symbolon* in patristic Greek as a term for a creed.[21] Reciting the creeds

---

21   According to Lampe, *Patristic Greek Lexicon*, s.v. '*symbolon, to*', the basic meaning of *symbolon* is a '*symbol* representing a reality (freq. supra-sensible) other than

impresses upon worshippers again and again the overarching meaning of the Bible and so shapes their capacity for hearing and heeding what specific passages of Scripture have to say to them. Reciting the creeds invites worshippers into diachronic solidarity with the saints gone before who for two millennia have confessed this story with these same words. Reciting the creeds declares worshippers' synchronic solidarity with sisters and brothers in Christ in other denominations who today embrace the story of the Triune God.

Having no fixed or mandated liturgy, Baptist churches are free to adopt whatever worship practices they find beneficial. Freely choosing to experience the benefits of rehearsing the divine story by confessing the ancient ecumenical creeds is a most Baptist thing for free and faithful Baptists to do. Regular recitation of the creed as an act of worship may be the single most important means by which Baptists can retrieve the patristic interdependence of theology and worship in their own weekly rehearsal of the Christian story.[22]

Prayer

All acts of worship function as forms of prayer, but spoken prayers addressed to God by the congregation and its members have particular functions in the narration of the story of God in worship. Robert Wilken observes that in patristic liturgy, prayer had 'a distinct narrative function', for 'to praise God is to narrate what he has done'.[23] Wilken illustrates this function of prayer in patristic worship by describing the prayer of thanksgiving in the fifth-century *Liturgy of Saint James*.

---

itself'. In the context of discussions of Christian worship, the fathers employed *symbolon* in the sense of a 'sacramental rite', with reference to the 'sacrament of baptism' and to the 'eucharistic elements both before and after consecration, as a symbol in some sense united with that which it signifies', and also to a 'ritual *formula*...hence *creed*'. This background and usage suggests a quasi-sacramental function for the creed as symbol, a function that is neither merely symbolic nor simply a matter of cognitive contemplation of the content of the story summarized by the creed. Corporate recitation of the creed is a means by which the congregation may participate in the divine life, just as the sacraments of baptism and the Eucharist are means of participation in the divine life—and among other liturgical acts that have a similar function, one might add the reading and proclamation of Scripture, which Baptists have invested with a de facto sacramentality.

22   Portions of the final three paragraphs in this subsection are adapted from S.R. Harmon, 'Do Real Baptists Recite Creeds?' *BapTod* 22.9 (September, 2004), p. 27.

23   R.L. Wilken, *The Spirit of Early Christian Thought: Seeking the Face of God* (New Haven: Yale University Press, 2003), pp. 32-33.

[T]he prayer of thanksgiving in the liturgy begins with praise and adoration of
God but then retells, in capsule form, the biblical story from creation through the
giving of the Law to the people of Israel to the coming of Christ, his death and
Resurrection, and the expectation of his coming again: 'You are holy, ruler of all
things...who made man from the earth in your own image, who did not forsake
him when he transgressed your command...who called him by the law and
instructed him by the prophets, and in the last times you sent your only begotten
Son our Lord Jesus Christ into the world that by his coming he might renew and
restore your image....In the night in which he was betrayed...he took
bread...saying, "Take eat this is my Body which is given for you".' The liturgy
kept intact the biblical narrative, and by recounting the story of Israel and Christ
in ritual form in confirmed Christian belief that God's fullest revelation came
through historical events.[24]

Such prayers were not merely recollections of God's past actions, however.
They made salvation-history present, so that 'the past becomes a present
presence that opens a new future'.[25] In prayers of adoration and
thanksgiving, worshippers offer themselves to God to become participants
in God's story, so that in prayer God's story and the worshipper's story
become intertwined.

Retrieval of the 'collect' form of prayer that originated in patristic
liturgy (and continues to be utilized in the contemporary liturgies of various
traditions) can contribute to the theological formation of worshippers
through its narrative dimensions. In the Latin liturgy around the time of Leo
I (440-461), the *collectio* was a prayer voiced by a leader of worship on
behalf of the congregation that had the function of collecting together the
prayers of the people. Patristic collects included the following elements:
'(1) an address to God; (2) a relative or participial clause referring to some
attribute or saving act of God; (3) the petition; (4) the purpose for which we
ask; (5) the conclusion', with the second and fourth elements sometimes
omitted.[26] The conclusion was either Christological (e.g., 'through Jesus
Christ our Lord') or Trinitarian (e.g., 'through Jesus Christ our Lord, who
lives and reigns with you and the Holy Spirit, one God, now and forever').
A collect from the late patristic/early medieval Gallican liturgy exemplifies
these elements:

O God the Trinity, Whose Name is ineffable, Who purifiest the cavern of man's
heart from vices, and makest it whiter than the snow; bestow on us Thy
compassions; renew in our inward parts, we pray Thee, Thy Holy Spirit, by
Whom we may be able to show forth Thy praise; that being strengthened by the

---

24   Wilken, *Spirit of Early Christian Thought*, p. 33.
25   Wilken, *Spirit of Early Christian Thought*, p. 35.
26   P.G. Cobb, 'The Liturgy of the Word in the Early Church', in *The Study of
Liturgy*, ed. Jones et al., pp. 224-25.

righteous and princely Spirit, we may attain a place in the heavenly Jerusalem; through Jesus Christ our Lord.[27]

It is not necessary to pray collects of patristic composition in order to benefit from the capacity of this patristic form of public prayer for narrating the divine story and inviting worshippers into it, although occasional use of a patristic collect may help to emphasize the connection of the Christian past to the prayers of the present in the communion of saints. The collect form may serve as the framework for the minister's composition of contemporary prayers intended to summarize and voice the prayers of the congregation, such as this collect written for the Sunday following 11 September 2001.

O God, you created us to live in families where love and gentleness are shared. Bless those whose homes have been shattered by the violence of war, theft, terrorism, and murder. Bless those who have died that they may rest in your eternal love and protection. Restore unto the survivors the gift of peace, tranquility, and trust that their world may be whole again; in the name of Christ who brought peace into this world, we pray. *Amen.*[28]

Careful and creative use of the collect form provides opportunities for the theological formation of the congregation through prayer. The address and subsequent relative or participial clauses serve to rehearse the story of what God has done or develop the character of the Triune God as the main character in the story through declarations of the attributes of the God to whom worshippers offer prayer. The petitions and the naming of the purposes of the petitions make explicit the worshippers' connections to this divine story and express their desire that they and their world move towards the eschatological future, towards God's goals for the transformation of the kingdom of this world into the kingdom of God. Given the lack of attention to the doctrine of the Trinity in much Baptist faith and practice, it would be well for worship leaders to end as many collects and other public prayers as possible with a Trinitarian conclusion.

These theological functions of prayer in the worship of the church are also operative in another practice of even earlier patristic origin, the corporate praying of the Lord's Prayer, in which divine and human participation in the story is framed by the already-but-not-yet-realized nature of biblical eschatology. The 'we' and 'our' first-person plural

---

27   W. Bright, *Ancient Collects and Other Prayers*, 7th edn. (Oxford: James Parker, 1902), p. 37.

28   'Collect for September 11', available online on the web site of St. Augustine by-the-Sea Episcopal Church, Santa Monica, California, USA at http://www.saint-augustine.org/_oct02/ef1002i.htm.

language in both the collect form and the Lord's Prayer also underscore the communal motif in the narration of the story and help prevent the rehearsal of the story from degenerating into a tale about the individual's relationship with God, as sometimes happens whenever leaders of public prayer use 'I' and 'me' first-person singular language. Corporate worship is not simply a gathering of people who engage in their individual devotions in close proximity to one another. The practice of voiced first-person plural communal prayers reminds the worshipper that as a new creation in Christ she is fundamentally an ecclesial person for whom 'we' and 'our' take precedence over 'I' and 'my'.

Confession and Pardon

A pre-Eucharistic confession of sin was a feature of ancient Christian worship as early as the *Didache*, a late first- or early second-century document that mentions the practice.[29] In various forms corporate confessions of sin and declarations of pardon have continued to be weekly practices in the worship of many Christian denominations. The *Book of Common Prayer*, for example, provides this prayer of confession and declaration of pardon in the spirit of the patristic tradition as part of the Sunday Eucharistic service:

Minister and People

Most merciful God, we confess that we have sinned against you in thought, word, and deed, by what we have done, and by what we have left undone. We have not loved you with our whole heart; we have not loved our neighbors as ourselves. We are truly sorry and we humbly repent. For the sake of your Son Jesus Christ, have mercy on us and forgive us; that we may delight in your will, and walk in your ways, to the glory of your Name. Amen.

The Bishop when present, or the Priest, stands and says

Almighty God have mercy on you, forgive you all your sins through our Lord Jesus Christ, strengthen you in all goodness, and by the power of the Holy Spirit keep you in eternal life. *Amen.*[30]

In keeping with traditional Baptist perspectives on the priesthood of all believers and the relationship between clergy and laity, Baptist congregations might wish to have the minister pronounce the declaration of pardon using the words specified by the *Book of Common Prayer* when a

---

29   *Didache* 14.1 (K. Lake, trans., *The Apostolic Fathers* [LCL, 24; Cambridge, Mass.: Harvard University Press, 1912], vol. 1, p. 331).

30   *Book of Common Prayer* (1979), p. 360.

deacon or layperson offers the declaration of pardon, substituting 'us' for 'you' and 'our' for 'your'.[31] *Gathering for Worship: Patterns and Prayers for the Community of Disciples* (Baptist Union of Great Britain) has adapted for Baptist use multiple prayers of confession and declarations of pardon from *Common Worship: Services and Prayers for the Church of England* and other sources along with confessions and assurances composed specifically for this book of worship resources,[32] including a prayer of confession—of Baptist composition—that incorporates as a repeated congregational response a prayer from ancient Greek liturgies that has survived, in Greek, in the Latin Mass and its vernacular translations and remains in Greek in this Baptist act of worship: *'Kyrie eleison'* ('Lord, have mercy').[33] If a key intersection of the divine story and the worshipper's story is the experience of being forgiven by God and the practice of granting forgiveness to others, this part of the story ought to be enacted every time believers gather for worship.

Passing of the Peace

Justin Martyr's *First Apology* attests to the greeting of one another with the kiss of peace between 'the prayers' and the bringing forward of the bread and the cup for the celebration of the Eucharist, a practice that probably is the continuation of the apostolic-era practice of greeting 'one another with a holy kiss' enjoined by Paul (Rom. 16.16, 1 Cor. 16.20, 1 Thess. 5.26).[34] As a result of the twentieth-century liturgical renewal movement and its retrieval of patristic patterns of liturgy, post-Vatican II Roman Catholic worship and the liturgies of several Protestant traditions have restored the passing of the peace to weekly worship. In an accommodation to modern Western greeting customs, Western worshippers today pass the peace to one another not with a kiss but by shaking hands and saying 'The peace of the Lord be with you.'

Like the practice of self-consciously communal prayer, the passing of the peace reinforces and enacts the 'horizontal' dimension of the Christian story. Someone once remarked to me that it irritated him when congregations stood up and greeted one another in the middle of the service, because 'I don't like having my worship interrupted.' The rationale offered for his aversion to contemporary versions of passing the peace reflects an individualistic understanding of worship as a private encounter between the individual worshipper and God, an understanding all too

---

31   *Book of Common Prayer* (1979), p. 80.
32   Baptist Union of Great Britain, *Gathering for Worship*, pp. 308-17.
33   Baptist Union of Great Britain, *Gathering for Worship*, pp. 312-13.
34   Justin Martyr *1 Apology* 65 (ET, ANF 1:185).

common among Baptists. Retrieving the passing of the peace can counter this understanding by providing a concrete way for the worshipper to act as an ecclesial self in the context of worship.

Lives of the Saints

The early church's rehearsal of the divine story in worship was not limited to word, table, prayer, and other verbal and symbolic means of telling the story. The story was also incarnated in exemplary persons whose life of Christian discipleship provided believers with concrete examples of what the Christian way of life, the life lived in light of and as part of the Christian story, 'looked' like. Within the framework of the Christian year, patristic Christianity also developed and followed a 'sanctoral', a listing of feast days for the commemoration of the saints. Initially these were martyrs whose stories of having confessed Christ even unto death were retold in worship on the days commemorating their deaths. Eventually the sanctoral after the 'peace of the church' also included ascetics, virgins, bishops, and other exemplary saints widely regarded as worthy models of the Christian life.[35]

Though lacking the formal canonization process that is prerequisite for inclusion in the modern Roman Catholic sanctoral, the *Book of Common Prayer*, the *Lutheran Book of Worship*, and some other Protestant books of worship have included calendars with commemoration days for saints ancient and modern, including more recent figures such as Dietrich Bonhoeffer and Martin Luther King, Jr. If Baptist historians were to propose additional exemplary Christians from the Baptist tradition to add to such calendars in producing a sanctoral that is both distinctively Baptist and broadly ecumenical, Baptist congregations might be able to include in their own weekly worship a few moments for telling the stories of men and women who have provided worthy examples of lives lived in the service of God and humanity. When the life of the model Christian being commemorated on a given Sunday serves to illustrate the living of the stories told in the lectionary texts for the day, the lives of the saints would serve as ideal sermon illustrations—lived biblical stories rather than anecdotes that parallel sermonic ideas. The late Baptist theologian James Wm. McClendon, Jr. offered seminal suggestions for incorporating the lives of the saints into Baptist worship in an appendix to his groundbreaking study in narrative theology *Biography as Theology*. In this treatment of 'Christian Worship and the Saints', McClendon developed a theology of the relation of the departed among the *communio sanctorum* to

---

35   K. Donovan, 'The Sanctoral', in *The Study of Liturgy*, ed. Jones et al., pp. 472-84.

the worship of the earthly church that is both consistent with the 'baptist' vision and yet broadly catholic. On the basis of these guiding theological principles, McClendon advocated a 'baptist' retrieval of the veneration (in the sense of honoring, not worshipping) of the saints in the worship and educational programs of congregations.[36] McClendon's suggestions are the starting point for future Baptist attempts to recover the patristic practice of the commemoration of the saints for contemporary Baptist worship.

Hymns

The singing of hymns is already the principal means by which Baptist congregations supplement the narration of the Christian story in the reading and proclamation of Scripture with other means of telling the story. In hymnals issued by Baptists during the twentieth century, hymns have also become the primary means by which the Baptist nuancing of the Christian story is linked with the versions of the Christian story told by other denominations, inasmuch as these recent Baptist hymnals incorporate a vast repertoire of hymnody of Baptist and non-Baptist composition. Some of these hymn texts are actually patristic in composition.

The Baptist Hymnal published in 1991 under the auspices of the Southern Baptist Convention is the hymnal currently used not only by most Southern Baptist congregations but also by those that now identify more closely with the Cooperative Baptist Fellowship. This hymnal includes seven hymns with hymn texts written during the patristic period (through the eighth century, though for the Western church in this period some scholars will date the beginnings of the medieval era earlier): 80 *Let All Mortal Flesh Keep Silence* from *The Liturgy of St. James* (fifth century); 126 *All Glory, Laud, and Honor* by Theodulph of Orleans (c. 750-821); 164 *The Day of Resurrection* by John of Damascus (c. 675-c. 749); 251 *Of the Father's Love Begotten* by Aurelius Clemens Prudentius (c. 348-after 405); 252 *Glory Be to the Father*, the anonymous Trinitarian doxology of the fourth century with wording reflecting the developments of the First Council of Constantinople (381); 356 *Christ Is Made the Sure Foundation*, an anonymous Latin hymn of the seventh century; and 414 *O Christ, Our Hope, Our Heart's Desire*, an anonymous Latin hymn of the eighth

---

36   McClendon, *Biography as Theology*, appendix, 'Christian Worship and the Saints', pp. 172-84. McClendon found the explanations of these practices and their theological presuppositions by Roman Catholic theologians K. Rahner and H. Vorgrimler (*Theological Dictionary*, ed. C. Ernst, trans. R. Strachan [New York; Herder and Herder, 1965], s.v. 'Veneration of Saints') helpful for putting the best face on these Catholic practices and concepts for 'baptist' and other non-Catholic readers (McClendon, *Biography as Theology*, pp. 181-82)

century.[37] All of these except *Glory Be to the Father* and *O Christ, Our Hope, Our Heart's Desire* were translated into English by John Mason Neale (1818-1866), an Anglican divine whose translations of Greek and Latin patristic and medieval hymns greatly enriched the hymnody of the Church of England.[38]

Baptist Praise and Worship, a hymnal produced in 1991 for the Baptist Union of Great Britain and utilized by about twenty-five percent of its member churches,[39] includes ten hymns with texts of patristic origin (only four of which parallel the patristic contents of *The Baptist Hymnal* [1991]): 145 *Of the Father's Love Begotten* by Aurelius Clemens Prudentius (c. 348-after 405); 216 *All Glory, Praise and Honor* by Theodulph of Orleans (c. 750-821; though attributed in *Baptist Praise and Worship* to John Mason Neale, the hymn text was translated rather than authored by Neale); 226 *Sing, My Tongue, the Glorious Battle* and 228 *The Royal Banners Forward Go* by Venantius Fortunatus (c. 530-609); 248 *Come, You Faithful, Raise the Strain* and 407 *Come, God's People, Sing for Joy* by John of Damascus (c. 675-c. 749); 434 *Father, We Thank You Now for Planting*, versified from a text in the second-century *Didache*; 441 *Let All Mortal Flesh Keep Silence* from *The Liturgy of St. James* (fifth century); 457 *Holy, Holy, Holy, God Almighty Lord*, based on the *Sanctus* that dates from the fourth-century liturgies; and 474 *Christ Is Made the Sure Foundation*, a seventh-century Latin hymn.[40]

Occasional singing of these hymns (and others of patristic origin found in other hymnals and books of worship) will allow the congregation to be formed by these ancient intersections of theology made present in the worship of today's church. If attention is called to their origin, singing these hymns may serve the secondary function of reminding worshippers that they are heirs to the church's telling of their story in the centuries that followed the New Testament. Weekly singing of *Glory Be to the Father* (the *Gloria Patri*) in particular will do much to help Baptist congregations become more consciously Trinitarian in their faith and practice.

Implementing *Lex Orandi, Lex Credendi* in Baptist Congregations

Recovery of various patterns and practices from patristic liturgy has already borne the fruit of liturgical renewal in some other Protestant denominations

---

37   W.L. Forbis, ed., *The Baptist Hymnal* (Nashville: Convention Press, 1991).

38   *Oxford Dictionary of the Christian Church*, s.v. 'Neale, John Mason'.

39   Ellis, *Gathering*, pp. 152, citing a survey of worship practices in churches of the Baptist Union of Great Britain conducted in 1996 and published as C.J. Ellis, *Baptist Worship Today* (Didcot: Baptist Union of Great Britain, 1999).

40   *Baptist Praise and Worship* (Oxford: Oxford University Press, 1991).

in the United States,[41] but as yet there is no widespread organized parallel movement in Baptist life. The current fragmentation of Baptist life in the Southern United States makes it unlikely that any new major Baptist hymnals or books of worship in which a more intentional retrieval of the early Christian interdependence of theology and worship might take place will be forthcoming from and for that context any time soon, nor is there likely to be any widespread interest in having such a resource until future generations of Baptist ministers have been theologically educated in a very different manner than their predecessors.[42] The recently published book of worship resources *Gathering for Worship: Patterns and Prayers for the Community of Disciples* is a promising step in this direction in the context of the Baptist Union of Great Britain, providing Baptist congregations with a wide range of flexible patterns for worship that incorporate many of the theologically formative patterns and practices of patristic worship treated in this chapter; an edition of this resource by a North American co-publisher is forthcoming. Pending the re-envisioning of the place of liturgical theology in Baptist theological education and the availability of a wider array of liturgical resources for Baptist churches, individual pastors and other worship leaders who have become interested in implementing 'ancient-future' worship[43] in their congregations will need to network with other ministers with similar hopes and locate like-minded theological educators who may be able to suggest resources and provide guidance.

Implementation of the *lex orandi, lex credendi* principle in a typical Baptist congregation through the retrieval of patristic patterns and practices of worship will require much wisdom and patience on the part of pastors and other involved church staff, and each small step toward retrieval will

---

41   G. Wainwright, 'Renewing Worship: The Recovery of Classical Patterns', *TheolTod* 48.1 (April, 1991), p. 46. Wainwright identifies as exemplary beneficiaries of this sort of patristic retrieval the Episcopal *Book of Common Prayer* (1979) and the *Lutheran Book of Worship* (1978), and to a lesser extent the worship materials produced during the same period by Methodist and Presbyterian churches in the United States.

42   Little progress can be made towards preparing Baptist ministers to draw extensively upon the liturgical tradition of the church in its catholicity in their planning and leadership of worship until Baptist institutions of theological education shift the primary curricular responsibility for courses in the leadership of worship away from an automatic assignment to teachers of church music and towards faculty with academic backgrounds in the history of liturgy and liturgical theology and the application of these fields of study to practical theology (and some persons with such qualifications may in fact also be teachers of church music, and indeed some are serving in such roles).

43   This is the language employed by R.E. Webber in *Ancient-Future Faith: Rethinking Evangelicalism for a Postmodern World* (Grand Rapids, Mich.: Baker Books, 1999), and also his *Worship Old and New: A Biblical, Historical, and Practical Introduction*, rev. edn. (Grand Rapids, Mich.: Zondervan, 1994).

need to be preceded and accompanied by careful Christian education within and without the context of the worship service. Even when all has been carefully explained, the minister should be prepared for objections to what some church members may view as (Roman) 'Catholic' practices. One of my former students who became pastor of a First Baptist Church in a rural town after completing his Master of Divinity degree held an Ash Wednesday service for the first time in the congregation's history, complete with the imposition of ashes. Having been very careful to explain the significance of everything involved in the service before and during worship, he experienced an enthusiastic response from the congregation. All was well until one woman returned from the service—with ashes on her forehead—to her husband, a retired pastor who was home sick that Wednesday. After several conversations with fellow church members in which he expressed his alarm over the Ash Wednesday service, however, he was assured that the service had been most meaningful to everyone present and that no one felt their participation in the service to have been contrary to who they were as Baptists. Such an experience is possible only when the whole congregation is given an opportunity to have ownership of experiments in worship.

For many Baptist congregations, the first small step toward ancient-future worship may need to be the introduction of corporate praying of the Lord's Prayer. Some Baptist churches have done this for years, but others have never done so, possibly because somewhere along the way they have had a preacher point out that Jesus intended us to follow the prayer as a model rather than recite the specific words. It is also good to pray the words of Jesus at least weekly. In two churches I served as pastor and in two interim pastorates, I have introduced this practice by preaching a sermon series on the petitions of the Lord's Prayer and having the congregation pray the Lord's Prayer together during those services. When the sermon series was concluded, we simply retained the practice of praying the Lord's Prayer each Sunday.

Another appropriate first step is to begin using the lectionary as a means of introducing additional Scripture readings into the service. At this stage it is not necessary to call attention to the fact that one is using the lectionary, as doing so might create resistance to an unfamiliar, 'Catholic'-sounding practice. Baptists, the 'people of the Book', ought to welcome gladly the pastor's suggestion that the congregation ought to read and hear more Scripture in its worship.

A congregation that has not previously followed the Christian calendar apart from Christmas and Easter might initially move towards a fuller celebration of the Christian year with Advent and Holy Week observances. Eventually Epiphany, Lent, Pentecost, Trinity Sunday, and the rest of the calendar may be introduced, but in many instances it is probably wise to do so gradually.

While a weekly service of word and table is the ideal pattern for the rehearsal of the Christian story and the formation of Christians through worship, that goal is a long time away for most typical Baptist congregations. If the current practice of a church is quarterly communion, one might begin by celebrating the Supper on other special occasions such as Christmas Eve or Maundy Thursday (another date on the calendar that may call for explanation to Baptist congregations). After the congregation comes to appreciate the opportunity to celebrate communion more than four times a year, monthly communion would be a reasonable goal. If leaders of worship succeed in making each monthly celebration of the Lord's Supper a meaningful act of worship, they may eventually succeed in proposing a weekly observance.

The single most significant contribution that patristic worship practices could make to a recovery of the patristic interdependence of theology and worship in a Baptist context is weekly recitation of the creed—the Apostles' Creed on Sundays when the Lord's Supper is not observed and the Nicaeno-Constantinopolitan Creed in connection with celebrations of communion. The introduction of the creed into Baptist worship is also likely to be the single most controversial experiment in the worship of a typical Baptist congregation in the United States. One strategy might be to begin with either a Sunday morning sermon series or mid-week Bible study series on the phrases of the Apostles' Creed (one of my students who served as a minister to youth had a good experience using the Apostles' Creed as the basis of an ongoing youth discipleship study). These sermons or studies should emphasize the biblical sources of the creeds, the nature of the creeds as concise narrative summaries of the whole biblical story, and the proper Baptist rejection of any coercive use of the creeds as tests of fellowship. Recitation of the creeds might initially be introduced into worship in connection with baptism, with both candidates and congregation reciting the Apostles' Creed as the story they are claiming as their own in baptism and to which they are re-committing themselves in a renewal of their baptismal vows. Recitation of the creed might later be introduced into services in which the Lord's Supper is celebrated. In time, when the congregation is ready, confession of the creeds may become a feature of weekly worship.

Similar strategies of Christian education and gradual introduction may be followed when introducing other patristic patterns and practices into Baptist worship. In cases in which there are already precedents these in typical Baptist worship, they may be adopted through subtle shifts in the leadership of those practices or through the explicit explanation of an existing worship practice. The 'pastoral prayer' may easily become a collect, the 'word of welcome' may easily become the passing of the peace, and the telling of a missionary story may easily become the commemoration of an exemplary Christian. Hymns with texts of patristic composition are already in the hymnals of most congregations and may be introduced at any time.

It cannot be emphasized enough that these suggestions for Baptist retrieval of patristic liturgical patterns and practices are not necessarily associated with a particular style of music or degree of formality or informality. One of the most meaningful worship services in which I have participated, and one of the most effective services I have experienced in terms of its rehearsal of the divine story along the lines proposed in this article, was a Roman Catholic Mass in a charismatic-influenced parish in Fort Worth, Texas. The service followed the traditional liturgy of the mass, but the tone was informal, the attire of worshippers was casual, and the music was contemporary, led by a four-piece 'praise and worship' band. That service was effective in my estimation where other 'contemporary' services in my experience had not been, primarily because the service, though contemporary in style, was built on ancient substance rather than contemporary style.[44] Perhaps shifting the focus of the worship wars currently being waged in Baptist congregations from matters of superficial musical style to recovery of the ancient patterns and practices of worship might provide a way beyond the current polarities towards the renewal of Baptist worship. Such renewal can help Baptists to become both a thinking people and a worshipping people—a people whose minds are formed by the story told in worship, a people who experience as Baptists the observation of Roman Catholic theologian Susan K. Wood that 'the Christian repeatedly participates in the liturgy in order to imprint that economy [of salvation-history] in his or her very being', so that 'worship provides the parameters for thinking about Scripture and theology by keeping these reflections oriented toward their proper object, God, and within their proper context, the Christian community'.[45]

Congregational worship is the primary means by which Baptists can be formed by the theological tradition of the church in its catholicity, but Baptist institutions of higher education also have an important role to play in the formation of the Christian minds of young adults through second-order reflection on the Christian theological tradition and exploration of the relationship of this tradition to all fields of academic study and vocational preparation. The next chapter turns to the implications of an intentional movement towards catholicity for the discussions of the proper relationship

---

44   I have since had similar experiences as a visitor in services of the Mass at an intentionally 'contemporary' Roman Catholic parish in Raleigh, North Carolina.

45   S.K. Wood, 'The Liturgy: Participatory Knowledge of God in the Liturgy', in *Knowing the Triune God: The Work of the Spirit in the Practices of the Church*, ed. J.J. Buckley and D.S. Yeago (Grand Rapids, Mich.: William B. Eerdmans, 2001), pp. 109-110.

between faith and learning in the Christian university currently underway in the United States and for the intra-faculty conflicts that have sometimes been occasioned by these deliberations.

CHAPTER 9

Contesting Our Story: Catholicity and Communal Conflict in Baptist Higher Education

'In a word, religious truth is not only a portion but a condition of general knowledge. To blot it out is nothing short, if I may so speak, of unravelling the web of university teaching. It is, according to the Greek proverb, to take the spring from out of the year; it is to imitate the preposterous proceeding of those tragedians who represented a drama with the omission of its principal part.' *John Henry Cardinal Newman*[1]

'[T]he university is, in God's good world, the principal community through which human rationality can examine all existing communities, families, and structures—including itself, but also including the One Holy Catholic and Apostolic Church—and thus can help them to become what they are.' *Jaroslav Pelikan*[2]

The current attention to the integration of faith and learning in Christian universities in the United States may prove to be the most significant development in the history of Christian higher education in that national context. In many cases, institutions are having the first serious conversation since their founding about their distinctiveness as church-related schools and what that might mean for the teaching of all university disciplines. Baptist colleges and universities are increasingly giving attention to this issue by sponsoring or sending representatives to conferences on faith and learning, founding interdisciplinary university centers and institutes for faith and learning, and implementing curricula that more intentionally correlate faith and learning across the university disciplines. Yet these discussions of the integration of faith and learning have sometimes resulted in much faculty uneasiness about such an enterprise at the local campus level, especially when the suggestion is made that theological reflection is

---

1   J.H. Cardinal Newman, *The Idea of a University* (Garden City, N.Y.: Image Books, 1959 [first published 1853 and 1858), p. 103.

2   J. Pelikan, *The Idea of a University: A Reexamination* (New Haven: Yale University Press, 1992), p. 67.

integral to the pursuit of diverse academic disciplines in a Christian intellectual community. Conflict over aspects of the ambitious 'Baylor 2012' institutional vision adopted in September 2001 by the Board of Regents of Baylor University (Waco, Texas, USA), in particular its call for a more intentional integration of faith and learning in the largest Baptist-related university in the world, has received considerable public attention recently.[3] Similar battles are being waged less publicly, however, at numerous colleges in the United States with historic denominational ties, many of them Baptist in foundation and constituency. Perhaps few Christian university professors have not had the experience of discussing religious matters at lunch with fellow faculty members from various departments of study and realizing during a less-than-cordial turn in the conversation that the cross-disciplinary integration of faith and learning in their own institution would be rough going indeed.

In some quarters, aversion to theological conversation across university disciplines threatens to paralyze these encouraging steps toward the integration of faith and learning before the movement is fully underway. Institutions of Christian higher education of all Christian traditions must recognize and address this paralysis in order to make substantive progress toward founding intellectual community upon Christian faith. After identifying the sources of the academic conflict avoidance that stifles interdisciplinary debate of matters of ultimate concern, this chapter contends that constructive conflict located within the tradition of the church in its catholicity and grounded in the practice of worship is vital for the integration of faith and learning in the postmodern context of today's Christian university. The observations and recommendations made here are applicable to Christian higher education in general, but they are addressed to Baptist higher education in particular because much recent discussion of these issues in Baptist circles has raised questions as to whether the Baptist tradition possesses sufficient intellectual resources in and of itself for interdisciplinary theological reflection on the university disciplines. If Baptist identity is primarily construed as that which distinguishes the Baptist tradition from other Christian traditions, then Baptist identity alone

---

3   R. Benne, 'Crisis of Identity: A Clash Over Faith and Learning', *ChrCent* 121.2 (27 January, 2004), pp. 22-26; R.C. Wood, 'The Heresy of Solitary Faith', *ChrTod* 48.1 (January, 2004), pp. 58-60; K.S. Mangan, 'Baylor President Faces the Test of His Tenure', *ChronHighEd* 50.4 (19 September, 2003), p. A27; K.S. Mangan, 'Baylor Professors Vote Against President', *ChronHighEd* 51.17 (17 December, 2004), p. A34; K.S. Mangan, R. Wilson, S. Smallwood, and P. Fogg, 'Baylor's President Will Become Its Chancellor', *ChronHighEd* 51.22 (4 February, 2005), p. A6. Documents articulating and commenting upon the 'Baylor 2012' vision are available online at http://www.baylor.edu/vision.

is an insufficient foundation for Christian intellectual community. The recovery of the catholic theological tradition as integral to Baptist identity that is urged in this book is therefore crucial for Baptist educational institutions if they are to have the theological resources that will sustain the minds of their Christian scholars in the correlation of Christian faith and academic inquiry.

Sources of Communal Conflict over Faith-and-Learning Proposals

The first step towards a recovery of the catholic tradition as the center of theological reflection on the university disciplines is the identification of the sources of conflict over proposals for intentionality in the integration of faith and learning. Faculty aversion to serious discussion of these proposals may be attributed to at least three factors.

Theological Controversies

First, many faculty members have personal experience of the theological controversies that have divided most American denominations in recent years. The real divisions in American Christianity today are not between denominations but rather within them.[4] My own experience has been of the theological-political controversy in the Southern Baptist Convention during the past three decades, but faculty from most other denominations can tell a similar story of bitter conflict over matters of faith and practice.[5] Consequently, many devoutly Christian professors are understandably uneasy about extending theological discussion, the source of so much divisiveness in their own Christian experience, beyond the classrooms of the religion department or divinity school.

Political Polarization

Second, the politicization of most academic disciplines and professional fields in the wake of the American 'culture wars' has been accompanied by diverse and conflicting Christian proposals as to the proper 'Christian' positions in these conflicts. Influencing the outcome of the 'culture wars' is

---

4   These developments and their implications are explored by R. Wuthnow, *The Restructuring of American Religion: Society and Faith Since World War II* (StudChSt, 1; Princeton, N.J.: Princeton University Press, 1988), esp. pp. 71-99 and 215-40.

5   E.g., the current controversies over same-sex unions and the ordination of homosexual persons in the Episcopal Church, U.S.A., the Presbyterian Church (USA), the United Methodist Church, and the Evangelical Lutheran Church in America.

not properly the concern of Christian higher education.[6] As Ralph Wood rightly urges, 'it is ever so important not to confuse Christian education with taking a position within the culture wars'; rather, 'our loyalty must always be to the transcendent and redeeming Lord who rules over all nations and all states'.[7] Nevertheless, Christian faculty who hear sermons, listen to Christian radio programs, or read Christian publications have had their thinking shaped by Christian arguments for or against capital punishment, for or against egalitarian gender relationships or gender-inclusive language, for or against various economic paradigms—the list of examples could continue *ad infinitum*. If faith is proposed as a foundation for intellectual community, which version of faith will it be? And how will faith be connected to the issues polarizing most academic and professional disciplines today, when possible Christian positions on the same issues cover the spectrum? A professor in the undergraduate religion department of my institution tells of having lunch with a professor in a non-theological discipline who is having a hard time fathoming how a relatively conservative Christian can be a straight-ticket Democrat; my colleague in turn has a hard time seeing how his lunch partner's support of the Republican party platform is compatible with Christian faith and its vision of social justice. Faculty members are well aware that any serious discussion of the integration of faith and learning must negotiate all sorts of sensitive political landmines.

---

6   This is not to suggest that Christians and Christian educators should refrain from take definite stands on controversial issues or retreat from Christian involvement in the public square; rather, Christian higher education must take great pains to avoid addressing such issues by lazily appropriating the assumptions, polarities, and rhetoric of the 'culture wars'. We must be 'in' this culture and its conflicts, but we must not 'belong' to them (John 17.11-18).

7 R.C. Wood, 'An Alternative Vision for the Christian University' (unpublished address to the faculty of Campbell University, Buies Creek, North Carolina, 30 March, 2004; a different version of this address, which does not include the material quoted here, is forthcoming as 'From Barren Modernism to Fruitful Post-Modernism: A Proposal for Christian Education in the Baptist Tradition' in *PRSt*). This caveat is rooted in the perspective on the relation of church to society exemplified by S. Hauerwas and W.H. Willimon, *Resident Aliens: Life in the Christian Colony* (Nashville, Tenn.: Abingdon Press, 1989); S. Hauerwas, *After Christendom: How the Church Is to Behave if Freedom, Justice, and a Christian Nation Are Bad Ideas* (Nashville, Tenn.: Abingdon Press, 1991); and R. Clapp, *A Peculiar People: The Church as Culture in a Post-Christian Society* (Downers Grove, Ill.: InterVarsity Press, 1996).

Mutual Suspicion

Third, faculty members in religious and theological studies, who were theologically formed by an academic theological education as well as by the church, and faculty members in other disciplines, whose theological formation took place primarily in church and para-church contexts, are frequently suspicious of one another's theologies. Theological professionals sometimes hear in the discourse of theological laypersons the fundamentalism they moved beyond during their academic theological educations, and theological laypersons sometimes hear in the discourse of theological professionals the positions their ministers or popular Christian media had led them to believe were sub-Christian or heretical. Such mutual mistrust reinforces a 'two-spheres' paradigm for faith and learning that from the outset precludes faith from becoming foundational for university-wide intellectual community, especially in the minds of theological professionals who would prefer that theological laypersons not introduce their 'naïve faith' into the teaching of university disciplines beyond the religion department or divinity school.[8]

Embracing Conflict as Contested Catholicity

The result of the combination of these factors is a fear not of communal theological reflection per se but rather of the intellectual conflict that inevitably arises from this much-needed conversation. The remainder of this chapter will address the temptation to retreat from the theological conflict necessarily involved in the integration of faith and learning in light of three developments in philosophy, theology, and liturgy that have relevance for the recovery of faith as a foundation for intellectual community in a postmodern context: first, the observations of moral philosopher Alasdair MacIntyre regarding the contested character of a community's tradition; second, the insights of postliberal narrative theology regarding the Christian story as the ground of communal theological reflection; and third, contemporary efforts to recover the early church's understanding of the inseparability of theology and worship. These

---

8   For case studies of the 'two-spheres' paradigm and reflections on its instability as a long-term strategy for relating faith and learning, see M. Beaty and L. Lyon, 'Integration, Secularization, and the Two-Spheres View at Religious Colleges: Comparing Baylor University with the University of Notre Dame and Georgetown College', *CSR* 29.1 (Fall, 1999), pp. 73-112; see also M. Beaty, T. Buras, and L. Lyon, 'Christian Higher Education: An Historical and Philosophical Perspective', *PRSt* 24.2 (Summer, 1997), pp. 145-65.

illuminate aspects of the sort of conscious catholicity that will sustain efforts towards Christian intellectual community in the denominationally diverse faculties that serve Baptist colleges and universities in the United States.

The Contested Character of the Christian Tradition

The work of Alasdair MacIntyre on the inescapably traditioned nature of rationality in general and moral reasoning in particular has received much attention in the twenty-three years since the publication of his book *After Virtue*. His definition therein of a 'living tradition' was quoted in chapter 3 of the present book but is repeated here for the sake of convenience: 'an historically extended, socially embodied argument, and an argument precisely in part about the goods which constitute that tradition'.[9] MacIntyre illustrates this understanding of tradition by pointing to specific institutional embodiments of this sort of 'living tradition', significantly including the university among them.

> When an institution—a university, say, or a farm, or a hospital—is the bearer of a tradition of practice or practices, its common life will be partly, but in a centrally important way, constituted by a continuous argument as to what a university is and ought to be or what good farming is or what good medicine is. Traditions, when vital, embody continuities of conflict.[10]

If a tradition does not embody this continuity of conflict, he warns, 'it is always dying or dead'.[11]

Such a MacIntyrean understanding of traditioned rationality has much potential for overcoming the aforementioned obstacles to engaging the theme of this book. Christian universities must reclaim the Christian tradition as the unifying center of their shared intellectual life, but they cannot reclaim the Christian tradition as the unifying center of intellectual community without also embracing conflict about that tradition. If there is an absence of conflict about a Christian university's understanding of the Christian tradition and its vision for the integration of faith and learning, then, in MacIntyre's words, 'it is always dying or dead'. In 'Reconceiving the University as an Institution and the Lecture as a Genre', the concluding lecture of his 1988 Gifford Lectures, MacIntyre envisioned a university 'as a place of constrained disagreement, of imposed participation in conflict, in which a central responsibility of higher education would be to initiate

---

9   MacIntyre, *After Virtue*, p. 222.
10   MacIntyre, *After Virtue*, p. 222.
11   MacIntyre, *After Virtue*, p. 222.

students into conflict' and 'as an arena of conflict in which the most fundamental type of moral and theological disagreement was accorded recognition'.[12] Yet it is precisely an aversion to conflict, especially to 'moral and theological disagreement', which threatens to keep many institutions from engaging fully the implications of their distinctiveness as Christian universities. If the administration, faculty, and constituencies of institutions of Christian higher education recognize at the outset of these discussions that they will necessitate conflict, and that such conflict is good, and that constructive dissension is welcome, then they may be more successful in navigating these stormy waters without the crew jumping ship or leading a mutiny along the way.[13]

MacIntyre's philosophical case for the necessity of intellectual conflict for the health of institutional bearers of a tradition must be supplemented by a twofold theological rationale for conflict in Christian institutions. First, because the matters contested in a Christian intellectual community are of ultimate concern, they are worth serious and spirited debate. Not to debate them would be to allow penultimate concerns to replace them. Second, because of the noetic limitations of the earthly church between the two advents,[14] Christian scholars must cultivate the epistemological humility to submit their perspectives on these matters of ultimate concern to be contested by the intellectual community to which they belong and to practice Christian hospitality towards those with whom they differ (unlike mere tolerance, hospitality encourages the debate of differences while showing regard for the other). Neglecting either part of this theological rationale for conflict can easily allow conflict to degenerate into the petty disputes and personal attacks that demoralize too many academic institutions.

The Narrative Shape of the Christian Tradition

But what is the tradition that constitutes the conflict Christian universities must embrace? An institution might identify a generic 'Christian

---

12   A.C. MacIntyre, *Three Rival Versions of Moral Inquiry: Encyclopedia, Genealogy, and Tradition. Being Gifford Lectures Delivered in the University of Edinburgh in 1988* (Notre Dame, Ind.: University of Notre Dame Press, 1990), pp. 230-31.

13   As Ralph Wood observed in response to reading an earlier version of this chapter, the ongoing conflict that constitutes the Christian tradition makes it immensely more interesting than secularism as a foundation for intellectual community.

14   Cf. the Apostle Paul's rationale for the necessity of contested 'heresies' in the life of the church this side of heaven, 'so it will become clear who among you are genuine' (1 Cor. 11.19).

worldview' as the common foundation of the university's intellectual life. Sometimes this is expressed in terms of adherence to a few basic Christian doctrines or positions on specific moral issues.[15] Some institutions might emphasize a particular denominational tradition as a foundation for intellectual community, though few (if any) faculties will be drawn entirely or even mostly from a single denominational tradition, and in any case no particular denominational tradition possesses in and of itself sufficient theological resources for making Christian faith foundational for the intellectual community of a university apart from the relationship of that denominational tradition to the church in its catholicity. Neither approach to defining foundational faith will be adequate for the postmodern milieu of our Christian universities if it frames either a Christian 'worldview'—a decidedly modern concept[16]—or a particular denominational perspective in terms of doctrinal or ethical propositions. Any understanding of the Christian tradition in its catholicity, or of a particular denominational tradition, that emphasizes a body of truly articulated propositions is liable to squelch healthy cross-disciplinary theological argumentation, especially within a denominationally and theologically diverse faculty. Some institutions may succeed in recruiting and retaining whole faculties committed to confessional specificity without compromising intellectual openness or stifling debate, but many more Christian university faculties share in common mainly a commitment to support the Christian purposes of the institution. These more confessionally diverse faculties may find a more

---

15   E.g., the 'Statement of Christian Affirmation' adopted by the board of trustees of the University of Mobile (Mobile, Alabama, USA), as explained by the president of the institution: M. Foley, '"Distinctively Christian": Higher Education for a Higher Purpose', available online at http://umobile.edu/foley.asp.

16   'Worldview' is a term laden with Enlightenment-era presuppositions about the capacity of human rationality to have what Hilary Putnam has called an 'externalist perspective' or 'God's Eye point of view' on the world (H. Putnam, *Reason, Truth and History* [Cambridge: Cambridge University Press, 1981], p. 49). According to Baptist theologian Dan Stiver (Logsdon School of Theology, Hardin-Simmons University, Abilene, Texas, USA), 'what virtually all postmodern thinkers would agree upon is that we do not have a transcendent, perspicuous vantage point, a God's-eye point-of-view…God may have, but not us!' (D.R. Stiver, 'Baptists: Modern or Postmodern?' *RevExp* 100.4 [Fall, 2003], p. 536). Christian educators seeking to respond constructively to the postmodern context would do well to dispense with the modern phraseology of a 'Christian worldview' in favor of an expressed commitment to 'the Christian tradition'. Fidelity to the catholic Christian tradition in the postmodern Christian university must be accompanied by an epistemological humility that takes seriously the Christian understanding of the fallenness of human rationality, even the rationality of the Christian mind on its way toward conformity to the mind of Christ—a transformation that is not fully realized in this present life.

viable model of faith as a foundation for postmodern Christian intellectual community in the narrative theology proposals of the 'New Yale' trajectory of postliberal theology introduced in chapter 3 of this book.

George Lindbeck and others have proposed that the first-order stuff of Christian faith is the Christian story that forms the identity of Christian community. Doctrine, in turn, is second-order reflection on the foundational narrative of the church. If we understand Lindbeck's observations on the nature of doctrine in MacIntyrean terms, doctrine is both the process and the product of second-order argumentation about the story we share in Christian community. Where do we find this story? It is told with rich particularity in the canonical Scriptures. Making faith the foundation of Christian intellectual community will therefore mean that in some manner the Christian university will identify the Bible as the normative expression of the Christian narrative. This story is also summarized in the ancient rule of faith underlying the Apostles' Creed and the Nicaeno-Constantinopolitan Creed. These ancient confessions of communal faith did not originate as lists of doctrinal propositions but rather as narrative rehearsals of the acts of the Triune God in creation, reconciliation, and consummation, intended to serve as liturgical expressions and instruments of Christian education.[17] While many Baptists would refrain from granting the ancient creeds an authority alongside the Bible, this book has already made the case that the liturgical and catechetical use of the creeds is not at all antithetical to Baptist faith and practice. Baptist universities and Christian universities of all denominational traditions alike would do well to reclaim these concise summaries of the Christian narrative as foci for interdisciplinary theological reflection. The Christian tradition is fundamentally the Christian story within which we understand our selves and our world. Reclaiming this story as the first-order foundation of Christian intellectual community would provide common ground on which faculty from multiple denominational traditions and theological perspectives may stand together while making their own distinctive contributions to the second-order argument that the integration of faith and learning entails.

The Liturgical Locus of the Christian Tradition

This narrative conception of the tradition which is to be contested by the university community will function best when the traditional narrative that forms Christian community, in particular Christian intellectual community, is given its proper locus: the worship of the community. Very few discussions of faith and learning in the Christian university have given

---

17   On the narrative shape and function of the ancient creeds, see Blowers, 'The *Regula Fidei* and the Narrative Character of Early Christian Faith', pp. 199-228.

attention to worship as the university's primary public expression of its foundational faith. Robert Benne's *Quality with Soul* is a notable exception to this tendency to ignore the liturgical life of Christian universities in literature on faith and learning.[18] If Baptist universities in particular are to recover faith as a foundation for intellectual community, they must recover the classical Christian context for the first-order narrative expression of that faith. Early Christianity understood doctrine and worship to be inseparable, an understanding expressed by the patristic axiom *lex orandi, lex credendi* explored in the previous chapter of this book. Worship is formative and normative for the theology of the church, and the theology of the church informs worship. If the central academic discipline in the integration of faith and learning is theology, and the proper context of the discipline of theology is the church at worship, then communal interdisciplinary theological reflection cannot be abstracted from a common liturgical life.

If Christian universities are serious about initiating cross-disciplinary conversation about the integration of faith and learning, they therefore ought first to seek ways to implement the *lex orandi, lex credendi* principle in the common life of the university community. This might be accomplished through weekly services of worship for faculty and students that tell the common Christian story through the systematic reading and proclamation of Scripture, the confession of the ancient ecumenical creeds, and—where ecclesiologically feasible—Eucharistic celebrations. The trend towards 'open communion' in many Baptist churches should make common Eucharistic celebrations ecclesiologically feasible for some Baptist universities with denominationally mixed faculty and students, though some non-Bapitst worshippers would have to abstain from receiving communion for ecclesiological reasons related to the discipline of their own communities. Baptist universities have much to gain from incorporating Eucharistic celebration into their common liturgical life, for the sacramental narration of God's relation to the world in the Eucharist that has been excised from much of the Baptist tradition is in fact an essential foundation for the integration of Christian faith with the arts, sciences, and any academic discipline that has to do with knowledge of the world—and what discipline does not have some aspect of knowledge of the world as its basic subject? As Robert Wilken has reminded readers of his delightful book *The Spirit of Early Christian Thought*, a key feature of early Christian thinking is the notion that in light of the incarnation, people may experience the presence of God by means of things—audible things such as words and

---

18   R. Benne, *Quality with Soul: How Six Premier Colleges and Universities Keep Faith with Their Religious Traditions* (Grand Rapids, Mich.: William B. Eerdmans, 2001), especially pp. 7, 11, 61-62, 145-46, 150, 155-57, 160-62, 165-66, 171, 193-94.

musical tones, tangible things such as water and bread and wine, and visible things such as icons and various media of the material and visual arts.[19] Regular university-wide services of word and table would help foster a shared first-order foundation upon which faculty and students alike could build in the second-order task of relating their faith to scholarship across the university disciplines.

Susan K. Wood's previously quoted observation that 'the Christian repeatedly participates in the liturgy in order to imprint that economy [of salvation-history] in his or her very being', so that 'worship provides the parameters for thinking about Scripture and theology by keeping these reflections oriented toward their proper object, God, and within their proper context, the Christian community'[20] suggests much about the potential contributions of worship to the integration of faith and learning. The primary setting for this liturgical formation of the Christian mind is of course the local church community, but a complementary university-wide shared liturgical life will help the Christian university to become a Christian intellectual community in more than name only. The liturgical rehearsal of the foundational narrative of Christian intellectual community would be reinforced by furnishing the campuses of Christian universities with architecture and art that communicate the Christian story in image and symbol throughout the campus (Baptist university campuses tend to be especially deficient at this point), but especially in a focal worship space that makes clear the university's identity as a worshiping community. It is not only with words that we tell the story of Christian faith that orients a Christian intellectual community in its pursuit of knowledge.

The Importance of Intra-Faculty Theological Education

The recovery of a common experience of worship would need to be preceded and supplemented by intentional interdisciplinary discussion, perhaps during faculty development workshops, of how the Christian

---

19   Wilken, *Spirit of Early Christian Thought*, p. xxi, referencing ch. 9, 'The Glorious Deeds of Christ' (pp. 212-36) and ch. 10, 'Making This Thing Other' (pp. 237-61); see also ch. 2, 'An Awesome and Unbloody Sacrifice' (pp. 25-49) and ch. 3, 'The Face of God for Now' (pp. 50-79). This point should not be taken as implying that it is only after the incarnation that the people of God are able to understand that they may encounter the divine via the material, for this was certainly already a feature of ancient Hebrew faith and practice. In Christian theology the import of the incarnation for understanding the relationship of God to the material order is in continuity with the pattern of God's saving acts already made known in Jewish salvation history, but it is also the definite word about this relationship and is the presupposition of Christian sacramental worship.

20   Wood, 'The Liturgy', pp. 109-110.

narrative might reframe disciplinary self-understandings in the context of a Christian university and also how the various university disciplines might make their own contributions to our understanding of the story. If this is to be a community-wide argument about the significance of our story, then the university faculty as a whole must become conversant with the biblical narrative, with the theological categories through which we reflect on this narrative and the faith and practices formed by it, with the story of the sponsoring denominational tradition, and with the stories of the other Christian traditions represented within the faculty and in the larger body of Christ. Christian universities that have attempted to be more intentional about the integration of faith and scholarship across the university disciplines have sometimes experienced some challenges related to the responses of faculty outside of departments of religion and schools of divinity to such proposals. On the one hand, some faculty in non-theological disciplines have balked at the prospect of a more explicit integration of their discipline with their Christian faith, protesting that they lack sufficient expertise in the Christian theological tradition to do such integration. On the other hand, some faculty in non-theological disciplines have been all too eager to teach their discipline from a Christian perspective, not realizing that they lack sufficient grounding in the Christian theological tradition for doing such integration in an academic setting. These challenges might be addressed by university faculties of religion and divinity if they embrace intra-faculty theological education as an important aspect of their contributions to the larger university.

Faculty members in the department of religious studies or divinity school will need to serve as the primary instructional resources for including theological education in a larger program of faculty development, but there are valuable resources for this work in the university community beyond the faculty in the explicitly theological disciplines. These resources include representatives of multiple denominational traditions throughout the faculty. Most institutions that publicly accept the challenge to make faith foundational for intellectual community will either fit or aspire to the 'critical-mass' category of Robert Benne's typology of church-related colleges.[21] Institutions of this type 'insist that a critical mass of adherents from their [sponsoring] tradition inhabit all the constituencies of the educational enterprise', including the faculty, but they also value the presence of other traditions in these constituencies for the contributions they make to the pursuit of truth.[22] The presence of faculty from traditions

---

21   Benne, *Quality with Soul*, pp. 48-68. See especially the summary table on p. 49 comparing the characteristics of 'Orthodox', 'Critical-Mass', 'Intentionally Pluralist', and 'Accidentally Pluralist' institutions.

22   Benne, *Quality with Soul*, p. 50.

other than the sponsoring tradition will ensure that the distinctive tellings of the Christian story in the multiple streams of the larger Christian tradition are heard. The faculty in a Baptist 'critical-mass' university needs to hear from Presbyterian, Catholic, Orthodox, or Pentecostal colleagues in various disciplines their perspectives on the significance of their own Christian traditions for the life of the mind. At the same time, the presence of a 'critical mass' of faculty members from the sponsoring tradition will help the denominational college to offer a public account of the unique contributions of a particular denominational telling of the Christian story to the intellectual life of the larger body of Christ. The encounter, and even conflict, of multiple denominational traditions in the Christian university is beneficial both to the sponsoring tradition and to the church catholic: it requires that our story be genuinely contested.

The collapse of modern foundational metanarratives provides Baptists and others involved in Christian higher education with an opportunity for re-founding the Christian university on Christian faith itself. A nonfoundational rationality need not mean a noncommittal relativism. Rather, it may liberate Christian thought from bondage to alien rationalities that never were as universal as they pretended to be.[23] Christian faith is grounded in nothing other than the shared Christian story, a story that invites argument among those who are shaped by it in worship. This sort of conflict is necessary and welcome, for it helps ensure the vitality of the tradition. If these proposals should elicit some disagreement from readers of this chapter with a stake in Christian higher education in Baptist and other contexts, any ensuing argument could lead to a more robust contesting of the story we share in Christian intellectual community.

---

23   For a constructive Christian response to the opportunity presented by the postmodern situation from an evangelical perspective, see Grenz and Franke, *Beyond Foundationalism*.

CHAPTER 10

'What Keeps You from Becoming a Catholic?' A Personal Epilogue

'While I most sincerely hold that there is in the Roman Church a traditionary system which is not necessarily connected with her essential formularies, yet, were I ever so much to change my mind on this point, this would not tend to bring me from my present position, providentially appointed in the English Church. That your communion was unassailable, would not prove that mine was indefensible. Nor would it at all affect the sense in which I receive our Articles; they would still speak against certain definite errors, though you had reformed them.' *John Henry Newman to a Roman Catholic correspondent, 5 May 1841 (four years prior to reception into the Roman Catholic Church)*[1]

'If, however, you saw our Church as we see it, you would easily understand that such a change of feeling, did it take place, would have no necessary tendency, which you seem to expect, to draw a person from the Church of England to that of Rome. There is a divine life among us, clearly manifested, in spite of all our disorders, which is as great a note of the Church as any can be. Why should we seek our Lord's presence elsewhere, when He vouchsafes it to us where we are? What *call* have we to change our communion?' *John Henry Newman to a Roman Catholic correspondent, 22 November 1842 (three years prior to reception into the Roman Catholic Church)*[2]

'Dr. Harmon, what keeps you from becoming a Catholic?' A couple of years ago one of my divinity school students addressed this question to me a few minutes before the beginning of class in a course on Augustine's *Confessions*. That day we were scheduled to discuss book 8 of the *Confessions*, in which Augustine recounts his conversion to Catholic Christianity. Hers was not a hostile or pejorative question. This student had been visiting Roman Catholic services of the Mass on occasion and had

---

1   J.H. Cardinal Newman, *Apologia Pro Vita Sua* (London: J.M. Dent & Sons, 1912 [1st edn. 1864]), p. 178.

2   Newman, *Apologia Pro Vita Sua*, p. 182.

incorporated some practices and patterns of prayer from the Roman Catholic tradition into her life of personal devotion, while remaining a Baptist and serving as a Baptist minister to youth. She had encountered in Roman Catholicism something that had been lacking in her own experience of the Baptist tradition, and she was earnestly wrestling with questions about her denominational future in light of that encounter. This epilogue chapter is a much more verbose (but hopefully more carefully nuanced) version of my brief response to her that day.

Precedents for 'Conversion'

The possibility that a Protestant minister and professor of theology might seriously consider embracing Roman Catholicism—or Eastern Orthodoxy or Anglicanism—is no longer as unthinkable as it might have been in the era of John Henry Newman's very public journey from the Church of England to reception into the Roman Catholic Church and eventual membership in the College of Cardinals. My student had read some of the writings of Scott Hahn, a former Presbyterian minister and alumnus of the evangelical Gordon-Conwell Theological Seminary (South Hamilton, Massachusetts, USA) who was later received into the Roman Catholic Church and now serves as Professor of Theology and Scripture at Franciscan University of Steubenville (Steubenville, Ohio, USA).[3] There are numerous other recent stories of 'conversions' (not really the most appropriate term for reception into one Christian communion of a baptized believer from another Christian communion) of ministers and theologians from various Protestant denominations to Roman Catholicism, Eastern Orthodoxy, or Anglicanism (or from Anglicanism to Roman Catholicism or Eastern Orthodoxy). Some have received much public attention, at least in theological circles; others are comparatively unknown. Robert Louis Wilken, a long-time Lutheran historian of patristic Christianity teaching on the faculty of the University of Virginia, was received into the Roman Catholic Church a few years ago. Not long after Wilken's departure from the Lutheran communion, his fellow Lutheran historical theologian Jaroslav Pelikan of Yale University was received into the fellowship of the Orthodox Church in America. In 2004 and 2005, a remarkable number of theologians in the United States found new ecclesial homes in the Roman Catholic Church: former Episcopalian Russell Reno of Creighton University (Omaha, Nebraska, USA) and former Lutherans Bruce Marshall (Southern Methodist University, Dallas, Texas, USA, formerly of St. Olaf College, Northfield, Minnesota, USA), David Fagerberg (University of

---

3   S. Hahn and K. Hahn, *Rome Sweet Home: Our Journey to Catholicism* (San Francisco: Ignatius Press, 1993).

Notre Dame, Notre Dame, Indiana, USA, formerly of Concordia College, Moorhead, Minnesota, USA), Reinhard Hütter (Duke Divinity School, Durham, North Carolina, USA, formerly of Lutheran School of Theology at Chicago, USA), and Mickey Mattox (Marquette University, Milwaukee, Wisconsin, USA, formerly of the Lutheran Ecumenical Institute, Strasbourg, France; readers of this book will be interested to know that Mattox was raised as a Baptist).[4]

While these recent examples of theological educators who have sought a fuller catholicity and found it beyond the denominations of their initial Christian nurture are from among the mainline Protestant churches, several evangelicals have made similar journeys. In the 1980s Robert Webber, then on the faculty of Wheaton College, walked the 'Canterbury Trail' into the Anglican communion along with several fellow evangelicals,[5] and Peter Gillquist and a sizeable number of other evangelicals (eventually including Francis Schaeffer's son Franky Schaeffer) embraced Orthodoxy.[6] One of my college classmates was raised as a Baptist, attended a Baptist college, became a Baptist pastor, and pursued graduate studies at a Baptist university where he wrote an M.A. thesis on the role of preaching in Greek Orthodox liturgy. He resigned his pastorate in order to do field research by attending a local Greek Orthodox church on Sundays and soon felt drawn to something present in Orthodoxy that had been lacking in his experience as a Baptist. He underwent the process that led to his reception into the Greek Orthodox Church and later realized that his sense of calling to vocational Christian ministry was still present with him in this new ecclesial home. He went on to earn an M.Div. from an Orthodox seminary, where he graduated as valedictorian of his class, was ordained as a deacon and then priest, and

---

4   These recent journeys towards Roman Catholicism by Lutheran theologians are recounted and their import discussed at length by Lutheran theologian Carl Braaten, co-founder of the Center for Catholic and Evangelical Theology and its journal *Pro Ecclesia*, in an open letter addressed to his bishop in the Evangelical Lutheran Church in America and disseminated widely on the Internet (C.E. Braaten, 'An Open Letter to Bishop Mark Hanson', 11 July 2005, available online at http://wordalone.org/docs/wabraaten.htm).

5   R.E. Webber, *Evangelicals on the Canterbury Trail: Why Evangelicals Are Attracted to the Liturgical Church* (Waco, Tex.: Word Books, 1985).

6   P.E. Gillquist, *Becoming Orthodox: A Journey to the Ancient Christian Faith* (Brentwood, Tenn.: Wolgemuth & Hyatt, 1989) and *Coming Home: Why Protestant Clergy Are Becoming Orthodox* (Ben Lomond, Calif.: Conciliar Press, 1992); F. Schaeffer, *Dancing Alone: The Quest for Orthodox Faith in the Age of False Religion* (Brookline, Mass.: Holy Cross Orthodox Press, 1994) and *Letters to Father Aristotle: A Journey through Contemporary American Orthodoxy* (Salisbury, Mass.: Regina Orthodox Press, 1995).

served on the staff of the Greek Orthodox Archdiocese of America before assisting in the planting of a mission Greek Orthodox congregation.

The possibility suggested by my student's question was not without precedent in more ways than one. Not only are there other theologians who have left their home communions for fuller ecclesial expressions of catholicity; one of my professional peers who made such a journey himself has wondered if I might be on a similar path. Not long after the essay upon which the first chapter of this book is based appeared in print in the annual volume of the College Theology Society, I received an e-mail message from Wilburn T. Stancil, a former professor of systematic theology at Midwestern Baptist Theological Seminary (Kansas City, Missouri, USA). After leaving the faculty of Midwestern when changes in that institution made it difficult for him to continue teaching there, Stancil became an Episcopalian and now serves as Chair of the Department of Theology and Religious Studies at Rockhurst University (Kansas City, Missouri, USA), a Roman Catholic university of Jesuit foundation. With his kind permission, the text of Stancil's message appears below.

Dear Steven,

Thank you for your very fine article on 'catholic Baptists' in vol. 50 of *New Horizons in Theology*. As a former Southern Baptist (now Episcopalian) and former theology teacher in SBC [Southern Baptist Convention] institutions…now at a Jesuit university, I wanted to share some reactions to the article.

My first impression was 'here is a man who is on his way to Rome, or perhaps Constantinople, or at least Canterbury'. Others (including myself) who have tried to map out a place in Baptist thought for these larger issues you raise have found the dissonance to be too great and eventually have had to cast our lots elsewhere.

I also raise this question for your reflection. Although what you propose is certainly more in line with views held by earlier Baptists, particularly British Baptists, to what extent can one turn back the time to a position that today is clearly outside the mainstream of the thinking of most Baptists? When I think of Baptists today, I picture in my mind either small, rural churches made up of sincere and simple people or large megachurches made up of sophisticated urbanites. I can't envision either group embracing your proposals, and I can envision both groups branding them as 'catholic' and 'unbaptist', no matter what funding in history they might have.

And I wonder if, in fact, it's fair to ask them to turn back the clock. When I made a decision to leave the SBC in 1994, I intentionally chose not to become a part of the Alliance [of Baptists] or the CBF [Cooperative Baptist Fellowship] as most of my friends and colleagues did. My thought was, 'here are two more breakaway groups from the one Church, and the body of Christ is already torn into too many parts'. Moreover, I felt that people who had chosen the Baptist way had chosen that way for some specific reasons, and that my attempt to introduce sacraments, liturgy, etc. was in a way unfair to what they had consciously chosen.

In the article you talk about this newer generation of Baptist theologians who are trying to move beyond the fundamentalist/liberal, conservative/moderate divide. I applaud that. I do want to point out, however, that many of us who were fighting for the 'moderate' cause in the 1980s and early 1990s did not want, nor did we expect, a return to the 1950s. There was much that was wrong with Baptist life when the 'moderates' ran it, and we knew that. But most of our time and energy was given over to simply surviving in a hostile situation, and of course, few of us did survive. I'm glad to see that the younger Baptist theologians are moving beyond the need to polarize into 'moderate/conservative' camps.

I did enjoy the article very much, and while I admire your efforts, I predict that if you remain a Baptist and continue in your present track, you'll end up a frustrated Baptist. Perhaps I'm wrong, but time will tell.

Best,
Wilburn (Bill) T. Stancil

Stancil's message raises two crucial questions about the enterprise upon which I have embarked with this book. First, is it inevitable that this quest for Baptist catholicity will be rejected by my fellow Baptists and that it will be realized only in a break with the Baptist tradition parallel to Newman's exit from the Church of England? In other words, is this book analogous to Newman's correspondence that prefaces this chapter (or perhaps to his book on the nature of doctrinal development that marked the final theological steps in his journey towards Rome[7]), one day to be read from the other side of the Tiber as a document that evidenced all the signs of where the journey was heading, even while contending that the signs need not point that direction? The pertinence of the latter way of putting the question is heightened by basic similarities between this book and books published by Russell Reno and Reinhard Hütter not long before their decisions to seek reception into the Roman Catholic Church.[8] Second, is it right to ask my fellow Baptists to reconsider the pattern of faith and practice that many of them have chosen with great intentionality—and that they sometimes have chosen precisely because it is other than the very pattern of catholic faith and practice that I have commended in this book? Both questions have troubled me long before Stancil raised them, and I am grateful that his questions have pressed me to articulate responses to them here in the course of elaborating my response to my student's question, 'What keeps you from becoming a Catholic?'.

---

7   J.H. Newman, *An Essay on the Development of Christian Doctrine* (London: J. Toovey, 1845).

8   R.R. Reno, *In the Ruins of the Church: Sustaining Faith in an Age of Diminished Christianity* (Grand Rapids, Mich.: Brazos Press, 2002); R. Hütter, *Bound to Be Free*.

Why Not Rome, Constantinople, or Canterbury?

What, then, would keep me from embracing Roman Catholicism, or Eastern Orthodoxy or Anglicanism, when these ecclesial communions already embody the very elements of faith and practice that I believe are found wanting in the Baptist tradition? A cynic might point out that the Baptist institutional sources of all three of my academic degrees would render such a transition professionally difficult at best, and that furthermore I have already carved out a niche for myself in the world of theological scholarship as a Baptist who does research and writing in patristics and ecumenical theology, areas in which few Baptist theologians work—a distinction that would be lost were I to leave Baptist life. I would be dishonest if I denied that those professional limitations have ever crossed my mind, but I hope I am not being falsely noble when I insist that those considerations would not by themselves preclude a decision to become Catholic, Orthodox, or Anglican. My student who inquired about what might keep me from becoming Catholic probably expected me to enumerate my theological objections to Roman Catholicism, but any reservations I have regarding elements of Catholic—or Orthodox or Anglican—faith and practice are ultimately negligible as arguments against becoming an adherent to any of those traditions.

Negligible Reservations

It should be clear to anyone who has read thus far that some typical Baptist objections to the doctrine, worship, and ecclesial practice of Roman Catholicism, Eastern Orthodoxy, and Anglicanism are not my own: tradition as a source of theological authority, fidelity to the ancient rule of faith and its conciliar clarifications, structured patterns of liturgy as bearers of the church's theology, and a more fully sacramental theology have already been incorporated into my own theological perspective. I now attribute most Baptist rejections of ancient catholic patterns of faith and practice that differ with what such Baptists believe the Bible teaches to the refusal of many Baptists to recognize that the New Testament canon to which they appeal to establish the legitimacy of their Baptist perspectives cannot be rightly interpreted apart from the theological assumptions of the fourth-century church regarding what made those texts reliable sources of authoritative doctrine.[9]

---

9   For an appropriately nuanced Baptist perspective on the relationship of the theological assumptions of the fourth-century church to the authority and meaning of the

Some remaining reservations about Catholicism and Orthodoxy are not so easy to dismiss, but neither are they insurmountable barriers to becoming Catholic or Orthodox (since these particular reservations do not apply to the *via media* of the Anglican tradition, it will be left to the side for the time being). Prayers addressed to the saints and to Mary among them do not necessarily threaten the role of Christ as sole mediator between humanity and God when they are understood within a robust theology of the communion of saints in which death cannot overcome the real communion that exists among those who belong to the one body of Christ, and even the Catholic Marian dogmas have been explained by magisterial teaching in such a Christocentric manner that the standard Protestant descriptions of Catholic Mariology now approach being caricatures.[10] The *Joint Declaration on the Doctrine of Justification* issued by the Roman Catholic Church and the Lutheran World Federation on 31 October 1999 renders null and void the soteriological objections to Catholicism that have been invoked as primary justifications for a separate Protestant ecclesial existence for almost five centuries, and I make bold to suggest here that the Doctrine and Interchurch Cooperation Commission of the Baptist World Alliance should now give serious consideration to whether Baptists might find a way to follow the Methodist World Council in joining the *Joint Declaration*.[11] The doctrine of Petrine primacy certainly gives pause, but the ecumenical reality is that there is no other viable institution for serving as a focal symbol of the unity of the church. Pope John Paul II saw his ecumenical role is such terms of service to the larger body of Christ, and some Baptists have explored ways to affirm this understanding of the ecumenical significance of the Petrine office.[12] As a Baptist I believe that

---

canon of Scripture, see D.H. Williams, 'The Patristic Tradition as Canon', *PRSt* 32.4 (Winter, 2005), pp. 357-79.

10   See the sections on 'The Communion of Saints' and 'Mary—Mother of Christ, Mother of the Church' in *Catechism of the Catholic Church* (Liguori, Mo.: Liguori Publications, 1994), §§ 946-75, pp. 247-54.

11   Lutheran World Federation and Roman Catholic Church, *Joint Declaration on the Doctrine of Justification* (Grand Rapids, Mich.: William B. Eerdmans, 2000). On the possibility of a Baptist affirmation of the *Joint Declaration*, see Toom, 'Baptists on Justification', pp. 289-306.

12   In the 1995 papal encyclical on ecumenism (*Ut Unum Sint: Encyclical Letter of the Holy Father John Paul II on Commitment to Ecumenism* [Vatican City: Libreria Editrice Vaticana, 1995]), Pope John Paul II encouragingly declared, 'As Bishop of Rome I am fully aware, as I have reaffirmed in the present Encyclical Letter, that Christ ardently desires the full and visible communion of all those communities in which, by virtue of God's faithfulness, his Spirit dwells. I am convinced that I have a particular responsibility in this regard, above all in acknowledging the ecumenical aspirations of the majority of the Christian communities and in heeding the request made of me to find

Baptists have made great contributions to the global cause of religious liberty, but since the Second Vatican Council publicly committed the Roman Catholic Church to this principle, one cannot charge any former Baptist who might be received into the membership of the Catholic Church with abandoning that Baptist conviction.[13] Catholics have common cause with Baptists and others who believe that faith should never be a matter of civil coercion.

The most significant personal reservation which I have about becoming Catholic or Orthodox is my support for the ordination of women to offices of pastoral ministry, which of course runs counter to the current ecclesial discipline of the Roman Catholic Church and Eastern Orthodoxy. It is my outsider perception that the limitation of the pastoral office to men in these communions is not necessarily set in stone for perpetuity, however, despite the obvious obstacles. Yet it would be theologically and pragmatically undesirable for such communions with a universal jurisdiction that includes not only Western nations with liberal democracies, but also nations with other societal patterns, to make rapid modifications in this aspect of ecclesiology, and it ought not to be pursued simply because Christians in more egalitarian societies prefer such ecclesial transformations. It is one thing for a congregationally-governed Baptist church in a North American metropolitan area to decide to ordain a woman for service as a pastor; it may be quite another matter for the Pope or the College of Cardinals to declare that women may serve as priests when the Roman Catholic Church encompasses multiple cultural contexts with varying patterns for the respective roles of men and women in familial and societal life. In the meantime, it seems to me that Roman Catholicism, for example, has already incorporated women into roles of ecclesial leadership much more thoroughly than have moderate to progressive streams of Baptist life in the United States. Roman Catholic women serving as theologians in Catholic universities in North America vastly outnumber their counterparts in Baptist theological education, and women more consistently serve in public roles during services of the Mass in Catholic parishes (at least in North

---

a way of exercising the primacy which, while in no way renouncing what is essential to its mission, is nonetheless open to a new situation' (§ 95). For a Baptist appreciation of this encyclical, along with reflections on its reception by the Baptist Union of Great Britain, see Wright, 'The Petrine Ministry: Baptist Reflections', pp. 451-65. A wider ranges of ecumenical reflections is collected in C.E. Braaten and R.W. Jenson, eds., *Church Unity and the Papal Office: An Ecumenical Dialogue on John Paul II's Encyclical Ut Unum Sint (That All May Be One)* (Grand Rapids, Mich.: William B. Eerdmans, 2001).

13   Vatican II, *Dignitatis Humanae*, 7 December 1965, translated as 'Declaration on Religious Liberty' in *Vatican Council II*, ed. Flannery, pp. 799-812.

America) than in many moderate to progressive Baptist congregations that have championed the cause of women in ministry. All this is to say that while I might retain some personal reservations about this or that aspect of Catholicism or Orthodoxy, none of these reservations would be significant enough to dissuade me from membership in those churches on theological grounds—if such a possibility were solely a matter of the personal choice of an ecclesial communion.

Ecclesial and Ecumenical Responsibility

As far as I know, the fuller catholicity that I wish for Baptists is not yet exemplified by any specific Baptist congregation. Yet even though there may be other communities that are in fact already living that which I seek, I do not intend to seek a new ecclesial home beyond Baptist life for two primary reasons. First, Baptist congregations nurtured me towards Christian faith, baptized me, formed me in the faith, recognized my areas of giftedness and encouraged me to exercise them in vocational Christian ministry, ordained me, funded my theological education, and have continued to support my ministry financially, through their prayers, and in countless other ways. I am now a theological educator because of the faithfulness of Baptists, and I believe that I owe Baptists in return a commitment to contribute to the theological formation of their ministers— even if I have also come to believe that Baptists will be best served if their future ministers are theologically formed in some ways that may differ substantially from the theological formation that I received in Baptist institutions in the course of my own theological education. Furthermore, for good and ill, I am a Baptist. If I were to be received into the membership of, say, an Episcopal church next week, such a transfer of church membership would not make me an Episcopal theologian, except in name. I have been traditioned as a Baptist, and I would never be able to teach and write from the perspective of one who has been traditioned as an Episcopalian. I am able to address this book to a Baptist readership because I have long and deep experience of what it means to belong to Baptist communities.

Second, I am not sure that the cause of ecumenism is best served through the movement of theologians and ministers from one imperfect communion to another in which they believe they have found truer expressions of Christian faith and practice. I do not call into question, but rather affirm, the decisions of those who have felt compelled by their consciences to undertake such movements. Many have done so, as noted above, and they are some of the brightest and best from among their former communions. They have not abandoned the cause of ecumenism, and they will no doubt make considerable contributions to the cause of Christian unity precisely because of their previous experiences in serving of the communions of their nurture and calling. These are also in their own way steps towards visible

Christian unity, and as such they should be affirmed and celebrated. Nevertheless, I am of the considered opinion that before the separated churches can move towards visible unity, they must first go deep within their own traditions in order to recover elements of catholicity that once characterized their own churches but have been subsequently neglected and in order to identify the sources of the present barriers to a mutually realized catholicity. This can happen only if theologians commit themselves to remaining with the communions of their nurture and calling, warts and all, and with great patience work to help their churches towards something that will probably not be realized within the temporal span of any living theologian's ministry. Ecclesiology and ecumenism are inescapably eschatological: they belong to the tension between the realized and the as-yet-unrealized aspects of the reign of God in which the church participates.

A More Precise Definition of 'Catholicity'

This book has not yet offered a definition of its sought-after 'catholicity' beyond the basic lexical definition given in chapter 1 of *katholikē*, the third of the Nicaeno-Constantinopolitan *notae ecclesiae*, as a reference to the 'general' or 'universal' church to which all Christians belong. This withholding of a more precise definition of catholicity until this point has been partly due to my desire to allow the chapters exploring the relevance of various facets of catholicity for Baptist faith and practice to speak for themselves. It is primarily due, however, to the fact that it had not been fully clear to me precisely what I meant by 'catholicity' until the manuscript for this book was almost complete. The writing of this epilogue chapter coincided with the preparation of a paper for a consultation convened to explore the factors necessary for successfully holding a Second Conference on Faith and Order in North America in the near future.[14] In my paper I interpreted the principal goal of classical Faith and Order ecumenism, 'to call the churches to the goal of visible unity in one faith and one Eucharistic fellowship, expressed in worship and in common life in Christ',[15] as a call to the churches to reevaluate the extent to which their ecclesial communities currently realize catholicity as a mark of the

---

14   The first and only such conference was held at Oberlin College in Oberlin, Ohio, USA, in 1957; see P.S. Minear, ed., *The Nature of the Unity We Seek: Official Report of the North American Conference on Faith and Order, September 3-10, 1957, Oberlin, Ohio* (St. Louis: Bethany Press, 1958).

15   By-laws of the Faith and Order Commission of the World Council of Churches, quoted in *Faith and Order: Toward a North American Conference. Study Guide*, ed. N.A. Hjelm (Grand Rapids, Mich.: William B. Eerdmans, 2004), p. vii.

church.[16] My equation of 'visible unity in one faith and Eucharistic fellowship' with a mutual fuller realization of catholicity was the outcome of the concentrated reflection on the precise nature of the catholicity I sought for evangelicals in general and for my own Baptist ecclesial communion in particular that the preparation of that paper occasioned.

Understandings of 'catholic' as a mark of the church range from the (invisible) oneness of the (invisible) universal church,[17] in which sense the first and third of the *notae ecclesiae* are almost indistinguishable, to the connotation of a 'diffuse inclusivism',[18] to an ecclesial status of communion with Rome.[19] Although the earliest ecclesiological use of

---

16   S.R. Harmon, 'Evangelical Catholicity and the Contestation of Faith and Order: Why We Need a Second North American Conference' (unpublished paper presented to the Consultation on a Conference on Faith and Order in North America, Graymoor Ecumenical and Interreligious Institute, Garrison, New York, 3-5 January 2006). A book collecting the papers presented at this consultation is forthcoming from William B. Eerdmans.

17   When Baptists have affirmed catholicity as a mark of the church, they have tended to understand catholicity in terms of the church's invisible or 'mystical' oneness. The *Orthodox Creed*, a confession adopted by a group of English General Baptist congregations in 1678, exemplifies this understanding: '[W]e believe the visible church of Christ on earth, is made up of several distinct congregations, which make up that one catholick church, or mystical body of Christ' ('The "Orthodox Creed"', article 30, in Lumpkin, *Baptist Confessions of Faith*, pp. 318-19). A similar theology of the church's catholicity is implied in the affirmation of the catholicity of the church in the 'Address of Welcome' of Judge Willis, President of the Baptist Union of Great Britain and Ireland, to the first Baptist World Congress in London in 1905: 'Let us, in all our supplications, remember all the members of other Churches, and ask that the choicest blessings may rest upon them. We believe, and our fathers have believed, in the Holy Catholic Church. The Church of Rome is right in affirming that the Church of Christ is catholic. The catholicity of the Church of Christ is not, however, a doctrine of Rome: it is an essential consequence resulting from the principles on which Christ's Church is founded. It is clearly written: "There is one body, and one Spirit, even as ye are called in one hope of your calling; one Lord, one faith, one baptism, one God and Father of all, who is above all, and through all, and in you all"' (Baptist World Alliance, *Baptist World Congress: London, July 11-19, 1905*, pp. 2-3).

18   A sense critiqued by D.H. Williams, 'The Disintegration of Catholicism into Diffuse Inclusivism', pp. 389-93.

19   So *Catechism of the Catholic Church*, § 834, p. 221: 'Particular Churches are fully catholic through their communion with one of them, the Church of Rome "which presides in charity" [quotation from Ignatius of Antioch *Romans* 1.1]. "For with this church, by reason of its pre-eminence, the whole Church, that is the faithful everywhere, must necessarily be in accord" [quotation from Irenaeus *Against Heresies* 3.3.2]. Indeed, "from the incarnate Word's descent to us, all Christian churches everywhere have held and hold the great Church that is here [at Rome] to be their only basis and foundation since, according to the Savior's promise, the gates of hell have never prevailed against

katholikē by Ignatius of Antioch certainly refers to a Christologically grounded universality of the church,[20] my call for Baptist and evangelical catholicity has in mind a much more narrow yet exceedingly common early Christian usage of the Greek *katholikē* and the Latin *catholica*: they are adjectives describing the fully orthodox pattern of faith and practice that distinguished early catholic Christianity from Gnosticism, Arianism, Donatism, and all manner of other heresies and schisms. Catholic Christianity in this ancient sense is the closest the post-New Testament church has come to a full realization of 'visible unity in one faith and one Eucharistic fellowship', even if the late patristic emergence of the non-Chalcedonian churches qualified the totality of that visible unity in the East, and even if the perfect realization of the church's catholicity lies in the eschatological future. Catholicity, then, has to do with a *qualitative* fullness of faith and order that is visibly expressed in one Eucharistic fellowship.

Although Baptists and other evangelicals sometimes attribute any feature of patristic Christianity that seems at odds with their own understanding of New Testament faith and practice to a Constantinian corruption of the church,[21] this understanding of catholicity in terms of one visible and orthodox Eucharistic fellowship is almost as old as the later New Testament documents. One paragraph prior to the description of the church as 'catholic' in the letter to the *Smyrneans*—and only a few years after the Christianity of the New Testament—Ignatius warned the church at Smyrna regarding the doctrine and practice of the Docetists, 'They abstain from the eucharist and prayer, since they do not confess that the eucharist is the flesh of our savior Jesus Christ, which suffered on behalf of our sins and which

---

her'" [quotation from Maximus the Confessor *Opuscula theologica et polemica*]. While the *Catechism* reserves the fullest sense of catholicity for churches in communion with Rome, in § 838 (p. 222) it also grants that there are other senses in which non-Roman Catholic churches and Christians participate in the catholicity of the church, though to a lesser extent: "'The Church knows that she is joined in many ways to the baptized who are honored by the name of Christian, but do not profess the Catholic faith in its entirety or have not preserved unity or communion under the successor of Peter" [quotation from *Lumen gentium* 15]. Those "who believe in Christ and have been properly baptized are put in a certain, though imperfect, communion with the Catholic Church" [quotation from *Unitatis redintegratio*]. *With the Orthodox Churches*, this communion is so profound "that it lacks little to attain the fullness that would permit a common celebration of the Lord's Eucharist"' [quotation from Paul VI, Discourse, 14 December 1975].

20   Ignatius of Antioch *Smyrneans* 8.2 (*The Apostolic Fathers*, ed. and trans. Ehrman, 1:304-05): 'Let the congregation be wherever the bishop is; just as wherever Jesus Christ is, there is the universal church (*katholikē ekklēsia*)'.

21   Cf. Williams, *Retrieving the Tradition and Renewing Evangelicalism*, pp. 101-31.

the Father raised in his kindness', and then exhorted them to 'flee divisions as the beginning of evils'.[22] What is explicit in the Ignatian correspondence around A.D. 110 is implicit in the New Testament itself, in particular the Gospel of John and its dominical sayings that have Eucharistic functions in the absence of a Johannine institution narrative: the insistence that those who eat Christ's flesh and drink Christ's blood are those who are one with Christ occasions the departure of some from one Eucharistic fellowship (John 6.52-69).

If, as I have suggested in this book, some aspects of Baptist patterns of faith and practice are currently insufficiently catholic in terms of this fuller qualitative catholicity, and if I do not intend to seek this qualitative catholicity within another ecclesial communion for the reasons given above, then my only recourse as a Baptist theologian is to advocate a renewal of qualitative catholicity within the Baptist tradition—especially when this is not a matter of mere personal preference but rather a settled conviction that such a renewal would contribute to 'building up the body of Christ' (Eph. 4.12). While it is too early to evaluate the role that the interest in 'ancient-future' Christianity manifested in the 'emergent church' movement may play in helping a younger generation of Christian leaders towards an appreciation for qualitative catholicity,[23] there have been some intentional catholic renewal movements within Protestant communions during the past two centuries. Any contemporary movement towards Baptist catholicity ought to keep in mind the strengths and weaknesses of these precedents outside of the Baptist tradition.

Precedents for Catholic Renewal within Protestant Denominations

There is a sense in which the Protestant Reformation was itself a catholic renewal movement within Roman Catholicism rather than an effort to establish a separate anti-Catholic ecclesial existence.[24] Many later Protestants did in fact come to understand the Protestant tradition in the

---

22   Ignatius of Antioch *Smyrneans* 7.1-2 (*Apostolic Fathers*, ed. and trans. Ehrman, 1:302-03). It is significant that immediately prior to this section, Ignatius linked the doctrinal errors of the Docetists, who lacked a truly embodied Christology, with their failures to embody the Christian way of life: 'But take note of those who spout false opinions about the gracious gift of Jesus Christ that has come to us, and see how they are opposed to the mind of God. They have no interest in love, in the widow, the orphan, the oppressed, the one who is in chains or the one set free, the one who is hungry or the one who thirsts' (*Smyrneans* 6.2).

23   See R.E. Webber, *The Younger Evangelicals: Facing the Challenges of the New World* (Grand Rapids, Mich.: Baker Books, 2002).

24   So the essays collected in C.E. Braaten and R.W. Jenson, eds., *The Catholicity of the Reformation* (Grand Rapids, Mich.: William B. Eerdmans, 1996).

latter terms, but there have also been groups of Protestants in the nineteenth and twentieth centuries that have sought to retrieve something that had been lost through this perpetuated separation from a communion that, for all its late medieval failings, had nonetheless remained in continuity with qualitative catholicity. The most significant among these are the nineteenth-century Oxford Movement within the Church of England that eventuated in the Anglo-Catholic tradition in Anglicanism, the 'Mercersburg Theology' that emerged within the German Reformed Church in the United States in the middle of the nineteenth century, and the Berneuchener liturgical renewal movement in twentieth-century Germany.

The Oxford Movement

Some Baptist ministers who learned a little about the Oxford Movement in a church history survey course may regard the Tractarians as odd group of Anglicans who lost their Protestant minds and tried to reverse the gains of the Reformation in the Church of England. Historians of the Baptist experience in England know that Baptist reactions against the emphases of the Oxford Movement led to the loss of a more robust sacramental life that British Baptist churches had once known.[25] Baptists may therefore be predisposed to be wary of any suggestion that the Oxford Movement might serve as a model for the recovery of catholicity within the Baptist tradition. Perhaps it might help Baptist champions of religious liberty towards some degree of sympathy with the aims of the Tractarians if it is pointed out that the Movement's public phase began as a protest against Erastianism, the supremacy of the state over the church in matters of religion.[26]

Led principally by John Keble (1792-1866), John Henry Newman (1801-90), and Edward Pusey (1800-82), the Oxford Movement called for the renewal of Anglicanism through the recovery of the more fully catholic patterns of faith and practice found in patristic Christianity. Supporters of the Movement advanced this cause not only through the publication of their essays in the serial *Tracts for the Times* that lent them the designation

---

25   On reactions to the Oxford Movement by Baptists in England, see J.H.Y. Briggs, *The English Baptists of the Nineteenth Century* (A History of the English Baptists, 3; Didcot: Baptist Historical Society, 1994), pp. 224-27.

26   Newman, *Apologia Pro Vita Sua*, p. 56, regarded John Keble's 14 July 1833 University sermon at St. Mary's Church in Oxford on 'National Apostasy', which took the Parliament to task for its introduction of a bill to dissolve ten Irish bishoprics, as the beginning of the public phase of the Oxford Movement. Most subsequent historians have followed Newman's lead and dated the formal or 'Tractarian' phase of the movement from Keble's sermon in 1833 to Newman's reception into the Roman Catholic Church in 1845.

'Tractarians' but also through energetic patristic, medieval, and Byzantine scholarship that resulted in the publication of the *Library of the Fathers*, an influential collection of English translations of patristic literature,[27] along with other significant contributions to historical, theological, and liturgical scholarship. The Movement initially encountered much popular and political opposition. Because Parliament was invested with the authority to approve the appointment of bishops in the Church of England, for a few decades the government was able to limit the advance of the Movement by choosing bishops from among the Movement's opponents, and the eventual reception into the Roman Catholic Church of Newman and a few others among the Tractarians fractured the movement internally. Yet the Movement ultimately succeeded in influencing the subsequent development of the Church of England beyond the wildest dreams of the Tractarians. During the remainder of the nineteenth century and into the twentieth century, the patterns of faith and practice they urged influenced the reintroduction of liturgical practices that had long been neglected and forgotten in the Church of England (some of which even a few Baptist congregations now practice, such as the exchange of the sign of peace), the founding of Anglican religious orders, and a heightened attention to addressing social injustices that included the commitment of Anglican clergy to service in the slums of English cities.[28] Now Anglo-Catholic and Evangelical clergy have for some time alternated in being elected as Archbishop of Canterbury, and even such a leading Evangelical Anglican as Alister McGrath can now praise the Oxford Movement as 'a renewing influence, bringing new life to the church and its worship'.[29]

The Mercersburg Theology

Although the Oxford Movement did exert some influence within Episcopalian circles in the United States (and in doing so created no small degree of controversy),[30] among non-Anglican Protestants in mid-nineteenth-century America another comparable movement was more influential—or more controversial, as the case might be. Theologian John Nevin (1803-86) and historian Philip Schaff (1819-93), professors in the

---

27   See R.W. Pfaff, 'The Library of the Fathers: The Tractarians as Patristic Translators', *StudPhil* 70 (1973), pp. 329-44.

28   C.B. Faught, *The Oxford Movement: A Thematic History of the Tractarians and Their Times* (University Park, Pa.: Pennsylvania State University Press, 2003), pp. 151-52.

29   A.E. McGrath, *The Renewal of Anglicanism* (Harrisburg, Pa.: Morehouse Publishing, 1993), p. 25.

30   Faught, *Oxford Movement*, pp. 146-50.

Theological Seminary of the German Reformed Church in the United States in Mercersburg, Pennsylvania, USA during the 1840s (Nevin resigned in 1850, Schaff continued until 1865 before joining the faculty of Union Theological Seminary, New York City, New York, USA in 1870), advocated an 'evangelical catholicism' that included efforts towards liturgical renewal, reverence for the ancient creeds and the writings of the church fathers, a Eucharistic theology of real presence, and an ecumenical openness that transcended Protestantism.[31] The Mercersburg theologians do not seem to have been influenced significantly by the Oxford Movement at first (although Nevin did ultimately find himself attracted in that direction), but like the Tractarians they advanced their cause through important literary contributions to historical and theological scholarship and the preparation of liturgical resources, and like Newman and his colleagues, Schaff helped make available in English translation the textual sources needed for an evangelical-catholic *ressourcement* by editing the two series of the *Nicene and Post-Nicene Fathers* and the three-volume collection of *The Creeds of Christendom*.[32]

Anti-Catholicism was then deeply entrenched in the German Reformed Church in the United States, as it was in all Protestant denominations of that day—in this case it featured a German Reformed version of the Landmark Baptist argument for an apostolic succession of 'true churches' that bypassed the 'false' Catholic Church, with special emphasis on the place of the persecuted Waldensians in the German Reformed pedigree[33]— and both Nevin and Schaff faced repeated charges of 'Romanism', with Schaff officially tried and acquitted (though not easily) of heresy. Their influence within their own denomination during their careers at Mercersburg was limited, though in the middle of the twentieth century the merger of the German Reformed Church with the Evangelical Synod of North America and then the Congregational Christian Churches would lay claim to the ecumenical emphases of the Mercersburg Theology. The more

---

31   For studies of the Mercersburg Theology, see L.J. Binkley, *The Mercersburg Theology* (FMCS, 7; Lancaster, Pa.: Franklin and Marshall College, 1953); J.H. Nichols, *Romanticism in American Theology: Nevin and Schaff at Mercersburg* (Chicago: University of Chicago Press, 1961); J.M. Maxwell, *Worship and Reformed Theology: The Liturgical Lessons of Mercersburg* (PTMS, 10; Pittsburgh: Pickwick Press, 1976).

32   P. Schaff, ed., *Nicene and Post-Nicene Fathers*, First Series, 14 vols. (New York: Christian Literature, 1886-89); P. Schaff and H. Wace, eds., *Nicene and Post-Nicene Fathers*, Second Series, 14 vols. (New York: Christian Literature, 1890-98); P. Schaff, *The Creeds of Christendom with a History and Critical Notes*, 6th edn., rev. D.S. Schaff, 3 vols. (New York: Harper & Row, 1931; reprint, Grand Rapids, Mich.: Baker Book House, 1990).

33   G.H. Shriver, *Philip Schaff: Christian Scholar and Ecumenical Prophet* (Macon, Ga.: Mercer University Press, 1987), pp. 21-23.

enduring influence of this movement came through Schaff's success in pushing the academic discipline of church history in the United States in more ecumenical directions. As George Shriver points out in his biography of Schaff, 'reading a list of twentieth-century presidents of the society [the American Society of Church History, which Schaff founded] is like reading the who's who of the ecumenical movement in the United States in this century'.[34]

The Berneuchener Movement

Beyond the English-speaking ecclesiastical world, the Berneuchener Movement, a liturgical renewal movement that began within the youth movement connected with the *Evangelisch* churches in Germany in the 1920s, also sought to renew the church through a retrieval of aspects of ancient catholicity. Led by Marburg theologian Karl Ritter (d. 1968) and Wilhelm Stählin (1883-1975), then professor of practical theology in the Protestant theological faculty in Münster (where for a time he was a colleague of Karl Barth) and later the Lutheran Bishop of Oldenburg, the initial Berneuchener Circle was a group of clergy and laypersons (including for a time Paul Tillich) that met periodically from 1923 to 1928 at the Berneuchen estate in East Brandenburg to consider how the spiritual needs of post-World War I Germany might be met through a more sacramental liturgical life. The meetings at Berneuchen led to the foundation in 1931 of the Brotherhood of St. Michael, a non-denominational and non-residential religious order that has maintained a retreat center at Kloster Kirchberg in the Black Forest and published a succession of journals and newsletters dealing with various issues in liturgy, theology, and ecclesial life. Today the Brotherhood has an international membership of around 400 men and women.[35]

The Anglophone theological world might be largely unaware of the existence of the Berneuchener Movement were it not for references to the Movement by Paul Tillich, Karl Barth, and Dietrich Bonhoeffer. Though they mention the Movement only briefly, their estimation of it was on the whole negative. Tillich was initially a member of the original Berneuchener Circle and was attracted to the Movement by the rigor of the reforms it sought, which 'did not limit itself to matters of ritual', but eventually left

---

34   Shriver, *Philip Schaff*, p. 98.
35   Little literature on the Movement is available in English. Publications associated with the Berneuchener Circle and the Brotherhood of St. Michael from 1924 through the present are available online at www.gottesjahr.de and www.quatember.de; other information may be found on the site of the Kloster Kirchberg retreat center, www.klosterkirchberg.de.

the Movement when he perceived that it trended towards 'an exclusive concern for sacramental realization (often in archaic forms)' rather than towards an active engagement with culture; he did, however, continue appreciate the Movement's recovery of a sacramental outlook that he believed had been lost by an overly intellectualized Protestantism.[36] In the course of lamenting the various matters of lesser importance with which various groups within German Protestantism occupied themselves after the retreat of the Confessing Church from political resistance, Stählin's former colleague Barth mentioned 'the Berneucheners...in their mysteries' in ironic juxtaposition with 'prisoners in their cells' who now 'discovered everywhere the wonder of solitary contemplation'.[37] In that connection Bonhoeffer's famous pronouncement to his Finkenwalde students, 'Only he who cries out for the Jews can sing the Gregorian chant', was directed against liturgists associated with the Berneuchener Movement whom Bonhoeffer regarded as indifferent to the political situation.[38]

While it would be an unfair caricature to portray the Berneuchener Movement solely in terms of an infatuation with ancient liturgical forms to the neglect of the social and political spheres of the church's existence in the world, the misgivings of Tillich, Barth, and Bonhoeffer about the Movement's preoccupations should give pause to Baptists who may become convinced of the need for a Baptist programme of catholic retrieval. Worship is indeed the most important locus for the recovery and transmission of catholicity in theology and praxis, but liturgical renewal must never devolve into mere formalism or antiquarianism. During an academic year spent at The Catholic University of America over a decade ago, I had a conversation with a young Jesuit priest enrolled in a doctoral program in liturgical studies who would regularly lead celebrations of the Mass based on patristic and medieval liturgies and incorporating Gregorian chant and medieval plainsong. When I told him that I was interested in attending those services in light of my own studies in patristics, he was

---

36   P. Tillich, *The Interpretation of History*, trans. N.A. Rasetzki and E.L. Talmey (New York: Charles Scribner's Sons, 1936), pp. 52-53.

37   K. Barth, letter to M. Niemöller (29 June 1946), quoted in Busch, *Karl Barth*, p. 273.

38   Recollection of H. Traub in *I Knew Dietrich Bonhoeffer: Reminiscences by His Friends*, ed. W.-D. Zimmermann and R.G. Smith, trans. K.G. Smith (New York: Harper and Row, 1966), p. 156, quoted in Bethge, *Dietrich Bonhoeffer*, p. 441. Many Baptists will resonate with this declaration of Bonhoeffer, but in light of the first-hand reports from the 1934 assembly of the Baptist World Alliance in Berlin that were published in Baptist newspapers in the United States and have been surveyed more recently by W.L. Allen, 'How Baptists Assessed Hitler', *ChrCent* 99.27 (1-8 September, 1982), pp. 890-91, Bonhoeffer could just as easily have said with Baptists in mind, 'Only those who cry out for the Jews can call for "world-wide evangelism"'.

quick to respond, 'But remember that worship is an encounter with the living God!' When the recovery of patterns of worship that bear the Christian tradition in its catholicity serves not as an end in itself but as means by which people are drawn into a sacramental encounter with the living God, people will be helped towards an embodied faith that seeks the transformation of society.

Without denigrating the quite legitimate concerns of the Berneuchener Movement or minimizing the contributions of the Mercersburg Theology along these lines to a more limited ecclesial context, I suggest that the Oxford Movement may offer the most appropriate model for Baptists who hope that Baptist congregations may become places in which that sort of formative sacramental encounter is the normative Baptist experience. The location of its principal exponents in influential centers of theological education, its contributions to theological scholarship that outlived the careers of the Tractarians, and its concern with the cure of souls in the practice of parish ministry were certainly some of the factors involved in the eventual success of the Oxford Movement, but I submit that the most significant reason for the ultimate emergence of Anglo-Catholicism as an enduring shaper of the Anglican ethos was the strength of the network of relationships among the Tractarians and their supporters.[39] These friendships sustained the Tractarians in the face of bitter opposition and public attacks on their work, and their encouragement of one another helped them continue patiently in their labors during the darkest days of their common project. The charges of 'Romanism' against both the Tractarians and the Mercersburg theologians are probable precedents for public reactions to any Baptists who might now urge a retrieval of qualitative catholicity, for as Barry Harvey has pointed out with regard to the context of Baptist life in the United States, anti-Catholicism is 'the one prejudice still socially acceptable among Baptists'.[40] Advocates of Baptist catholicity will need each other as they seek to convince their fellow Baptists that they need their sisters and brothers in the *communio sanctorum*.

An Invitation to a Conversation

I remain troubled by the possibility that a quest for a fuller catholicity among Baptists might do violence to people who have chosen to be Baptist because they perceived that the Baptist tradition lacked some of those

---

39   See Faught, *Oxford Movement*, pp. 73-99 (ch. 3, 'Friendship: Fraternity and Farewell'), in which Faught defends the thesis that 'Friendship was intrinsic to the Oxford Movement' (p. 73).

40   Harvey, 'Where, Then, Do We Stand?', p. 377, n. 69.

aspects of a qualitative catholicity—e.g., a sacramental spirituality—that I have identified in this book as desirable amendments to typical Baptist faith and practice, but which these people may already have rejected as characteristics of the communions they left in order to identify with Baptists. This is a legitimate concern, especially if any transformation of the Baptist vision in this direction were to be implemented through authoritarian abuses of the pastoral office. The last thing I would want theological students or ministers to do with my proposals is to become pastors who implement changes in worship or other aspects of congregational life contrary to the wishes of the membership of a congregation. I am not asking any Baptist to give up anything that he or she has chosen through the exercise of an uncoerced conscience. Rather, I want to invite Baptist theological educators and students, Baptist ministers, and Baptist laypersons to an ongoing conversation about the nature of Baptist identity and its relationship to catholic Christian identity. The conversation for which I hope is a contested conversation in the MacIntyrean sense, one in which all Baptists have a voice in a community-wide argument about these matters, but also in which all Baptists have ears that will hear and minds that will give genuine consideration to perspectives on Baptists and the catholic tradition that are not presently their own.

British Baptist theologian John Colwell began the preface to his recent book on sacramental theology, 'I suspect that some may view this work as an inexcusably long letter of resignation'.[41] Some readers of my own book might have similar perceptions—or perhaps even hopes—but its author has no plans to resign either from the Baptist tradition or from the responsibility for the theological formation of future ministers in that tradition. I wholeheartedly concur with Stephen Holmes, another British Baptist theologian, who began his own book on the value of tradition for present-day Christians by insisting that 'I remain grateful for all I have learnt and received from this background, and I feel as comfortable within such circles as I ever expect to feel anywhere, this side of the return of Christ'.[42] I do love the Baptist tradition, and I offer here my apologies to any Baptist readers who may feel that I have been unduly harsh on some of their most deeply cherished beliefs and practices in these pages. It is precisely because I love the Baptists whom I serve as a theological educator that I have carried out this book-length argument with my own tradition. I hope that others will join this argument, and I hope that all involved in the conversation will love Christ's church deeply enough to regard our cherished constructions of Baptist identity as temporary way stations en

---

41   Colwell, *Promise and Presence*, p. ix.
42   Holmes, *Listening to the Past*, p. xi.

route to the realization of the visible unity of the body of Christ in one Eucharistic fellowship.

Re-Envisioning Baptist Identity: A Manifesto for Baptist Communities in North America

Dear Baptist Sisters and Brothers,

We are writing to ask you to consider the following theological proposal. Baptists in North America have long been fragmented, and far too often the fragmentation has been for most unworthy reasons. In the contemporary theological milieu, many Baptist theologians have remained timid about stepping forward to make constructive theological proposals. Even criticism of the status quo popular theology is either excessively muted, or so heavily ideological that it seldom gets to the heart of what the Baptist theological heritage has stood for.

For too long Baptist theology has railed against Catholics, Anglicans, Campbellites, and Methodists, not to mention liberals, fundamentalists, pedobaptists, holy rollers, or whoever are identified as the current 'bad guys' in other churches or theological camps. But Baptist theology ought not to be against the church. Baptist theology needs to be for the church and the gospel in a hostile world.

We believe that there are a growing number of Baptists who would like to see a new theological direction. We think you may also be among them. That is why we are asking you to examine the statement Re-Envisioning Baptist Identity. Please read it carefully and give it your consideration. It is not a perfect statement. It is a beginning. We hope that it will begin a framework for dialogue among Baptists of all sorts. We are inviting you to help us place the issues raised in these affirmations before other Baptists. Let us know by mail or email if you would like to be in conversation with a growing number of people who want to pursue the task of re-envisioning Baptist identity.

Hopefully,

Mikael Broadway	Barry Harvey	Elizabeth Newman
Curtis Freeman	James Wm. McClendon, Jr.	Philip Thompson

Re-Envisioning Baptist Identity: A Manifesto for Baptist Communities in North America

To the people called Baptist in North America who in Jesus Christ have 'like living stones' been 'built into a spiritual house, to be a holy priesthood, to offer spiritual sacrifices acceptable to God through Jesus Christ, may grace and peace be yours in abundance' (1 Pet. 2.4-5). From our beginnings, we Baptists have celebrated the freedom graciously given by God in Jesus Christ (Gal. 5.1; John 8.31-32). Freedom in Christ is a gift, not a given. This freedom does not subsist merely in self-determination. It is not rooted in what the world calls natural rights or social entitlements. It cannot be claimed, possessed, or granted by any human institution, community, or individual. It belongs to God's gift of the new creation in which we share through our faithfulness to Christ (2 Cor. 5.17; Rom. 5.15).

God's freedom is the pattern for the gift of freedom in Jesus Christ. This freedom which is ours in Christ therefore cannot be understood apart from the fellowship of the Holy Spirit (2 Cor. 13.13; 3.17) who convicts us of sin (John 16.8-11), leads us to repentance (Rom. 2.4; Acts 5.31), converts us to faith (Rom. 8.9; 1 Cor. 12.3), renews us through regeneration (John 3.5-6; Tit. 3.4-5), sanctifies us to holiness (Rom. 15.16; Gal. 5.16; 1 Pet. 1.2), assures us of salvation (Rom. 8.15; Gal. 4.6; Eph. 1.13-14), incorporates us into the church (1 Cor. 12.13), guides us in discernment (John 14.26, 20.22-23; 1 Cor. 2.14-16, 12.10), and readies us for ministry (1 Cor. 12.11). Human freedom exists only in relationship with the triune God who lovingly creates, wisely governs, mercifully redeems, and justly judges the world. It is into this relationship of freedom that God calls a people from every tribe and language, nation and race...to be a royal house of priests, to serve our God and to rule upon the earth (Rev. 5.9-10).

The freedom of God's people is freedom *from* the domination of sinful and selfish human impulses (Rom. 7.24-25; Eph. 2.1-10). We are free *for* serving Christ and one another (Gal. 5.1, 13), free to be sisters and brothers of the firstborn Jesus (Rom. 8.14-17, 29; Col. 1.15, 18; John 1.12-13), and free in our participation in the new humanity that God is calling out from among the nations (Eph. 2.15; 2 Cor. 5.17; James 1.18; Rev. 14.4). Because freedom comes to us as gift, it is not something that we possess for ourselves to use for our own ends. It is something we encounter through the divine community of the triune God and with the Christian fellowship that shares in this holy communion (1 John 1.3). Human freedom in the new creation is the image of the Creator's freedom who does not will to be free in solitude but for creation (Gen. 1.26-30).

Baptists at the outset faithfully bore witness to this freedom in their common life. For these early Baptists, liberty of conscience was not a libertarian notion. It was a conviction that faith must not, indeed cannot, be coerced by any power or authority. This understanding of freedom is very different from the modern account in which the mere expression of the will is the greatest good. We concede nevertheless that the conception of freedom we oppose became deeply entrenched in the North American Baptist tradition by the mid-eighteenth century. Baptist heritage, however, predates the formation of modern democratic societies in North America. We have, therefore, drawn from earlier sources of the Baptist heritage and from other examples in the believers church (or baptist) tradition that have resisted modern notions of freedom and have practiced a more communal discipleship. We thus seek an understanding of freedom that is true to the biblical witness and the earliest insights of the Baptist heritage.

Two mistaken paths imperil this precious freedom in contemporary Baptist life. Down one path go those who would shackle God's freedom to a narrow biblical interpretation and a coercive hierarchy of authority. Down the other path walk those who would sever freedom from our membership in the body of Christ and the community's legitimate authority, confusing the gift of God with notions of autonomy or libertarian theories. We contend that these two conceptions of freedom, while seemingly different, both define freedom as a property of human nature apart from the freedom of God in Jesus Christ and the Holy Spirit. We reject both of them as false and prefer neither, for false freedom will only lead Baptists to exchange the glory of God for the shame of idols (Rom. 1.21-23). Only the freedom of the gospel liberates us from the worship of idols, including the idolatry of the self, so that we might serve the living and true God and await the Son from heaven whom God raised from the dead (1Thess. 1.9-10; Tit. 2.11-14; Acts 1.11). We invite Baptists in the fellowship of kindred minds to join us in resisting all destructive ideologies that subvert the gospel. To that end we offer the following affirmations as a description of freedom, faithfulness, and community.

1. *We affirm Bible Study in reading communities* rather than relying on private interpretation or supposed 'scientific' objectivity. We believe that we are engrafted anew into God's freedom whenever we gather around the open Bible, because it is the truth of God's Word that sets us free (Rom. 11.17; John 8.31-32). Such freedom is a consequence, not a condition, of reading the Scriptures. God therefore calls us to freedom through the faithful and communal study of the Scriptures (John 5.39; Acts 17.11). Because all Christians are graciously gifted everyone has something to bring to the conversation, but because some members are specifically called 'to equip the saints' everyone has something to learn from those with equipping gifts (Eph. 4.7-16). We thus affirm an open and orderly process whereby faithful communities deliberate together over the Scriptures with sisters and brothers of the faith, excluding no light from any source. When all exercise their gifts and callings, when every voice is heard and weighed, when no one is silenced or privileged, the Spirit leads communities to read

wisely and to practice faithfully the direction of the gospel (1 Cor. 14.26-29).

We reject all forms of authoritarian interpretation, whether they come from the ranks of the academy or the clergy. Consequently, we deny that the Bible can be read as Scripture by any so-called scientific or objective interpretive method (e.g., literal-grammatical, historical-critical, etc.) apart from the gospel and the community in which the gospel is proclaimed. Scripture wisely forbids and we reject every form of private interpretation that makes Bible reading a practice which can be carried out according to the dictates of individual conscience (2 Pet. 1.20-21). We therefore cannot commend Bible study that is insulated from the community of believers or that guarantees individual readers an unchecked privilege of interpretation. *We call others to the freedom of faithful and communal reading of Scripture.*

2. *We affirm following Jesus as a call to shared discipleship* rather than invoking a theory of soul competency. We believe that by following the call to discipleship we discover true freedom (Matt. 4.19; 8.22; 9.9; 10.38; etc.). Just as the pattern of God's freedom became flesh in Jesus of Nazareth, we who are his followers partake of the gift of freedom as we offer our bodies to God as living sacrifices, thus exalting Christ in our living and in our dying (John 1.14; Rom. 12.1; Phil. 1.20). God therefore calls us to the freedom of faithful discipleship by participating in the way of Jesus, which begins with our confession of faith (Matt. 16.15; Rom. 10.9-13) and is lived out under the shadow of the cross which is ours to bear (Luke 9.23). Such discipleship requires a shared life of mutual accountability in the church. Disciples may not remain aloof from the church and its life, its proclamation, its fellowship, its ministry, its suffering, its peace (Luke 4.16; Acts 2.42; 1 Cor. 12.12-26; Heb. 10.25). Only as we stand together under the Lordship of Christ can we discern by the Spirit that from which we are liberated and that to which we are obligated (Matt. 18.15-20; John 20.22-23). In this life together, God has chosen us to serve as priests, not for our own selves, but to one another. Through our mutually reciprocal priestly actions, confessions of faith and of fault are heard by the church to the end that together we might proclaim the mighty acts of God's mercy (Isa. 61.6; 1 Pet. 2.9-10; James 5.16; Rev. 1.6; 5.10; 20.6).

We reject all accounts of following Jesus that construe faith as a private matter between God and the individual or as an activity of competent souls who inherently enjoy unmediated, unassailable, and disembodied experience with God. We further reject all identifications of the priesthood of believers with autonomous individualism that says we may do and believe what we want regardless of the counsel and confession of the church. We finally reject the false teaching that redefines gospel freedom as the pursuit of self-realization apart from the model of Jesus Christ (Phil.

2.5-11). *We call others to the freedom of faithful and communal discipleship.*

3. *We affirm a free common life in Christ in gathered, reforming communities* rather than withdrawn, self-chosen, or authoritarian ones. We believe that, along with other Christians, the Holy Spirit gathers us from the nations (Isa. 56.7; Mark 11.17; Rev. 5.9-10) and empowers us to share in the gift of God's freedom so that in our bodies the Lord's mission of reconciling the world might continue (1 Cor. 6.19-20; 2 Cor. 5.18). We further believe that Baptists have an important contribution to make in God's mission of freedom. The practices of believers baptism and called-out church membership display a distinctive vision of the church as a community of shared response to God's mission, message, and renewal (Matt. 28.19-20; Acts 2.38; 22.16). As we strive to embody this vision, our life together suggests an alternative to the undisciplined practice of baptism. We find it alarming that for many Christians the fact of their baptism into the death, burial, and resurrection of Christ is of little or no consequence to them. Our call for a believers church, however, is not a condescension to other traditions. It is first a summons to close off nominal Christianity in our own ranks. It is only second a gesture toward other traditions and communities to the end that they might make disciples of those whom they baptize. Insofar as we are faithful in our common witness to a believers church, we embody afresh the church to which God's call to mission is given (Matt. 28.19-20; Mark 16.15; Luke 24.46-48; John 20.21; Acts 1.8).

In humility, we recognize the failures of the believers church to be a faithful witness to its own ecclesial vision, and we look to the church catholic as it appears throughout the world and through history for other examples of faithful communities. Because we affirm that there is much the believers church can and must learn from other Christian traditions, we reject as false all ecclesiologies which claim either that the aggregate of Baptist (or Evangelical) congregations is the whole of God's people (1 Cor. 3.16-17; 12.12) or that any one congregation (or association of congregations) exists autonomously without connection to the whole people of God (John 17.21; 1 Cor. 12.12-26; Eph. 4.4-6; 1 Pet. 2.4-5). *We call others to the freedom of a faithful and communal embodiment of a believers church.*

4. *We affirm baptism, preaching, and the Lord's table as powerful signs that seal God's faithfulness in Christ and express our response of awed gratitude* rather than as mechanical rituals or mere symbols. We do not deny that God may strengthen the faith of believers in new forms and in providential ways. Nevertheless baptism, proclamation, and the Lord's table, which were ordained by the Lord to be observed faithfully until the end of the age (Matt. 28.19-20; Mark 16.15; 1 Cor. 11.23-26; Matt. 26.26-29; Mark 14.22-25), have sustained and nourished the people of God through the ages as we make our way through this world. In and through

these remembering practices, God's grace and Christian obedience converge in a visible sign of the new creation. By repeating these signs we learn to see the world as created and redeemed by God. The Spirit who proceeds from the Father through the Son makes the performance of these practices effectual so as to seal and nourish the faith and freedom of believers.

Baptism is a sign of our fellowship with the crucified and risen Lord. We are buried with Christ in a watery grave (Rom. 6.3; Col. 2.12), and we are raised by the Spirit to walk in the resurrection life of the new creation (Rom. 6.4-5; 2 Cor. 5.17; Gal. 3.27-28; 6.15; Col. 3.1). Our rebirth through the Holy Spirit (John 3.3, 6; 1.12-13; Tit. 3.5; 1 Pet. 1.3, 23) is sealed in baptism until the Lord comes to consummate our salvation (Acts 2.38; 10.47-48; 19.5-6; 1 Pet. 3.21-22; 1 Cor. 12.13; 2 Cor. 1.21-22; 5.5; Eph. 1.13-14; Rom. 8.23). Because we have been claimed in the waters of baptism, we are reminded that our lives are not our own but have been bought with a price (Col. 2.20; 3.3; 1 Cor. 6.19-20). Thus by baptism we enter into a covenant of mutual accountability and discipleship with the community of the faithful (Matt. 18.15-20).

Preaching becomes a sign when those who preach and listen witness the judging and reconciling grace of God's Word (Eph. 1.13-14; 1 Cor. 14.24-25; Tit. 3.9; Heb. 4.12). Gospel proclamation is more than the utterance of human words. Preaching is the Word of God only when by the power of the Holy Spirit it becomes God's own speech that brings the new creation within sight. Whether it is in hot gospel preaching, elegantly intoned sermons, or plain and simple messages, God graciously declares the liberating Word which seals salvation through our proclamation of the gospel (Acts 10.44; Rom. 10.13-17; 1 Pet. 1.23). Gospel proclamation may be performed by all who are gifted by the Spirit and called by the church (Acts 11.19-21; 1 Pet. 4.10-11).

The bread is a sign of Christ's body, and the cup is a sign of the new covenant in his blood (Luke 22.19-20; 1 Cor. 11.23-26). As we remember Jesus in communion through the bread of fellowship and the cup of life (1 Cor. 11.24-25), the Lord himself is with us (Matt. 26.26; Mark 14.22; Luke 22.19; 1 Cor. 11.24, 27-29) declaring that we who are many are one body (1 Cor. 10.17; Eph. 4.4-6). In the Lord's Supper the Spirit thus signifies and seals the covenant that makes us one with Christ and one in Christ with one another. Yet we must continually strive to learn in the company of our sisters and brothers what it means to be a people that are reconciled and reconciling, forgiven and forgiving (1 Cor. 11.17-22; 2 Cor. 5.17-21). Thus each time we remember Jesus in communion we renew our pledge of faith and are renewed by the grace of God as we envision the coming fullness of the new creation (Matt. 14.25; 26.29; Luke 14.15; 22.18, 30; Rev. 19.9).

Baptist reflections on 'the sacraments' have for too long been fixed on late medieval and early modern theories. As modernity draws to a close, it is a fitting time to revisit afresh these practices and their significance for the people of God. We reject all accounts of these practices that would limit the presence of the risen Lord to the performance of the enacted signs as we also reject all accounts that deny the reality of his presence in their enactment. The Lord is present and active both in the performance of these remembering signs and with the community that performs them. Yet the greater threat in the believers church is not from false understandings but from neglect of practice. Baptism has been superseded by the evangelical invitation. Preaching is being displaced by other media. The Supper is so infrequently observed that Christians starve for lack of nourishment. We reject all attempts to make the church and its practices incidental to our relationship with Christ and one another. *We call others to the freedom of the faithful communal enactment of the Lord's remembering signs.*

5. *We affirm freedom and renounce coercion as a distinct people under God* rather than relying on political theories, powers, or authorities. We believe that when God's people live together as a colony of heaven (Phil. 1.27; 3.20; Col. 3.1-4; Heb. 11.8-10), the gift of God's freedom will keep them from the reach of all worldly rulers, powers, and authorities. We therefore affirm the historic free church conviction that the church is to be disestablished from the control of the state (Matt. 22.15-22; 1 Pet. 2.11-17) and from the use of coercive power to enforce and extend the gospel (Matt. 5.21-26, 38-48; 26.52; Luke 9.51-56; Rom. 12.14-21). We further believe that in order for our free church witness to be faithful we must do more than seek institutional independence of civil authorities. We must also continue to press for the independence of the church from the idols of nationalism, racism, ethnocentrism, economic systems, gender domination, or any other power that resists the Lordship of Jesus Christ (Gal. 3.27-28; Acts 10.34), who disarmed and triumphed over the rebellious powers in the cross (Col. 2.15). We cannot merely accept the disestablishment of the church through the cultural forces of secularity, the political measures of government, or the judicial interpretations of courts. The disestablishment of the church is constitutive of its identity as God's called-out community which foreshadows the coming reign of God as does no other community. Nor can we accept terms of agreement with nation-states which sequester the authority of faith to a private, internal, individual, and narrow sphere. The gospel we proclaim is a public message for all people. It speaks to the external lives of believers. It calls out a distinctive community seeking to embody the reign of God. It makes all-encompassing claims about the world. We affirm the disestablishment of the church as the faithful form of the church's social existence.

The disestablishment of the church is not just a curious fragment of Baptist folklore, but if the designation 'free church' is to be more than an empty phrase it must refer to a distinctive way of living in and engaging the world. We believe that in the pluralistic society of North America, only a church that is politically and culturally independent can convince its own and others of gospel truth (Rom. 1.16). The community of people that is to be a 'city built on a hill' (Matt. 5.14) is not any worldly power or authority. This exemplary community is the free and faithful church of Jesus Christ. Gospel freedom misunderstood and misused turns the church into a tool of the powers and authorities (Eph. 1.21; 2.2; 3.10; 6.12; Col. 1.16; 2.10, 15; Tit. 3.1). The skills we learn in the baptized and remembering community help us to resist these powers that otherwise would determine our lives. Only such a distinct people can make known to the powers and authorities of the present age the plan of the mystery hidden for ages in God who created all things (Eph. 3.10). In a free and faithful church, the community of the baptized together with the whole of creation can know that there is a God who is the beginning and end of all things and especially of our freedom (Rev. 1.8).

We reject any attempt to establish a vision of the church, whether Baptist or any other, by means of civil or political power. We thus reject all such constantinian strategies. Although we attempt to live at peace with all people (Rom. 2.10; 14.19; 2 Tim. 2.22; Heb. 12.14) and to seek the peace of the earthly city (Jer. 29.7), we do so with our eyes on the peace of the other city (1 Cor. 7.15; Heb. 11.10; Rev. 21.1-2), whose citizenship we share (Eph. 2.19-22), whose politics we practice (Phil. 1.27; 3.20; 1 Pet. 2.11-12), and whose Lord alone is our peace (Eph. 2.14-15; Col. 1.21-22; Heb. 7.2, 15-17; Rev. 1.4). Thus we heed the call to be salt and light, engaging the world and challenging the powers with the peace and freedom of the gospel (Matt. 5.13-14). We therefore reject any and all efforts to allow secular political versions of church-state separation to define the boundaries or the nature of our witness as the free and faithful people of God. *We call others to the freedom of faithful and communal witness in society.*

Among Baptists today this witness is in danger of falling to ideologies of the right and of the left that are foreign to the content and direction of the gospel. To many observers the crisis may appear to be merely a manifestation of the culture wars that pit conservatives against liberals, people of color against 'white America', women against men, interest group against interest group. What these agendas call freedom is what the gospel calls bondage to the false gods of nationalism, classism, or narcissism. The tragedy for Christians is that the culture wars have overwhelmed and co-opted the agenda of the church. The struggle for the soul of Baptists in North America is a struggle against all these false gods. It is, therefore, not a struggle between one such god and another. Yet some Baptists believe that it is. We disagree.

Ideologies and theologies of the right and the left, as different as they may appear, are really siblings under the skin by virtue of their accommodation to modernity and its Enlightenment assumptions. Some

Baptists (in the tradition of E.Y. Mullins' *Axioms of Religion* or D.C. Macintosh's *Personal Religion*?) embraced modernity by defining freedom in terms of the Enlightenment notions of autonomous moral agency and objective rationality. Others (in the tradition of the Princeton Theology and *The Fundamentals*?) have reacted against modernity, but ironically they perpetuated the same modern assumptions through the individualism of revivalistic religious experience and through the self-evidence of truth available by means of common sense reason. It is not a question of whether these adversaries have adopted modernity. Both drank deeply from the same waters even if they have done so at different wells. We believe that this accommodation to the individualism and rationalism of modernity weakens the church by transforming the living and embodied Christian faith into an abstract and mythic *gnosis* (1 Tim. 1.3-7).

Since the patterns of certitude, privilege, and power that modernity engendered are passing away (1 Cor. 7.31), it is time to admit that all theologies tied to the foundational assumptions of the Enlightenment will share the same fate. We thus urge our fellow Baptists to say farewell to modernity and its theological offspring because there is no other foundation for our faith than Jesus Christ (1 Cor. 3.11). We further believe that the real struggle facing Baptist Christians today is for the embodiment of free, faithful, and communal discipleship that adheres to the gospel rather than submitting to intellectual and social agendas that have no stake in the gospel (Rom. 1.16; Gal. 1.6).

We embrace neither modern alternative. We call instead for a reclaiming of the Baptist heritage as we re-envision the study of Scripture, the life of discipleship, the embodiment of a faithful church, the enactment of remembering signs, and the disestablishment of the church from worldly powers. We believe these affirmations to be true to the gospel and to the best of our heritage as Baptists. We are convinced that by proclaiming this vision of freedom, faithfulness, and community the church can be renewed through the Holy Spirit. We invite those who disagree with us or have questions to engage us in conversation. Through such interaction we gain a clearer understanding of these issues which are essential for the flourishing of the church of Jesus Christ. We call upon all those who can join us in this declaration to do so, and more importantly to display it in the worship, work, and witness of the free and faithful people of God.

Confessing the Faith

On July 5, 1905 the Baptist World Alliance met in London for its first congress. Its president, Alexander Maclaren, addressed the assembly and proposed that their very first act be an affirmation of the historic Christian faith. Such a step, he said, would clear away misunderstanding and put an end to slander. It would have been predictable if he had invited the participants to recite a passage of Scripture like John 3.16, but instead Maclaren asked his fellow Baptists to rise to their feet and confess the Apostles' Creed. Affirming the creed was a surprising act for a people who are typically perceived as avowing 'no creed but the Bible' and emphasizing the liberty of each individual conscience. Why would they take such an unusual step?

Many Baptists acquired an allergy to creeds because of the illegitimate ways they have been used to bind the individual conscience, to substitute for a personal confession of faith, or to underwrite an established church-state order. Creeds are misused whenever they become instruments of coercion, just as religious liberty is abused when it is invoked to legitimate deviation from the living witness of apostolic faith. Maclaren, however, called for the affirmation of the creed, 'not as a piece of coercion or discipline, but as a simple acknowledgment of where we stand and what we believe'.

The staunch anti-creedalism in Baptist life often leads to the faulty assumption that modern Christians can leapfrog from the primitive Christianity of the Bible to the contemporary situation with relative ease. This hermeneutical naïveté fails to offer any realistic means for present day Bible readers to discern the central themes of Scripture that give a sense of its whole message as good news. Ironically, in the wake of the Baptist encounter with modernity those from both ends of the theological spectrum employed the slogan 'no creed but the Bible' in their theological arguments. Serious Bible readers will find much needed hermeneutical guidance by returning to the ancient creeds of the church.

The creeds contain a basic outline of apostolic preaching and teaching to which the Scriptures attest. They do not possess an authority independent of Scripture, but derive their authority from the biblical story which they summarize and ultimately from the Triune God whose voice is heard in it.

They are not full accounts of 'the faith once delivered to the saints', but they do provide a kind of 'rule of faith' which effectively regulates and guides the reading of interpretive communities. The creeds thus name what C.S. Lewis called 'mere Christianity' which all Christians can in good conscience affirm: the Father Almighty who made heaven and earth, Jesus Christ the only Son our Lord, the Holy Spirit, the universal church, the communion of saints, the forgiveness of sins, the resurrection of the body, and the life everlasting. Conspicuously absent is any reference to biblical inspiration, atonement theories, baptismal practices, communion theologies, church polity, millennial views, or gender pronouncements.

Affirming one of the ancient ecumenical creeds guards against the twin dangers posed by those who would either add to or take away from the gospel. As the BWA prepares to meet for the centennial world congress next year in London a few outspoken detractors have questioned its orthodoxy. They demand capitulation to a new set of fundamentals which include narrow theories of biblical inerrancy and the subordination of women to men in domestic and church life as articles of faith, while also tolerating no criticism of the United States and its foreign policy. At the same time, others reduce the richness of the apostolic faith to what seems at the time to be most rational or most relevant. The worldwide community of Baptists has wisely resisted both sorts of narrowing that produce further fragmentation and division.

We encourage the Baptist World Congress to follow again the wise counsel of Alexander Maclaren and show the shrills on the extremes to be wrong by joining voices with a great cloud of witnesses in 'the unanimous acknowledgement of our Faith' by reaffirming either the Apostles' Creed or the 'Nicene' Creed. Such a free and faithful declaration is a commendable act that bears repeating—at least once every century! Indeed we encourage all congregations to confess the faith by reciting one of the ancient ecumenical creeds each Lord's Day. If faith is the assurance of things hoped for, then such acts of confession move us toward the unity for which our Lord prayed and which we seek.

Curtis W. Freeman   Elizabeth Newman
Steven R. Harmon   Philip E. Thompson

(The statement was prefaced by the following cover letter, which was signed by twenty-eight Baptist principals, deans, and theologians from institutions of theological education in Australia, Brazil, Canada, the Czech Republic, England, India, Scotland, and the United States of America.)

23 June 2004

Revd Keith G. Jones, Chair
BWA Resolutions Committee
Nad Habrovkou 3
164 00 PRAHA 6
Czech Republic

Dear Keith Jones and BWA Resolutions Committee:

On July 5, 1905 the first act of the BWA World Congress as a community of baptized believers was to confess the faith by reciting the Apostles' Creed. It was an historic event that we hope will be repeated, not only at the Centenary Congress at Birmingham next summer, but in congregations of Baptists worldwide.

To that end as Baptist theologians and educators we want to affirm and encourage your plans to recite either the Apostles' Creed or the Niceno-Constantinopolitan Creed at the BWA Congress in 2005. We have expressed our support for this action in the statement 'Confessing the Faith'. These are important times for us as a worldwide community of Baptists to declare together the unity of the faith. If our confession inspires others to follow and stirs a conversation about the unity we seek, then it will be a positive step.

Your fellow Baptist sisters and brothers,

Mikael Broadway	Shaw University Divinity School Raleigh, North Carolina
Biju Chacko	India Baptist Theological Seminary Kottayam, India
Christopher J. Ellis	Bristol Baptist College Bristol, England
Rosalee Velloso Ewell	South American Theological Seminary Londrina, Brazil
Paul Fiddes	Regent's Park College, University of Oxford Oxford, England

Curtis W. Freeman	Duke Divinity School Baptist House of Studies Durham, North Carolina
James Gordon	Scottish Baptist College Paisley, Scotland
Doug Harink	King's University College Alberta, Canada
Steven R. Harmon	Campbell University Divinity School Buies Creek, North Carolina
Barry Harvey	Baylor University Waco, Texas
Stephen Holmes	King's College London, England
Willie J. Jennings	Duke Divinity School Durham, North Carolina
Barry A. Jones	Campbell University Divinity School Buies Creek, North Carolina
Roy Kearsley	South Wales Baptist College Cardiff, Wales
Ken R. Manley	Whitley College, University of Melbourne Melbourne, Australia
Nathan Nettleton	Whitley College, University of Melbourne Melbourne, Australia
Elizabeth Newman	Baptist Theological Seminary at Richmond Richmond, Virginia
Parush R. Parushev	International Baptist Theological Seminary Prague, Czech Republic
Frank Rees	Whitley College, University of Melbourne Melbourne, Australia
Luis Rivera	Princeton Theological Seminary Princeton, New Jersey
J. Deotis Roberts	Eastern Baptist Theological Seminary (retired) Philadelphia, Pennsylvania
Karen Smith	South Wales Baptist College Cardiff, Wales

Philip E. Thompson	North American Baptist Theological Seminary Sioux Falls, South Dakota
John Weaver	South Wales Baptist College Cardiff, Wales
Daniel H. Williams	Baylor University Waco, Texas
Jonathan Wilson	Acadia Divinity College Wolfville, Nova Scotia
Ralph Wood	Baylor University Waco, Texas
Nigel G. Wright	Spurgeon's College London, England

*Institutions are named only for the purpose of identifying the signatories and are not intended to speak on behalf of the institutions.

Bibliography

Ancient Texts

Alexander of Alexandria. 'Letter to Alexander of Thessalonica', in *The Trinitarian Controversy*, ed. and trans. W.G. Rusch (SEChrTh; Philadelphia: Fortress Press, 1980), pp. 33-44.

Ambrose of Milan. 'Concerning Repentance' (NPNF[2] 10:329-59).

Arius. 'Letter to Alexander of Alexandria', in *The Trinitarian Controversy*, ed. and trans. W.G. Rusch (SEChrTh; Philadelphia: Fortress Press, 1980), pp. 31-32.

— 'Letter to Eusebius of Nicomedia', addressed to Eusebius of Nicomedia, in *The Trinitarian Controversy*, ed. and trans. W.G. Rusch (SEChrTh; Philadelphia: Fortress Press, 1980), pp. 29-30.

Augustine of Hippo. *De Baptismo contra Donatistas* (PL 43:107-244; ET, NPNF[1] 4:411-514).

— *De Trinitate* (PL 42:819-1098; ET, NPNF[1] 3:1-228).

Basil of Caesarea. *De Spiritu Sancto* (PG 32:67-217; ET, *St. Basil the Great: On the Holy Spirit*, trans. D. Anderson [Crestwood, N.Y.: St. Vladimir's Seminary Press, 1980].

Cassiodorus. *Expositio epistulae ad Hebraeos* (PL 68:685-794).

Cyril of Alexandria. *Fragmenta in epistulam ad Hebraeos* (PG 74:953-1005).

Cyril of Jerusalem. *Catecheses* (PG 33:331-1180; ET in *The Works of Saint Cyril of Jerusalem*, trans. L.P. McCauley and A.A. Stephenson [FC, 61, 64; Washington, D.C.: The Catholic University of America Press, 1969], vol. 1, pp. 91-249; vol. 2, pp. 4-140).

Didache. In *The Apostolic Fathers*, trans. and ed. K. Lake (LCL, 24; Cambridge, Mass.: Harvard University Press, 1912), vol. 1, pp. 309-33.

Didymus the Blind. *Fragmenta in epistulam ad Hebraeos (in catenis)*, in *Pauluskommentare aus der griechischen Kirche: aus Katenenhandschriften gesammelt und herausgegeben*, 2nd edn., ed. K. Staab (NTAbh, 15; Münster: Aschendorff, 1984), pp. 83-112.

Ephrem the Syrian. *Commentary on the Epistle to the Hebrews* (in Armenian), in *Srboyn Ep'remi matenagrut'iwnk'* (Venetik, Armenia: Tparani Srboyn Ghazaru, 1836), vol. 3.

Epiphanius. *Panarion Adversus LXXX Haereses* (PG 41-42; ET, *The Panarion of Epiphanius of Salamis*, 2 vols., trans. F. Williams [NHS, 35-36; Leiden: E.J. Brill, 1987-1994]).

Eusebius of Caesarea. *Historia Ecclesiastica* (PG 20:45-906; ET, *Eusebius: The Ecclesiastical History*, trans. J.E.L. Oulton, 2 vols. [LCL, 264-265; Cambridge, Mass.: Harvard University Press, 1932]).

Evagrius of Pontus. 'Chapters on Prayer', ch. 8 in *Evagrius of Pontus: The Greek Ascetic Corpus. Translation, Introduction, and Commentary*, trans.

and ed. R.E. Sinkewicz (OECS; Oxford: Oxford University Press, 2003), pp. 191-209.

Gennadius of Constantinople. *Fragmenta in epistulam ad Hebraeos* (PG 85:1664-65).

Gregory of Nazianzus. 'The Theological Orations', trans. C.G. Browne and J.E. Swallow, in *Christology of the Later Fathers*, ed. E.R. Hardy (LCC; Louisville: Westminster John Knox Press, 1954), pp. 128-214.

Gregory of Nyssa. *Ad Ablabium quod non sint tres dii* (GNO III/1:37-57; ET, 'Answer to Ablabius', trans. C. Richardson, in *Christology of the Later Fathers*, ed. E. Hardy (LCC, 3; Philadelphia: Westminster Press, 1954), pp. 256-67.

— *Contra Eunomium* (GNO I-II; ET, NPNF[2] 5:33-248).

— *In Canticum canticorum homiliae* (GNO VI:3-467; ET, *Saint Gregory of Nyssa: Commentary on the Song of Songs*, trans. Casimir McCambley [AILEHS, 12; Brookline, Mass.: Hellenic College Press, 1987).

Hilary of Poitiers. *De Trinitate* (PL 10:9-472; ET, NPNF[2] 9).

Hippolytus *Contra Haeresin Noeti* (PG 10:817; ET, ANF 5:223-31).

— *The Refutation of All Heresies* (GCS 26:1-293; ANF 5:9-153).

Ignatius of Antioch. 'Letters of Ignatius', in *The Apostolic Fathers*, ed. and trans. B.D. Ehrman (LCL, 24; Cambridge: Harvard University Press, 2003), vol. 1, pp. 218-321.

Jerome. *Commentary on Isaiah* (PL 24:17-349).

John Chrysostom. *In epistulam ad Hebraeos argumentum et homiliae1-34* (PG 63:13-236).

— *Homilies on the Epistle to the Hebrews* (NPNF[1] 14:363-522).

John of Damascus. *De Fide Orthodoxa* (PG 94; ET, NPNF[2] 9:1-101).

John of Damascus (?). *Commentarii in epistolam ad Hebraeos* (PG 95:929-97).

Justin Martyr. *1 Apologia* (*Die ältesten Apologeten*, ed. E.J. Goodspeed [Göttingen: Vandenhoeck & Ruprecht, 1915], pp. 26-77; ET, ANF 1:163-87).

— *2 Apologia* (*Die ältesten Apologeten*, ed. E.J. Goodspeed [Göttingen: Vandenhoeck & Ruprecht, 1915], pp. 78-89; ET, ANF 1:188-93).

— *Dialogus cum Tryphone Judaeo* (*Die ältesten Apologeten*, ed. E.J. Goodspeed [Göttingen: Vandenhoeck & Ruprecht, 1915], pp. 90-265; ET, ANF 1:194-270).

Oecumenius. *Commentarii in epistolam ad Hebraeos*, in *Pauluskommentare aus der griechischen Kirche: aus Katenenhandschriften gesammelt und herausgegeben*, 2nd edn., ed. K. Staab (NTAbh, 15; Münster: Aschendorff, 1984), pp. 462-69.

Origen. *Commentarii in Iohannem* (*Commentaire sur saint Jean*, ed. C. Blanc, vols. 1-2 [SC, 120, 157; Paris: Éditions du Cerf, 1966-92]; ET, *Origen: Commentary on the Gospel According to John, Books 1-10*, trans. R.E. Heine [FC, 80; Washington, D.C.: The Catholic University of America Press, 1989]).

— *De Principiis* (*Vier Bücher von den Prinzipien*, ed. H. Görgemanns and H. Karpp [TF, 24; Darmstadt: Wissenschaftliche Buchgesellschaft, 1976], pp. 462-560 and 668-764; ET, *Origen: On First Principles*, trans. G.W. Butterworth [Gloucester, Mass.: Peter Smith, 1973]).

— *Fragmenta in Epistulam ad Hebraeos homiliae* (PG 14:1308-09).

Paulinus of Nola. *Carmina* (CSEL, 30; ET in *Documents of the Marriage Liturgy*, ed. and trans. M. Searle [Collegeville, Minn.: Liturgical Press, 1992], pp. 31-32).

Photius. *Fragmenta in epistulam ad Hebraeos* 6.6, in *Pauluskommentare aus der griechischen Kirche: aus Katenenhandschriften gesammelt und herausgegeben*, 2nd edn., ed. K. Staab (NTAbh, 15; Münster: Aschendorff, 1984), p. 646.

Prosper of Aquitaine. *Praeteritorum Sedis Apostolicae episcoporum auctoritates, de gratia Dei et libero voluntatis arbitrio* (PL 45:1756-60, 51:205-212, 50:531-37; ET 'Official Pronouncements of the Apostolic See on Divine Grace and Free Will', in *Defense of St. Augustine*, trans. P. de Letter [ACW, 32; Westminster, Md.: Newman Press, 1963], pp. 178-85).

Richard of St. Victor. *De Trinitate* (*De Trinitate: Text critique avec introduction, notes et tables*, ed. J. Ribaillier [TPMA, 6; Paris: J. Vrin, 1958]; ET, 'Book Three of the Trinity', in *Richard of St. Victor: The Twelve Patriarchs, The Mystical Ark, Book Three of the Trinity*, trans. G.A. Zinn [CWS; New York: Paulist Press, 1979], pp. 373-97.

Severian of Gabala. *Fragmenta in epistulam ad Hebraeos (in catenis)*, in *Pauluskommentare aus der griechischen Kirche: aus Katenenhandschriften gesammelt und herausgegeben*, 2nd edn., ed. K. Staab (NTAbh, 15; Münster: Aschendorff, 1984), pp. 213-351.

Synodal Letter of the Council of Antioch. In *The Trinitarian Controversy*, ed. and trans. W.G. Rusch (SEChrTh; Philadelphia: Fortress Press, 1980), pp. 45-48.

Tertullian. *Adversus Praxean* (CSEL 47:227-89; ET, ANF 3: 597-627).

Theodore of Mopsuestia. *Fragmenta in epistulam ad Hebraeos (in catenis)*, in *Pauluskommentare aus der griechischen Kirche: aus Katenenhandschriften gesammelt und herausgegeben*, 2nd edn., ed. K. Staab (NTAbh, 15; Münster: Aschendorff, 1984), pp. 113-212.

Theodoret of Cyrus. *Interpretatio in epistulam ad Hebraeos* (PG 82:673-785).

— 'Interpretation of Hebrews', in *Theodoret of Cyrus: Commentary on the Letters of St. Paul*, trans. and ed. R.C. Hill (Brookline, Mass.: Holy Cross Orthodox Press, 2001), vol. 2, pp. 136-207.

Theophilus of Antioch. *Ad Autolycum* (*Theophilus of Antioch: Ad Autolycum*, ed. R.M. Grant [Oxford: Clarendon Press, 1970], pp. 2-146; ET, ANF 2:89-121.

Vincent of Lérins. *Commonitorium* (G. Rauschen and P.B. Albers, eds., *Florilegium Patristicum*, vol. 5, *Vincentii Lerinensis Commonitoria*, ed. G. Rauschen [Bonn: P. Hanstein, 1906]; ET, NPNF[2] 11:131-56).

Modern Literature

Allen, W.L. 'How Baptists Assessed Hitler', *ChrCent* 99.27 (1-8 September, 1982), pp. 890-91.

Altaner, B. and Stuiber, A. *Patrologie: Leben, Schriften und Lehre der Kirchenväter*, 8th edn. (Freiburg im Breisgau: Herder, 1978).

Ammerman, N.T. *Baptist Battles: Social Change and Religious Conflict in the Southern Baptist Convention* (New Brunswick, N.J.: Rutgers University Press, 1990).

Anglican Communion Office and Baptist World Alliance. *Conversations around the World 2000-2005: The Report of the International Conversations between the Anglican Communion and the Baptist World Alliance* (London: Anglican Communion Office, 2005).

Armstrong, A.H. 'Karl Barth, the Fathers of the Church, and "Natural Theology"', *JTS* n.s. 46.1 (April, 1995), pp. 191-93.

Backus, I. 'Ulrich Zwingli, Martin Bucer and the Church Fathers', in *The Reception of the Church Fathers in the West: From the Carolingians to the Maurists*, ed. I. Backus (Leiden: E.J. Brill, 1997), vol. 2, pp. 627-60.

Baker, R.A., ed. *A Baptist Source Book* (Nashville, Tenn.: Broadman Press, 1966).

Balthasar, H.U. von. *Presence and Thought: An Essay on the Religious Philosophy of Gregory of Nyssa*, trans. Marc Sebanc (San Francisco: Ignatius Press, 1995).

Baptist Union of Great Britain. *Gathering for Worship: Patterns and Prayers for the Community of Disciples*, ed. C.J. Ellis and M. Blyth (Norwich, England: Canterbury Press, 2005).

Baptist World Alliance. *The Baptist World Congress: London, July 11-19, 1905. Authorised Record of Proceedings*, ed. J.H. Shakespeare (London: Baptist Union Publication Dept., 1905).

Bardsley, H.J. 'The Testimony of Ignatius and Polycarp to the Writings of St. John', *JTS* 14 (1913), pp. 207-220.

Bardenhewer, O., Schermann, T., and Weyman, C., eds. *Bibliothek der Kirchenväter*, 2nd edn. (Kempten and Munich: J Kösel, 1911-).

Bardenhewer, O., Zellinger, J., and Martin, J., eds. *Bibliothek der Kirchenväter*, 2nd series (Munich: J. Kösel, 1932-).

Barth, K. *Unterricht in der christlichen Religion*, vol. 1, *Prolegomena (1924)*, ed. H. Reiffen, Karl Barth-Gesamtausgabe pt. 2, vol. 9 (Zürich: Theologischer Verlag, 1985).

— *Unterricht in der christlichen Religion*, vol. 2, *Die Lehre von Gott/Die Lehre vom Menschen (1924/1925)*, ed. H. Stoevesandt, Karl Barth-Gesamtausgabe, pt. 2, vol. 10 (Zürich: Theologischer Verlag, 1990).

— *Unterricht in der christlichen Religion*, vol. 3, *Die Lehre von der Versöhnung/Die Lehre von der Erlösung (1925/1926)*, ed. H. Stoevesandt, Karl Barth-Gesamtausgabe, pt. 2, vol. 13 (Zürich: Theologischer Verlag, 2003).

— *Die christliche Dogmatik im Entwurf*, vol. 1, *Die Lehre vom Worte Gottes: Prolegomena zur christlichen Dogmatik (1927)*, ed. G. Sauter, Karl Barth-Gesamtausgabe, pt. 2, vol. 7 (Zürich: Theologischer Verlag, 1982).

— *Der Römerbrief*, 5th edn. (Münich: Chr. Kaiser Verlag, 1929).

— *God in Action: Theological Addresses*, trans. E.G. Homrighausen and K.J. Ernst (Edinburgh: T & T Clark, 1937).

— *Church Dogmatics*, vols. I-IV, ET eds. G.W. Bromiley and T.F. Torrance (Edinburgh: T & T Clark, 1956-75).

— *The Göttingen Dogmatics: Instruction in the Christian Religion*, ed. H. Reiffen, trans. G.W. Bromiley (Grand Rapids, Mich.: William B. Eerdmans, 1991).

— *The Holy Spirit and the Christian Life: The Theological Basis of Ethics*, trans. R.B. Hoyle (Louisville, Ky.: Westminster John Knox, 1993).

Bauckham, R. 'The Study of Gospel Traditions Outside the Canonical Gospels: Problems and Prospects', in *Gospel Perspectives*, vol. 5., *The Jesus Tradition Outside the Gospels*, ed. D. Wenham (Sheffield: JSOT Press, 1984), pp. 369-403.

Beaty, M., Buras, T., and Lyon, L. 'Christian Higher Education: An Historical and Philosophical Perspective', *PRSt* 24.2 (Summer, 1997), pp. 145-65.

Beaty, M. and Lyon, L. 'Integration, Secularization, and the Two-Spheres View at Religious Colleges: Comparing Baylor University with the University of Notre Dame and Georgetown College', *CSR* 29.1 (Fall, 1999), pp. 73-112.

Benne, R. *Quality with Soul: How Six Premier Colleges and Universities Keep Faith with Their Religious Traditions* (Grand Rapids, Mich.: William B. Eerdmans, 2001).

— 'Crisis of Identity: A Clash Over Faith and Learning', *ChrCent* 121.2 (27 January, 2004), pp. 22-26.

Benoit, A. and Prigent, P., eds., *La Bible et les Pères: Colloque de Strasbourg (1er-3 Octobre 1969)* (Paris: Presses Universitaires de France, 1971).

Benoit, A., Prigent, P., Aland, K., Duplancy, J., and Fischer, B. 'Pour un inventaire général de citations patristiques de la Bible Grecque: Appel et propositions aux Patrologues et aux Biblistes', *Greg* 51 (1970), pp. 561-65.

Bethge, E. *Dietrich Bonhoeffer: A Biography*, rev. edn., trans. E. Mosbacher (Minneapolis: Fortress Press, 2000).

Binkley, L.J. *The Mercersburg Theology* (FMCS, 7; Lancaster, Pa.: Franklin and Marshall College, 1953).

Black, M. 'The Christological Use of the Old Testament in the New Testament', *NTS* 18 (1971), pp. 1-14.

Bloom, H. *The American Religion: The Emergence of the Post-Christian Nation* (New York: Simon & Schuster, 1992).

Blowers, P.M. 'The *Regula Fidei* and the Narrative Character of Early Christian Faith', *ProEccl* 6 (Spring, 1997): 199-228.

Boff, L. *Trinity and Society*, trans. P. Burns (TLS; Maryknoll, N.Y.: Orbis Books, 1988),

Boring, M.E. *Disciples and the Bible: A History of Disciples Biblical Interpretation in North America* (St. Louis: Chalice Press, 1997).

Braaten, C.E. 'An Open Letter to Bishop Mark Hanson', 11 July 2005, available online at http://wordalone.org/docs/wa-braaten.htm).

Braaten, C.E. and Jenson, R.W., eds. *The Catholicity of the Reformation* (Grand Rapids, Mich.: William B. Eerdmans, 1996).

— *Church Unity and the Papal Office: An Ecumenical Dialogue on John Paul II's Encyclical Ut Unum Sint (That All May Be One)* (Grand Rapids, Mich.: William B. Eerdmans, 2001).

— *In One Body through the Cross: The Princeton Proposal for Christian Unity* (Grand Rapids, Mich.: William B. Eerdmans, 2003).

Briggs, J.H.Y. *The English Baptists of the Nineteenth Century* (A History of the English Baptists, 3; Didcot: Baptist Historical Society, 1994).

Bright, P. 'The Epistle to the Hebrews in Origen's Christology', in *Origeniana Sexta: Origène et la Bible/Origen and the Bible*, ed. G. Dorival and A. le Boulluec (BETL, 118; Leuven: Leuven University Press, 1995), pp. 559-65.

Bright, W. *Ancient Collects and Other Prayers*, 7th edn. (Oxford: James Parker, 1902).

Broadway, M., Freeman, C., Harvey, B., McClendon, J.W. Jr., Newman, E., and Thompson, P.E. 'Re-Envisioning Baptist Identity: A Manifesto for Baptist Communities in North America', *BapTod* (26 June, 1997), pp. 8-10.

Bultmann, R. *Die Geschichte der synoptischen Tradition*, 3d edn. (Göttingen: Vandenhoeck und Ruprecht, 1958).

— *History of the Synoptic Tradition*, trans. J. Marsh (New York: Harper and Row, 1963).

Burghardt, W.J. 'Did Saint Ignatius of Antioch Know the Fourth Gospel?' *TS* 1 (1940), pp. 7-15.

Bush, L.R. and Nettles, T.J. *Baptists and the Bible*, rev. edn. (Nashville, Tenn.: Broadman & Holman, 1999).

Busch, E. *Karl Barth: His Life from Letters and Autobiographical Texts*, trans. J. Bowden (Grand Rapids, Mich.: William B. Eerdmans, 1994).

Campbell, T.A. 'The "Wesleyan Quadrilateral": The Story of a Modern Methodist Myth', in *Doctrine and Theology in the United Methodist Church*, ed. T.A. Langford [Nashville, Tenn.: Abingdon, 1991], pp. 154-61.

Capes, D.B. *Old Testament Yahweh Texts in Paul's Christology* (WUNT^2, 47; Tübingen: J.C.B. Mohr [Paul Siebeck], 1992).

Carroll, J.M. *The Trail of Blood* (Lexington, Ky.: American Baptist Pub. Co., 1931).

Charlesworth, J.H. and Culpepper, R.A. 'The Odes of Solomon and the Gospel of John', *CBQ* 35 [1973], pp. 298-322.

Childs, B.S. *The New Testament as Canon: An Introduction* (Philadelphia: Fortress Press, 1984).

Clapp, R. *A Peculiar People: The Church as Culture in a Post-Christian Society* (Downers Grove, Ill.: InterVarsity Press, 1996).

Clark, N. *Call to Worship* (London: SCM Press, 1960).

Clarke, W.N. *An Outline of Christian Theology* (New York: Charles Scribner's Sons, 1898).

Coakley, S. '"Persons" in the "Social" Doctrine of the Trinity: A Critique of Current Analytic Discussion', in *The Trinity: An International Symposium on the Trinity*, ed. S.T. Davis, D. Kendall, and G. O' Collins (New York: Oxford University Press, 1999), pp. 123-44.

Cockerill, G.L. 'Heb 1:1-14, *1 Clem.* 36:1-6 and the High Priest Title', *JBL* 97.3 (September, 1978), pp. 437-40.

Cobb, P.G. 'The History of the Christian Year', in *The Study of Liturgy*, rev. edn., ed. C. Jones, G. Wainwright, E. Yarnold, and P. Bradshaw (London: SPCK/New York: Oxford University Press, 1992), pp. 459-60.

— 'The Liturgy of the Word in the Early Church', in *The Study of Liturgy*, ed. Jones et al., pp. 224-25.

Colwell, J.E. 'The Sacramental Nature of Ordination: An Attempt to Re-Engage a Catholic Understanding and Practice', in *Baptist Sacramentalism*, ed. A.R. Cross and P.E. Thompson (SBHT, 5; Carlisle: Paternoster Press, 2003), pp. 228-46.

— *Promise and Presence: An Exploration of Sacramental Theology* (Milton Keynes: Paternoster, 2006).

Committee of the Oxford Society of Historical Theology. *The New Testament in the Apostolic Fathers* (Oxford: Clarendon Press, 1905).

Conference on Biblical Inerrancy. *The Proceedings of the Conference on Biblical Inerrancy, 1987* (Nashville, Tenn.: Broadman Press, 1987).

Congar, Y. *Divided Christendom: A Catholic Study of the Problem of Reunion*, trans. M.A. Bousfield (London: G. Bles, 1939).

Conner, W.T. *A System of Christian Doctrine* (Nashville: Sunday School Board of the Southern Baptist Convention, 1924).

— *Revelation and God: An Introduction to Christian Doctrine* (Nashville, Tenn.: Broadman Press, 1936).

Corwin, V. *St. Ignatius and Christianity at Antioch* (New Haven: Yale University Press, 1960.

Cross, A.R. '"One Baptism" (Ephesians 4.5): A Challenge to the Church', in *Baptism, the New Testament, and the Church: Historical and Contemporary Studies in Honour of R.E.O. White* (JSTNSup, 171; Sheffield: Sheffield Academic Press, 1999), pp. 173-209.

— 'Spirit- and Water-Baptism in 1 Corinthians 12.13', in *Dimensions of Baptism: Biblical and Theological Studies*, ed. S.E. Porter and A.R. Cross (JSNTSup, 234; Sheffield: Sheffield Academic Press, 2002), pp. 120-48.

— 'Baptism, Christology and the Creeds in the Early Church: Implications for Ecumenical Dialogue', in *Ecumenism and History: Studies in Honour of John H.Y. Briggs*, ed. A.R. Cross (Carlisle: Paternoster, 2002), pp. 23-49.

— 'The Pneumatological Key to H. Wheeler Robinson's Baptismal Sacramentalism', in *Baptist Sacramentalism*, ed. A.R. Cross and P.E. Thompson (SBHT, 5; Carlisle: Paternoster Press, 2003), pp. 151-76.

— 'Being Open to God's Sacramental Word: A Study in Baptism', in *Semper Reformandum: Studies in Honour of Clark H. Pinnock*, ed. S.E. Porter and A.R. Cross (Carlisle: Paternoster, 2003), pp. 355-77.

— 'Faith-Baptism: The Key to an Evangelical Baptismal Sacramentalism', *JEBapSt* 4.3 (May, 2004), pp. 5-21.

Cross, A.R. and Thompson, P.E., eds. *Baptist Sacramentalism* (SBHT, 5; Carlisle: Paternoster Press, 2003).

Cross, F.L. and Livingstone, E.A., eds. *The Oxford Dictionary of the Christian Church*, 2nd edn. (Oxford: Oxford University Press, 1974).

D'Ambrosio, M. 'Ressourcement Theology, Aggiornamento, and the Hermeneutics of Tradition', *Communio* 18 (Winter, 1991), pp. 530-55.

Daniélou, J. *From Glory to Glory: Texts from Gregory of Nyssa's Mystical Writings*, trans. and ed. H. Musurillo (New York: Charles Scribner's Sons, 1961; reprint, Crestwood, N.Y.: St. Vladimir's Seminary Press, 1995).

Denzinger, H., Bannwart, C., and Umberg, J.B. eds. *Enchiridion Symbolorum: Definitionum et declarationum de rebus fidei et morum*, 14th and 15th edn. (Freiburg im Breisgau: Herder, 1922).

Denzinger, H. and Schönmetzer, A., eds. *Enchiridion Symbolorum: definitionum et declarationum de rebus fidei et morum*, 36th edn. (Freiburg: Herder, 1976).

Dhôtel, J.-C. 'La "sanctification" du Christ d'après *Hébreux*, II, 11: Interprétations des Pères et des Scholastiques médiévaux', *RSR* 47 (1959), pp. 515-43.

Dibelius, M. *Die Formgeschichte des Evangeliums*, 2nd edn. (Tübingen: J.C.B. Mohr, 1933).

— *From Tradition to Gospel*, trans. B.L. Woolf (New York: Charles Scribner's Sons, 1934).

Donovan, K. 'The Sanctoral', in *The Study of Liturgy*, rev. edn., ed. C. Jones, G. Wainwright, E. Yarnold, and P. Bradshaw (London: SPCK/New York: Oxford University Press, 1992), pp. 472-84.

Dorrien, G. *The Barthian Revolt in Modern Theology: Theology without Weapons* (Louisville, Ky.: Westminster John Knox, 2000).

Elliott, R.H. *The Message of Genesis* (Nashville, Tenn.: Broadman Press, 1961).

— *The 'Genesis Controversy' and Continuity in Southern Baptist Chaos: A Eulogy for a Great Tradition* (Macon, Ga.: Mercer University Press, 1992).

Ellis, C.J. *Baptist Worship Today* (Didcot: Baptist Union of Great Britain, 1999).

— 'Baptist Worship: Liturgical Theology from a Free Church Perspective' (PhD thesis, University of Leeds, 2002).

— *Gathering: A Theology and Spirituality of Worship in the Free Church Tradition* (London: SCM Press, 2004).

Ellis, E.E. *The Making of the New Testament Documents* (BIS, 39; Leiden: Brill, 1999).

Episcopal Church in the United States of America. *The Book of Common Prayer and Administration of the Sacraments and Other Rites and Ceremonies of the Church, together with the Psalter or Psalms of David, according to the Use of the Episcopal Church* (New York: Oxford University Press, 1979).

Erickson, M.J. *Christian Theology* (Grand Rapids, Mich.: Baker Book House, 1983-85).

— *Postmodernizing the Faith: Evangelical Responses to the Challenge of Postmodernism* (Grand Rapids, Mich.: Baker Books, 1998).

Estep, W.R. 'A Response to *Baptism, Eucharist and Ministry*: Faith and Order Paper No. 111', in W.H. Brackney and R.J. Burke, eds., *Faith, Life and Witness: The Papers of the Study and Research Division of the Baptist World Alliance 1986-1990* (Birmingham, Ala.: Samford University Press, 1990), pp. 2-16.

Faught, C.B. *The Oxford Movement: A Thematic History of the Tractarians and Their Times* (University Park, Pa.: Pennsylvania State University Press, 2003).

Fiddes, P.S. *Participating in God: A Pastoral Doctrine of the Trinity* (Louisville, Ky.: Westminster John Knox, 2000).

— *Tracks and Traces: Baptist Identity in Church and Theology* (SBHT, 13; Carlisle: Paternoster Press, 2003).

Fitzmeyer, J.A. 'The Semitic Background of the New Testament *Kyrios*-Title', ch. in *A Wandering Aramean: Collected Aramaic Essays* (SBLMS, 25; Missoula, Mont.: Scholars Press, 1979), pp. 124-25

Flannery, A., ed. *Vatican Council II: The Conciliar and Post Conciliar Documents*, rev. edn. (Northport, N.Y.: Costello Publishing, 1992).

Forbis, W.L., ed. *The Baptist Hymnal* (Nashville, Tenn.: Convention Press, 1991).

Ford, D. *Barth and God's Story: Biblical Narrative and the Theological Method of Karl Barth in the 'Church Dogmatics'* (SIHC, 27; Frankfurt: Peter Lang, 1981).

Fowler, S.K. *More Than a Symbol: The British Baptist Recovery of Baptismal Sacramentalism* (SBHT, 2; Carlisle: Paternoster Press, 2002).

Freeman, C.W. 'A Confession for Catholic Baptists', in *Ties That Bind: Life Together in the Baptist Vision*, ed. G. Furr and C.W. Freeman (Macon, Ga.: Smyth & Helwys, 1994), p. 85.

— 'Can Baptist Theology Be Revisioned?' *PRSt* 24.3 (Fall, 1997), pp. 273-310.

— 'E.Y. Mullins and the Siren Songs of Modernity', *RevExp* 96.1 (Winter, 1999), pp. 23-42.

— 'A New Perspective on Baptist Identity', *PRSt* 26.1 (Spring, 1999), pp. 59-65.

— '"To Feed Upon by Faith": Nourishment from the Lord's Table', in *Baptist Sacramentalism*, ed. A.R. Cross and P.E. Thompson (SBHT, 5; Carlisle: Paternoster Press, 2003), pp. 194-210.

— 'God in Three Persons: Baptist Unitarianism and the Trinity', *PRSt* 33.3 (Fall, 2006; forthcoming).

Freeman, C.W., Harmon, S.R., Newman, E., and Thompson, P.E. 'Confessing the Faith', published online by the *Baptist Standard* (9 July, 2004) at www.baptiststandard.com/postnuke/pdf/Confessing_the_Faith_Draft.pdf.

Frei, H. *The Eclipse of Biblical Narrative: A Study in Eighteenth and Nineteenth Century Hermeneutics* (New Haven: Yale University Press, 1974).

— *Theology and Narrative: Selected Essays*, ed. G. Hunsinger and W.C. Placher (Oxford: Oxford University Press, 1993).

Frishman, J. and Van Rompay, L., eds. *The Book of Genesis in Jewish and Oriental Christian Interpretation: A Collection of Essays* (Louvian: Peeters, 1997).

Gadamer, H.-G. *Wahrheit und Methode: Grundzüge einer philosophischen Hermeneutik*, 2nd edn. (Tübingen: J.C.B. Mohr, 1965).

— *Truth and Method*, 2nd rev. edn., trans. J. Weinsheimer and D.G. Marshall (New York: Crossroad, 1989).

Garnet, P. 'Hebrews 2:9: χάριτι or χωρίς?', in *StudPat* 18.1, *Historica-Theologica-Gnostica-Biblica*, ed. E.A. Livingstone (Kalamazoo, Mich.: Cistercian Publications, 1985), pp. 321-25.

Garrett, J.L. Jr. 'Sources of Authority in Baptist Thought', *BHH* 13 (1978), pp. 41-49.

— *Systematic Theology: Biblical, Historical, and Evangelical*, 2 vols. (Grand Rapids, Mich.: William B. Eerdmans, 1990-1995; 2nd edn., North Richland Hills, Tex.: BIBAL Press, 2000-2001).

Garrett, J.L. Jr., Hinson, E.G., and Tull, J.E. *Are Southern Baptists "Evangelicals"?* (Macon, Ga.: Mercer University Press, 1983).

Gavrilyuk, P.L. *The Suffering of the Impassible God: The Dialectics of Patristic Thought* (OECS; New York: Oxford University Press, 2004).

Geitz, E.R. *Gender and the Nicene Creed* (Harrisburg, Pa.: Morehouse Publishing, 1995).

George, T. 'An Evangelical Reflection on Scripture and Tradition', *ProEccl* 9.2 (Spring, 2000), pp. 184-207.

— 'The Sacramentality of the Church: An Evangelical Baptist Perspective', *ProEccl* 12.3 (Summer, 2003), pp. 309-23.

— 'John Paul II: An Appreciation', *ProEccl* 14.3 (Summer, 2005), pp. 267-70.

Gerhardsson, B. *Memory and Manuscript: Oral Tradition and Written Transmission in Rabbinic Judaism and Early Christianity* (ASNU, 22; Lund: C.W.K. Gleerup, 1964).

— *The Origins of the Gospel Traditions* (Philadelphia: Fortress Press, 1979).

Gillquist, P.E. *Becoming Orthodox: A Journey to the Ancient Christian Faith* (Brentwood, Tenn.: Wolgemuth & Hyatt, 1989).

— *Coming Home: Why Protestant Clergy Are Becoming Orthodox* (Ben Lomond, Calif.: Conciliar Press, 1992).

Goh, J.C.K. *Christian Tradition Today: A Postliberal Vision of Church and World* (LTPM, 28; Louvain: Peeters Press, 2000).

Gonnet, D. 'L'Utilisation Christologique de l'Épître aux Hébreux dans les *Oarationes contra Arianos* d'Athanase d'Alexandrie', in *StudPat* 32, ed. E.A. Livingstone (Leuven: Peeters Press, 1997), pp. 19-24.

Grant, R.M. *The Early Christian Doctrine of God* (Charlottesville: University Press of Virginia, 1966).

Graves, J.R. *Old Landmarksim: What Is It?* (Memphis, Tenn.: Baptist Book House, 1880).

Green, J.B. 'Biblical Authority and Communities of Discourse', in *Baptists in the Balance: The Tension between Freedom and Responsibility*, ed. E.C. Goodwin (Valley Forge, Pa.: Judson Press, 1997), pp. 151-73.

Greer, R.A. *The Captain of Our Salvation: A Study in the Patristic Exegesis of Hebrews* (BGBE, 15; Tübingen: J.C.B. Mohr [Paul Siebeck], 1973).

Grenz, S.J. *Theology for the Community of God* (Grand Rapids, Mich.: William B. Eerdmans, 2000).

— *The Social God and the Relational Self: A Trinitarian Theology of the Imago Dei*, The Matrix of Christian Theology, vol. 1 (Louisville, Ky.: Westminster John Knox, 2001).

Grenz, S.J. and Franke, J.R. *Beyond Foundationalism: Shaping Theology in a Postmodern Context* (Louisville, Ky.: Westminster John Knox, 2001).

Hahn, S., and Hahn, K. *Rome Sweet Home: Our Journey to Catholicism* (San Francisco: Ignatius Press, 1993).

Hallman, J.M. 'The Communication of Idioms in Theodoret's *Commentary on Hebrews*', in *In Dominico Eloquio/In Lordly Eloquence: Essays on Patristic*

Exegesis in Honor of Robert L. Wilken, ed. P.M. Blowers et al. (Grand Rapids, Mich.: William B. Eerdmans, 2002), pp. 369-79.

Hankins, B. *Uneasy in Babylon: Southern Baptist Conservatives and American Culture* (Tuscaloosa, Ala.: University of Alabama Press, 2002).

Hanson, R.P.C. *The Search for the Christian Doctrine of God: The Arian Controversy 318-381* (Edinburgh: T. & T. Clark, 1988).

Harmon, S.R. 'Baptist Confessions of Faith and the Patristic Tradition', *PRSt* 29.4 (Winter, 2002), pp. 349-58.

— 'A Note on the Critical Use of *Instrumenta* for the Retrieval of Patristic Biblical Exegesis', *JECS* 11.1 (Spring, 2003), pp. 95-107.

— 'The Authority of the Community (of All the Saints): Toward a Postmodern Baptist Hermeneutic of Tradition', *RevExp* 100.2 (Fall, 2003), pp. 587-621.

— *Every Knee Should Bow: Biblical Rationales for Universal Salvation in Early Christian Thought* (Lanham, Md.: University Press of America, 2003).

— 'Baptist Understandings of Theological Authority: A North American Perspective', *International Journal for the Study of the Christian Church* 4.1 (2004), pp. 50-63.

— 'Do Real Baptists Recite Creeds?', *BapTod* 22.9 (September, 2004), p. 27.

— 'Praying and Believing: Retrieving the Patristic Interdependence of Worship and Theology', *RevExp* 101.4 (Fall, 2004), pp. 667-95.

— '"Catholic Baptists" and the New Horizon of Tradition in Baptist Theology', in *New Horizons in Theology*, ed. Terrence W. Tilley (Maryknoll, N.Y.: Orbis Books, 2005), pp. 117-34.

— 'Hebrews in Patristic Perspective', *RevExp* 102.2 (Spring, 2005), pp. 215-33.

— 'Between Text and Sermon: Hebrews 2:10-18', *Int* 59.4 (October, 2005), pp. 404-406.

— 'Communal Conflict in the Postmodern Christian University', in *Christianity and the Soul of the University: Faith as a Foundation for Intellectual Community*, ed. Douglas V. Henry and Michael W. Beaty (Grand Rapids, Mich.: Baker Academic, 2006), pp. 133-44.

— 'Karl Barth's Conversation with the Fathers: A Paradigm for *Ressourcement* in Baptist and Evangelical Theology', *PRSt* 33.1 (Spring, 2006), pp. 7-23.

— 'From Triadic Narrative to Narrating the Triune God: The Development of Patristic Trinitarian Theology', *PRSt* 33.3 (Fall, 2006).

'"Doctrines in the Form of a Story": Narrative Theology in Gregory of Nyssa's *Oratio Catechetica Magna*', in *Studia Patristica: Papers Presented at the Thirteenth International Conference on Patristic Studies held in Oxford, 2003*, ed. E.J. Yarnold and M. Wiles (Louvain: Peeters Publishers, forthcoming 2006).

— 'Evangelical Catholicity and the Contestation of Faith and Order: Why We Need a Second North American Conference' (unpublished paper presented to the Consultation on a Conference on Faith and Order in North America, Graymoor Ecumenical and Interreligious Institute, Garrison, New York, 3-5 January 2006).

Harnack, A. von. *Lehrbuch der Dogmengeschichte*, 3 vols. in 2 (Freiburg im Breisgau: J.C.B. Mohr, 1886-90).

— *Das Wesen des Christentums: sechzehn Vorlesungen vor Studierenden aller Facultäten im Wintersemester 1899/1900 an der Universität Berlin gehalten* (Leipzig: Hinrichs, 1908).

— *What Is Christianity?*, trans. T.B. Saunders (New York: Harper, 1957).

— *History of Dogma*, trans. N. Buchanan, 7 vols. in 4 (New York: Dover Publications, 1961).

Hart, D.B. *The Beauty of the Infinite: The Aesthetics of Christian Truth* (Grand Rapids, Mich.: William B. Eerdmans, 2003).

Harvey, B. *Another City: An Ecclesiological Primer for a Post-Christian World* (Harrisburg, Pa.: Trinity Press International, 1999).

— 'Doctrinally Speaking: James McClendon on the Nature of Doctrine', *PRSt* 27.1 (Spring, 2000), pp. 39-61.

— 'The Eucharistic Idiom of the Gospel', *ProEccl* 9.3 (Summer, 2000), pp. 297-318.

— 'Review Essay: M.B. Copenhaver, A.B. Robinson, and W.H. Willimon, *Good News in Exile*; M.J. Dawn, *A Royal 'Waste' of Time*; C. Van Gelder, ed., *Confident Witness-Changing World*; J.R. Wilson, *Living Faithfully in a Fragmented World*', *ProEccl* 10.4 (Fall, 2001), pp. 487-90.

— 'Where, Then, Do We Stand? Baptists, History, and Authority', *PRSt* 29.4 (Winter, 2002), pp. 359-80.

— 'Re-Membering the Body: Baptism, Eucharist and the Politics of Disestablishment', in *Baptist Sacramentalism*, ed. A.R. Cross and P.E. Thompson (SBHT, 5; Carlisle: Paternoster Press, 2003), pp. 96-116.

Hauerwas, S. *After Christendom: How the Church Is to Behave if Freedom, Justice, and a Christian Nation Are Bad Ideas* (Nashville, Tenn.: Abingdon Press, 1991).

Hauerwas, S. and Jones, L.G., eds. *Why Narrative? Readings in Narrative Theology* (Grand Rapids, Mich.: William B. Eerdmans, 1989).

Hauerwas, S. and Willimon, W.H. *Resident Aliens: Life in the Christian Colony* (Nashville, Tenn.: Abingdon Press, 1989).

Heen, E.M. and Krey, P.D.W., eds. *Hebrews* (ACCS.NT, 10; Downers Grove, Ill.: InterVarsity Press, 2005).

Hefley, J. *The Conservative Resurgence in the Southern Baptist Convention* (Hannibal, Mo.: Hannibal Books, 1991).

Hinson, E.G. 'The Nicene Creed Viewed from the Standpoint of the Evangelization of the Roman Empire', in *Faith to Creed: Ecumenical Perspectives on the Affirmation of the Apostolic Faith in the Fourth Century. Papers of the Faith to Creed Consultation Commission on Faith and Order NCCCUSA October 25-27, 1989—Waltham, Massachusetts*, ed. S.M. Heim (Grand Rapids, Mich.: William B. Eerdmans, 1991), pp. 117-28.

Hjelm, N.A., ed. *Faith and Order: Toward a North American Conference. Study Guide* (Grand Rapids, Mich.: William B. Eerdmans, 2004).

Holmer, P.L. *The Grammar of Faith* (San Francisco: Harper & Row, 1978).

Holmes, S.R. 'The Justice of Hell and the Display of God's Glory in the Thought of Jonathan Edwards', *ProEccl* 9.4 (Fall, 2000), pp. 389-403.

— 'The Authority of the Christian Tradition: Introductory Essay', in *The Practice of Theology: A Reader*, ed. C.E. Gunton, S.R. Holmes, and M.A. Rae (London: SCM Press, 2001), pp. 55-59.

— *Listening to the Past: The Place of Tradition in Theology* (Carlisle: Paternoster and Grand Rapids, Mich.: Baker Academic, 2002).

— *Tradition and Renewal in Baptist Life: The Whitley Lecture 2003* (Oxford: Whitely Publications, 2003).

Humphreys, F. Review of C.E. Braaten and R.W. Jenson, eds., *The Catholicity of the Reformation*, A. Dulles, *The Catholicity of the Church*, and G. Weigel, *Soul of the World: Notes on the Future of Public Catholicism*, in *PRSt* 26.1 (Spring, 1999), pp. 91-95.

Hunsinger, G. 'Karl Barth's Christology: Its Basic Chalcedonian Character', in *The Cambridge Companion to Karl Barth*, ed. J.B. Webster (Cambridge: Cambridge University Press, 2000), pp. 127-42.

Hütter, R. *Bound to Be Free: Evangelical Catholic Engagements in Ecclesiology, Ethics, and Ecumenism* (Grand Rapids, Mich.: William B. Eerdmans, 2004).

Hyman, G. *The Predicament of Postmodern Theology: Radical Orthodoxy or Nihilist Textualism?* (Louisville, Ky.: Westminster John Knox Press, 2001).

International Council on Biblical Inerrancy. 'Chicago Statement on Biblical Inerrancy', *JETS* 21 (December, 1978), pp. 289-96.

James, R.B., ed. *The Unfettered Word: Confronting the Authority-Inerrancy Question* (Macon, Ga.: Smyth & Helwys, 1994).

Jenson, R.W. *Systematic Theology*, 2 vols. (New York: Oxford University Press, 1997-99).

John Paul II. *Ut Unum Sint: Encyclical Letter of the Holy Father John Paul II on Commitment to Ecumenism* (Vatican City: Libreria Editrice Vaticana, 1995).

Johnson, W.B. 'The Southern Baptist Convention, To the Brethren in the United States; To the Congregations Connected with the Respective Churches; and to All Candid Men', in *Proceedings of the Southern Baptist Convention in Augusta, Georgia, 8-12 May 1845* (Richmond: H.K. Ellyson, 1845), pp. 17-20.

Jones, C., Wainwright, G., Yarnold, E., and Bradshaw, P., eds. *The Study of Liturgy*, rev. edn. (London: SPCK/New York: Oxford University Press, 1992).

Jones, R.P. 'Re-Visioning Baptist Identity from a Theocentric Perspective', *PRSt* 26.1 (Spring, 1999), pp. 35-57.

Jungmann, J.A. *The Place of Christ in Liturgical Prayer*, 2nd rev. edn. (Staten Island, N.Y.: Alba House, 1965).

Kelly, J.N.D. *Early Christian Creeds*, 2nd edn. (New York: David McKay Co., 1960).

— *Early Christian Doctrines*, rev. edn. (San Francisco: Harper & Row, 1978).

Kelsey, D.H. *The Uses of Scripture in Recent Theology* (Philadelphia: Fortress Press, 1975).

Kerr, F. 'French Theology: Yves Congar and Henri de Lubac', in *The Modern Theologians: An Introduction to Christian Theology in the Twentieth Century*, 2nd edn., ed. D.F. Ford (Cambridge, Mass.: Blackwell, 1997), pp. 105-17.

Kobler, J.F. 'On D'Ambrosio and Ressourcement Theology', *Communio* 19 (Summer, 1992), pp. 321-25.

Köbler, R. *In the Shadow of Karl Barth: Charlotte von Kirschbaum*, trans. K. Crim (Louisville, Ky.: Westminster/John Knox, 1989).

Köster, H. *Synoptische Überlieferung bei den apostolischen Vätern* (TU, 17; Berlin: Akademie-Verlag, 1957).

Kolb, R. and Wengert, T.J., eds. *The Book of Concord: The Confessions of the Evangelical Lutheran Church*, trans. C.P. Arand (Minneapolis: Fortress Press, 2000).

La Bonnardière, A.-M. 'L'épître aux Hébreux dans l'œuvre de saint Augustin', *RÉAug* 3 (1957), pp. 137-62.

LaCugna, C.M. *God for Us: The Trinity and Christian Life* (New York: HarperCollins, 1991).

Lampe, G.W.H. *A Patristic Greek Lexicon* (Oxford: Clarendon Press, 1961).

Lehmann, P. 'The Ant and the Emperor', in *How Karl Barth Changed My Mind*, ed. D.K. McKim (Grand Rapids, Mich.: William B. Eerdmans, 1986), pp. 36-46.

Leonard, B. *God's Last and Only Hope: The Fragmentation of the Southern Baptist Convention* (Grand Rapids, Mich.: William B. Eerdmans, 1990).

Lightfoot, J.B. *The Apostolic Fathers: Clement, Ignatius, and Polycarp*, 2nd edn., pt. 2, *Ignatius and Polycarp* (London: Macmillan, 1889, 1890; reprint, Peabody, Mass.: Hendrickson, 1989).

Lindbeck, G.A. *The Nature of Doctrine: Religion and Theology in a Postliberal Age* (Louisville, Ky.: Westminster John Knox Press, 1984).

Loughlin, G. *Telling God's Story: Bible, Church, and Narrative Theology* (Cambridge: Cambridge University Press, 1996).

Louis, C.J., ed. *Rome and the Study of Scripture: A Collection of Papal Enactments on the Study of Holy Scripture Together with the Decisions of the Biblical Commission*, 5th edn. (St. Meinrad, Ind.: 1953).

Lubac, H. de. *Exégèse médiéval: Les quatres sens de l'Écriture*, 2 vols. (Paris: Aubier, 1959).

— *Medieval Exegesis*, 2 vols. (Grand Rapids: William B. Eerdmans, 1998).

Ludlow, M. *Universal Salvation: Eschatology in the Thought of Gregory of Nyssa and Karl Rahner* (OTM; Oxford: Oxford University Press, 2000).

Lumpkin, W.L. *Baptist Confessions of Faith*, rev. edn. (Valley Forge, Pa.: Judson Press, 1969).

— 'The Nature and Authority of Baptist Confessions of Faith', *RevExp* 76 (Winter, 1979), pp. 17-28.

Lutheran World Federation and Roman Catholic Church. *Joint Declaration on the Doctrine of Justification* (Grand Rapids, Mich.: William B. Eerdmans, 2000).

MacIntyre, A. *After Virtue: A Study in Moral Theory*, 2nd edn. (Notre Dame, Ind.: University of Notre Dame Press, 1984).

— *Whose Justice? Which Rationality?* (Notre Dame, Ind.: University of Notre Dame Press, 1988).

— *Three Rival Versions of Moral Inquiry: Encyclopedia, Genealogy, and Tradition. Being Gifford Lectures Delivered in the University of Edinburgh in 1988* (Notre Dame, Ind.: University of Notre Dame Press, 1990).

Maddox, T. 'Revisioning Baptist Principles: A Ricoeurian Postmodern Investigation' (PhD thesis, The Southern Baptist Theological Seminary, 1997).

Mangan, K.S. 'Baylor President Faces the Test of His Tenure', *ChronHighEd* 50.4 (19 September, 2003), p. A27.

— 'Baylor Professors Vote Against President', *ChronHighEd* 51.17 (17 December, 2004), p. A34.

Mangan, K.S., Wilson, R., Smallwood, S., and Fogg, P. 'Baylor's President Will Become Its Chancellor', *ChronHighEd* 51.22 (4 February, 2005), p. A6.

Mansell, S. *A Second Address to Mr. Huntington* (London: J. Parsons, 1797).

Margerie, B. de. *An Introduction to the History of Exegesis*, vol. 1, *The Greek Fathers*, trans. L. Maluf (Petersham, Mass.: Saint Bede's Publications, 1993).

Marshall, M.T. 'Southern Baptist Theology Today: An Interview with Molly Marshall-Green', *TheolEd* 40 (Fall, 1989, pp. 25-34.

— *Joining the Dance: A Theology of the Spirit* (Valley Forge, Pa.: Judson Press, 2003).

— 'A Conversation with Molly Marshall', *BapTod* 23.1 (November, 2005), pp. 2-3, 16-17.

Massaux, É. *Influence de l'Évangile de saint Matthieu sur la littérature chrétienne avant saint Irénée* (Leuven: University Press, 1950).

— *The Influence of the Gospel of Saint Matthew on Christian Literature before Saint Irenaeus*, vol. 1, *The First Ecclesiastical Writers*, trans. N.J. Belval and S. Hecht, ed. A.J. Bellinzoni (NGS, 5; Macon, Ga.: Mercer University Press, 1990).

Mauldin, F.L. *The Classic Baptist Heritage of Personal Truth: The Truth as It Is in Jesus* (Franklin, Tenn.: Providence House Publishers, 1999).

Maurer, C. *Ignatius von Antiochien und das Johannesevangelium* (ATANT, 18; Zürich: Zwingli-Verlag, 1949), pp. 25-43 and 92-93.

Maxwell, J.M. *Worship and Reformed Theology: The Liturgical Lessons of Mercersburg* (PTMS, 10; Pittsburgh: Pickwick Press, 1976).

McClendon, J.W. Jr. *Biography as Theology: How Life Stories Can Remake Today's Theology* (Philadelphia: Trinity Press International, 1974).

— *Systematic Theology*. 3 vols. (Nashville: Abingdon, 1986-2000).

McCormack, B.L. *Karl Barth's Critically Realistic Dialectical Theology: Its Genesis and Development 1909-1936* (Oxford: Oxford University Press, 1997).

McGlothlin, W.J. *Baptist Confessions of Faith* (Philadelphia: American Baptist Publication Society, 1911).

McGrath, A.E. *The Renewal of Anglicanism* (Harrisburg, Pa.: Morehouse Publishing, 1993)

McWilliams, W. 'Why All the Fuss about *Filioque*? Karl Barth and Jürgen Moltmann on the Procession of the Spirit', *PRSt* 22.2 (Summer, 1995), pp. 167-81.

Medley, M.S. 'Catholics, Baptists, and the Normativity of Tradition,' *PRSt* 28.2 (Summer, 2001), pp. 119-29.

— *Imago Trinitatis: Toward a Relational Understanding of Becoming Human* (Lanham, Md.: University Press of America, 2002).

— Review of S.J. Grenz and J.R. Franke, *Beyond Foundationalism: Shaping Theology in a Postmodern Context* [Louisville, Ky.: Westminster John Knox Press, 2000], in *IJST* 4.1 (March, 2002), pp. 83-90.

— '"Do This": The Eucharist and Ecclesial Selfhood', *RevExp* 100.3 (Summer, 2003), pp. 383-401.

— 'The Use of Theosis in Contemporary Baptist Theology' (unpublished paper presented to the annual meeting of the American Academy of Religion— Southeast Region, Atlanta, Georgia, 5-7 March 2004, and the joint annual meeting of the College Theology Society and National Association of Baptist Professors of Religion Region-at-Large, Washington, D.C., 3-6 June 2004).

Meijering, E.P. *Von den Kirchenvätern zu Karl Barth: Das altkirchliche Dogma in der 'Kirchlichen Dogmatik'* (Amsterdam: J.C. Gieben, 1993).

Merkt, A. *Das patristische Prinzip: Eine Studie zur theologischen Bedeutung der Kirchenväter* (SVC, 58; Leiden: Brill, 2001), pp. 121-53.

Metz, J.B. 'A Short Apology of Narrative', in *Why Narrative? Readings in Narrative Theology*, ed. S. Hauerwas and L.G. Jones (Grand Rapids, Mich.: William B. Eerdmans, 1989), pp. 251-62.

Milbank, J., Pickstock, C., and Ward, G., eds. *Radical Orthodoxy: A New Theology* (London: Routledge, 1999).

Minear, P.S., ed. *The Nature of the Unity We Seek: Official Report of the North American Conference on Faith and Order, September 3-10, 1957, Oberlin, Ohio* (St. Louis: Bethany Press, 1958).

Moltmann, J. *Der gekreuzigte Gott: Das Kreuz Christi als Grund und Kritik christlicher Theologie* (Munich: Chr. Kaiser Verlag, 1972).

— *The Crucified God: The Cross of Christ as the Foundation and Criticism of Christian Theology*, trans. R.A. Wilson and J. Bowden (Minneapolis: Fortress Press, 1993).

— *The Trinity and the Kingdom: The Doctrine of God*, trans. M. Kohl (Minneapolis: Fortress Press, 1993).

Moody, D. *The Word of Truth: A Summary of Christian Doctrine Based on Biblical Revelation* (Grand Rapids, Mich.: William B. Eerdmans, 1981).

Moore, S.H. 'The End of Convenient Stereotypes: How the First Things and Baxter Controversies Inaugurate Extraordinary Politics', *ProEccl* 7 (Winter, 1998), pp. 17-47.

Morgan, D.T. *The New Crusades, the New Holy Land: Conflict in the Southern Baptist Convention, 1969-1991* (Tuscaloosa, Ala.: University of Alabama Press, 1996).

Mullins, E.Y. *The Axioms of Religion: A New Interpretation of the Baptist Faith* (Philadelphia: American Baptist Publication Society, 1908).

— *The Christian Religion in Its Doctrinal Expression* (Philadelphia: Judson Press, 1917).

Nettleton, N.C. 'The Liturgical Expression of Baptist Identity' (ThM thesis, Melbourne College of Divinity, 2000).

Newman, E. 'The Lord's Supper: Might Baptists Accept a Theory of Real Presence?', in *Baptist Sacramentalism*, ed. A.R. Cross and P.E. Thompson (SBHT, 5; Carlisle: Paternoster Press, 2003), pp. 211-227.

— 'The Priesthood of All Believers and the Necessity of the Church', in *Recycling the Past or Researching History? Studies in Baptist Historiography and Myths*, ed. P.E. Thompson and A.R. Cross (SBHT, 11; Milton Keynes: Paternoster, 2005), pp. 50-66.

Newman, J.H. (Cardinal). 'Remarks on Certain Passages in the Thirty-Nine Articles', *Tracts for the Times* 90 (London: J.G.F. & J. Rivington, 1841), pp. 1-83.

— *An Essay on the Development of Christian Doctrine* (London: J. Toovey, 1845).

— *The Idea of a University* (Garden City, N.Y.: Image Books, 1959 [first published 1853 and 1858).

— *Apologia Pro Vita Sua* (London: J.M. Dent & Sons, 1912 [1st edn. 1864]).

— *The Arians of the Fourth Century*, 4th edn. (London: Longmans, Green, and Co., 1876).

Nichols, J.H. *Romanticism in American Theology: Nevin and Schaff at Mercersburg* (Chicago: University of Chicago Press, 1961).

O'Connor, S.B. '*Lex Orandi, Lex Credendi*: An Investigation into the Liturgy and Theology of New Zealand Baptists' (ThM thesis, University of Auckland, 2001).

Oden, A., ed. *In Her Words: Women's Writings in the History of Christian Thought* (Nashville: Abingdon, 1994).

Oden, T.C. *Agenda for Theology: Recovering Christian Roots* (San Francisco: Harper & Row, 1979).

— *The Living God* (San Francisco: Harper & Row, 1987).

— *Classical Pastoral Care*, 4 vols. (Grand Rapids, Mich.: Baker Books, 1987-94).

— 'Then and Now: The Recovery of Patristic Wisdom', *ChrCent* 107 (12 December 1990), pp. 1164-1168.

— *The Word of Life* (San Francisco: Harper & Row, 1992).

— *Life in the Spirit* (San Francisco: Harper & Row, 1994).

— *Requiem: A Lament in Three Movements* (Nashville: Abingdon Press, 1995).

Oden, T.C., ed. *The Ancient Christian Commentary on Scripture* (Downers Grove, Ill.: InterVarsity Press, 1998-).

Oden, T.C. and Hall, C. Reply to R.D. Young's 'Texts Have Consequences'. *FT* 94 (June/July, 1999), pp. 2-7.

Olson, R.E. 'Whales and Elephants: Both God's Creatures, but Can They Meet? Evangelicals and Liberals in Dialogue', *ProEccl* 4 (Spring, 1995), pp. 165-89.

Outler, A.C. 'The Wesleyan Quadrilateral—in John Wesley', in *The Wesleyan Theological Heritage: Essays of Albert C. Outler*, ed. T.C. Oden and L.R. Longden (Grand Rapids, Mich.: Zondervan, 1991), pp. 21-37.

Parker, G.K. *Baptists in Europe: History & Confessions of Faith* (Nashville, Tenn.: Broadman Press, 1982).

Parvis, P.M. 'The *Commentary on Hebrews* and the *Contra Theodorum* of Cyril of Alexandria', *JTS* n.s. 26 (October, 1975), pp. 415-19.

Pelikan, J. *The Christian Tradition: A History of the Development of Doctrine*, vol. 1, *The Emergence of the Catholic Tradition (100-600)* (Chicago: University of Chicago Press, 1971).

— *The Vindication of Tradition* (New Haven: Yale University Press, 1984).

— *The Idea of a University: A Reexamination* (New Haven: Yale University Press, 1992).

— *Credo: Historical and Theological Guide to Creeds and Confessions of Faith in the Christian Tradition* (New Haven: Yale University Press, 2003).

Pendleton, J.M. *An Old Landmark Re-set* (Nashville, Tenn.: South-Western Publishing House, 1859).

Pfaff, R.W. 'The Library of the Fathers: The Tractarians as Patristic Translators', *StudPhil* 70 (1973), pp. 329-44.

Pickstock, C. *After Writing: On the Liturgical Consummation of Philosophy* (CCT; Oxford: Blackwell, 1998).

Pius XII. *Divino Afflante Spiritu*, in *AAS* 35 (Rome: 1943), pp. 297-326.

Placher, W.C. 'Postliberal Theology', in *The Modern Theologians: An Introduction to Christian Theology in the Twentieth Century*, 2nd edn., ed. D.F. Ford (Cambridge, Mass.: Blackwell, 1997), pp. 343-56.

Pontifical Biblical Commission. *The Interpretation of the Bible in the Church* (Washington, D.C.: United States Catholic Conference, 1993).

Pool, J.B. '"Sacred Mandates of Conscience": A Criteriology of Credalism for Theological Method Among Baptists', *PRSt* 23.4 (Winter, 1996), pp. 353-86.

— 'Christ, Conscience, Canon, Community: Web of Authority in the Baptist Vision', *PRSt* 24.4 (Winter, 1997), pp. 417-45.

Presbyterian Church (U.S.A.). *The Constitution of the Presbyterian Church (U.S.A.): Part 1, Book of Confessions* (Louisville, Ky.: Office of the General Assembly, 1996).

Prestige, G.L. *God in Patristic Thought* (London: S.P.C.K., 1936).

Psalms and Hymns Trust. *Baptist Praise and Worship* (Oxford: Oxford University Press, 1991).

Putnam, H. *Reason, Truth and History* [Cambridge: Cambridge University Press, 1981.

Quasten, J. *Patrology*, 4 vols. [vol. 4 edited by A. Di Berardino] (Westminster, Md.: Christian Classics, 1990-91).

Quinot, B. 'L'influence de l'Épître aux Hébreux dans la notion augustinienne du vrai sacrifice', *RÉAug* 8 (1962), pp. 129-68.

Rahner, K and Vorgrimler, H. *Theological Dictionary*, ed. C. Ernst, trans. R. Strachan (New York; Herder and Herder, 1965).

Ramm, B. *After Fundamentalism: The Future of Evangelical Theology* (San Francisco: Harper & Row, 1983).

Rathke, H. *Ignatius von Antiochien und die Paulusbriefe* (TU, 99; Berlin: Akademie-Verlag, 1967).

Reithmayr, F.X. and V. Thalhofer, V., eds. *Bibliothek der Kirchenväter* (Kempten: J. Kösel, 1860-88).

Reno, R.R. *In the Ruins of the Church: Sustaining Faith in an Age of Diminished Christianity* (Grand Rapids, Mich.: Brazos Press, 2002).

Richardson, C.C. *The Christianity of Ignatius of Antioch* (New York: Columbia University Press, 1935).

Ricoeur, P. *The Symbolism of Evil*, trans. Emerson Buchanan (Boston: Beacon Press, 1967).

— *Freud and Philosophy: An Essay on Interpretation* (New Haven, Conn.: Yale University Press, 1970).

— 'Ethics and Culture: Habermas and Gadamer in Dialogue', *PhilTod* 17 (1973), pp. 153-65.

— *Interpretation Theory: Discourse and the Surplus of Meaning* (Fort Worth: Texas Christian University Press, 1976).

— 'The Model of the Text: Meaningful Action Considered as a Text', in *Hermeneutics and the Human Sciences: Essays on Language, Action, and Interpretation*, ed. J.B. Thompson (Cambridge: Cambridge University Press, 1981), pp. 131-44.

Riesenfeld, H. *The Gospel Tradition and its Beginnings: A Study in the Limits of 'Formgeschichte'* (London: A.R. Mowbray, 1957).

Riesner, R. *Jesus als Lehrer: Eine Untersuchung zum Ursprung der Evangelien-Überlieferung* (WUNT², 7; Tübingen: J.C.B. Mohr, 1981).

Roberts, A. and Donaldson, J., eds. *Ante-Nicene Fathers*, 10 vols. (Buffalo, N.Y.: Christian Literature, 1885-1896).

Robinson, R.B. *Roman Catholic Exegesis Since Divino Afflante Spiritu: Hermeneutical Implications* (SBLDS, 111; Decatur, Ga.: Scholars Press, 1988).

Roman Catholic Church. *Catechism of the Catholic Church* (Liguori, Mo.: Liguori Publications, 1994).

Russell, R.G. 'Q&A with Timothy George: "I'm a Firm Believer in Creeds"', *Dallas Morning News* (2 July 2005), pp. 1G, 4G.

Sayers, D.L. *Creed or Chaos?* (New York: Harcourt, Brace and Co., 1949).

Scalise, C.J. 'Patristic Biblical Interpretation and Postmodern Baptist Identity', *RevExp* 101.4 (Fall, 2004), pp. 615-28.

Schaeffer, F. *Dancing Alone: The Quest for Orthodox Faith in the Age of False Religion* (Brookline, Mass.: Holy Cross Orthodox Press, 1994).

— *Letters to Father Aristotle: A Journey through Contemporary American Orthodoxy* (Salisbury, Mass.: Regina Orthodox Press, 1995).

Schaff, P., ed. *Nicene and Post-Nicene Fathers*, First Series, 14 vols. (New York: Christian Literature, 1886-89).

— *The Creeds of Christendom with a History and Critical Notes*, 6th edn., rev. D.S. Schaff, 3 vols. (New York: Harper & Row, 1931; reprint, Grand Rapids, Mich.: Baker Book House, 1990).

Schaff, P., and Wace, H., eds. *Nicene and Post-Nicene Fathers*, Second Series, 14 vols. (New York: Christian Literature, 1890-98).

Schlier, H. '*haireomai, hairesis*' in *Theological Dictionary of the New Testament*, ed. G. Kittel, trans. G.W. Bromiley (Grand Rapids, Mich.: William B. Eerdmans, 1964), vol. 1, pp. 180-85.

Schoedel, W.R. *Ignatius of Antioch: A Commentary on the Letters of Ignatius of Antioch* (Hermeneia; Philadelphia: Fortress Press, 1985).

Schulze, M. 'Martin Luther and the Church Fathers', in *The Reception of the Church Fathers in the West: From the Carolingians to the Maurists*, ed. I Backus (Leiden: E.J. Brill, 1997), vol. 2, pp. 573-626.

Selinger, S. *Charlotte von Kirschbaum and Karl Barth: A Study in Biography and the History of Theology* (PSSLRE; University Park, Pa.: Pennsylvania State University Press, 1998).

Shriver, G.H. *Philip Schaff: Christian Scholar and Ecumenical Prophet* (Macon, Ga.: Mercer University Press, 1987).

Shurden, W.B. 'The Baptist Identity and the Baptist Manifesto', *PRSt* 25.4 (Winter, 1998), pp. 321-40.

Shurden, W.B., ed. *The Struggle for the Soul of the SBC: Moderate Responses to the Fundamentalist Movement* (Macon, Ga.: Mercer University Press, 1993).

Sibinga, J.S. 'Ignatius and Matthew', *NovT* 8 (1966), pp. 263-83.

Sidebottom, E.M. *The Christ of the Fourth Gospel in the Light of First-Century Thought* (London: S.P.C.K., 1961).

Sieben, H.J. *Kirchenväterhomilien zum Neuen Testament: Ein Reperorium der Textausgaben und Übersetzungen, mit einem Anhang der Kirchenväter-kommentare* (InstrPat, 22; The Hague: Martin Nijhoff International, 1991).

Simmons, L.K. *Creed without Chaos: Exploring Theology in the Writings of Dorothy L. Sayers* (Grand Rapids, Mich.: Baker Academic, 2005).

Smart, J.D., ed. and trans. *Revolutionary Theology in the Making: Barth-Thurneysen Correspondence, 1914-1925* (Richmond, Va.: John Knox Press, 1964).

Smith, J.W. 'Suffering Impassibly: Christ's Passion in Cyril of Alexandria's Soteriology', *ProEccl* 11.4 (Fall, 2002), pp. 463-83.

Smith, M.A. 'The Early English Baptists and the Church Fathers' (PhD thesis, The Southern Baptist Theological Seminary, 1982).

Southern Baptist Convention. *The Baptist Faith and Message: A Statement Adopted by the Southern Baptist Convention June 14, 2000* (Nashville, Tenn.: LifeWay Christian Resources, 2000).

Stassen, G.H. 'Baptist Identity for a New Millennium' (unpublished presidential address, National Association of Baptist Professors of Religion annual meeting, Nashville, Tennessee, November 18, 2000).

Stiver, D.R. *Theology after Ricoeur: New Directions in Hermeneutical Theology* (Louisville, Ky.: Westminster John Knox Press, 2001).

— 'Baptists: Modern or Postmodern?', *RevExp* 100.4 [Fall, 2003], p. 536.

Strong, A.H. *Systematic Theology: A Compendium*, 3 vols. in 1 (Valley Forge, Pa.: Judson Press, 1907).

Studer, B. *Trinity and Incarnation: The Faith of the Early Church*, trans. M. Westerhoff, ed. A. Louth (Collegeville, Minn.: Liturgical Press, 1993).

Sutton, J. *The Baptist Reformation: The Conservative Resurgence in the Southern Baptist Convention* (Nashville, Tenn.: Broadman & Holman, 2000).

Symonds, H.E. 'The Heavenly Sacrifice in the Greek Fathers', in *StudPat*, vol. 8, ed. F.L. Cross (TU, 93; Berlin: Akademie-Verlag, 1966), pp. 280-85.

Tabbernee, W. 'Unfencing the Table: Creeds, Councils, Communion, and the Campbells', *Mid-Stream* 35.6 [1966], pp. 417-32.

— 'Alexander Campbell and the Apostolic Tradition', in *The Free Church and the Early Church: Bridging the Historical and Theological Divide*, ed. D.H. Williams (Grand Rapids, Mich.: William B. Eerdmans, 2002), pp. 163-80.

Thiselton, A.C. *New Horizons in Hermeneutics: The Theory and Practice of Transforming Biblical Reading* (Grand Rapids, Mich.: Zondervan, 1992).

Thompson, P.E. 'A New Question in Baptist History: Seeking a Catholic Spirit among Early Baptists', *ProEccl* 8.1 (Winter, 1999), pp. 51-72.

— 'Re-envisioning Baptist Identity: Historical, Theological, and Liturgical Analysis', *PRSt* 27.3 (Fall, 2000), pp. 287-302.

— 'Sacraments and Religious Liberty: From Critical Practice to Rejected Infringement', in *Baptist Sacramentalism*, ed. A.R. Cross and P.E. Thompson (SBHT, 5; Carlisle: Paternoster Press, 2003), pp. 36-54.

— '"As It Was in the Beginning"(?): The Myth of Changelessness in Baptist Life and Belief', in *Recycling the Past or Researching History? Studies in Baptist Historiography and Myths*, ed. P.E. Thompson and A.R. Cross (SBHT, 11; Milton Keynes: Paternoster, 2005), pp. 184-206.

Thurian, M., ed. *Churches Respond to Baptism, Eucharist and Ministry*, 6 vols. (Geneva: World Council of Churches, 1986-88).

Thurneysen, E., ed. *Karl Barth—Eduard Thurneysen Briefwechsel*, vol. 2, *1921-1930*, Karl Barth-Gesamtausgabe, vol. 5, *Briefe* (Zürich: Theologischer Verlag, 1974).

Tilley, T.W. *Inventing Catholic Tradition* (Maryknoll, N.Y.: Orbis Books, 2000).

Tillich, P. *The Interpretation of History*, trans. N.A. Rasetzki and E.L. Talmey (New York: Charles Scribner's Sons, 1936).

Toom, T. 'Baptists on Justification: Can We Join the Joint Declaration on the Doctrine of Justification?' *ProEccl* 13.3 (Summer, 2004), p. 289-306.

Torrance, T.F. 'Karl Barth and Patristic Theology', in *Theology Beyond Christendom: Essays on the Centenary of the Birth of Karl Barth, May 10, 1886*, ed. J. Thompson (Allison Park, Pa.: Pickwick Publications, 1986), pp. 215-39.

Trevett, C. *A Study of Ignatius of Antioch in Syria and Asia* (Lewiston, N.Y.: Edwin Mellen, 1992).

Tull, J.E. *High-Church Baptists in the South: The Origin, Nature, and Influence of Landmarkism*, ed. M. Ashcraft (Macon, Ga.: Mercer University Press, 2000).

Tupper, E.F. 'Biblicism, Exclusivism, Triumphalism: The Travail of Baptist Identity', *PRSt* 29.4 (Winter, 2002), pp. 411-26.

Underhill, E.B. *Confessions of Faith and Other Public Documents Illustrative of the History of the Baptist Churches of England in the 17th Century* (London: Haddon Brothers, 1854).

Van Oort, J. 'John Calvin and the Church Fathers', in *The Reception of the Church Fathers in the West: From the Carolingians to the Maurists*, ed. I. Backus (Leiden: E.J. Brill, 1997): vol. 2, pp. 661-700.

Vanhoye, A. 'Esprit éternel et feu du sacrifice en He 9,14', *Bib* 64.2 (1983), pp. 263-74.

Voicu, S.J. 'Gennadio di Costantinopoli: La trasmissione del frammento *In Hebr* 9, 2-5', *OCP* 84 [1982], pp. 435-37.

Wainwright, A.W. *The Trinity in the New Testament* (London: S.P.C.K., 1962).

Wainwright, G. *Eucharist and Eschatology* (New York: Oxford University Press, 1978).

— *Doxology: The Praise of God in Worship, Doctrine, and Life. A Systematic Theology* (New York: Oxford University Press, 1980).

— 'Renewing Worship: The Recovery of Classical Patterns', *TheolTod* 48.1 (April, 1991), p. 45-55.

— *For Our Salvation: Two Approaches to the Work of Christ* (Grand Rapids, Mich.: William B. Eerdmans, 1997).

Wallace, M.I. *The Second Naiveté: Barth, Ricoeur, and the New Yale Theology*, 2nd edn. (SABH, 6; Macon, Ga.: Mercer University Press, 1995).

Wallace-Hadrill, D.S. *Christian Antioch: A Study of Early Christian Thought in the East* (Cambridge: Cambridge University Press, 1982).

Ward, G. 'Barth, Modernity, and Postmodernity', in *The Cambridge Companion to Karl Barth*, ed. J.B. Webster (Cambridge: Cambridge University Press, 2000), pp. 274-95.

Webber, R.E. *Evangelicals on the Canterbury Trail: Why Evangelicals Are Attracted to the Liturgical Church* (Waco, Tex.: Word Books, 1985).

— *Worship Old and New: A Biblical, Historical, and Practical Introduction*, rev. edn. (Grand Rapids, Mich.: Zondervan, 1994).

— *Ancient-Future Faith: Rethinking Evangelicalism for a Postmodern World* (Grand Rapids, Mich.: Baker Books, 1999).

— *The Younger Evangelicals: Facing the Challenges of the New World* (Grand Rapids, Mich.: Baker Books, 2002).

Wilken, R.L. *The Spirit of Early Christian Thought: Seeking the Face of God* (New Haven: Yale University Press, 2003).

Wilken, R.L., ed. *The Church's Bible* (Grand Rapids: William B. Eerdmans, 2003-).

Williams, D.H. *Ambrose of Milan and the End of the Nicene-Arian Conflicts* (OECS; New York: Oxford University Press, 1995).

— *Retrieving the Tradition and Renewing Evangelicalism: A Primer for Suspicious Protestants* (Grand Rapids, Mich.: William B. Eerdmans, 1999).

— 'The Disintegration of Catholicism into Diffuse Inclusivism', *ProEccl* 12.4 (Fall, 2003), pp. 389-93.

— *Evangelicals and Tradition: The Formative Influence of the Early Church* (ERASCF, 1; Grand Rapids, Mich.: Baker Academic, 2005).

— 'The Patristic Tradition as Canon', *PRSt* 32.4 (Winter, 2005), pp. 357-79.

Williams, R. *Arius: Heresy and Tradition*, rev. edn. (Grand Rapids, Mich.: William B. Eerdmans, 2002).

Wilson, J.R. *Living Faithfully in a Fragmented World: Lessons for the Church from MacIntyre's After Virtue* (CMMC; Harrisburg, Pa.: Trinity Press International, 1997).

Wilson-Kastner, P. *Faith, Feminism, and the Christ* (Philadelphia: Fortress Press, 1983).

Winslow, D.F. 'The Idea of Redemption in the Epistles of St. Ignatius of Antioch', *GOTR* 11 (1965), pp. 120-21

Winward, S.F. *The Reformation of Our Worship* (Richmond, Va.: John Knox Press, 1965).

Wood, R.C. 'Review Essay: D.W. Fagerberg, *The Size of Chesterton's Catholicism*', *ProEccl* 9.2 (Spring, 2000), pp. 236-40.

— *Contending for the Faith: The Church's Engagement with Culture* (ICTT, 1; Waco, Tex.: Baylor University Press, 2003).

— 'The Heresy of Solitary Faith', *ChrTod* 48.1 (January, 2004), pp. 58-60.

— 'An Alternative Vision for the Christian University' (unpublished address to the faculty of Campbell University, Buies Creek, North Carolina, 30 March, 2004.

Wood, S.K. 'The Liturgy: Participatory Knowledge of God in the Liturgy', in *Knowing the Triune God: The Work of the Spirit in the Practices of the Church*, ed. J.J. Buckley and D.S. Yeago (Grand Rapids, Mich.: William B. Eerdmans, 2001), pp. 95-118.

World Council of Churches. *Baptism, Eucharist and Ministry*, Faith and Order Paper No. 111 (Geneva: World Council of Churches, 1982).

— *Baptism, Eucharist and Ministry 1982-1990: Report of the Process and the Responses*, Faith and Order Paper No. 149 (Geneva: World Council of Churches, 1990).

— *Confessing the One Faith: An Ecumenical Explication of the Apostolic Faith as it is Confessed in the Nicene-Constantinopolitan Creed (381)*, Faith and Order Paper No. 153 (Geneva: WCC Publications, 1991).

Wright, L.E. *Alterations of the Words of Jesus As Quoted in the Literature of the Second Century* (HHM, 25; Cambridge: Harvard University Press, 1952).

Wright, N.G. 'The Petrine Ministry: Baptist Reflections', *ProEccl* 13.4 (Fall, 2004), pp. 451-65.

Wuthnow, R. *The Restructuring of American Religion: Society and Faith Since World War II* (StudChSt, 1; Princeton, N.J.: Princeton University Press, 1988).

Yocum, J. 'What's Interesting about Karl Barth? Barth as Polemical and Descriptive Theologian', *IJST* 4.1 (March, 2002), pp. 29-44.

Young, F.M. 'Christological Ideas in the Greek Commentaries on the Epistle to the Hebrews', *JTS* n.s. 20 (April, 1969), pp. 150-63.

— *From Nicaea to Chalcedon: A Guide to the Literature and Its Background* (Philadelphia: Fortress Press, 1983).

Young, F.M., Ayres, L., and Louth, A., eds. *The Cambridge History of Early Christian Literature* (Cambridge: Cambridge University Press, 2004).

Young, R.D. 'Texts Have Consequences', *FT* 91 (March, 1999), pp. 40-43.

Zimmermann, W.-D., and Smith, R. G. *I Knew Dietrich Bonhoeffer: Reminiscences by His Friends*, trans. K.G. Smith (New York: Harper and Row, 1966).

Index of Scripture References

Index of Names

Index of Subjects

Studies in Baptist History and Thought

(All titles uniform with this volume)
Dates in bold are of projected publication
Volumes in this series are not always published in sequence

David Bebbington and Anthony R. Cross (eds)
Global Baptist History
(SBHT vol. 14)

This book brings together studies from the Second International Conference on Baptist Studies which explore different facets of Baptist life and work especially during the twentieth century.

2006 / 1-84227-214-4 / approx. 350pp

David Bebbington (ed.)
The Gospel in the World
International Baptist Studies
(SBHT vol. 1)

This volume of essays from the First International Conference on Baptist Studies deals with a range of subjects spanning Britain, North America, Europe, Asia and the Antipodes. Topics include studies on religious tolerance, the communion controversy and the development of the international Baptist community, and concludes with two important essays on the future of Baptist life that pay special attention to the United States.

2002 / 1-84227-118-0 / xiv + 362pp

John H.Y. Briggs (ed.)
Pulpit and People
Studies in Eighteenth-Century English Baptist Life and Thought
(SBHT vol. 28)

The eighteenth century was a crucial time in Baptist history. The denomination had its roots in seventeenth-century English Puritanism and Separatism and the persecution of the Stuart kings with only a limited measure of freedom after 1689. Worse, however, was to follow for with toleration came doctrinal conflict, a move away from central Christian understandings and a loss of evangelistic urgency. Both spiritual and numerical decline ensued, to the extent that the denomination was virtually reborn as rather belatedly it came to benefit from the Evangelical Revival which brought new life to both Arminian and Calvinistic Baptists. The papers in this volume study a denomination in transition, and relate to theology, their views of the church and its mission, Baptist spirituality, and engagements with radical politics.

2007 / 1-84227-403-1 / approx. 350pp

Damian Brot
Church of the Baptized or Church of Believers?
A Contribution to the Dialogue between the Catholic Church and the Free Churches with Special Reference to Baptists
(SBHT vol. 26)

The dialogue between the Catholic Church and the Free Churches in Europe has hardly taken place. This book pleads for a commencement of such a conversation. It offers, among other things, an introduction to the American and the international dialogues between Baptists and the Catholic Church and strives to allow these conversations to become fruitful in the European context as well.

2006 / 1-84227-334-5 / approx. 364pp

Dennis Bustin
Paradox and Perseverence
Hanserd Knollys, Particular Baptist Pioneer in Seventeenth-Century England
(SBHT vol. 23)

The seventeenth century was a significant period in English history during which the people of England experienced unprecedented change and tumult in all spheres of life. At the same time, the importance of order and the traditional institutions of society were being reinforced. Hanserd Knollys, born during this pivotal period, personified in his life the ambiguity, tension and paradox of it, openly seeking change while at the same time cautiously embracing order. As a founder and leader of the Particular Baptists in London and despite persecution and personal hardship, he played a pivotal role in helping shape their identity externally in society and, internally, as they moved toward becoming more formalised by the end of the century.

2006 / 1-84227-259-4 / approx. 324pp

Anthony R. Cross
Baptism and the Baptists
Theology and Practice in Twentieth-Century Britain
(SBHT vol. 3)

At a time of renewed interest in baptism, *Baptism and the Baptists* is a detailed study of twentieth-century baptismal theology and practice and the factors which have influenced its development.

2000 / 0-85364-959-6 / xx + 530pp

Anthony R. Cross and Philip E. Thompson (eds)
Baptist Sacramentalism
(SBHT vol. 5)

This collection of essays includes biblical, historical and theological studies in the theology of the sacraments from a Baptist perspective. Subjects explored include the physical side of being spiritual, baptism, the Lord's supper, the church, ordination, preaching, worship, religious liberty and the issue of disestablishment.

2003 / 1-84227-119-9 / xvi + 278pp

Anthony R. Cross and Philip E. Thompson (eds)
Baptist Sacramentalism 2
(SBHT vol. 25)

This second collection of essays exploring various dimensions of sacramental theology from a Baptist perspective includes biblical, historical and theological studies from scholars from around the world.

2006 / 1-84227-325-6 / approx. 350pp

Paul S. Fiddes
Tracks and Traces
Baptist Identity in Church and Theology
(SBHT vol. 13)

This is a comprehensive, yet unusual, book on the faith and life of Baptist Christians. It explores the understanding of the church, ministry, sacraments and mission from a thoroughly theological perspective. In a series of interlinked essays, the author relates Baptist identity consistently to a theology of covenant and to participation in the triune communion of God.

2003 / 1-84227-120-2 / xvi + 304pp

Stanley K. Fowler
More Than a Symbol
The British Baptist Recovery of Baptismal Sacramentalism
(SBHT vol. 2)

Fowler surveys the entire scope of British Baptist literature from the seventeenth-century pioneers onwards. He shows that in the twentieth century leading British Baptist pastors and theologians recovered an understanding of baptism that connected experience with soteriology and that in doing so they were recovering what many of their forebears had taught.

2002 / 1-84227-052-4 / xvi + 276pp

Steven R. Harmon
Towards Baptist Catholicity
Essays on Tradition and the Baptist Vision
(SBHT vol. 27)

This series of essays contends that the reconstruction of the Baptist vision in the wake of modernity's dissolution requires a retrieval of the ancient ecumenical tradition that forms Christian identity through rehearsal and practice. Themes explored include catholic identity as an emerging trend in Baptist theology, tradition as a theological category in Baptist perspective, Baptist confessions and the patristic tradition, worship as a principal bearer of tradition, and the role of Baptist higher education in shaping the Christian vision.

2006 / 1-84227-362-0 / approx. 210pp

Michael A.G. Haykin (ed.)
'At the Pure Fountain of Thy Word'
Andrew Fuller as an Apologist
(SBHT vol. 6)

One of the greatest Baptist theologians of the eighteenth and early nineteenth centuries, Andrew Fuller has not had justice done to him. There is little doubt that Fuller's theology lay behind the revitalization of the Baptists in the late eighteenth century and the first few decades of the nineteenth. This collection of essays fills a much needed gap by examining a major area of Fuller's thought, his work as an apologist.

2004 / 1-84227-171-7 / xxii + 276pp

Michael A.G. Haykin
Studies in Calvinistic Baptist Spirituality
(SBHT vol. 15)

In a day when spirituality is in vogue and Christian communities are looking for guidance in this whole area, there is wisdom in looking to the past to find untapped wells. The Calvinistic Baptists, heirs of the rich ecclesial experience in the Puritan era of the seventeenth century, but, by the end of the eighteenth century, also passionately engaged in the catholicity of the Evangelical Revivals, are such a well. This collection of essays, covering such things as the Lord's Supper, friendship and hymnody, seeks to draw out the spiritual riches of this community for reflection and imitation in the present day.

2006 / 1-84227-149-0 / approx. 350pp

Brian Haymes, Anthony R. Cross and Ruth Gouldbourne
On Being the Church
Revisioning Baptist Identity
(SBHT vol. 21)

The aim of the book is to re-examine Baptist theology and practice in the light of the contemporary biblical, theological, ecumenical and missiological context drawing on historical and contemporary writings and issues. It is not a study in denominationalism but rather seeks to revision historical insights from the believers' church tradition for the sake of Baptists and other Christians in the context of the modern–postmodern context.

2006 / 1-84227-121-0 / approx. 350pp

Ken R. Manley
From Woolloomooloo to 'Eternity': A History of Australian Baptists
Volume 1: Growing an Australian Church (1831–1914)
Volume 2: A National Church in a Global Community (1914–2005)
(SBHT vols 16.1 and 16.2)

From their beginnings in Australia in 1831 with the first baptisms in Woolloomooloo Bay in 1832, this pioneering study describes the quest of Baptists in the different colonies (states) to discover their identity as Australians and Baptists. Although institutional developments are analyzed and the roles of significant individuals traced, the major focus is on the social and theological dimensions of the Baptist movement.

2 vol. set 2006 / 1-84227-405-8 / approx. 900pp

Ken R. Manley
'Redeeming Love Proclaim'
John Rippon and the Baptists
(SBHT vol. 12)

A leading exponent of the new moderate Calvinism which brought new life to many Baptists, John Rippon (1751–1836) helped unite the Baptists at this significant time. His many writings expressed the denomination's growing maturity and mutual awareness of Baptists in Britain and America, and exerted a long-lasting influence on Baptist worship and devotion. In his various activities, Rippon helped conserve the heritage of Old Dissent and promoted the evangelicalism of the New Dissent

2004 / 1-84227-193-8 / xviii + 340pp

Peter J. Morden
Offering Christ to the World
Andrew Fuller and the Revival of English Particular Baptist Life
(SBHT vol. 8)

Andrew Fuller (1754–1815) was one of the foremost English Baptist ministers of his day. His career as an Evangelical Baptist pastor, theologian, apologist and missionary statesman coincided with the profound revitalization of the Particular Baptist denomination to which he belonged. This study examines the key aspects of the life and thought of this hugely significant figure, and gives insights into the revival in which he played such a central part.

2003 / 1-84227-141-5 / xx + 202pp

Peter Naylor
Calvinism, Communion and the Baptists
A Study of English Calvinistic Baptists from the Late 1600s to the Early 1800s
(SBHT vol. 7)

Dr Naylor argues that the traditional link between 'high-Calvinism' and 'restricted communion' is in need of revision. He examines Baptist communion controversies from the late 1600s to the early 1800s and also the theologies of John Gill and Andrew Fuller.

2003 / 1-84227-142-3 / xx + 266pp

Ian M. Randall, Toivo Pilli and Anthony R. Cross (eds)
Baptist Identities
International Studies from the Seventeenth to the Twentieth Centuries
(SBHT vol. 19)

These papers represent the contributions of scholars from various parts of the world as they consider the factors that have contributed to Baptist distinctiveness in different countries and at different times. The volume includes specific case studies as well as broader examinations of Baptist life in a particular country or region. Together they represent an outstanding resource for understanding Baptist identities.

2005 / 1-84227-215-2 / approx. 350pp

James M. Renihan
Edification and Beauty
The Practical Ecclesiology of the English Particular Baptists, 1675–1705
(SBHT vol. 17)

Edification and Beauty describes the practices of the Particular Baptist churches at the end of the seventeenth century in terms of three concentric circles: at the centre is the ecclesiological material in the Second London Confession, which is then fleshed out in the various published writings of the men associated with these churches, and, finally, expressed in the church books of the era.

2005 / 1-84227-251-9 / approx. 230pp

Frank Rinaldi
'The Tribe of Dan'
A Study of the New Connexion of General Baptists 1770–1891
(SBHT vol. 10)

'The Tribe of Dan' is a thematic study which explores the theology, organizational structure, evangelistic strategy, ministry and leadership of the New Connexion of General Baptists as it experienced the process of institutionalization in the transition from a revival movement to an established denomination.

2006 / 1-84227-143-1 / approx. 350pp

Peter Shepherd
The Making of a Modern Denomination
John Howard Shakespeare and the English Baptists 1898–1924
(SBHT vol. 4)

John Howard Shakespeare introduced revolutionary change to the Baptist denomination. The Baptist Union was transformed into a strong central institution and Baptist ministers were brought under its control. Further, Shakespeare's pursuit of church unity reveals him as one of the pioneering ecumenists of the twentieth century.

2001 / 1-84227-046-X / xviii + 220pp

Karen Smith
The Community and the Believers
A Study of Calvinistic Baptist Spirituality in Some Towns and Villages of
Hampshire and the Borders of Wiltshire, c.1730–1830
(SBHT vol. 22)

The period from 1730 to 1830 was one of transition for Calvinistic Baptists. Confronted by the enthusiasm of the Evangelical Revival, congregations within the denomination as a whole were challenged to find a way to take account of the revival experience. This study examines the life and devotion of Calvinistic Baptists in Hampshire and Wiltshire during this period. Among this group of Baptists was the hymn writer, Anne Steele.

2005 / 1-84227-326-4 / approx. 280pp

Martin Sutherland
Dissenters in a 'Free Land'
Baptist Thought in New Zealand 1850–2000
(SBHT vol. 24)

Baptists in New Zealand were forced to recast their identity. Conventions of communication and association, state and ecumenical relations, even historical divisions and controversies had to be revised in the face of new topographies and constraints. As Baptists formed themselves in a fluid society they drew heavily on both international movements and local dynamics. This book traces the development of ideas which shaped institutions and styles in sometimes surprising ways.

2006 / 1-84227-327-2 / approx. 230pp

Brian Talbot
The Search for a Common Identity
The Origins of the Baptist Union of Scotland 1800–1870
(SBHT vol. 9)

In the period 1800 to 1827 there were three streams of Baptists in Scotland: Scotch, Haldaneite and 'English' Baptist. A strong commitment to home evangelization brought these three bodies closer together, leading to a merger of their home missionary societies in 1827. However, the first three attempts to form a union of churches failed, but by the 1860s a common understanding of their corporate identity was attained leading to the establishment of the Baptist Union of Scotland.

2003 / 1-84227-123-7 / xviii + 402pp

Philip E. Thompson
The Freedom of God
Towards Baptist Theology in Pneumatological Perspective
(SBHT vol. 20)

This study contends that the range of theological commitments of the early Baptists are best understood in relation to their distinctive emphasis on the freedom of God. Thompson traces how this was recast anthropocentrically, leading to an emphasis upon human freedom from the nineteenth century onwards. He seeks to recover the dynamism of the early vision via a pneumatologically-oriented ecclesiology defining the church in terms of the memory of God.

2006 / 1-84227-125-3 / approx. 350pp

Philip E. Thompson and Anthony R. Cross (eds)
Recycling the Past or Researching History?
Studies in Baptist Historiography and Myths
(SBHT vol. 11)

In this volume an international group of Baptist scholars examine and re-examine areas of Baptist life and thought about which little is known or the received wisdom is in need of revision. Historiographical studies include the date Oxford Baptists joined the Abingdon Association, the death of the Fifth Monarchist John Pendarves, eighteenth-century Calvinistic Baptists and the political realm, confessional identity and denominational institutions, Baptist community, ecclesiology, the priesthood of all believers, soteriology, Baptist spirituality, Strict and Reformed Baptists, the role of women among British Baptists, while various 'myths' challenged include the nature of high-Calvinism in eighteenth-century England, baptismal anti-sacramentalism, episcopacy, and Baptists and change.

2005 / 1-84227-122-9 / approx. 330pp

Linda Wilson
Marianne Farningham
A Plain Working Woman
(SBHT vol. 18)

Marianne Farningham, of College Street Baptist Chapel, Northampton, was a household name in evangelical circles in the later nineteenth century. For over fifty years she produced comment, poetry, biography and fiction for the popular Christian press. This investigation uses her writings to explore the beliefs and behaviour of evangelical Nonconformists, including Baptists, during these years.

2006 / 1-84227-124-5 / approx. 250pp

Other Paternoster titles
relating to Baptist history and thought

George R. Beasley-Murray
Baptism in the New Testament
(Paternoster Digital Library)

This is a welcome reprint of a classic text on baptism originally published in 1962 by one of the leading Baptist New Testament scholars of the twentieth century. Dr Beasley-Murray's comprehensive study begins by investigating the antecedents of Christian baptism. It then surveys the foundation of Christian baptism in the Gospels, its emergence in the Acts of the Apostles and development in the apostolic writings. Following a section relating baptism to New Testament doctrine, a substantial discussion of the origin and significance of infant baptism leads to a briefer consideration of baptismal reform and ecumenism.

2005 / 1-84227-300-0 / x + 422pp

Paul Beasley-Murray
Fearless for Truth
A Personal Portrait of the Life of George Beasley-Murray

Without a doubt George Beasley-Murray was one of the greatest Baptists of the twentieth century. A long-standing Principal of Spurgeon's College, he wrote more than twenty books and made significant contributions in the study of areas as diverse as baptism and eschatology, as well as writing highly respected commentaries on the Book of Revelation and John's Gospel.

2002 / 1-84227-134-2 / xii + 244pp

David Bebbington
Holiness in Nineteenth-Century England
(Studies in Christian History and Thought)

David Bebbington stresses the relationship of movements of spirituality to changes in their cultural setting, especially the legacies of the Enlightenment and Romanticism. He shows that these broad shifts in ideological mood had a profound effect on the ways in which piety was conceptualized and practised. Holiness was intimately bound up with the spirit of the age.

2000 / 0-85364-981-2 / viii + 98pp

July 2005

Clyde Binfield
Victorian Nonconformity in Eastern England 1840–1885
(Studies in Evangelical History and Thought)
Studies of Victorian religion and society often concentrate on cities, suburbs, and industrialisation. This study provides a contrast. Victorian Eastern England—Essex, Suffolk, Norfolk, Cambridgeshire, and Huntingdonshire—was rural, traditional, relatively unchanging. That is nonetheless a caricature which discounts the industry in Norwich and Ipswich (as well as in Haverhill, Stowmarket and Leiston) and ignores the impact of London on Essex, of railways throughout the region, and of an ancient but changing university (Cambridge) on the county town which housed it. It also entirely ignores the political implications of such changes in a region noted for the variety of its religious Dissent since the seventeenth century. This book explores Victorian Eastern England and its Nonconformity. It brings to a wider readership a pioneering thesis which has made a major contribution to a fresh evolution of English religion and society.
2006 / 1-84227-216-0 / approx. 274pp

Edward W. Burrows
'To Me To Live Is Christ'
A Biography of Peter H. Barber
This book is about a remarkably gifted and energetic man of God. Peter H. Barber was born into a Brethren family in Edinburgh in 1930. In his youth he joined Charlotte Baptist Chapel and followed the call into Baptist ministry. For eighteen years he was the pioneer minister of the new congregation in the New Town of East Kilbride, which planted two further congregations. At the age of thirty-nine he served as Centenary President of the Baptist Union of Scotland and then exercised an influential ministry for over seven years in the well-known Upton Vale Baptist Church, Torquay. From 1980 until his death in 1994 he was General Secretary of the Baptist Union of Scotland. Through his work for the European Baptist Federation and the Baptist World Alliance he became a world Baptist statesman. He was President of the EBF during the upheaval that followed the collapse of Communism.
2005 / 1-84227-324-8 / xxii + 236pp

Christopher J. Clement
Religious Radicalism in England 1535–1565
(Rutherford Studies in Historical Theology)
In this valuable study Christopher Clement draws our attention to a varied assemblage of people who sought Christian faithfulness in the underworld of mid-Tudor England. Sympathetically and yet critically he assess their place in the history of English Protestantism, and by attentive listening he gives them a voice.
1997 / 0-946068-44-5 / xxii + 426pp   July 2005

Anthony R. Cross (ed.)
Ecumenism and History
Studies in Honour of John H.Y. Briggs
(Studies in Christian History and Thought)
This collection of essays examines the inter-relationships between the two fields in which Professor Briggs has contributed so much: history—particularly Baptist and Nonconformist—and the ecumenical movement. With contributions from colleagues and former research students from Britain, Europe and North America, *Ecumenism and History* provides wide-ranging studies in important aspects of Christian history, theology and ecumenical studies.
2002 / 1-84227-135-0 / xx + 362pp

Keith E. Eitel
Paradigm Wars
The Southern Baptist International Mission Board
Faces the Third Millennium
(Regnum Studies in Mission)
The International Mission Board of the Southern Baptist Convention is the largest denominational mission agency in North America. This volume chronicles the historic and contemporary forces that led to the IMB's recent extensive reorganization, providing the most comprehensive case study to date of a historic mission agency restructuring to continue its mission purpose into the twenty-first century more effectively.
2000 / 1-870345-12-6 / x + 140pp

Ruth Gouldbourne
The Flesh and the Feminine
Gender and Theology in the Writings of Caspar Schwenckfeld
(Studies in Christian History and Thought)
Caspar Schwenckfeld and his movement exemplify one of the radical communities of the sixteenth century. Challenging theological and liturgical norms, they also found themselves challenging social and particularly gender assumptions. In this book, the issues of the relationship between radical theology and the understanding of gender are considered.
2005 / 1-84227-048-6 / approx. 304pp

David Hilborn
The Words of our Lips
Language-Use in Free Church Worship
(Paternoster Theological Monographs)
Studies of liturgical language have tended to focus on the written canons of
Roman Catholic and Anglican communities. By contrast, David Hilborn
analyses the more extemporary approach of English Nonconformity. Drawing
on recent developments in linguistic pragmatics, he explores similarities and
differences between 'fixed' and 'free' worship, and argues for the
interdependence of each.

2006 / 0-85364-977-4

Stephen R. Holmes
Listening to the Past
The Place of Tradition in Theology
Beginning with the question 'Why can't we just read the Bible?' Stephen
Holmes considers the place of tradition in theology, showing how the doctrine
of creation leads to an account of historical location and creaturely limitations as
essential aspects of our existence. For we cannot claim unmediated access to the
Scriptures without acknowledging the place of tradition: theology is an
irreducibly communal task. *Listening to the Past* is a sustained attempt to show
what listening to tradition involves, and how it can be used to aid theological
work today.

2002 / 1-84227-155-5 / xiv + 168pp

Mark Hopkins
Nonconformity's Romantic Generation
Evangelical and Liberal Theologies in Victorian England
(Studies in Evangelical History and Thought)
A study of the theological development of key leaders of the Baptist and
Congregational denominations at their period of greatest influence, including
C.H. Spurgeon and R.W. Dale, and of the controversies in which those among
them who embraced and rejected the liberal transformation of their evangelical
heritage opposed each other.

2004 / 1-84227-150-4 / xvi + 284pp

Galen K. Johnson
Prisoner of Conscience
John Bunyan on Self, Community and Christian Faith
(Studies in Christian History and Thought)
This is an interdisciplinary study of John Bunyan's understanding of conscience across his autobiographical, theological and fictional writings, investigating whether conscience always deserves fidelity, and how Bunyan's view of conscience affects his relationship both to modern Western individualism and historic Christianity.

2003 / 1-84227- 151-2 / xvi + 236pp

R.T. Kendall
Calvin and English Calvinism to 1649
(Studies in Christian History and Thought)
The author's thesis is that those who formed the Westminster Confession of Faith, which is regarded as Calvinism, in fact departed from John Calvin on two points: (1) the extent of the atonement and (2) the ground of assurance of salvation.

1997 / 0-85364-827-1 / xii + 264pp

Timothy Larsen
Friends of Religious Equality
Nonconformist Politics in Mid-Victorian England
During the middle decades of the nineteenth century the English Nonconformist community developed a coherent political philosophy of its own, of which a central tenet was the principle of religious equality (in contrast to the stereotype of Evangelical Dissenters). The Dissenting community fought for the civil rights of Roman Catholics, non-Christians and even atheists, on an issue of principle which had its flowering in the enthusiastic and undivided support which Nonconformity gave to the campaign for Jewish emancipation. This reissued study examines the political efforts and ideas of English Nonconformists during the period, covering the whole range of national issues raised, from state education to the Crimean War. It offers a case study of a theologically conservative group defending religious pluralism in the civic sphere, showing that the concept of religious equality was a grand vision at the centre of the political philosophy of the Dissenters.

2007 / 1-84227-402-3 / x + 300pp

Donald M. Lewis
Lighten Their Darkness
The Evangelical Mission to Working-Class London, 1828–1860
(Studies in Evangelical History and Thought)
This is a comprehensive and compelling study of the Church and the complexities of nineteenth-century London. Challenging our understanding of the culture in working London at this time, Lewis presents a well-structured and illustrated work that contributes substantially to the study of evangelicalism and mission in nineteenth-century Britain.
2001 / 1-84227-074-5 / xviii + 372pp

Stanley E. Porter and Anthony R. Cross (eds)
Semper Reformandum
Studies in Honour of Clark H. Pinnock
Clark Pinnock has clearly been one of the most important evangelical theologians of the last forty years in North America. Always provocative, especially in the wide range of opinions he has held and considered, Pinnock, himself a Baptist, has recently retired after twenty-five years of teaching at McMaster Divinity College. His colleagues and associates honour him in this volume by responding to his important theological work which has dealt with the essential topics of evangelical theology. These include Christian apologetics, biblical inspiration, the Holy Spirit and, perhaps most importantly in recent years, openness theology.
2003 / 1-84227-206-3 / xiv + 414pp

Meic Pearse
The Great Restoration
The Religious Radicals of the 16th and 17th Centuries
Pearse charts the rise and progress of continental Anabaptism – both evangelical and heretical – through the sixteenth century. He then follows the story of those English people who became impatient with Puritanism and separated – first from the Church of England and then from one another – to form the antecedents of later Congregationalists, Baptists and Quakers.
1998 / 0-85364-800-X / xii + 320pp

Charles Price and Ian M. Randall
Transforming Keswick
Transforming Keswick is a thorough, readable and detailed history of the convention. It will be of interest to those who know and love Keswick, those who are only just discovering it, and serious scholars eager to learn more about the history of God's dealings with his people.
2000 / 1-85078-350-0 / 288pp

Jim Purves
The Triune God and the Charismatic Movement
A Critical Appraisal from a Scottish Perspective
(Paternoster Theological Monographs)
All emotion and no theology? Or a fundamental challenge to reappraise and realign our trinitarian theology in the light of Christian experience? This study of charismatic renewal as it found expression within Scotland at the end of the twentieth century evaluates the use of Patristic, Reformed and contemporary models (including those of the Baptist Union of Scotland) of the Trinity in explaining the workings of the Holy Spirit.
2004 / 1-84227-321-3 / xxiv + 246pp

Ian M. Randall
Evangelical Experiences
A Study in the Spirituality of English Evangelicalism 1918–1939
(Studies in Evangelical History and Thought)
This book makes a detailed historical examination of evangelical spirituality between the First and Second World Wars. It shows how patterns of devotion led to tensions and divisions. In a wide-ranging study, Anglican, Wesleyan, Reformed and Pentecostal-charismatic spiritualities are analysed.
1999 / 0-85364-919-7 / xii + 310pp

Ian M. Randall
One Body in Christ
The History and Significance of the Evangelical Alliance
In 1846 the Evangelical Alliance was founded with the aim of bringing together evangelicals for common action. This book uses material not previously utilized to examine the history and significance of the Evangelical Alliance, a movement which has remained a powerful force for unity. At a time when evangelicals are growing world-wide, this book offers insights into the past which are relevant to contemporary issues.
2001 / 1-84227-089-3 / xii + 394pp

Ian M. Randall
Spirituality and Social Change
The Contribution of F.B. Meyer (1847–1929)
(Studies in Evangelical History and Thought)
This is a fresh appraisal of F.B. Meyer (1847–1929), a leading Free Church minister. Having been deeply affected by holiness spirituality, Meyer became the Keswick Convention's foremost international speaker. He combined spirituality with effective evangelism and socio-political activity. This study shows Meyer's significant contribution to spiritual renewal and social change.
2003 / 1-84227-195-4 / xx + 184pp

Geoffrey Robson
Dark Satanic Mills?
Religion and Irreligion in Birmingham and the Black Country
(Studies in Evangelical History and Thought)
This book analyses and interprets the nature and extent of popular Christian belief and practice in Birmingham and the Black Country during the first half of the nineteenth century, with particular reference to the impact of cholera epidemics and evangelism on church extension programmes.
2002 / 1-84227-102-4 / xiv + 294pp

Alan P.F. Sell
Enlightenment, Ecumenism, Evangel
Theological Themes and Thinkers 1550–2000
(Studies in Christian History and Thought)
This book consists of papers in which such interlocking topics as the Enlightenment, the problem of authority, the development of doctrine, spirituality, ecumenism, theological method and the heart of the gospel are discussed. Issues of significance to the church at large are explored with special reference to writers from the Reformed and Dissenting traditions.
2005 / 1-84227330-2 / xviii + 422pp

Alan P.F. Sell
Hinterland Theology
Some Reformed and Dissenting Adjustments
(Studies in Christian History and Thought)
Many books have been written on theology's 'giants' and significant trends, but what of those lesser-known writers who adjusted to them? In this book some hinterland theologians of the British Reformed and Dissenting traditions, who followed in the wake of toleration, the Evangelical Revival, the rise of modern biblical criticism and Karl Barth, are allowed to have their say. They include Thomas Ridgley, Ralph Wardlaw, T.V. Tymms and N.H.G. Robinson.
2006 / 1-84227-331-0

Alan P.F. Sell and Anthony R. Cross (eds)
Protestant Nonconformity in the Twentieth Century
(Studies in Christian History and Thought)
In this collection of essays scholars representative of a number of Nonconformist traditions reflect thematically on Nonconformists' life and witness during the twentieth century. Among the subjects reviewed are biblical studies, theology, worship, evangelism and spirituality, and ecumenism. Over and above its immediate interest, this collection provides a marker to future scholars and others wishing to know how some of their forebears assessed Nonconformity's contribution to a variety of fields during the century leading up to Christianity's third millennium.

2003 / 1-84227-221-7 / x + 398pp

Mark Smith
Religion in Industrial Society
Oldham and Saddleworth 1740–1865
(Studies in Christian History and Thought)
This book analyses the way British churches sought to meet the challenge of industrialization and urbanization during the period 1740–1865. Working from a case-study of Oldham and Saddleworth, Mark Smith challenges the received view that the Anglican Church in the eighteenth century was characterized by complacency and inertia, and reveals Anglicanism's vigorous and creative response to the new conditions. He reassesses the significance of the centrally directed church reforms of the mid-nineteenth century, and emphasizes the importance of local energy and enthusiasm. Charting the growth of denominational pluralism in Oldham and Saddleworth, Dr Smith compares the strengths and weaknesses of the various Anglican and Nonconformist approaches to promoting church growth. He also demonstrates the extent to which all the churches participated in a common culture shaped by the influence of evangelicalism, and shows that active co-operation between the churches rather than denominational conflict dominated. This revised and updated edition of Dr Smith's challenging and original study makes an important contribution both to the social history of religion and to urban studies.

2006 / 1-84227-335-3 / approx. 300pp

David M. Thompson
Baptism, Church and Society in Britain from the Evangelical Revival to
Baptism, Eucharist and Ministry
The theology and practice of baptism have not received the attention they
deserve. How important is faith? What does baptismal regeneration mean? Is
baptism a bond of unity between Christians? This book discusses the theology of
baptism and popular belief and practice in England and Wales from the
Evangelical Revival to the publication of the World Council of Churches'
consensus statement on *Baptism, Eucharist and Ministry* (1982).
2005 / 1-84227-393-0 / approx. 224pp

Martin Sutherland
Peace, Toleration and Decay
The Ecclesiology of Later Stuart Dissent
(Studies in Christian History and Thought)
This fresh analysis brings to light the complexity and fragility of the later Stuart
Nonconformist consensus. Recent findings on wider seventeenth-century
thought are incorporated into a new picture of the dynamics of Dissent and the
roots of evangelicalism.
2003 / 1-84227-152-0 / xxii + 216pp

Haddon Willmer
Evangelicalism 1785–1835: An Essay (1962) and Reflections (2004)
(Studies in Evangelical History and Thought)
Awarded the Hulsean Prize in the University of Cambridge in 1962, this
interpretation of a classic period of English Evangelicalism, by a young church
historian, is now supplemented by reflections on Evangelicalism from the
vantage point of a retired Professor of Theology.
2006 / 1-84227-219-5

Linda Wilson
Constrained by Zeal
Female Spirituality amongst Nonconformists 1825–1875
(Studies in Evangelical History and Thought)
Constrained by Zeal investigates the neglected area of Nonconformist female
spirituality. Against the background of separate spheres, it analyses the
experience of women from four denominations, and argues that the churches
provided a 'third sphere' in which they could find opportunities for
participation.
2000 / 0-85364-972-3 / xvi + 294pp

Nigel G. Wright
Disavowing Constantine
Mission, Church and the Social Order in the Theologies of
John Howard Yoder and Jürgen Moltmann
(Paternoster Theological Monographs)

This book is a timely restatement of a radical theology of church and state in the Anabaptist and Baptist tradition. Dr Wright constructs his argument in dialogue and debate with Yoder and Moltmann, major contributors to a free church perspective.

2000 / 0-85364-978-2 / xvi + 252pp

Nigel G. Wright
Free Church, Free State
The Positive Baptist Vision

Free Church, Free State is a textbook on baptist ways of being church and a proposal for the future of baptist churches in an ecumenical context. Nigel Wright argues that both baptist (small 'b') and catholic (small 'c') church traditions should seek to enrich and support each other as valid expressions of the body of Christ without sacrificing what they hold dear. Written for pastors, church planters, evangelists and preachers, Nigel Wright offers frameworks of thought for baptists and non-baptists in their journey together following Christ.

2005 / 1-84227-353-1 / xxviii + 292

Nigel G. Wright
New Baptists, New Agenda

New Baptists, New Agenda is a timely contribution to the growing debate about the health, shape and future of the Baptists. It considers the steady changes that have taken place among Baptists in the last decade – changes of mood, style, practice and structure – and encourages us to align these current movements and questions with God's upward and future call. He contends that the true church has yet to come: the church that currently exists is an anticipation of the joyful gathering of all who have been called by the Spirit through Christ to the Father.

2002 / 1-84227-157-1 / x + 162pp

Paternoster
9 Holdom Avenue,
Bletchley,
Milton Keynes MK1 1QR,
United Kingdom

July 2005

Web: www.authenticmedia.co.uk/paternoster